MISSIONARY PRACTICES
and
SPANISH STEEL

MISSIONARY PRACTICES

and

SPANISH STEEL

*The Evolution of Apostolic Mission
in the Context of New Spain Conquests*

ANDREW L. TOTH

iUniverse, Inc.
Bloomington

MISSIONARY PRACTICES AND SPANISH STEEL
The Evolution of Apostolic Mission in the Context of New Spain Conquests

iUniverse books may be ordered through booksellers or by contacting:

iUniverse
1663 Liberty Drive
Bloomington, IN 47403
www.iuniverse.com
1-800-Authors (1-800-288-4677)

ISBN: 978-1-4759-4743-4 (sc)
ISBN: 978-1-4759-4744-1 (hc)
ISBN: 978-1-4759-4745-8 (ebk)

Library of Congress Control Number: 2012916472

Printed in the United States of America

iUniverse rev. date: 10/01/2012

To Dorciane, my wife and co-worker during
our four decades of Christian missionary work and
to each of our four children and their families
who have always been so much a part
of those ministries.

"All authority has been given to me in Heaven and on earth. Go therefore and make disciples of all the nations . . ."

Jesus of Nazareth

TABLE OF CONTENTS

PREFACE

This book examines the missionary work, principally of the Franciscans but also some of the Jesuit ministries as they were influenced by the doctrines of the Council of Trent in their encounters with the indigenous people of the North American continent during the Spanish conquests of the New World. By considering their missionary charge, the world context bearing on their work, the local context of their ministries, the values of the missionaries, and the goals or expectations of their ministries, an attempt is made to determine the missiological methodologies. Then by comparison of the periods of conquest, discover the evolution of Tridentine Missiology as it develops into a functional field of theology. This is done by dividing the 300 year apostolic period of New Spain into eight *epochs* of ministry and evaluating the ministries of each epoch through a five-point missiological framework.

The work and ministries of the Roman Catholic Friars that gave their lives, both as martyrs for the cause of their church, or in many years of hard and often thankless labor are the inspiration and basis for this attempt to remember and understand their accomplishments in Christian mission. Their goals were simplistic and their methods were a bit crude at first, though correct by their contemporary standards. Their labor, though at times not appreciated, was seldom in vain. In the great majority of the cases studied, their objectives as men, and as ambassadors of the Roman Catholic Church, were completely accomplished by the evidence of over 12,000 churches founded. The author's 40 years of experience in Christian mission coupled with academic degrees in missiology and theology have given us a clear and thought provoking approach to understanding the ministries of the friars sent to New Spain.

It is a goal of this book to see light shed upon the actual task the friars faced, the difficulties they encountered in their fields of service, and how they overcame and accomplished their missiological purposes in being chosen and sent as Christian missionaries. In doing so it is the author's objective to bring remembrance, honor, and understanding to the memory of the deserving missionary friars.

To each of my colleagues and family members I extend my heartfelt thanks for their time, effort, comments, and recommendations that have made this work possible. Such a work as this is built upon the foundation of works done by many scholars in the areas of history, theology, and also the ministries of practitioners of Christian mission. To each of them that have gone before I acknowledge my debt of gratitude for their contribution to our understanding of how Christian mission has been such an integral part of what we as people in North America, neighbors both near and far, have become today.

CHAPTER I

INTRODUCTION

The sweat-soaked missionary struggled both to maintain his balance and to keep up with Rutillio, his Native American guide. The humid air brought no relief on the steep, rocky, and muddy jungle trail. Rutillio had pastored the small congregation for several years in the Pame village that was their objective for that day. Spanish was the common language of these two apostles of the Christian faith, though Rutillio also spoke Tenek, Aztec, and even a little English. Neither of them spoke Pame or *Xi'iuy*, as the North American indigenous people of the village call themselves.

Cresting another hill, they paused for the missionary to catch his breath and slow down his heart rate. They noticed an opening to a cave close by and the missionary got up to explore it. Rutillio nearly panicked and demanded the missionary stay away from the sacred cave. With concern for the possibility of snakes and large cave spiders, the missionary retreated, asking why the sudden alarm. Rutillio explained that in this area the people believed spirits lived in the underground and could come out through that cave. Some believed babies lived when born because good spirits came from the cave and inhabited the newborn baby giving them spirit and life. Other times, bad spirits came out from the same cave and the baby only lived a short while or died at birth. This belief explained why the mortality rate of the newborn babies was over 50% in this village—there were just too many bad spirits coming out from this cave.

As they moved along, the missionary attempted to grasp the implications of this Mexican pastor's explanation. What were the historical roots of this strange mixture of animistic and Christian beliefs? After three hours of walking mountain trails from the nearest road, they arrived at a beautiful, high valley with the Pame village scattered over one side of it. People had lived there for many hundreds of years, and it was as if time had stood still. The rugged mountains of the Sierra Madre Occidentales were considered unfit for human habitation by the Spanish—certainly not worth fighting for them. This left the culture of the indigenous Pame people relatively undisturbed as the centuries went by.

The homes there were mud and stick walls with thatched roofs; three to seven one-room houses together defined a family complex. There were several natural springs that supplied water for the village and their animals—all drinking from the same crude cistern. There were no roads, no electricity, almost no outside interference with the daily lives and routines of these subsistence farmers. They ate what they grew or starved if there was not enough—and no one from the outside seemed to care one way or another. After all, they were just *Indios*. For more than 500 years, the gospel of Jesus Christ had been in the land. Why then was this village so unaffected spiritually, without the normal lifting of moral and living standards that usually accompanies the entrance of the gospel message into a new culture?

The missionary went to the village *Juez*, the judge or leader, to introduce himself and was informed that, "In this village we are all Catholic." He was also informed that no other religions were permitted there. There were no church buildings in the valley of any kind. Worship consisted of processions to sacred places where men and women would drink themselves into a stupor while sacrificing small animals or birds. Once per year a Roman Catholic priest would try to come up the trail, if it was passable, to celebrate the Eucharist, baptize living babies for that year, collect tithes and offerings to cover the costs of his trip, and then leave. There was a cross which was also considered a sacred place set up on a hill in the distance overlooking the valley. For daily worship, a number of houses had a type of altar set up in a corner, often with a picture of Mary and baby Jesus or the popular Spanish Virgin of Guadalupe—usually with a garlic wreath as an adornment and a candle to burn on special occasions. When the missionary asked, "Who does this represent?" The typical answer was usually: God.

Most of life's milestones were still held in the traditional Pame ways. Marriages were done without the benefit of church, clergy, or even a celebration.[1] Burials were a cause for drunken excesses and ancient Pame customs. In fact, the burial place was the most sacred place of all and the only one strictly maintained by the villagers. Every year on *Day of the Dead* the whole village turned out to clean away rubbish, restore the rock walls, and spend a day or two in feasting and drunkenness. It was from here that the departed spirits left the bodies and fled out over the eastern sea and then returned to the ground until new life called them forth from the caves again. The missionary marveled at just what it meant for these indigenous villagers to be *Catholic,* or what they really understood of the Christian faith as expressed in the biblical concepts of sin, propitiation, redemption, forgiveness, being in Christ, and filled with the Spirit of the Living God.

The Roman Catholic Church states that these indigenous people in the Mexican rural villages are *Catholic*. The village leaders themselves in many of these nearly forgotten rural towns also say that they are *Catholic*. But aside from a few borrowed Christian symbols here and there, and perhaps a visit from some outsider that represents being *Roman Catholic* to the rest of the world, one would look in vain for any semblance of Christianity in any of its multicultural manifestations. The rituals, the world views, and most of the Pame symbols were and are a continuation of ancient indigenous religious practices. These practices included animal sacrifices, drunkenness, and many other practices well outside the bounds of any definition of biblical morality.

Pondering the situation, it can be concluded, as the Friar Bernardino de Sahagún did over 490 years ago: "Whatever evangelism was done here did not work out the way it was intended." A goal of this book is to understand why. What theological teachings or practical applications of Christian principles resulted in these North American indigenous people believing as their animistic forefathers did, while claiming to be ardent Roman Catholics to the exclusion of all other outside religious expressions?

The Spanish Mission and the friars that penetrated indigenous lands undertaking the spiritual conquest for their king and God have inspired countless biographies and histories. The reports of clerics and friars that came to the New World would indicate a mighty movement toward Latin Catholicism unprecedented in history. Juan Zumárraga,[2] writing just seven years after the first missionaries arrived in Mexico, declared that the Franciscan friars had baptized more than one and a half million indigenous converts. The warrior and conqueror, Hernán Cortés, himself a Brother of Penance Tertiary, a third Order of Franciscans, can be presented as a Christian with apostolic zeal, insisting upon religious conformity both in his own ranks and among the masses of new converts, long before any religious professionals appeared on the scene of the conquest of Mexico.[3]

Many great stories emerged from the conquest—of valor, of controversy, and at times, of utter confusion. Following the stories came numerous interpretations of what had taken place, or defenses and justifications of policies, all of which have continued to circulate since 1492. The Black Legend[4] contends that the Spanish murdered, maimed, tortured, and in general, made life miserable for the indigenous Americans through cruelty, exploitation, religious intolerance, enslavement, and sexual abuse. This continues to be thought of as fact by many, even among some in higher education, though the legend could be equally applied to many of the other European colonists at some point in their conquests of the American lands.

Most people have some idea of what a Spanish Catholic mission settlement was. They may even understand who the indigenous people of the missions were and probably have some impression of the alleged mistreatment of the mission coverts to Roman Catholicism. There are stereotypes of the friars that would have them appear to us as saintly; some indeed have been canonized by the Roman Catholic Church. Yet there are a number of murals on subway walls and public buildings in Mexico City that present the friars as demonic taskmasters. Neither view does justice to the facts of life common to most of the early Spanish settlements and missions. Today the polarization of perceptions has made it very difficult to discern just what really happened so long ago. The confusion goes all the way back to Cortéz and his letters[5] to the Crown of Spain stating the accomplishments of his armies and defending his courses of action.

The letters and reports[6] coming from explorers and colonists ignited a passion in the hearts of the people on the Iberian Peninsula. The stories of these encounters, as told from a European perspective, raged throughout Europe. They were at once liberating for the archaic, medieval, and decaying European upper crust of society and, at the same time, depressing for many of the European Christians to discover the world was still so populated by pagans and infidels.

Many clerics felt the end of times prophetically predicted in the Scriptures was already upon them. Muslims still held Africa; they had just recently taken Constantinople and were systematically taking central Europe as far north as Hungary. The Holy Roman Empire stood alone, the great Eastern Orthodox Church having already been overrun by Roman Catholic and then later by Muslim armies. In the midst of this corporate, besieged state of mind, Columbus verified rumors[7] that there were indeed heavily populated lands to the west. Populations that needed to have the gospel preached to them. Columbus thought he had found some islands off India and that a new water route to the Spice Islands had been found. After four voyages to the Gulf of Mexico and stumbling on South and Central America, Columbus died still believing he had found India by circumnavigation of the globe.

However, later it was discovered that Columbus had actually stumbled upon a huge obstacle in the Western route to Asia. Not only were there two whole unexplored continents that now belonged to Queen Isabella, but they were full of pagans who were so culturally different from anything the Europeans had seen to date as to raise the question regarding whether they were completely human.[8] Some reports described the indigenous people of the Caribbean as docile children.[9] In another report they were described in the worst imaginable way as savage cannibals preying upon each other.[10] Either way they were seen by the early explorers as pagans in great need of the one true Holy Roman Catholic Church, and obviously someone had to make them into civilized, tax-paying citizens of the Spanish Empire. Only mendicant friars could do that.

New Spain was the name that was used for all the Spanish claims on mainland North America until much later when the sheer size of what they had discovered became known. This name will continue to be used for consistency and as a reminder of who owned the Americas for the next several hundred years. As the Spanish continued to expand to fill its claims of territory and to *Christianize* the tribes and nations, a responsibility bestowed upon them by the Pope Alexander VI in 1501,[11] each geographic area presented physical challenges not experienced before. Each indigenous American group presented a new way of life, a new language, and new ways to scratch out basic survival needs from the often barren, inhospitable land. Too often they were hostile toward the Spanish due to tales of slavery raids that preceded the friar's incursion, or due to the horrible, usually fatal sicknesses that too often appeared just before or after first contact with the Spanish.

Most indigenous people wanted nothing to do with the European strangers. The city of Matehuala was so named for the often repeated word used by the natives upon their first encounters with the Spanish. Later it was found that the word meant: *Do not come.* But the Spanish had come to stay.

Friars were to expunge and replace the indigenous religions with a new faith. The new, Southern European faith was defined by the Council of Trent in a marathon sixteenth century response to the reformation movements within the European Roman Catholic Church. Trent gave Roman Catholic leaders a fixed doctrinal position and required that the Latin Church traditions be locked into a rigid, unchangeable, hierarchal structure centered in Rome. This was a response to those reformation movements that were questioning the Roman church's legitimacy and challenging the Southern Church's spiritual authority and political structure.

A second mandate of the friars during the conquest was to make Spanish *citizens* out of the indigenous groups by teaching them gainful employment and Spanish cultural mores, and then to incorporate them into the imperial economy. Eventually employment meant agriculture, ranching, and limited cottage industry, all of which the friar was to be proficient in and able to teach his flock. Often the survival of the mission and its converts depended upon their self-sufficiency. An evaluation of the degree of success of this missionary enterprise must take into consideration the degree of success of both of these primary objectives.

The King of Spain was the civil head of government, but he was also the Emperor of the Holy Roman Catholic Empire. The Council of Trent defined in clear, concise terms what being a Roman Catholic meant; the religious police of the Inquisition enforced Roman Catholic doctrinal purity. The civil law that came down from the King, through the Viceroy and his magistrates, and eventually to the priests and friars, was also very clearly defined for each stage of the conquest of New Spain. To fulfill his mission the friar morally and legally had to accomplish both, i.e. make these indigenous Americans Roman Catholic Christians and make them culturally Spanish citizens of the Empire.

The methodologies of the friars and their missiological framework need to be examined, and how those missiological principles evolved as they approached the herculean tasks set before them. Missionary work was always constrained within the greater framework of the colonists, civil government, and a military presence, as well as the mission organization's own assigned purposes. It quickly becomes obvious that New Spain was not a monolithic imperial system applying its imperial policies equally throughout the empire.[12] Local interpersonal and interregional dynamics shaped the course of law application, if indeed the imperial laws were ever implemented at all. Very often, the friars were the civil government as they attempted to contact, subjugate, convert, and disciple the indigenous people. When the indigenous people turned hostile, the friars also became the military presence seeking to defend themselves and their converts from the pagan hordes. When the Spanish presence was sufficiently great to warrant its own civil authorities and/or military presence in strength, then the civil authority was removed from the friars. That was often accomplished with a bit of animosity from both sides, but the missionary was usually seen as a tool to accomplish specific purposes for the Crown and the Church, and then to be sent somewhere else to repeat the process.

It is difficult, though necessary, to limit the scope of this study to something less than the whole existence and ever-changing geography of New Spain. The conquests of the multitude of indigenous nations, and then the colonization to permanently hold the newly conquered territory, took more than 300 years and were still in progress when Mexico threw off the shackles of colonial government, winning their independence from Spain in 1829. It is in many ways precisely these centuries long processes of conquest and colonization that are in and of themselves the causes of much confusion when one attempts historical understanding of the religious foundations of the conquest of New Spain.

This venture will take on the form of a comparative survey of the conquest period, focusing on the ministries of the friars as they attempted to fulfill their purposes as missionaries and cultural change agents in the various indigenous contexts. In the process of survey the evolution or progressive developments in methodology in the fundamental missionary work of the friars will be noted, as well as their strategies in coping with the perceived extremes in the value systems of the indigenous cultures. This study will focus on the entrance of the friars into their particular Epoch of conquest and how their ministries were established, that is the formation of, or application of, their methodologies.

Although the way they went about their work was often modified as friars adjusted to changing circumstances, sometimes over several generations, it was usually the entrance and initial evangelistic efforts that established basic patterns of indigenous worship for as long as the indigenous cultures would last as distinct elements of New Spain society. As the study moves through the different Epochs of conquest we can also observe the actual results of the missionary efforts in the indigenous cultural adaptations and responses to the friars' Tridentine Roman Catholic evangelism.

The basic question to be considered is this: How did post-Tridentine Roman Catholicism affect the missiology of the mendicant friars in the New Spain context of indigenous American conquest and domination by Spain? Corollaries to this question would be: Given their historical context, their geographic assignment, and the expected indigenous groups to be subjugated, how did the friars adapt their methods and expectations for ministry? What did the friars actually accomplish, or perhaps better expressed, for what did they give their lives? The latter question is demanded by the lists of deaths from hardship, murder, and drownings from among the different mendicant orders.[13]

To answer these questions, several underlying questions surface. Who were these friars upon which such a heavy mantle of responsibility was to be shouldered? What was the historical context from which these missionaries were drawn? What was the geography of New Spain in their eyes, at the time of their ministry? Who were these 'heathen' nations? What were the assigned purposes of the friars as men under rule and as missionaries? Obviously, each underlying question introduces another whole order of sub questions that should to be answered to grasp the meaning of the primary question.

It was asked, "For what did they give their lives?" Scores of friars and priests gave their lives quite literally as martyrs for their church and Lord. Some through ghastly torture and very slow death, accompanied by the most humiliating treatment one can conceive. For a great many others, the lives they gave were many years of hard labor, loneliness, and frustration that destroyed lesser men. For some was given the delight of seeing the success of their ministries and to partake of the fruits of their labors. The Scriptures declare that we shall know them by their fruit.[14]

What was the fruit, the long-term legacy, of the Friar-Indian encounter in New Spain? These all form a part of the primary question this book will attempt to answer.

Seldom are the missionary tasks of these friars investigated in a context sensitive manner. Many generations of friars came and went over the centuries of mission work. They came from many different backgrounds, spoke different languages, their training differed widely, and their Orders had different emphases in life and in ministry. They ministered in divers' geographical areas from steaming jungles to arid mountains, and hazardous deserts. Many were killed by the very people they had come to transform, to bless with the precepts of their one true religion as understood by the friars, and the benefits of Spanish civilization—whether the people wanted those benefits or not.

The magnitude of the task facing these friars could have wilted the strongest human will. First, they were to bring the Tridentine Roman Catholic Faith to a continent. A continent with hundreds of separate indigenous nations, each with varying degrees of social development, radically different customs and cultures, many different families of languages, dialects, and still more sub dialects, and each group with its own, well developed religion. The time span in which the whole enterprise was undertaken, more than 300 years, and given the technology of the times would have been a discouragement, probably in some cases it was an impossible undertaking. Most of these friars had no idea what was in the surrounding geographic areas to which they were assigned, or what cataclysmic events might lie ahead. The ideological and legal controversy in which the whole task was embroiled most of the time might have stopped the whole process, and indeed it did in some geographic areas.

The Dominicans, Franciscans, Augustinians, Mercedarians, and the Jesuits all have extensive written histories of their ministries in North America, as they have understood them.[15] Some were written as a defense of their methodologies, their doctrine, and either for or against the treatment of the indigenous people by the Spanish civil governments, colonists, and militia forces. Others were written to establish sainthood for a particularly effective missionary. Some were written to attack another order such as the attacks on the Jesuit Order which resulted in their expulsion from all of Spain's empire. These histories make a valuable contribution to our understanding when read with discrimination as to when it was written, who wrote it, and for what purposes.

One tantalizing category of primary sources would be missionary reports to their superiors, requests for supplies, and personal correspondence to family, friends, and business associates. Civil leaders also frequently had to make reports, defend their actions, and wrote to family and business associates. However, the archaic language and location of the many surviving documents of the various Orders make their accessibility difficult. Much of what was written concerning New Spain missions was destroyed, or is still hidden in archives, in monasteries, in convents, and library storerooms throughout the Iberian Peninsula, and Latin America. For example, most of what was written by Franciscans in Mexico that survived the Mexican Revolution with its library burnings has been gathered in store rooms such as in the Franciscan Convent in Celaya, Guanajuato. There the material is un-catalogued for the most part, and simply waiting for researchers to penetrate the mysteries they might contain. They are written in antiquated Spanish, in individualized longhand styles, many with improvised phonetic alphabets, and are in varying degrees of preservation. Few of these sources have been translated and random samplings would indicate it will be rare indeed to find them speaking to this missiological research question.

This study will examine the data recorded by early historians of the conquest of New Spain, along with the writings of more contemporary authors, to gain a better understanding of the mission of the friars, their ministries, and the results of their work. An observation from this research is that there is a reticence to accept primary historical documents that are written by clerics at their face value, more so than any investigation or normal discernment would warrant. The reasons often cited[16] for this reluctance are that the reality of mission life and dealing with indigenous people has been misrepresented and skewed for a defense of personal ministries, for self-serving purposes, or to justify continuing support of the local mission by far off authorities. Some secular historians have by-passed primary sources because a 'miracle' is stated as actually happening, and for the secular mind-set that just can't be.[17] Revisionist historians have attributed the motives of clerics[18] to something other than the obvious fact that a minister of the gospel is called of God and serving God to the best of his ability.

The sacrifice of one's life in humble servitude, or facing torture or violent death for personal beliefs, is normally taken as a confirmation of intrinsic motives. An investigator must be discerning, but not to such an extreme as to overlook the obvious.

At times historical data has been deliberately misconceived for political or personal reasons. An example would be the adamant denial of modern Carib or Aztec indigenous leaders of their ritual cannibalistic heritage,[19] both in the face of overwhelming historical evidence to the contrary. Another example would be the omissions in South Carolina museums and school texts that have little or nothing to say about early English colonists arming and leading pagan Creeks on raids to burn churches, murder indigenous Christians, and to capture those who survived the raids to sell them into slavery in the Caribbean plantations. Neither do they emphasize that Charleston harbor was a center for the slave trade to sell captured indigenous Carolinians as slaves into the plantations of the Indies long before it became a center for the importation of black slaves to the colonies.[20] History by definition has happened; it is dishonest to attempt to change it or forget it is part of who we are as a people and from where we have come.

Also an objective of this study is to glean from the historical record the context of the missionary enterprise, to better understand the conditions of the indigenous people the missionaries attempted to reach, and what the missionaries actually did to bring about cultural and political change. Some would say that history is interpretations of interpretations and that it is unrealistic to seek the truth in history.[21] Still, it is an objective of this study to discern what information is most consistent with the context and known facts of the epoch, the nature of the friars and their commission, and attempt to tone down the inherent political and personal bias of the times to reach an understanding of the way in which missionary practices took place during each epoch of Spanish conquest.

The methodology of this study will be to briefly summarize the Spanish secular conquest, and/or the religious missionary charge at the point of contact with the indigenous nation for each epoch under consideration. The indigenous context at the time of the conquest will need to be surveyed for insight as to the indigenous reaction to the strategies and methodologies the friars actually implemented. An analysis will be attempted to discern how efficacious the ministry was for accomplishing their objectives of making Roman Catholic Christians and Spanish citizens of the indigenous nations subjugated. It will then be possible to attempt to determine the advancement of missiological strategies, methods, and the positive results, or explanations as to why the missionary objectives were not accomplished.

With these considerations I have defined an *epoch* of the New Spain conquest by considering the geography of New Spain, the chronology of the conquest, the cultural/linguistic homogeneity of the indigenous people, and which orders were assigned to the tasks of *Reduction*[22] and evangelization of the people. All these parameters applied simultaneously would result in eight[23] major *epochs* for the conquest of New Spain spanning three centuries.

Naming these epochs by geographic regions in more or less chronological order of conquest they would be: the Florida/Caribbean Region; the Central Valleys (Nahuatl/Tarascan) Region; the Yucatan (Maya) Region; the Central High Deserts (Chichimeca), the Nueva Vizcaya and Baja California Region; the New Mexico Region (Pueblos); the Nuevo Leon, Santander/Texas Region (Coahuiltecan); and the Upper California Region. Overlap and the incredibly drawn out order of conquest still leaves these *epochs* a bit fuzzy, but they are sufficiently defined for these purposes.

My hypothesis for this book is that the Council of Trent so constrained the missiology of the mendicant friars that they seldom if ever preached the gospel of Jesus Christ as the Lord commanded when he said, "Go therefore and make disciples of all the nations, baptizing them . . . teaching them to observe all that I commanded you."[24] The anemic gospel that was preached by the friars could not have been construed as redemptive, as a rule. However, the Word of God was there, and the Holy Spirit was there, because the friars were there. God in his sovereignty could call indigenous Americans to himself because the Roman Pontiff and the King of Spain in obedience to God's command in His Word had sent the mendicant friars to New Spain.

CHAPTER II

THE PRECONQUEST
EUROPEAN CONTEXT

Europe, at the time of its discovery of America, was in chaos. The Renaissance was full blown bringing humanism and a return to the philosophy of secularism, worldly pleasures, personal independence, and individual expression. In contrast, the Latin Catholic church at the time officially ignored both man and nature; it restricted individual expression, fostered self-abnegation and self-annihilation, demanded implicit faith and unquestioning obedience. For what was thought to be the only remaining true church in the world, life revolved around the community rather than the individual, collective and corporate liberty rather than individual freedom. The individual who attempted to challenge authority or traditions, in matters of thought or action, was either discouraged or silenced by the church.[1]

The end of the fifteenth century also saw the conclusion of a long period of ethnic cleansing within the Iberian Peninsula. The Jewish population had been a part of the Iberian Peninsula since the Romans ruled the area, yet they were never assimilated into the various Iberian cultures. There had been repeated attempts at conversion of the Jews, most peaceful, some forceful, a few of them quite violent. Then in the middle of the 14th century the Spanish Crown ordered free access to both Jewish and Moorish communities for evangelism. The edict was met with resistance, and more serious trouble soon followed. In 1391, in Seville, Synagogues were closed or burned, and thousands of Jews killed or violated. The persecution of Jews then spread to the whole Iberian Peninsula, with entire Jewish communities in 70 Spanish towns destroyed. In Valencia not a single known Jew was left alive in the

Kingdom. The total number of Jewish dead by some estimates was over 50,000.

What made this persecution different was that with few exceptions in the past, the Jews died for their faith. This time the morale of the Jews corporately broke, possibly for the first and only time in the long, bloody history of these people. A very large proportion of these Jews chose life rather than martyrdom, and converted to Latin Catholicism. Large bodies of Jews, often led by their Rabbis and scholars, accepted mass baptism. Thus the fourteenth century saw vast numbers of both Jew and Moor, enter into the Spanish Roman Catholic faith, with very little knowledge of it. They accepted Christianity to spare their lives, but continued the practice of their previous cultural expressions and many secretly practiced the tenants of their previous faith.

"The survivors of the persecutions were Jews in all but name and Christian in nothing but outward form."[2] Their Jewish and Moorish cultural expressions did not change, nor did their economic status change. Therefore assimilation into the dominant culture still failed to occur. Hiebert explains this phenomenon in terms of conversion.[3] He sees three levels of conversion: First, is that which affects surface culture, behavior, and rituals. At this level the ways of the dominant Christian culture are adopted such as clothing, food, memorization of rules and sayings, etc. The second level of conversion is that which affects beliefs and belief systems. This can be understood in repentance and confession of sins, belief and following the teaching of the Scriptures, and voluntary participation in the Christian society. The third level is that which changes the world view from the popular society view to a fundamentally biblical world view. Few of the Jewish and Moorish converts ever made it past the first level of outward change, but continued to practice their own belief systems and world views.

The Jewish-Spanish Catholics were derogatorily known as *Marranos* (pigs). This apparent syncretism of the Jewish-Catholic beliefs was a principle motivation for the Spanish Inquisition—the Crown was concerned, as proof of secret Jewish practices was given, that many Jews had made false professions and that they would contaminate the Jewish Catholics that were sincere in their faith. Something had to be done but the King of Spain did not trust the Pope enough to involve Rome. Finally the King was able to secure permission from Rome to appoint his own inquisitors.[4] The Spanish Inquisition was intended to be used against the Jewish and Moorish sham proselytes, but soon spread to anyone suspected of heresy. The trial of the Inquisition not only provided a legal means to destroy the individuals, it also meant the confiscation of their wealth, properties, and businesses. Even dead individuals were tried and effigies burned at the stake so that the properties of their descendents could be confiscated. Persecution and popular fanaticism, coupled with both church and State acquiescence, led to continuing massacres of Jews with impudence all over Spain during the latter fourteenth century. Later, with the fall of the last Moorish Caliph in Granada, the time had come for the Crown to act against the remaining Jews.

The Jews' expulsion had long been an objective of the Spanish Inquisition headed up by Father Tomas de Torquemada. Ferdinand and Isabella had rejected up until that time Torquemada's demands that the Jews be expelled. Then in 1492, after the Spanish Army had defeated Muslim forces in Granada and all of Spain was established under Roman Catholic rule, the time was ripe. With the country's unification complete, the king and queen concluded that the Jews were now expendable. On March 30, they issued the infamous expulsion decree with the order to take effect four months later.[5]

This edict applied only to the *Jews* of Spain, while the ethnic Moors of Granada were still exempt due to the generous treaty granted by Ferdinand and Isabella in 1492, which guaranteed freedom of worship for the Muslims within their Mosques. The Spanish even allowed Muslims expelled from Portugal to settle in Spain. But due to the inquisition methods of Archbishop Ximenes Cisneros, pressure was put on the Muslims, in violation of the Spanish sovereigns' decrees and also in violation of the provisions of the Treaty of Grenada. Many Muslims were forced to convert to Catholicism. Mosques were the local center of studies and for the preparation of Imanes, their leaders. To put a stop to leadership training, Cisneros ordered the destruction of thousands of rare manuscripts in the Muslim study centers. When accused by the Muslims of breaking the treaty, the Spanish Sovereigns did nothing to stop the out-of-control, fanatical Bishop. He was cited to give account and after his defense before the King, Cisneros returned and forced the baptism of 50,000-70,000 Muslims.[6] In 1502, Ferdinand ordered the expulsion edict against all Muslims but in such strict terms that compliance was impossible and the only real choice was to convert.

A Bishop from this epoch wrote that anyone might with impunity slay a heretic (evangelical), an infidel (Jew or Muslim), or a renegade (a defector from Roman Catholicism that became a Muslim—these were especially hated).[7] Of these three, the evangelical who wished to reform the Roman Catholic hierarchy or its dogmas was considered the most dangerous. Heresy was considered treason against the State as well as the church, being as the two were so closely linked. The evangelical that questioned any element of the Catholic Church's dogma or tradition was the anarchist of the middle Ages[8] and viewed with revulsion by the faithful Roman Catholic.

About 250,000 Jewish people were affected by the eviction notice of intolerance and desperate to find a way out of Spain. Every Spanish seaport was congested with refugees.[9] The Jewish and Moorish expulsions affected the mentality and world view of most Spaniards of that time. The Jews were converted, dead or gone. The Moors were defeated, converted, or dead and no longer visible in society. The evangelical Roman Catholic reformers had no footholds on the Iberian Peninsula and the common understanding was that Spain would be of one religion: Roman Catholic. None other would be tolerated. The friars carried to New Spain this attitude of Spanish intolerance towards the religions of all other peoples. If a religious practice was not of the Latin Catholic Church, it was of the devil, set against the Spanish monarchy, and set against God. The missiological pattern was already set by the crusades of the re-conquest and ethnic cleansings of Spain: anything other than Roman Catholicism would not be tolerated and therefore must be eliminated by any means possible.

In the early sixteenth century the Holy Roman Empire was facing grave threats from without, as well as Christian evangelical diversity from within, but Charles V rose to the occasion. His great success in defending the Habsburg realm (Austria) against France from the west, the Ottoman Turks from the east, and the emerging German Protestants from the north, led many to believe he was divinely appointed to be *God's Standard-Bearer* and to spread the Southern European Latin version of Christianity to the New World.[10] He took that commission seriously. The previous administrations had dealt with the Jews and Muslims, evicting them from Spain. Spain was Spanish, and Spain was Roman Catholic. Some were saying that it was more Catholic than the

Vatican itself. The Spanish Inquisition was established to keep all of the Spanish Empire that way.

It has been said that medieval warfare and pogroms against the cultures of Islam and Judaism gave Spanish Roman Catholicism a militant edge not found elsewhere in Europe.[11] Throughout the Empire, that militancy was turned against the new reformers and reformation movements that spontaneously kept appearing in different places. Within the Holy Roman Empire it was decided that these reformation movements should be ended immediately and by force if necessary. But what was to be the standard of measurement for correct doctrine and practice? Reformation movements and contradictions between the Bible and popular Christian practices had totally muddied the waters. The Council of Trent was called to establish the standard for correct doctrine and practice that would be enforced for all Roman Catholics wherever they were for centuries to come.

The fifteenth century represented years of the ethnic cleansing and religious purification in Spain. During that time several precedents were set that would come back into vogue in New Spain as the crusades[12] against the American indigenous people unfolded. These precedents were:

- The mass conversions of ethnic groups to Roman Catholicism through the application of water baptism.
- The concept that clerics must obey the dictates of the Roman church over the King's commands.
- The precedent of book-burning campaigns using all the opposition's ethnic literature in an attempt to eradicate the subculture.

These precedents can be viewed as the rudiments of Spanish Roman Catholic missiology that would be implemented in New Spain. Missiology is the division of theology that studies the practice of cross-cultural evangelism, discipleship, and the founding of Christian Churches in a new cultural context. These three precedents that grew out of the Spanish ethnic cleansing and religious purification on the Iberian Peninsula were the guidelines for the friars as they faced this huge challenge of communicating Christianity to the indigenous Americans and founding an American Roman Catholic Church.

The first precedent of mass conversion of both Jews and Muslims along with their leadership, without any individual preparations, and without any discipleship by religious leaders, meant that the local churches were full of what Hiebert called first-level converts that understood almost nothing of their new religion but the name. When the ethnic community leadership were left to continue in their same roles after baptism, a covert continuation of former cultural practices was almost inevitable. This had the effect of introducing many syncretic practices of the old religions into the Roman Catholic cultural expressions. Baptisms without teaching or discipleship would necessarily result in a fusion of belief systems and detract from the significance of the Christian baptism as an initiation rite to the new religion. The lack of doctrinal teaching opens the door to a continuation of the previous religious world views as an underground cultural expression and can manifest itself as resistance to the importation of new expressions with their original meanings.

This practice of mass conversions by water baptism would be confirmed as legitimate by the Council of Trent due to their acceptance of the view of baptismal regeneration—the doctrine that water baptism truly affects, or marks, the soul of an individual.[13] Coupled with the concept of Purgatory, baptism implied arrival into God's presence in eternity regardless of one's behavior in this earthly life and suggested no clear moral responsibility on the part of the individual. Mass baptisms would be used extensively in New Spain with many of the same moral and ethical problems found in the Spanish Crusade against the Moors and Jews of Old Spain.[14]

The second precedent to emerge from this period of political and religious upheaval was the activities of Ximenes Cisneros, the Archbishop of Toledo. With the full knowledge of Ferdinand and Isabella, the Cardinal proceeded to violate the guarantees of the 1492 Treaty of Grenada for Muslim citizens of Spain.[15] Bringing the Inquisition against the Moors of Spain, Ximenes forced the mass baptism of Muslims that had opted against returning to Africa. In 1500, he caused the collection of all books written in Aramaic, especially copies of the Qur'an, to be burned in public. More than 1,000,000 volumes, including unique works of Moorish culture were destroyed. Later on in New Spain Bishop Juan Zumárraga would claim this precedent as justification for the utter destruction of the Aztec Codices—and the loss of written Aztec history to the world.[16]

Because the friars that were sent to New Spain always had to obey two authorities, the King and the Pope, Bishop Ximenes also set the precedent that the religious must obey the dictates of the church over the King's command or over the laws of the land. In the case of the Treaty of Grenada, when it came into conflict with the Inquisition, the King decided in favor of the arguments of Ximenes over his own word codified and sworn before God in the treaty. This precedent became the basis of endless sparring between the secular priests, the friars, and the Spanish civil authorities in New Spain. In reality, the same basic arguments would continue throughout the history of Mexico and into our own time.

Northern Europe Becomes Protestant

Before, and coinciding with the events within Spain during the first part of the sixteenth century, were the escalating events of the Protestant Reformation—the *enlightened* Roman Catholics that *protested* against the dominance of the Roman Church in every aspect of life. First, there was John Wycliffe (1324-1384) and his followers, the Lollards, with the first English translation of the Bible. There had been Bible portions before Wycliffe, but he believed that the Sacred Scriptures were meant to be the property of the people. In his time, the Black Death swept England taking nearly half of the population of London and causing grave doubts about the efficacy of religion. Wycliffe had a theological doctorate and was a professor at Oxford University. He preached against the scandalous conduct of the friars of the Dominican and Franciscan Orders. His pamphlets attacked the doctrines of the Latin Church that violated clear Scriptural teaching. His followers, the Lollards, accepted no authority but Scripture, practiced believer's baptism, and declared the doctrine of transubstantiation false.[17] Wycliffe was finally burned at the stake; his followers formed an army and rebelled against the Crown of England, but were defeated. Yet his teachings prevailed and continued to influence many later reform movements.

Then followed the Bohemian John Huss, and after his martyrdom the Hussite Church was organized, which became the first Protestant movement to succeed from the Latin Church, after fighting the holy Roman armies to a standstill. Huss was heavily influenced by Wycliffe's writings and attacked the abuses of the clergy, thus earning the hostility of many priests. He was appointed rector of the university but was later excommunicated (in 1410) by the archbishop, along with his followers. Huss denied the infallibility of an immoral pope, asserted the ultimate authority of Scripture over the traditions of the Church, and accorded the State the right and duty to supervise the Church.[18] Because of these ideas he is generally considered a forerunner of what was to become the Evangelical or Protestant Reformation. He was granted a safe-conduct by Pope Sigismund to visit Rome and defend his doctrines, a safe conduct which was then violated by the Roman Church. Huss was imprisoned and tried as a heretic and later burned at the stake by this same *infallible* Pope that had issued the safe-conduct.

Then along came Martin Luther (1483-1546) with his Bible translation into the German language and his Lutheran movement which, with support of the German princes, directly challenged the authority of the Pope, the counsels, and many of the traditions of the Latin Catholic church. Luther consolidated the elements of the evangelical reformations to date when he nailed his Ninety-Five Theses to the door of the Wittenberg Church.[19] This symbolic, direct challenge to the Latin Church went unanswered until the Council of Trent, and then the points of doctrine and traditional practices were largely answered in the negative. The Trent participants could not handle the doctrine of justification by faith—the teaching that Christ's own righteousness is imputed to those who believe, and that on that ground alone, those who believe are accepted by God. This doctrine, more than all the moral issues, initiated the great division between the Northern European and the Southern European churches. Luther's teachings are summarized in the following documents: Shorter Catechism (in 1529); The Augsburg Confession (in 1530); The Larger Catechism (in 1530). Though Luther is often seen as the greatest of the evangelical reformers, he retained much of the former Roman Catholic practices and traditions in the new Lutheran church movements.

John Calvin (1509-1564) and the Huguenot movement in France developed an entirely different approach to theology based upon Scriptures alone. Luther started with the Roman Church and eliminated anything he could not find in Scripture; Calvin started with the Scriptures and built whole new expressions of church practice based only upon the biblical principles. In Geneva, Calvin introduced much of what would become known as the Reformed Traditions, which included much greater participation by the laity in church government. Calvin went to the University of Paris where he studied theology, then law, then back to Paris again to study Greek. He became an admirer of Erasmus and was greatly influenced by the humanist while becoming highly critical of the abuses in the French Catholic Church. The French Crown was strongly Roman Catholic forcing Calvin to flee to Geneva, a French-speaking Swiss city, which became the centre of his work. In May, 1536, the city adopted his religious reform which included 1) the dissolving of monasteries, 2) the abolishment of the Holy Mass, and 3) the renunciation of Papal authority.[20]

It took Calvin 14 years before he could fully impose his version of liturgy, doctrine, organization of the church, and biblical moral behavior on Geneva. It was expected that many French Huguenots would head for the university to train as missionaries, and they did. Calvin's dream was fulfilled by 1654, with over 1,500 students studying in the university, and most of them were French. Educated merchants were drawn to Calvinism with its strong work ethic and individual responsibility. A number of noble French families converted to Calvinism, although it was illegal to do so by French law. The Huguenots were concentrated on the coast of France, mainly in the west (La Rochelle) and in the southeast. They developed their own cavalry force and openly worshipped in their own churches with armed guards at the doors for security.[21]

By 1561, there were 2,150 Huguenot churches in France and Calvinists were estimated to be about 10% of the population—about one million people. The French Reformed churches continued to spread until the Jesuit advisor to the King convinced him to prepare secretly and strike at the Huguenots by surprise. On August 24, 1572 the French army and brigades of the Holy Roman Empire's army, attacked most of the French Huguenot communities simultaneously. After one week of bloodshed, over 100,000 Huguenots were murdered in what became known as the St. Bartholomew Massacre.[22] With Charles IX, the St. Bartholomew Massacre, and the intolerable persecutions of the bloody tyrant Louis XIV, it has been estimated that almost two million Huguenots died or had to flee France.[23] In the final expulsion order

---

of Louis XIV in 1685, the last 400,000 Huguenots were driven out of France,[24] leaving only a few very isolated pockets of evangelicals in France known as Desert Huguenots.

Switzerland at the time of the Evangelical Reformation was not so much a single country as a confederacy of 13 city-states or *cantons*. Several of these cantons broke away from the Roman Catholic Church and became Evangelical. Ulrich Zwingli, a humanist scholar and leader of the evangelical reformation in Switzerland, accepted Luther's ideas which began to pore over from the German borders and from the cantons that adopted Luther's views; the most important was the city-state of Zurich, under the capable leadership of Zwingli.

Zwingli brought to Luther's revolution an education steeped in northern humanism, particularly that of Desiderius Erasmus. He was popular in the extreme among the people of Zurich for his opposition to Swiss mercenary service in foreign wars, for his attacks on indulgences, and for the fact that he was as significant a player in the critique of indulgences as Luther himself.[25] Zwingli's theology and morality were based on a single principle of hermeneutics: if the Old or New Testament did not say something explicitly and literally, then it was not binding upon the Christian. This resulted in an important shift in understanding and use of the Scriptures in practice. The literal reading of the Old and New Testaments and their application to life brought a whole new meaning to popular Christianity and to secular authority.

The most important doctrinal issue of contention between Zwingli and Luther was that they disagreed on the nature of the Eucharist. Zwingli believed the elements only *symbolized* the body and blood of Christ, while Luther held to a Roman Catholic understanding that the elements *became* the body and the blood. This theological division prevented an alliance between the German and Swiss States, as intelligent and necessary as this was politically for their survival against Rome. They met at Marburg and attempted to forge a common understanding, but in the end, they failed. After Marburg, the unification of the various Evangelical movements seeking reform in the Roman Catholic Church became untenable.

All of these evangelical movements and their leadership became abhorrent to the Spanish. Their very existence was intolerable to the Latin Catholic expression of Christianity and their followers became fair game for the pyres of the inquisition. Because of the inability of the evangelical reformation movements to join forces, none of them individually were a match for the Holy Roman Empire's armies. Therefore much of what was gained by the evangelical movements was soon to be lost in the wars that followed, historically and corporately to be known as the Roman Catholic Church's Counter Reformation.

The evangelical movements focused upon biblical theology, and then the practical application of that theology to life, especially Christian morality fueled by a universal rebellion against flagrant immorality within the Roman Catholic Church. The Roman Church focused upon its traditions and practice, and then concentrated upon how to substantiate those practices with a plausible theology. But the way the Roman Catholic Church attempted to crush the evangelical movements and murder their adherents spawned such deep rooted hatreds and fundamental distrust among the evangelicals, that any form of reconciliation became simply untenable. This became the foundation and heritage of what otherwise seemed like unprovoked slaughter of each other as the two ideologies encountered one another in the later epochs of evangelism in North America.

For the Roman Catholic hierarchy, biblical morality was not an issue. It would be correct to take a closer look at the moral and ethical behavioral problems of the Spanish at the time of conquest because of the way they affect the indigenous Americans of this study.

Sixteenth Century Roman Catholic Moral Practices

Religious unity, consolidation under the one Roman Catholic expression, did not bring about a uniform, individual response of the Spanish people to the moral code of their faith. Religion for the newly baptized adult was, in reality, a formal acceptance of what the Roman Catholic Church taught with neither a real moral influence, nor a demand to see a change in the character of the person as evidence of regeneration. In Tridentine, Roman Catholic theology baptism was to accomplish that, with or without outward evidence.

It has been said that the conquistadores were men of their times.[26] That we cannot condone what they did, but we must understand their morality, ethical conditions, and beliefs in the context of the times.

It is said that we must not judge history based upon the morality of our own times.[27] Perhaps it would be more appropriate to have our perceptions of the times formulated upon biblical, absolute truth as opposed to a secular perspective, or rather than a modern verses historical perspective. It is easy to overlook the fact that men of all times are at least equally intelligent.[28] In the cases of Roman Catholic or Evangelical Catholic morality, both expressions of New Testament Christianity are originally based upon the same Scriptures,[29] both are guided and enlightened by the same Holy Spirit in understanding of those Scriptures. All Christian movements have their confessions and creeds that were passed down from the ancients that formed the dogmas of their faith. The early separatist evangelical movements of this period retained far more of the religious expressions of the Latin Catholic church than they would like to publicly admit. Universally, believers of both these expressions of faith today would heartily and completely condemn the violence, torture, and murder so commonly found in the Iberian and American crusades against Jews, Muslims and indigenous Americans, as well as condemn the many wars these two expressions of Christianity have fought against each other over the years.

Therefore it is not the elements of enlightenment or of knowledge of right and wrong or of good and evil that are lacking on the parts of Roman or Evangelical Catholic traditions. What Christian men do must be evaluated, not by what their society or their conscience says is right, but by what their moral and ethical foundations based upon God's special revelation say is right. The behavioral problems of the Spanish crusade against the indigenous Americans are really based, not upon the actions of those who practice the moral precepts of their Christianity, but upon those who do not, or only practice a secular or social expression of their Christianity—whether friar, colonist, or soldier. As the Apostle Paul would say to the Corinthian Christians it's the works of the spiritual man verses the works of the carnal man. This type of division highlights the terrible results of a populace that fails to grasp the morality of their own religious expression, and only adheres to the religious motions or customs of their traditions without any change of heart attitude, or, as the theologians would say, without regeneration or change in their spiritual nature.

It has been suggested that the many reform movements taking place in the fourteenth and fifteenth century churches were indeed affecting the leadership of the church, but leaving the body of the church still basically unaffected.[30] Could it be some massive flaw in the dogmas of the Roman Catholic Church itself that condones, or at least permits, immoral behavior on the part of its adherents, even on a scale such as practiced in the conquest of New Spain? By assuming the position that a priest by his work can transmit saving grace through the administration of the sacrament of baptism, the Council of Trent was laying upon the priesthood a work that only the Spirit of God can perform in a human being. A ritual performed by man was replacing the atoning work of the Holy Spirit of God Himself. This was indeed at the heart of what the reformation movements were opposing. That water baptism was not changing the nature of the newly baptized was obvious among the many Jews and Moors that had been baptized by force. The dreaded inquisition still had to be brought into being to deal with the many baptized Spanish people that wanted nothing to do with Latin Christianity.

A secular or anthropological approach, putting aside all pretext of religion, would serve the same ends as this Tridentine doctrine. The anthropologist Sweet expressed this thought when he said that conversion cannot be done to people. It is undergone voluntarily by rational adults who have learned something new that makes sense to them and that seems so important as to cause them to want to adjust the rest of their thinking and behavior to it. It is an active and not passive experience.[31] Tridentine dogma says holy water can regenerate; the anthropologist says knowledge can regenerate and alter behavior. Both leave God out of the equation. The evangelical reformers of the Catholic Church were taking exactly the opposite tact saying only God can regenerate and change the inner man, which then permits a change in the outer man to begin to take place, the doctrine of sanctification, and cause a change in his moral perspective.

Another approach to this dilemma of baptismal regeneration might be to compare the Roman Catholic concept of corporate liberty verses the reformers' more humanistic concept of individual liberty. The underlying philosophy of the Trinity is that of internal relationships. Personal relationship and plural relationships exist within the Godhead; man created in his image reflects the same basic relationships, or need for relationships as seen in man and God interacting. God takes the initiative in pursuing relationship with each of us individually as seen in his interaction with Old Testament characters and then culminating in the sending of his Son, Jesus Christ, into the world to interact face to face, *Immanuel*—God with man. The reformers were teaching that it is relationship with the Triune God that changes the heart of a man giving him true individual liberty. It is a mystical, graceful relationship, initiated by God himself, based upon the finished work of Christ on the cross and his victory over death in the resurrection, all applied by the Holy Spirit to the individual setting him free from judgment and condemnation, liberating man's will. A priest with water and an institutional blessing cannot do this. The church on earth cannot assume the right to regenerate an individual by its own declaration over all the people that receive the church's baptism. The personal God of Salvation liberates individually as he calls each one of us to Himself; we are not saved corporately by church dogma.

How then can we understand this baptism of an individual apart from knowledge of God or of the Scriptures? First, baptism is an ecclesiastical act, an action sanctioned and performed by the Roman Catholic Church on an individual. As such it is, in part, an initiation into the visible church on earth. Confess with your mouth and believe in your heart are also requirements,[32] but in the case of uninformed baptism those two elements are missing. In a theocracy such as that of the Aztec society and a mono-religious empire such as that of the Spanish empire, the State and the state religion are inseparable. It was not possible to be a part of one without being a part of the other. Therefore water baptism became the initiation rite for entrance into the combined whole. As Rivera would say, baptism "became a political act, an affirmation of Spanish imperial sovereignty."[33] Therefore from the act of ecclesiastical baptism we see political subjugation taking place—subjugation to the new political/religious system of the conquerors but with no understanding of Christian spirituality or moral precepts on the part of the baptized. They became Spanish citizens, and therefore they were also Roman Catholic; as Spanish citizens they could be no other.

Without a doubt, God has accomplished his work apart from the knowledge of these intricacies of Christian doctrine. Saving faith, changed moral constitutions, and new life come from God through his Spirit and the Word of God. Both the Spirit of God and the Word of God were working in America because the mendicant friars were

in America. It was still God's choice as to who was to be called to be
sons, and those who were called Roman Catholics because of the water.
Obviously then, many Latin Catholics continued in their old natures,
with an unregenerate soul and the lack of Christian morality in their
hearts. That could explain the excesses of the confrontations between
Spanish and Native American armies: the Spanish branded with hot
irons, roasted men alive, dismembered, mangled, whipped, racked,
beheaded in sport, drowned, dashed against the rocks, drove them
until famished, fed them to mastiffs,[34] and in general, broke the spirit
of the indigenous people with senseless murder and torture designed to
shock the indigenous people into submission.[35] And this was all done
by educated, civilized Spanish men of "untainted blood" and called
Roman Catholic Christians. While other Spanish men looked on in
horror at what was happening and dedicated their lives to stopping the
outrages that were being done to the newly conquered people wherever
the Spanish conquistadores and colonists set foot.[36]

Under the evangelical movements of Europe in the sixteenth century,
whole new structures and philosophies of life were coming into being
in direct opposition to the Roman Catholic systems of government and
religious expressions, doctrines that would destroy the Latin-Roman
Catholic hierarchy if accepted. The Evangelical Reformation broke the
autocratic control of the Catholic Church on nearly all aspects of life
within the Reformed communities giving a whole new definition to
the meaning of liberty. The doctrine of the priesthood of all believers
highlighted individual liberty and undermined the Roman Catholic
concepts of corporate liberty.[37] The lasting results of the Protestant
Reformation for Northern Europe was an economic trend towards
capitalism, liberty for the individual, and a trend towards separation of
the politics of church and State. Calvin's experiments in Geneva led to
participation of the general public in the administration of their own
religious institutions and eventually of the institutions of their civil
governments as well.[38]

There was a special animosity for the French and the French
Evangelical Huguenots by the Spanish during the first epochs of the
conquest of New Spain. Back in Europe, the Spanish held that it
was the French that challenged the Hapsburg Empire and stole the
Papacy. It was the French that fought the Hapsburgs during the Thirty
Years War simply to stop Spanish dominance of Europe. Pure Roman

Catholic Spain watched in horror as the French evangelicals nearly won control of France and then cheered the expulsion of the last 400,000 Huguenots from France. However, what Spain did not anticipate was that many of these French evangelicals would find their way to the Americas, and Spain would soon have to deal with them directly upon her own soil of New Spain.

All of these European religious intrigues were factors when the leaders and theologians of the Southern European Roman Catholic Church met together at the Counsel Trent to determine just what was to be the Roman Catholic Church of the future. Their decisions would have a great impact upon the new content and methods of the evangelization of New Spain.

Therefore in the European context at the time of the discovery of the Americas, evangelical reformations as part of the Renaissance stood in direct contrast to the Roman Catholic Dark Age institution of corporate community, implicit faith, and unquestioned obedience. The fifteenth century also saw the conclusion of ethnic wars of Spain with the Roman Catholic armies dominating the Jews and the Muslims, forcing their conversion or expulsion from the Iberian Peninsula. The Spanish Inquisition was initiated to keep the forced converts to Roman Catholicism pure externally, although it was soon used against evangelical reformers and other political opponents as well. Spain became Rome's champion warriors, the intolerant 'terrorists' of their day that would do anything to another people as long as it resulted in their becoming a part of the Roman Catholic Church—slavery or death were the only other alternatives.

CHAPTER III

THE COUNCIL
OF TRENT

The Council of Trent straddled the partition of a European world in upheaval. At its beginning it included people who had experienced the institutional domination of the Roman Catholic Church over all aspects of life. At the conclusion of the meeting 16 years later, it included people who would experience Catholicism as only one force in a political and cultural marketplace that included many other religious and social forces.[1] According to Vecsey, "One must understand the post-Tridentine Church in its Spanish, French, and later Irish and German manifestations, as well as American-isms, in order to understand adequately the type of Christianity that [indigenous Americans] have met when they have encountered Catholicism."[2]

In order to bring together a formal church council in a reasonably neutral place, the town of Trent was finally decided upon. The agenda: to deal with the Lutherans and other evangelical reformers. It was necessary to wait until a conservative Pope was in control of the Catholic Church to accomplish the purposes formally assigned to the council by Paul III in 1542. These were to define doctrine, correct morals, restore peace among Christians, and repel infidels.[3] Towards the end of the Council, Pius IV made it more explicit that an objective was also "that schisms and heresies may be destroyed."[4]

Some salient factors of the European context at the time of Columbus and leading up to the Council of Trent have been noted. Consideration should also be given to the more immediate cultural and historical factors fermenting among the delegates to this historic conference which may have affected their perceptions as each orator spoke. There was a continual state of war going on with England, the Low Countries, and France at this point in history. There was a militant hatred for the reformation movements, for Protestantism, for the Muslims, and for the Jews. The inquisition was gaining strength carrying with it a constant foreboding by each delegate of being found in heresy by design or by omission. Any individual, regardless of rank or class that deviated from expected norms could expect to be tortured and/or suffer violent death by burning at the stake by the inquisitors.

Religious leaders usually had more influence and authority than most civil leaders in fifteenth and sixteenth century Europe. This meant that the Counsel was a powerful assembly politically. Outward appearance of conformity and submission to the church hierarchy were essential, yet no personal morality was really expected of clerics. The political intrigues they practiced would of themselves verify this. This was the normal environment of the delegates to the Council of Trent.

Added to this state of affairs the Roman Catholic Evangelicals and the Evangelical Reformers who had already declared themselves outside of the Roman Church were proposing interpretations of biblical doctrines that were seen to be attacking the very foundations of the Roman Church's beliefs, as well as the church's hierarchal authority. The evangelical attacks on the questionable foundations of many traditions were rocking the millennial Roman Church to the core. Not only that, but if based upon the Scriptures and sound hermeneutical principles alone, the arguments put forth against many of the Roman Church's traditions had the ring of truth. To base any debate upon the Cannon of the Scriptures would lead to a certain collapse of the traditional church structure whose foundations were really hundreds of years of traditions and evolution of traditions, not the Scriptures. What could be the authoritarian foundation of the Latin Church and its' councils if not the Scriptures? If the practices of the Roman Church could not be brought into alignment with Scriptures, how could they be justified? These were the real foundational issues set before the Council of Trent.

This is why those with a vested interest in the continuation of the traditional church were very careful to insure that a conservative Pope was reigning at the time of the council. Ward says, "Nothing, as had probably been foreseen at Rome, could have better facilitated the immediate establishment of the ascendancy in the counsel of the papal policy than the composition of its opening meeting. Of the 34 ecclesiastics present, only five were Spanish and two French bishops, and no German bishop had crossed the Alps. Nor had any secular power except the Emperor and King Ferdinand sent their ambassadors."[5] The Southern European powers had complete control of the council. The Northern European powers, where most of the evangelical reformations were taking place, remembered well what had happened to John Huss when he was issued a papal safe-conduct pass. They stayed home.

A philosophy of life flows from the values and belief system of the person. A very large part of the belief system is expressed in the theology to which one adheres. The theology which flowed out of the Council of Trent was clear, concise, and absolutely to be adhered to by all Roman Catholics.[6] But Rome, while waiting for the optimum conditions for their council, had waited too long to deal with the issues that the evangelical reformers were raising. The reformers were no longer dealing with the moral abuses in the church offices. They were dealing with the bad theology and hierarchal structure of the Roman Church that allowed the abuses a foothold in the first place. The Evangelical Reformation justified defiance of the Roman Catholic Church by claiming higher authority than the Church on earth—the Scriptures, God's Word. "Only the Scriptures" had become a watch-word of the Evangelical Reformation.

New, evangelical theologies and new structures for the church were being implemented and consolidated by these reformers while the Roman Catholic conservatives squabbled among themselves as to how, and when, to deal with the issues they were raising. The political squabbles seemed irreconcilable being as neither Pope nor monarchs could trust one another. The council could not be called until a Pope that would rule in the conservative's favor was in place to guarantee a continuation of the traditional churches' monolithic hierarchy. The church was willing to deal with the moral abuses and, with the passing of nearly a century, it did. The Latin Church was not capable of dealing with the new theological interpretations without self-destructing; neither could they accept the restructuring of the Holy Roman Catholic Church that was beginning to take place piecemeal by default while they delayed.

However, Spain was unaffected by all this controversy with the exception of making sure that *all* religious controversies stayed out of Spain. For over seven centuries Spain had reclaimed itself from

African dominance, had purged itself of all the Jews and Muslims, and had eliminated any evangelical reformers, all in order to assure that there was only going to be one religion in Spain and in the Spanish territories. The Spanish *religious cleansing* was nearly complete by the end of the fifteenth century. The self-conscious, traditional version of Southern European Christianity was thoroughly entrenched in the Iberian Peninsula by then. It was that version of Roman Catholicism which was set as their system of belief and would be defined in writing at Trent. So for the Iberian Peninsula, and for New Spain, no other religion could even be considered.

What the Council of Trent accomplished was to define the dogma of the Roman Catholic Church in such a way that allowed the church to continue to be the monolithic, top down church of the previous 1,000 years since the fall of the Roman Empire. Fancying themselves the one and only true religion, the only valid expression of Christianity, they made themselves an introverted sect, way off center from Biblical doctrine. Of the reformers that were invited to the council, those within and those already outside of the Roman Church, few came, and of those reformers that came, most left never to return after the first sessions. Obviously the deck was stacked against them. The council rejected the major doctrinal interpretations and arguments of the evangelical reformers outright. They then proceeded to fix for the centuries to come just what the Roman Catholic Church structure should be, making it even heavier at the top with the addition of the Congregations for administrative purposes. They fixed what traditions were *inspired by God* and what doctrinally all Roman Catholics had to believe. To counter the reformers, they claimed higher authority than even the Scriptures—God himself in their midst, the author of Scriptures, as their authority in a system of progressive revelation of His will through the Pope and the councils of the Church,[7] thus justifying their extra-biblical doctrines.

For the Council of Trent, ultimate authority for the counsel's decisions had to be based upon the Latin/Roman Church and none other, acting for God on earth in a unique and authoritative manner. This had the affect of logically requiring that the Roman Catholic expression of the church be the *only* true expression of the church, that it be exclusive and distinctively authoritative. This was the route chosen by the council. In attempting to protect the dogma of the

Roman Church, they took the expedient, political route and made the Roman Catholic Church into an exclusive sect of Christianity. Conversely, it also had the effect of denying the authority of any other expression of the Church on earth, as all sects do. This route left all would-be reformers in an irreconcilable position with the Roman Catholic Church. As Diamond has said: "Because of selfish actions taken for short-term gain, the Renaissance Popes deliberately provoked the Protestant succession."[8]

Therefore the Council of Trent established the doctrine that God spoke through the Popes and the Councils of the Church in authoritative revelation. Also, the unwritten apostolic traditions, whether dictated orally by Christ or by the Holy Spirit (through the Pope and councils), were also to be considered a source of saving truths and rules of conduct.[9] They established the Cannon of Scripture as including the Apocrypha books. The Council decreed that justification was an unmerited gift of God, but that man could *cooperate* with grace through good works. The council established the traditional seven sacraments (baptism, confirmation, Eucharist, penance, extreme unction, holy orders, and matrimony) as having been instituted by Christ and that they contained the grace they signify. The council confirmed that baptism by water was a requirement for salvation. Concerning the Eucharist the council upheld the theory of transubstantiation and confirmed that the Mass was therefore a sacrifice. Verbal confession of one's mortal sins to a priest was made a requirement. To be valid, marriage, as a sacrament of the church, was to be contracted before a Roman Catholic priest, and witnesses. The council confirmed the existence of a place called purgatory and the traditions it involved.[10] They made the veneration of saints, relics, and sacred images mandatory.[11] The *interpretation* of all doctrines verified or established by the Council of Trent could only be made by the Roman Catholic Church. No more room would be left for any new reformers to maneuver.

One must observe what is missing from the dogma of the Council of Trent. The whole concept of Christian morality in practice is not incorporated. It can be argued that the moral abuses of the church leadership were already being laid to rest by the renewal movements in the orders, and that there was no cause to deal with the obvious moral issues at this level. But we also notice the underlying concepts of Christian fellowship within the Body of Christ, the fellowship of the saints in unity, is missing. The Scriptures command all Christians to love the brethren. There is a special relationship shared by all who are of the household of faith. The enemy is not the Christian brothers we disagree with in doctrine. Even wicked or depraved people are not the enemy according to Jesus Christ; they are the victims of the enemy of our souls. Jesus Christ tells us to love our enemies and serve them, and thus bring them into the fold of the church.

The violence of the Roman Church against the evangelical reformers that were already outside of their expression of the church through open warfare, coupled with the implementation of the inquisition acting internally against all nonconformists, did work to a certain degree, to maintain the outward purity of the Spanish Latin expression of the Roman Catholic Church. Yet a Christian does not judge by whether a policy is working or accomplishing its purposes, but by whether it is *right* as judged by the fundamental principles of the faith. The failure to address morality issues being raised by the Roman Catholic evangelicals, and the violence being done against the Christian brothers seeking reform within the church, was the greatest single failure of the Council of Trent. This single concern, if it had been properly dealt with, had the potential to undermine and stay the hand of war, torture, and bloodshed for the centuries to come, but it failed to materialize. Sadly, it would be the American indigenous people that would pay an incredibly high price for this moral failure of the Council of Trent.

It may be said that the author's reluctance to acknowledge so different a moral standard now in existence from that of the sixteenth century is unfair. The response is: What difference is there in the standard? The moralities of all branches of Christianity are based upon the principles derived from Scripture, since the time of Christ, no particular century being an exception. The secularization of the church can bring into common practice a morality that is decidedly anti-Christian, but that is never a justification for the resulting immoral behavior. The church's failure to condemn violations of Biblical morality is never an excuse but a condemnation of the state of the church. Every man is still held accountable to God for his actions and that accountability will be based upon the principles of the Scriptures, not on the secular society's current standards.

The effect of the Council of Trent was to place the dogmas of the Roman Catholic Church in concrete. After the 16-year meeting there would be no more *reformation* of the church's doctrine until the first Vatican Council, nearly three centuries later.[12] After the meetings of the council the decisions of the Sacred Congregations[13] imposed on Latin Roman Catholicism uniformity and a passive deference to Rome that became known as *Tridentinism*14. The Council of Trent ensured that a Spanish version of traditional Roman Catholicism had made it through the Renaissance virtually unscathed. Spanish Roman Catholicism was able to stand firm through the age of rationality, science, and reason of the eighteenth century, known as the Enlightenment, to be one of the few surviving European dark-age institutions in the midst of modernism. The Roman Catholic Church neither lost its institutional mysticism nor did it give up any of its tyrannical authority over religious expression. It was with this dogmatic philosophy of Roman Catholicism that all mendicant friars and churchmen were required to indoctrinate the nations and tribes of America in what was to become known for the next several hundred years as New Spain.

In translating the theology of the Council of Trent into practice, some fundamental precepts should be noted. After Trent, all non-Roman Catholic worship was of the devil, it was heresy, and it was unacceptable practice that must be eliminated by inquisition within and war without the Holy Roman Empire. Utter destruction of other religions was the duty of all Roman Catholics. The books of the Bible were established, with the so called Apocrypha books, but only to be interpreted by the professional clergy. The Scriptures were to be kept out of the hands of laymen to avoid any chance of further reformation. The seven sacraments that were understood to be instituted by Christ contained grace, and therefore must be performed by a priest. Veneration of saints, relics, and sacred images was made a mandatory practice by all Roman Catholics. Water baptism contained grace for regeneration and was therefore required for salvation. Baptism for salvation without instruction or discipleship was an acceptable form of evangelism for Moors, Jews, and pagans, the outward forms of religion being sufficient signs of obedience. The Pope and the counsels of the Roman Catholic Church spoke with divine authority and therefore, were infallible. The Mass was a sacrifice through transubstantiation and therefore, a requirement for religious worship. Purgatory and all of its corollary doctrines and practices were decreed true and necessary. No further reform of the church was needed or allowed. The fires of inquisition awaited anyone, no matter what their rank or position, who dared to violate any of these doctrines or practices.[15]

One of the strengths of the Roman Catholic Church was its ability to incorporate renewal movements into its structure. One of the greatest of these renewal movements occurred in the thirteenth century. The mendicant orders that came out of that renewal period were the Franciscans (1221), Dominicans (1216), and Augustinians (1244). These orders underwent considerable reformation themselves during the fifteenth and into the sixteenth centuries. They experienced the restoration of primitive observances, a more strict application of their rules, and the reform of individuals through spiritual disciplines and evangelistic services. These reform movements raised the moral and educational standards of the clergy within the orders, manifested a renewed zeal and ardor for the faith, and a more spiritual, personal lifestyle. The renewal was also manifested in an attitude of intolerance toward the heresy of evangelical reformers who rejected pure tridentine doctrine and resulted in animosity toward the groups becoming known as *Protestants* in general.

Several new religious orders emerged at this time and were a fundamental part of this tridentine renewal trend, orders such as the Capuchins, Ursulines, Theatines, Barnabites, and especially the Jesuits. They strengthened rural parishes, improved popular piety, helped to curb corruption within the church, set examples that would be a strong impetus for Roman Catholic renewal, and proved to be foundational for the missions' calling that would come with the circulation of notices from the newly discovered Americas. As the magnitude of the American missionary calling became evident, and the tremendous needs of the pagan inhabitants became known, men of the orders began to respond to the missionary calling.

They were men under the rule (submitted to regulations of piety) of religious orders. This implies a very strict hierarchy of authority and service. They were better educated than most of the people by standards of the day. Many had advanced degrees of philosophy and theology. In the case of the Franciscans, their vows of poverty, demonstrated in their clothing and going bare footed, would earn the respect of the indigenous Americans. They were mostly Spanish and Italian, but many came from European countries of the Holy Roman Empire. They were called by God, confirmed by their orders, and sent for a purpose, usually with a service term of ten years. They were financed, provisioned, and protected by the Crown of Spain as part of the King's obligations for subjugating the Americas.

Yet more than the authority of the king and church, most of the friars also had the spiritual authority of personally knowing their God through their disciplines, the personal calling of God for missionary work, and the knowledge that the God who called them is faithful and will also do the work for his own glory. This calling and personal faith was based upon many years of training and preparation in convents, monasteries, and through their religious practices in the ministries of the church throughout Spain and Italy. They were men who had responded of their own free will to the same call as Isaiah of old saying, "Here am I. Send me!"[16] Their desperation to go was born of their obedience to God, to be found faithful to the end, to bring the *One true Church* to the heathen lands.

From their arrival in New Spain, the clerics were nearly always embroiled in disputes. They would be in constant turmoil with the colonizers over control of the indigenous people. The friars would try to protect the native inhabitants from obvious abuses and some of the most horrible treatment imaginable rendered to fellow human beings. They saw the colonizers as law breakers and bad Christians who corrupted morals and violated women. The colonizers, in turn, saw the friars as hypocrites that used the indigenous as slaves for their own personal gain. There were also quarrels between orders over geographical jurisdiction. There were bitter disputes between the regular friars and the secular priests over ecclesiastical authority for ministries. Then there were the fights between clerics and civil authorities that became so out-of-hand that they ended up in discipline by higher authorities. All this was background to their spiritual ministries in North America.

CHAPTER IV

FIRST EPOCH: DISCOVERY — CARIBBEAN/FLORIDA

Epoch One Introduction

We can now focus on *The Evolution of Apostolic Mission in the Context of New Spain Conquests,* starting by examining the Caribbean/Florida Epoch. The reasons for this designation of the first epoch are the time of discovery, the similarity of the geography which includes the many Caribbean Islands and costal lowlands of the mainland, the network of indigenous trade routes that tied them all together, the geographic distribution of the Arawak peoples, and the shared characteristics of the Spanish behavior in subjugation and exploitation of these geographic areas. Christopher Columbus did stumble into the Bahamas in 1492.[1] But there are two good reasons for not starting this study with Columbus. The first is that the Spanish conquest and subjugation of the Caribbean Islands did not start with the Caribbean area but off the coast of Africa in the Canary Islands. The second is that the Caribbean area was discovered, explored, and inhabited, and again invaded probably at least twice, long before Columbus came on the scene.

Canary Islands

As one makes an effort to understand why historical events take place, precedence begins to take on a great deal of importance. The precedent of the Spanish entrance into the Caribbean area can be traced directly back to the conquest and evangelization of the Canary Islands during the century preceding Columbus's great stumble. Originally known as the *Fortunate Islands* by ancient mariners, the conquest of the Canaries was not an easy task. They were the home to about 80,000 indigenous peoples called Guanches,[2] probably of North African Berber decent, and could be placed in the Neolithic Revolution stage of societal development.

Due to their isolated island geography and lack of the use of boats, the Guanches were not exposed to European culture or many of the European/African plagues and common sicknesses. They lived in loosely organized kingdoms with a ruler, nobles, and a lower class. Clan warfare was common among them and they were quite skilled at it. Their religion was pantheistic, worshiping the sun god, the earth goddess, and a demon associated with the islands' volcanoes.[3] Until 1404, sporadic slave raids by outsiders were part of the life of the Canary Islands.

It was at that time Juan Bethencourt of Castile built a castle in true crusader fashion as his military base for a planned invasion of Lanzarote in the Canary Islands. By 1408, three additional islands were dominated. Bethencourt brought two Franciscan friars with him as chaplains and chroniclers, plus two baptized Guanche natives as translators. After military preparations were made, the force landed on Lanzarote, only to be welcomed as saviors by the Guanche natives, who had suffered greatly from piratical raids and slavers the previous year, and saw in Bethencourt a chance for protection. While Bethencourt returned to Spain for a heroes' welcome, his men left at Lanzarote fought among themselves and the indigenous people became involved in the treason and treachery so common among the Spanish conquistadores throughout their history. Bethencourt returned, brought peace, and the Franciscans baptized all the people of the four conquered islands.[4]

Because each island was totally independent of the other, each had to be conquered in turn. However, the islanders of Tenerife, very effective fighters who used their terrain well, were not conquered until 1494. Alonzo Fernandez de Lugo used a force of 2,500 Spanish and a large number of Christianized Guanches. The first battle went to the Guanches due to their knowledge of the terrain; the second battle was a route, due to Spanish cavalry and crossbow. Then during the siege of the last stronghold, the Guanche warriors fell under a plague brought by the Europeans and died by the hundreds. Thus so weakened, they could no longer resist the Spanish army.[5]

Therefore the roots of the modern, Western missionary movement out of Europe were first put down in the Canaries after Castilians established their presence there. More Franciscans were later sent from Castile's most southern province, Andalusia.[6] In their ministries they spoke out strongly against enslaving native people who had converted to Christianity. The Franciscans persuaded the authorities in Rome to allow for the ordination of natives and a native clergy was developed.[7] Elements of this Canary Island model were precedence for what the Franciscans could eventually apply in the New World as they encountered very similar situations.

What was learned by the Spanish conquerors from the Canary Islands' precedent was that a relatively small group of well armed, well led soldiers, could defeat a vastly superior force; that pestilence was a very effective weapon when it struck a large number of indigenous people in close quarters, because of their proximity to the Europeans; that an army could be organized out of indigenous allies to be used against their traditional enemies, and thus greatly even the odds when doing battle in a foreign land. Because of the loosely organized political situation in the Canaries and the independent nature of the clans, the long drawn-out conquest also forced the Spanish to deal with guerrilla warfare in small pockets of resistance on the various islands once the majority of the population was secured. The crusader castles built by Bethencourt to secure a toe-hold on the islands were the forerunners of the borderland presidios used throughout the conquest of the Americas. But for the Guanche people, the conquered people, Spanish victory would mean enslavement and slow death through forced labor and malnutrition for those that resisted the Spanish—another terrible precedent. The populace that did submit to baptism and integration into Spanish cultural mores and survived the sicknesses that the Spanish soldiers introduced became the Roman Catholic Spanish citizens of the islands.[8] These ends, citizenship and Christianization fully justified conquest in the Spanish mindset.

Perhaps the attitudes demonstrated by the Spanish in the Canary Island conquest were not contemporary, but learned from of old in their centuries of battle with the Moors: that the superiority in arms entitles one nation to subdue another; that land can be taken from a people if we deem them, or their use of land, to be deficient by our standards; or that all cultures should be judged by our own to determine whether they should be allowed to persist. These perceptions were certainly to be carried over to the Americas. What the Spanish failed to notice was that, in taking the offensive invasion against a passive people, they had traded places with and had become themselves, the abhorred Moor.[9] The Guanche had not made war on Christians; they were not an occupying, foreign power—but now it was the Spanish that had become the dreadful invaders. This precedent would also be carried to the Americas.

For the Canary Islands the entire society and ecology of the islands were forever changed. The crusading Spanish brought with them the Europeanization of the land. Livestock, with all the infrastructure of ranch living, and sugar plantations, with slave labor and market based economy, replaced all native industries and native society. However, the bottom line from Canary Island history was the fact that inoffensive, native societies were forcibly destroyed simply because they lived on land desired by the European invaders and that was justified because the Europeans saw themselves as superior in culture and value systems. Being technologically more advanced was sufficient justification to destroy a less advanced society if in the process, Christianity, the one true religion, was imposed upon the conquered race. Precisely the same attitude demonstrated by the Muslim Moors who imposed their religion on the Iberian Peninsula centuries before. Although the imposition of Christianity was really just an afterthought in the case of the Canary Islands, it would become the dominant excuse in the Americas. Both Muslim and Christian were using their religion as an excuse to conquer.

The missiological implications of the Spanish Canary Island crusade and eventual conquest need to be noticed. First, it was the clerics under *rule*, the Franciscan Order, who sent the first two missionaries as chaplains with Bethencourt, not the secular clergy. The orders, originally counter-cultural and set up for personal, internal and spiritual growth in a complete separation from pagan society, would spearhead the outreach and growth of Christianity in pagan societies.[10] Second, the Orders had to function under direct authority of the Pope, there being no secular church in place to assist them, or in need of revival. In the future conquest of North America all the mendicant orders would seek Papal permission and authority before venturing into pagan lands, to the utter frustration of the secular clergy when they would eventually become established in the same places. We also should note that the mendicant friars went forth with full authority, by papal bull, of a ministering priest in their administration of the sacraments.

A third missiological implication was the need to communicate with the pagans. Evangelism is proclamation of the gospel of Jesus Christ, and as St. Paul asks, "How shall they believe in Him whom they have not heard? And how shall they hear without a preacher?"[11] Two Christian native translators were brought along by Bethencourt for military purposes, but it would have been nearly impossible to communicate the spiritual truths the Franciscan friars preached without the translators. And as anyone who has attempted to preach through a translator knows, it is better for all involved for the missionary to learn the native tongue. We later see learning the native language a nearly universal requirement for the friars sent to New Spain. That lesson was learned in the Canary Islands. In the Canaries, the Franciscans had fought the administrative battles all the way to the halls of Rome to win freedom for Christian natives so that they could not later be enslaved and sold. The friars also secured from Rome permission to establish a native clergy. This guaranteed the establishment of the Guanche native church. That was a valuable missiological lesson that was forgotten by the Spanish when the opportunity came up in New Spain. However, many valuable lessons for the physical and spiritual conquest of the Americas were learned in the Canary Islands.

Lastly, the concept of sovereignty should be considered: By what right did the Crown assume total lordship over New Spain? "From the outset the Indies were treated as the direct and exclusive possession of the Crown of Castile."[12] Isabella had financed the discovery voyages and the profits of the venture accrued to her and to her heirs. The overseas possessions were not an integral part of the Kingdom of Castile, not colonies of Spain or even the Spanish in the strictest sense. They were the possessions of the Crown of Castile—Isabella owned America. The Queen of Castile possessed not only sovereign rights of the new possessions, but the property (and mineral) rights as well. Every privileged position whether economic, political, or religious, came from the Queen of Castile, and when she died, it passed over to her heir, the King of Aragon—Fernando. The Pope had ceded power over the church to the Crown of Spain in exchange for their evangelism of the Americans. "Consequently the laws and institutions of Spanish America were modeled on those of Castile, often modified in form and in function to meet local needs, but always emanating from the Crown and kept under royal control."[13]

The Florida-Caribbean People

The second reason for not starting with Columbus is the history of the Caribbean area itself. Eight hundred years before Columbus encountered the Lucayan branch of the Taino people in the Bahamian archipelago, the class of people called Arawakans began their migrations out of the Amazonia, through Northeastern South America, up through the arc of Windward Islands, through the Greater Antilles, and into the Bahaman chain and Florida mainland.[14] In this migration they evidently displaced some of the Ciboney people already established in the islands, or possibly both these peoples came from the same source at the same or different times. There are, of course, no written histories for these peoples. The widely separated island groups dictated separate cultural developments, and eventually different subgroup names such as the Taino as the Arawak of the Greater Antilles were known. In general the Arawakan societies had a sophisticated government of chiefdoms, a well developed cosmology, a tradition of crafts with stone tools for carpentry, and a very well developed system of trade routes that loosely tied the many groups together.[15] On the Florida mainland the Arawak-Taino were expressed in the Calusa society of the Tekesta in the south and as the Timucuan people of Northern Florida.[16]

When the Spanish stumbled onto the scene, the indigenous cultures of the region included ceremonial ball parks marked by upright stone dolmens, houses were round stick-and-thatch construction, but the *cacique* (chief) lived in a larger rectangular building in the center of the compound. The floors were earthen, and the whole compound at times was surrounded by a palisade. This construction was sturdy enough to resist hurricanes—examples can still be seen in the Northern Yucatan villages of the Maya.[17] The Arawak personal items consisted of wooden stools, hammocks of cotton cloth for sleeping, clay and wooden bowls for eating, gourds for drinking, and large, sea-going canoes.[18] Clothing was not necessary for warmth and was not used.

The religion consisted of hierarchies of deities who inhabited the sky. *Yocahu* was the supreme creator; *Jurakán* was the perpetually angry god of the storms. *Zemi* were lesser gods of both sexes that were represented by icons and had to be kept in good graces by offerings of manioc (yucca) bread, beverages, and tobacco. *Maboyas* was a nocturnal deity who destroyed crops and was greatly feared, requiring elaborate sacrifices to placate him. There were ceremonial dances to drumbeats, oral traditions, and ceremonial ball games with a rubber ball and teams from different villages in competition. These were theocratic kingdoms with a chief, sub chiefs, nobles which were priests and medicine men, and the working class or commoners.[19] At the time of Columbus, there were five different kingdoms on Hispaniola. They were patriarchal societies and polygamy was practiced with two or three wives being normal, although a chief would often have as many as 30 wives.[20]

One other Caribbean migration of a people must be considered. The Carib people are thought to have originated in the rain forests of Venezuela. They began migrating up the island chains about 100 years before Columbus, displacing the peoples of the southern Lesser Antilles as each group was conquered. The Carib seem to have been patriarchal. Women carried out primarily domestic duties and farming, while living in separate houses from the men. The Carib were more egalitarian than most indigenous Caribbean people with only a war leader and no multitier society such as the Taino. Their religion was polytheism, and it is understood from early testimony that cannibalism was part of a special ceremony in which even children would participate. The Carib apparently had gained control of the lower Caribbean up to and including the Virgin Islands. Puerto Rico seems to have been the southeastern limit of the Taino at the time of Spanish subjugation. The Taino were often terrorized by raids from Carib fleets.[21] The northern coast of South America was under similar oppression by Carib raiders.[22]

The subject of cannibalism seems to have raised a considerable discord among historians with a revisionist school vigorously denying the cannibalistic life style of many indigenous American groups against all early evidence and testimony of the Spaniards. The revisionist schools notes that the Spanish Crown had ruled cannibals could be legally taken as slaves, which they claim gave the Spanish an incentive to identify various groups as cannibals. The logic is good, but whether or not indigenous people practiced cannibalism does not seem to be a factor; the Spanish colonists enslaved anyone they wanted for labor and domestic help. Alan Riding says, "Mexicans prefer to ignore evidence that their Aztec ancestors practiced cannibalism."[23] Drawings of Aztec sacrifices as imagined by various artists and the temples where sacrifices took place are common; the meat market at the foot of the temple[24] as described in detail by eye witness Bernal Díaz is very seldom visualized for obvious reasons.

Yet the sacrifice of human beings and the eating of human flesh seem to be a part of many of the histories of indigenous Americans from the high cultures of Mexico[25] to the Anastasia[26] and on up to the tribes of the Iroquois League.[27] The reasons for cannibalism may be ceremonial, domination, starvation, a habitat that lacks protein in the diet, or because a taste for human flesh has been developed.[28] Prescott says, "Still, cannibalism, under any form or whatever sanction, cannot but have a fatal influence on the nation addicted to it."[29] Spanish clerics did see their conquest as a judgment of God for the indigenous American's devilish practices.

The fact is the Carib people were cannibalistic according to nearly all historical data. Not only were they known by all groups from the coast of South America to Florida for their ferocity and cannibalism but also renowned as great warriors. Their primary targets were the Arawak men who were captured for food or exterminated; women and children were taken as wives or slaves. The Ciboney were believed to be the original inhabitants of the Lesser Antilles but seem to have succumbed to the same fate that the Arawak experienced. Soon after the Spanish arrived, the last enclaves of Ciboney disappeared,[30] with the possible exception of Cuba.[31]

Therefore the descendants of the Arawak peoples of the northern Caribbean and the Carib peoples of the southern Caribbean were the two principle native cultures encountered by the Europeans in 1492.

Christopher Columbus

Before setting sail, Columbus secured several titles from the Queen of Castile for the lands he might discover. Probably thinking in terms of the Canary Islands, the Queen accorded the hereditary title of Viceroy of the lands he expected to discover, together with those of governor, captain-general, and admiral.[32] These powers made Columbus sole judge in cases arising out of trade in the new territories. As Viceroy and Governor he was to have a tenth part of all royal revenues due the Crown from the Indies. He was the commander of any militia that might be raised in New Spain and he was to appointed candidates for all political offices. However, with great powers come great responsibilities—the two cannot be separated. It is doubtful that any man could have been equal to the many responsibilities that Columbus undertook when conferred with such titles. Perhaps it could work for a few islands, certainly not for two continents.

When Columbus dropped anchor in the Bahamas, the Lucayan people greeted the strange ships and stranger people in friendship. He had been five weeks at sea when the unknown island with the naked humans that he mistakenly called *Indians* appeared. In his journal Columbus wrote: "It appears to me that the people are ingenious, and would be good servants and I am of opinion that they would very readily become Christian, as they appear to have no religion."[33] It would seem that the intuition of Columbus was somewhat lacking in regard to discernment of the spiritual nature of man.

Columbus went on to discover the Northeast coast of Cuba and the North coast of Hispaniola where one of his ships, the *Santa Maria*, ran aground and destroyed itself on a reef on Christmas day. The Taino cacique or chief in that region gave him permission to leave 39 of his men in a makeshift fort constructed with timbers from the Santa Maria. This was to be the first settlement of Europeans in New Spain, La Navidad, on what is today the north coast of Haiti. For more than a year, his men lived among the Arawak Indians exploring the island, and looking for gold, before their lust of gold and women so alienated the Taino that they rose up and killed all the Spaniards and destroyed their settlement.[34] Columbus had returned to Spain and then the following year set sail on his second voyage (1493) with 17 ships and 1,500[35] men.

On this second voyage the route of his fleet is not certain. He seems to have sailed through the Lesser Antilles, the Virgin Islands, and then the Greater Antilles where he landed on Puerto Rico, which he named *San Juan Bautista*. When they landed a party there was a brief skirmish, the first between Europeans and Americans since the days of Viking excursions into the Americas. During the skirmish they rescued two boys[36] that had just been castrated by their captors (Caribs), just as ranchers castrate steers.[37] The fleet then returned to Hispaniola where they found the previous settlement of Navidad in ruins and the men long dead. He re-established a new settlement 100 kilometers east of La Navidad called La Isabella, but it also proved to be unsuitable for a base in the Caribbean.

Columbus then sailed on to Cuba, explored its southern coast, and continued sailing on to Jamaica. He retraced his route to Hispaniola and then returned to Spain. On the third voyage with six ships (1498) he made landfall at Trinidad and explored the north coast of South America discovering Tobago and Grenada. He then returned to Hispaniola to find his colony full of discontent at not finding riches as promised. He repeatedly had to deal with treason and seditions among his settlers and the Tainos. Columbus did note in his journal an important comment about Hispaniola. He wrote that "From here one might send . . . as many slaves as could be sold."[38]

On his fourth and last voyage to New Spain (1502) with four ships, Columbus made landfall at Santo Domingo but was denied port by the new governor. He continued on to Jamaica, then to the coast of Honduras. From there Columbus spent two months exploring what are now the coasts of Honduras, Nicaragua, Costa Rica, and Panama. The admiral and his men survived a violent storm that destroyed his ships which he beached on Jamaica stranding them there for a year. Survival came from the assistance of the natives and grudging help from the governor of Hispaniola who earlier had refused assistance and then hindered all attempts to save the shipwrecked explorers. When finally rescued, Columbus returned to Spain.

These four voyages with a total of 30 ships, and an estimated total of about 2,200 men, allowed Columbus to visit all the major island groups of the Caribbean. Some islands were only noted in passing but many others saw prolonged visits and the beginnings of permanent European settlements. Cook[39] reminds us that voyages of coastal discovery meant intermittent stops for fresh water and any foods that could be secured in whatever manner. Also stops were made, for emergencies, for repairs, and for safe havens during storms. Direct contact was usually made with indigenous people during these stops. Trade was often attempted and at times kidnappings took place in an attempt to understand what was inland, or to glean more knowledge of the coast. The fact is that during the ten years of the four Columbus voyages, continual interchange was taking place between Europeans and the indigenous Americans throughout the Caribbean basin.

Colonialists of the Caribbean

The colonists, exclusively male as a rule, brought with them both plants and animals from Europe to plant and ranch in New Spain according to the pattern established in the Canary Islands which had proven very successful there. Pigs, chickens, dogs, cats, cattle, horses, sheep, and goats began to thrive wherever they settled. Significantly, some of the animals were noted to be sick during the second voyage.[40] The ecology of the Caribbean was forever changed with the introduction of so many foreign flora and fauna, and especially with the diseases they carried.

The Spanish that enlisted were men of all types and strata of society who essentially left nothing or very little in Spain to follow Columbus west to the New World with hopes of carving out their fortunes from the newly discovered territories. Some were desperate men—such as the second sons of nobles without inheritance, some simply went for adventure, some to escape their past, but most saw a second chance to make their fortunes. For many, the voyage was a gamble: first, that they would arrive at all given the difficulty of sea travel in the sixteenth century, and second, that upon arrival their hands and their wits would be sufficient to prevail against all encounters to survive and then to take whatever fate would offer and make it pay off.

These explorers, soldiers of fortune, and colonizers would do whatever had to be done, in any way it could be done to make their own fortunes whether in pueblos, or on plantations, in mines, or on ranches—to produce and develop a way of living. All this was to make of themselves a new elite class in the new land. Without production there could be no wealth, there could be no European society and no future for the colonists. Without labor, there was no production. The only laborers available were the indigenous people—hundreds of thousands of local people—that in some areas were accustomed to dictatorial leaders and hierarchal society. The Spanish had to put them to work for a new Spanish society if their New Spain was to survive.

Indigenous Americans and European Diseases

Two results of these visitations of Columbus and his crews to the various islands are of importance to our study: first, the introduction of European and African diseases to the Americas, and second, the introduction of Roman Catholic clerics and other lay religious leaders with their exclusive Spanish-Latin version of Roman Catholicism.

Much has been written about the effects of European disease upon the Americans in this first epoch.[41] Columbus left 39 men on Hispaniola after the grounding of his ship the Santa Maria. Those men survived possibly as long as a year before being wipe out by the offended Taino people. That means that before their deaths in 1493, the first of many epidemics[42] broke out in the Caribbean region. Cook reported that the first major influenza epidemic, probably swine flu, spread throughout the region in 1493, and lasted until 1498.[43] He concluded that it must have followed the extensive trade routes to spread from island to island. There are no pre-second voyage records to indicate how extensive the epidemic was, although it had the potential of affecting all the islands and the mainland coast lines of South America and Florida which all lie within that trade network. This may have been the epidemic of *romadizo* (an unidentified sickness) reported to have occurred in Panama in that time. No data exist recording either the extent or the mortality rates, only that this first epidemic of European disease in America did occur before any European set foot on most of the islands, and it was extensive.

When the colonists arrived in the Caribbean with the massive second Columbus voyage, almost immediately the sickness that had come with the fleet began to spread. Five of the seven Lucayo Americans who had gone to Spain with the first Columbus trip and were returning with him on the second trip died in route. There is no record of how many Europeans died during the voyage. The highly contagious sickness debilitated the Spaniards—Columbus himself fell ill—and it spread quickly to the indigenous population. One of the few indications of mortality of the indigenous population was that 550 Taino Amerindians were sent back to Spain, but 200 of them died in route having been already infected with the unidentified malady. Cook reported that a third of the population (European) fell sick within a few days; they fell sick with high fevers and many died. Mortality among Spaniards was also so severe that they were reduced to a third of their former strength. Cook also reports that more than half of the 1,500 first settlers perished before Columbus returned to Spain, and an untold number of the Taino natives perished.

The above description of the sickness during the second voyage of Columbus, compounded by the continuing complications from the influenza of the first voyage, paints a picture of what was happening throughout the Caribbean. Although the numbers of indigenous peoples were far greater than those of Europeans, both peoples seemed to be suffering and dying in proportion to their numbers. Many estimates exist as to the size of that indigenous population of Hispaniola at the time of the Spanish invasion. The general agreement of modern scholars is between 300,000 and 400,000 people in 1492. By 1508, that population was down to 60,000, and two years later it was cut in half again.[44]

On his third voyage to the Caribbean with six ships, Columbus stopped at Santiago to take on cattle for Hispaniola, but he did not because the island was most unhealthy, and his men began to fall sick. When he again arrived at Hispaniola, Columbus found that another 300 of the second voyage colonists had died and the rest were suffering from an unknown affliction, later concluded to be an American strain of syphilis. It appears this strain had been exported to Europe by men of the first Columbian voyage, and an unwitting Europe was paying a price for its immoral behavior.

Also, during the time of this third voyage, other fleets began arriving from Southern Spain triggering a rapid expansion of European colonists in both numbers and geographic area being settled. Cook says to argue that no disease transfer took place on these other voyages is to assume the highly improbable. In 1502, the fleet of the new governor, Nicolás de Ovando, sailed from Spain with 30 ships and 2,500 men and women including 12 Franciscans. But the infrastructure in Hispaniola did not yet exist to receive such a large number. With rampant sickness and inadequate supplies, in a short period of time over 1,000 of the new arrivals were dead. Still, the die-off of Europeans did not match the soaring number of deaths of the indigenous people. Before their eyes the native population was disappearing, and the Spanish could do nothing about it.

Columbus started off on his fourth and last voyage three months after Ovando. What is significant to this research is that after exploring the coastal areas and then being shipwrecked on Jamaica, Columbus sent by canoe one of his lieutenants—Diego Méndez who had all the symptoms of recurrent malaria—to Hispaniola for help. Soon after this, malaria began to break out along the coast of Central America, though no direct connection has ever been identified with Méndez.

This very brief survey of just the ten years of explorations by Columbus reveals the extent of the damages being done to the population of both the Native Americans and the European colonists. It is probable that as many as half of the population of Americans in the Caribbean died in the first ten years after contact with Europeans.[45] Approximately the same proportion of colonists died after contact with the Americas. The more severe killer epidemics were still in the very near future for the Americans—smallpox, measles, cholera, bubonic and pneumonic plagues, and yellow fever. The precedent experienced by Spaniards in the conquest of the Canary Islands when indigenous people were exposed to the sicknesses that Europeans were accustomed to carry should have given them an anticipation of problems in the Caribbean. But in reality, nothing, not even the hundreds of deaths on the Canary Island of Tenerife, could have foreshadowed the annihilation of such a multitude of people as the indigenous Taino and Carib were experiencing in the Caribbean.

The First Clerics in New Spain

After noting the diseases brought by the voyages of Columbus, the second item of interest for this epoch of New Spain conquest was the Roman Catholic clerics and other lay religious leaders that accompanied them. In 1493, Pope Alexander VI gave Spanish Kings permission to subjugate the islands and the lands of the American continent, thus making the conquest a religious, evangelistic campaign. The Spanish Crown in turn then asked, "The Orders' provincials, either through letters, or summoning them in person to the Court, to look in their communities for the most suitable and willing religious who wanted to go to convert non-Christians, in order to send them to the new continent for at least ten years."⁴⁶ With the door to the Americas wide open, the various mendicant Orders began to gear-up for the task.

The procedure for religious communities was to appoint a commissioner themselves who assembled a number of brothers from monasteries in Spain and other European nations who were willing to go and serve in the Americas. The commissioner then applied to the *Casa de la Contratación* (Department of Government Contracts) in Seville, which paid for the equipment needed by the missionaries such as clothing, vestments, sacred utensils, books and provisions. They also made the arrangements for shipping and passage for the friars. Each individual friar received travel funds for layovers and personal costs in route. This was the procedure for all missionaries going to America under the auspices of the Spanish Crown.⁴⁷ Secular clergy usually had to make their own arrangements for the voyage and lived from the tithes and offerings of the church community once they arrived. Thus the seeds of animosity and jealousy were being sewn before the two major divisions of the church, modality and sodality, set foot in New Spain.

Once the friars arrived in New Spain, they submitted to the authority of the communities of each order, according to the peculiarities and philosophical ideals of each tradition. But even in the convents they never escaped from the long arm of the Crown. The local governors, the *audiencias* (administrative committees), and the Viceroys all were responsible for overseeing the operation and details of the monasteries in their jurisdictions. Once every three years all of these authorities were required to report to the Crown their observations and concerns about the friars and their ministries. The Crown also reserved the right to send inspectors unannounced from time to time. The civil authorities were authorized to support, in every respect, the religious who were engaged in the conversion and instruction of the indigenous Americans.

Throughout the history of the conquest of New Spain, it was very rare indeed that an exploratory adventure would be undertaken without the inclusion of some clerics.⁴⁸ Bethencourt had included two Franciscans as his scribes and personal counselors in the conquest of the Canary Islands. In the Americas evangelization and the establishment of the Roman Catholic Church was a legal requirement as well as a desired part of the conquest.

Whereas on the first voyage of Columbus it appears that there were no clerics, on the massive second voyage of Columbus, there were five priests:[49] a Benedictine Father Buil, the Jeronymite Father Ramon Pane, and three Franciscan missionaries, and in addition three lay brothers accompanied them. Father Buil was appointed by Pope Alexander VI as *Vicar Apostolic* of all the newly discovered territories and he was sent under the authority of the Crown of Spain.[50] Also there is record of two Mercedarian friars and two other religious[51] workers who accompanied the second voyage. Because of the disaster that had befallen the original *La Navidad* settlement, a new settlement was initiated farther east along the coast of Hispaniola called *La Isabella*. It was here that all the clerics joined together on the day of the Three Kings, January 6, 1494, and held what was probably the first mass said in the New World. It should be noted that this was done for the benefit of the Spanish explorers and colonists rather than to fulfill the Great Commission of evangelizing the indigenous people.

Painfully missing is any record of ministry being instigated by these priests other than secular, priestly obligations to the European communities. They had little fortitude or understanding of the missions' mandate and soon returned to Spain with their observations of the situation. Only the three lay brothers, two Franciscans, and the Jeronymite, remained and survived the raging diseases to actually attempt evangelism among the indigenous Taino people.[52] Columbus had commissioned the Jeronymite Pane to study the language and the customs of the Tainos, which was later published in Europe.[53] A record exists of the two Franciscan lay brothers, who returned to Spain in 1499, they claimed they had baptized Tainos and plead for more Franciscan brothers to come over and join in the ministry because the needs were so great.[54] The order responded and three more Franciscans were dispatched with the Bobadilla delegation in 1500. Seventeen more Franciscans accompanied the delegation of Governor Ovando in 1502. These Franciscans built a *meeting house* in the new capital of *Santo Domingo* which became the first church building in New Spain.[55]

The brother of Columbus, Bartholomew, founded the town of *Santo Domingo* in 1498. When the site of *La Isabella* had proven unsatisfactory, the whole town was moved to a new site at the mouth of the Ozama River in 1496, and despite hurricanes, earthquakes, and repeated attacks, has continued to this day as the oldest continually inhabited European city in the Americas. It was Santo Domingo that was to become the hub for Roman Catholic ministry in the Caribbean and the center for secular church life in this epoch of study.

Please take a moment to imagine the context in which these clerics were to begin to build the church in New Spain during this epoch. The vast majority of the colonists during this first ten years came to exploit the land and its people, not to develop them. Their primary interest was in high value items such as gold, silver, gems, and pearls that could economically be shipped back to Spain. These items were already in circulation within native societies of this region, and they had to be found, expropriated, mined, or stolen from the natives. For the colonists to continue to exist they had to be self-sufficient in basic commodities, especially food; starvation was a common factor as cultural disintegration and forced labor severed native food sources. These needs fostered a Spanish dependency on native labor, on tribute, and a subjugated population.[56] In the midst of this Spanish-European rape of the Caribbean Islands and their people a hand full of men that accompanied these cruel invaders were going to try and teach the basic principles of Roman Catholic Christianity, surrounded by the worst possible examples of what a Christian man was supposed to be.

The perception about the indigenous peoples held by the colonists in general at this time was that the Caribbean native was an underdeveloped race, subhuman, and perhaps closer to the animal world than to that of people. They saw the hunter-gatherers as naked savages, running like a herd of beasts,[57] without civilized customs or institutions, or even "normal" family relationships. Already noted is the statement of Columbus that they had no apparent religion. European morality caused them to view cultural practices when present—incest, sodomy, cannibalism, and human sacrifice—as indications of a strange race totally given over to the devil. From this European perspective, the rules of human decency did not apply to the indigenous peoples. If they were really mere animals, they had no soul to lose. They were a commodity to be used or discarded at will, just as the Spanish used their war dogs or donkeys. Add to this perception the greed for wealth, the arrogance of men without the presence of wives or family values and unrestrained by superiors many thousands of miles away, and one may begin to understand the context and attitude of the Spanish colonist in which the friars were to minister.

Again the effects of diseases in this colonial context must be considered which were causing the deaths of nearly half of all the Europeans in the first ten years. Most frightening of all, however, was the death toll that was going on among the "savages." It was perceived as God's judgment against these "Satan followers" for their wicked ways. This was the social context of the island of Hispaniola when the clerics of the second voyage of Columbus arrived to begin their ministry in the New World.

The Foundation of the Colonies

Though the clerics came as missionaries, they were really under the authority of the secular Roman Church with the exception of the three lay brothers. Friar Buil, a Benedictine monk had been appointed to his apostolic position by Ferdinand and was instructed to bring missionaries with him to the Americas. Upon arrival they began their ministries by doing normal church functions for the colonist. The exceptions were the three lay brothers who came as missionaries with a zeal for conversion of souls. Almost nothing is known about the actual work of these lay brothers. But enough can be discern to understand a contrast in the approach of the *churchmen* that is, the secular priests, and the *missionaries*. Churchmen, in this first epoch, fulfilled the functions of a priest ministering to their flock. Surely most of their time was spent burying the dead, the friends with whom they had journeyed to the Americas. They must have seen the multitudes of indigenous people and must have seen these multitudes dying and suffering horrible treatment by the European colonists. But they were evidently blind to the needs of those people, or so overwhelmed by the needs of the Europeans they could not consider the sufferings of the indigenous Tainos.

The missionary lay brothers, by contrast, had to have gone out into the Taino areas or ministered to the Tainos who were enslaved, forced to work in mines, or on plantation *encomiendas*. They claimed to have baptized natives when attempting to recruit more Franciscans in Spain in 1499. Nothing more can be said, except that they seem to have fulfilled their calling to evangelize the indigenous people as they understood evangelism.

The last thing of note for this initial epoch was the actual events of conquest taking place in the first ten years. The problem with further implementation of a Canary Island model of subjugation in the Caribbean was the contrasting and appalling record of those colonial adventurers who undertook Spain's forward movement in the Greater Antilles. The stories of unprovoked aggression, treachery, theft, slavery, and genocide[58]—all the fruits of unrestrained greed—but mostly a desperate striving for survival by the Spanish colonists worked absolute havoc on the Taino people of Hispaniola. When Columbus returned to La Navidad and found the fort destroyed and the men dead, two of Columbus' subordinates took revenge on the Tainos near La Navidad first slaughtering and then capturing a large number of Tainos for use as slaves.[59]

In 1495, Columbus initiated a determined conquest of Hispaniola, spreading devastation among the Taino who were already ravaged by disease. There is evidence, especially in the objections of Bernardo Buil,[60] that Columbus's methods in this conquest were cruel and extreme. The Tainos had found gold and used it for adornments. The Spanish colonists confiscated their trinkets and then their mines, and forced the Taino slaves to work them until they literally dropped dead from overwork and starvation.[61] Columbus was very sick most of the time, frustrated, and unable to control the Spaniards on the island in their abuse of the Tainos, probably due to poor governing skills. He personally seized more than a thousand indigenous people making them his slaves.[62]

The Taino were forced to produce their own food, the primary staple being the yucca root, and also produce food for the Spanish while laboring in the mines and developing plantations for the colonists. Sugar cane, another import from the Canary Islands, was planted as part of a labor intensive plantation economy; however, the indigenous Americans were not accustomed to such labor, which left no time for the private cultivation of food with the enforced labor demands of the colonists. And as always, since the arrival of the Spanish colonists, the people kept on dying of the strange new sicknesses that swept over them in waves. The breaking point finally came and full-scale war with the Taino broke out when Columbus seized the thousand free Taino and made them his slaves.[63]

Rebellion was immediately crushed by the colonists whose European style of warfare was incomprehensible to the island Taino.[64] Savage attack dogs caused shock, fear, and bloody devastation among the naked Taino warriors. The steel armor worn by soldiers, the steel-tipped lance and war horse, the harquebus, and the crossbow were weapons used in tight, well organized formations that made the Spanish appear invincible. These Caribbeans were accustomed to warfare and the defense of their islands against the Caribs,[65] but they were helpless against these men of steel. Another incomprehensible factor was that the Spanish used the conquered Tainos as allies against their own people. In essence the indigenous people became the armies of their enemies, the foot soldiers of the Spanish in further conquests. Never had the Tainos faced anything such as these European weapons and tactics. These tactics of horror were designed to instill such fear that further rebellion would never again be considered an option. The Taino rebels who survived the battles were sold into slavery—a sentence of death by labor and malnutrition.

Easily winning all military engagements, the Spanish ended up with thousands of slaves. The colonists then demanded from the remaining free Taino people a tribute in gold to begin building their European economy in Hispaniola. This tribute was far more gold than the free Taino could ever collect, and when they failed to pay, their lands were confiscated. Taino clans who had been pursued into the mountains during the wars lost their lands confiscated as war prizes—if the Spanish had use for those lands. When the war was finished, the colonists found themselves with most of the good farm land and thousands of slaves to put to work.

In 1498, when Columbus arrived at Hispaniola on his third trip, he found the Europeans of the island in a state of rebellion and virtual anarchy. The brother of Columbus who was left in charge was incapable of governing. To resolve the mess, Columbus eventually agreed to grant each Spaniard a substantial tract of cultivated land with a number of Indians to till it.[66] Obviously the colonists had already taken both the land and the indigenous people as their slaves. Columbus simply gave in and legalized the very hostile takeover. This was the origin of the *repartimiento* or *encomienda* system, formalized into law on Hispaniola in 1503.

When Bobadilla arrived at Hispaniola in 1500 as the new governor under orders to investigate the administration of Columbus, he put Columbus under arrest, seized his papers and property, and sent him back to Spain in chains. After a brief time in prison the Crown released him and allowed a fourth exploratory trip to be taken, but the governorship of Hispaniola was not restored. The third governor, Nicholas de Ovando, was sent out in 1501 with orders to force Bobadilla to restore the property he had taken from Columbus. Ovando decided in favor of the *encomienda* system, and made it government policy, but from then on only the governor (himself) had the power to grant an *encomienda*. The Crown required each *encomendero,* or owner, to care for the indigenous people without the use of violence, to settle them in villages, and to build churches and schools for them.[67] Although it was the law, it very seldom ever happened.

Columbus was never the systematic oppressor of the Taino, but simply unable to control the colonists on land who came under his jurisdiction.[68] The population of Hispaniola fell from the estimated 300,000-400,000 Taino indigenous residents in 1492, to approximately 60,000 in 1507, and then dropped to 600[69] in 1531. The very few clerics laboring on Hispaniola at this time viewed with consternation the demise of the Taino and could not fathom the reason the Tainos, once so prevalent, seemed to be doomed to extinction. Theologians concluded that the cause must be providential; God had predestined the indigenous Caribbean people to destruction for their devil worship and immoral practices.[70] But regardless of the theology or the practice, the reality was that the Taino of Hispaniola to whom the clerics had been sent to the Americas to make into Roman Catholic, Spanish citizens, were gone. The extent of the friars' total failure in their primary purpose for being sent to New Spain had to be burning in their hearts. The church was simply part of the conquering power; missionaries and clergy, in the eyes of the natives, were part of the same class as conquistadores, colonials, and traders.[71] It was clear to the friars that a whole new methodology had to be found to evangelize the indigenous Americans.

The Caribbean: A Spanish Lake

From Santo Domingo on Hispaniola the Spanish struck out in all directions to explore and conquer. Columbus had given Spain a new world; now others rose to the challenge of discovery. In 1508, Ocampo sailed around Cuba proving it was an island. In 1510, Velázquez arrived at a small island just off of Cuba with 300 men and prepared for the conquest of Cuba. With the party of invaders was a young man named Bartolomé de Las Casas[72] who had come to New Spain on Columbus's third voyage. From 1511-1515, Velázquez waged a series of campaigns of extermination against the Taino and Ciboney chiefdoms and villages of Cuba. On horseback, accompanied by infantry and war dogs, the conquistadores destroyed at will the hunting and gathering tribes of the island. They murdered and subjugated, burned and utterly destroyed all indigenous villages they could find, sparing neither women nor children, until all who were left were totally passive. Slaves were gathered for *encomiendas* when it was convenient, and any other resistance was put down mercilessly.[73] In four years Velázquez had nearly exterminated the indigenous people of Cuba. Some pockets had escaped him and encomiendas did contain large numbers of indigenous slaves. But for Las Casas, "a few months had been enough to show [him] the horrors of this system. The [indigenous Caribbean people] on Cuba were literally worked to death. Those who resisted were tormented into the grave, in ingenious and spectacular ways . . ."[74]

Puerto Rico had been a stopping place for water and repairs but no settlements had been attempted until 1508. The island had been populated by Tainos, but they were constantly under attack by the Caribs. Both groups were living on the island at the time of Spanish invasion with a total population of between 20,000 to 50,000 people.[75] Ponce de Leon had sailed on the second voyage of Christopher Columbus to the Americas in 1493. He did not return to Spain with Columbus but stayed on in Hispaniola. He heard of gold on the island of Borinquen (Puerto Rico). Securing permission for an invasion, De Leon entered the island with 200 men "classified as government officials, old conquerors, new hirelings, and converted Jews."[76] With this group he brutally conquered the island, using the same methodology so successful in Cuba, claiming it for Spain. He was then appointed governor of Puerto Rico. The Taino people formed an alliance with their enemies the Caribs, and rebelled, trying to throw out the Spanish. Between 80 and 100 of de Leon's men were killed by the Puerto Ricans. But the surviving conquistadores were reinforced with another 300 men and de Leon crushed the rebellion.[77] Due to his extreme brutality to Native Americans, de Leon was removed from office in 1511. The census taken in 1515 showed the island population had dropped to 4,000 due to maltreatment, war, flight to other islands, and sickness. By 1544, there only remained 60 Tainos in Puerto Rico.[78]

Jamaica had a pattern of conquest that would be more typical of the rest of the inhabitable Caribbean Islands. In 1494, Columbus, on his second voyage, landed on the shore of Jamaica at a place now called Discovery Bay. The Taino population was estimated at 100,000[79] people at that time. Nine years later on Columbus' fourth voyage, what was left of one ship after his small fleet was battered by a hurricane, was beached on Jamaica where they stayed for one year. In 1509, in a settlement with the son of Columbus regarding his inheritance, the Crown gave Diego Columbus[80] Jamaica, and the rights to develop the island. Columbus appointed Alfonzo de Ojeda and Diego Nicuissa as joint leaders of a colonization effort.[81] When they arrived on Jamaica, they divided up the island and its Taino people and promptly began to engage in civil war with each other. Villages were burned, hundreds died, and the native economy was destroyed. After an uneasy peace began between the Europeans, the colonists began rounding up Tainos and selling them off as slaves to other islands. Sugar cane and other domestic crops, cattle, swine, and goats were introduced to the island and the animals prospered. But by 1558, the Taino of the island were extinct.[82]

The author has not found any record, nor any mention of any friars or other clerics in these first decades of conquest who had come to Jamaica for the purpose of evangelizing or building the Church. In the 64 years after first contact between 80,000 to 100,000 Taino people were killed, died from disease, or were sold into slavery, never having seen a cleric, or ever having heard of the Christian gospel in any form. The *Christian* men they saw acted worse than devils. Jamaica represents the single, most complete failure of evangelism of indigenous

Americans in the Caribbean. Jamaica also represents, in its truest form, the capability of uncontrolled Spanish colonists when left to their own devices thousands of miles from accountability. Jamaica could easily have been the true foundation for the *Black Legend*.

With the Greater Antilles firmly under Spanish control, the smaller islands began to receive the attention of the explorers, colonists, and that of the secular church. In 1504, Pope Julius II founded the first three dioceses in America: Baynua, Magua, and Yaguata. King Ferdinand of Spain objected as this power had been given to the Crown of Spain in 1493, and patronage over the church in the Indies was established under the Crown. Ferdinand then nominated three bishoprics: Santo Domingo, San Juan, and Concepcion de la Vega in 1511.[83] Santo Domingo was the first to build a cathedral; each Diocese then began to establish its own geographical administration. After the 1511 rebellion on Puerto Rico, Bishop Alonso Manso established his diocese at San Juan and soon added Trinidad, Margarita, Barcelona, Cumana, and Guyana to the diocese. However, no record exists of Manso doing anything to reach out to the indigenous people who were so quickly perishing all around him. It would seem that the secular church simply could not see the spiritual needs and hopeless plight of the native Caribbean people—or they felt incapable of doing anything about them. The secular church continued what it did know and understand as their mission: they ministered to the colonists and used their own *encomiendas* of native Tainos to build their cathedrals and established the institutional church in the Caribbean Islands.

The mendicant friars were coming to America—but too few, and too late to impact the fate of the Taino or Carib indigenous people. In 1509, the Dominicans were authorized to enter the Caribbean. In 1510, both Franciscan and Dominicans were arriving to the Caribbean, but far too few to affect the still large yet rapidly declining numbers of Tainos who were fleeing the presence of all Europeans at this time. It was obvious to the New Spain friars that whatever had been happening to the indigenous people to that point was very, very wrong. Letters began to arrive in Spain explaining the incredibly out-of-control nature of the colonization process in the Caribbean. Las Casas had witnessed the conquest of Cuba and was so repulsed by what he had witnessed being done by the men of the Velázquez force, that he became a Dominican monk and spent the rest of his life championing[84] the Caribbean natives and attacking the methods of the Colonists and the militia.

The Crown of Spain began to understand something of the chaos going on in America and responded with laws for the operation of New Spain. In 1512, the Laws of Burgos were issued to govern Spanish-Indigenous American relations. An important aspect of this legislation was the adaptation of Castilian administrative and judicial institutions to the governmental needs of the New World. The Laws regulated relations between Spaniards and the conquered people particularly to ensure the Tainos' spiritual and material welfare.[85] They also attempted to dismantle the *encomienda* system of virtual slavery because the colonists were not upholding their part of the obligation to teach Roman Catholic Christianity to the Tainos.

In 1513, the *Requirement* was created. This document stipulated a decree with the full authority of God and the Holy Roman Catholic Church, that all lords, kings, and the lands they governed were to be turned over peacefully, and that all inhabitants of the lands were to become Roman Catholics or that the lands would be taken by force, if necessary, to accomplish the task of conversion.[86] This *Requirement* was to be read to all unconquered people, and in the mind of some lawyer sitting in an office in Spain, it was to give the indigenous Americans a chance to surrender their lives and property before being killed by the conquistadores. Of course, the Tainos did not understand the Spanish, and even if they did, it was really a declaration of war, not the intended call for peace. However, Spain was very far away and the colonists were very much in control of what was happening in New Spain.

By 1518, about 122 friars had set out for the Caribbean from Spain. These were Franciscans (89), Dominicans (32), and one Mercedarian. A fourth diocese of Cuba had been set up in Havana that included all of Louisiana and La Florida to the north—nearly half of what is the continental United States today. The Franciscan convent in La Vega, Hispaniola, was constructed. The Mercedarian convent in Santo Domingo was built and became the center for that orders' ministries. The secular church was becoming established as the colonists were settling into their ranches, plantations, and utilizing their *encomiendas* to build up their holdings. The Tainos were greatly reduced in numbers from the first few years but their dying seemed to have slowed to just those that died from overwork and cultural disintegration.[87] But none realized that only the first and second waves of disease had passed over the Caribbean; the third was coming.

Cook, in reference to the smallpox epidemic of 1519-21 said, "There occurred an epidemic of smallpox so virulent that it left Hispaniola, Puerto Rico, Jamaica, and Cuba desolated of Indians or with so few that it seemed a great judgment from heaven."[88] For the people of the Caribbean, such a sickness had never been seen before. The indigenous population had been halved, and then halved again; this smallpox pandemic completely decimated the indigenous inhabitants on a number of small islands and greatly reduced the existing population on the larger ones to a few thousand scared, sickly, horror-filled people. Cook says the memory of that tragic event persisted long in the mind of the survivors, both the indigenous Americans who suffered its debilitating scourge and the Europeans who witnessed their abundant labor force being annihilated.

The ministry of the few score friars laboring among the indigenous people was reduced to baptizing dying people and doing their best to bury the piles of corpse. They also found ministry in helping the children and adolescents who had survived once their parents were dead and the indigenous societies had ceased to function. This was not the end of the indigenous races. Some families, some groups were devastated; others were inexplicably spared. But those who had first escaped were hit by later waves of the disease. The smallpox epidemic of 1519-21 made it clear to all that the indigenous people were vanishing from the Caribbean. They could not be counted on for labor, as servants, or even to exist in the near future. Again, to the common Spanish interpretation of the situation, it seemed God was judging the Tainos for their immoral ways. At the end of the first 25 years after Old and New World contact, the Taino and their circum-Caribbean neighbors were approaching extinction.

Nonresident Indigenous Colonial Slavery

The mines and the plantations needed laborers. Spanish noblemen, or those plantation and hacienda owners that now thought of themselves as noblemen, did not work with their hands. The indigenous Americans never did make good slaves; they escaped too easily and were very difficult to find in their home territory. Poor whites that had fallen into slavery for various reasons complained to authorities and also were hard to find when they escaped. In 1502, the first black slaves from Europe arrived in Hispaniola; they were domesticated descendents from African slaves. In 1505, the first black slaves, coming direct from Africa, arrived in the Caribbean.[89] Las Casas, in a zealous move to protect the natives from the treatment of Spanish colonials, proposed to the king in 1517 to allow the planters to have a dozen black slaves each. There was a yearly average of less than 2,000 African slaves imported to the Americas in the sixteenth century,[90] but that was never enough to meet the needs of the mines and plantations, and there were large numbers of other indigenous Americans on the nearby continent, according to the reports of older explorers.

In 1513, Ponce de Leon had stumbled onto the east coast of Florida, probably near the future site of San Augustín. He attempted a colonization of the Florida peninsula in 1521 at Charlotte Harbor on the southwest coast of Florida but was met by indigenous warriors who showered them with arrows wounding many of the men, including Ponce de Leon. He later died in Havana, Cuba, from this wound.[91] This event occurred in the midst of the first great smallpox epidemic. His men were only too glad to get out of the islands for a time, but one wonders if the disease might not have been brought with them to La Florida. There is no written record of its spreading to the mainland at that time.

Juan de Grijalva went to Hispaniola in 1508 and then on to the conquest of Cuba with Velázquez in 1511. He became one of the earliest to explore the shores of the mainland. De Grijalva left Cuba with four ships in April 1518. After rounding the Cape of Guaniguanico on Cuba, he sailed along the Yucatan coast and explored the Tabasco region on the southern shore of the Gulf of Mexico. He discovered the Río Grijalva, and it was named for him. In Grijalva's interaction with the Mayan speaking people, the word *Mexico* kept coming up, and it seemed that the gold the Spanish had always sought was in this land to the west. Grijalva immediately dispatched a boat to tell Velásquez the news of the existence of this new Western empire called Mexico.[92]

Herdando Cortéz had arrived in Hispaniola at the age of 18 years and had sailed with Velázquez in the conquest of Cuba after which he was appointed a judge. When Juan de Grijalva reported his discovery of the mainland to the southwest in 1518, Velázquez picked Cortéz to build a colony there. Velázquez soon suspected that Cortéz would go beyond his orders and investigate this new empire, so he attempted to cancel the expedition. Unfortunately for Velázquez, Cortéz had already assembled men and equipment and set sail. He rounded the Yucatan peninsula and touched the southern coast of the Gulf of Mexico in what is now the state of Tabasco. During battle with a Maya group there, he took many captives including a young Aztec woman who would become his interpreter, advisor, and mistress. Through her Cortéz learned something of the mighty empire that lay inland over the high mountains. Cortéz continued with his explorations up the coast, and on April 21, 1519, he landed and established a settlement at Villa Rica near today's city of Veracruz.[93] Thus began the conquest of the Aztec empire.

Velázquez then sent Pánfilo de Narvaez after Cortéz for exceeding his orders, but Cortéz, upon hearing of the new force coming behind him, took 300 men and surprised the 900 man force of de Narvaez and captured the captain. De Narvaez was held prisoner for several years while appeal was made to the King. The judgment favored Cortéz who was now conquering the Aztec empire.[94] It should again be remembered that this was the time of the first great plague of smallpox. It was undoubtedly carried to the mainland by either the men of Cortéz or those of de Narvaez who joined Cortéz after their encounter. One might say it was the smallpox that conquered Tenochtitlán[95] not the small band of invaders.

Also about this time the governor of Jamaica, Francisco de Garay, authorized an expedition to explore the west coast of the Gulf of Mexico. Alonso Álvarez de Pineda, in 1519, led an expedition which essentially sailed around the west end of Cuba, followed the Gulf coast west, and then south until he found the small settlement of Villa Rica.[96] He was accosted by Cortéz, escaped and returned north, founding a settlement on the Pánuco River where he stayed.[97] The following year a supply ship found the Pánuco settlement under attack by Huastecos and evacuated the 60 survivors. De Pineda died defending his settlement. Pánuco would become the center for expansion on the Gulf coast, for a base of government administration, and for slave raiders capturing Huastecos to be shipped to the Indies. This was the time of the first smallpox plague, and it can be assumed that the previous two plagues were also running their course through the Huastecos.

Another visitor to Hispaniola, Nuño Beltrán de Guzmán, was born in Guadalajara, Spain, to an old family of the hidalgo class. He studied law, becoming a licentiate. He arrived in 1526, and traveled to Pánuco, the failed settlement of De Pineda six years previously. The area was now occupied by *encomenderos* due to the great Huasteco population loss after contact with the de Pineda's settlement. Guzmán was appointed governor of Pánuco, where he first showed his rapaciousness by taking thousands of indigenous prisoners and selling them as slaves to the islands of the Caribbean.[98] The way Zumárraga described the administration of Guzman was, "They impoverished the Indians by taxes, sold them into slavery . . . sent shiploads to the Antilles, offered violence to Indian girls . . . these immoral and unprincipled men."[99]

Though Guzmán was the kind of man who verified the shocking details of the Black Legend, there are two facts that should be noted in this episode of conquest: first, the very rapid de-population of the aggressive Huasteco people after the de Pineda settlement, probably due to the introduction of disease—a combination of influenza and smallpox, and the second, that the primary purpose of Guzman's administration was to enslave the population to supply the plantations and mines of the Greater Antilles. It can be concluded that the Huastecos on the continent were dying out rapidly due to disease long before any clerics came on the scene. Again, the coastal areas of the continent were being used to supply the slave markets of the islands before any attempts were made to evangelize the Native Americans on the continent.

Though Spain did not uphold the complaints of Narvaez against Cortéz, they did give him the right to colonize La Florida giving him the title of Adelantado of all the lands he could conquer there. In 1528, he landed in the Tampa Bay area and then marched 600 men up towards Tallahassee looking for the gold of *Apalachee*. The party returned to the gulf coast near modern day Panama City, built shallow-draft ships, and then set out along the coast to the northwest. They were battered by storms, and disasters struck many of the small boats.[100] Only four men of the entire party eventually made it all the way back to Mexico on their now famous seven-year journey.[101]

As a reward, Hernando De Soto, one of the conquerors of the Inca Empire, had asked the Crown for the governorship of Guatemala but instead was given Cuba. Based on information from the Narvaez-Cabeza de Vaca expedition, De Soto wanted to conquer the whole of La Florida. He selected 620 eager Spanish and Portuguese volunteers, embarked from Havana on nine ships with tons of heavy armor and equipment, a livestock count of 237 horses, 200 pigs, and a host of European germs. He made landfall in 1538, near Tampa Bay and began a four-year trek of exploration that would take him throughout La Florida and Louisiana territories: Georgia, the Carolinas, Tennessee, Alabama, Mississippi, Arkansas, and Texas. The remnants of his expedition returned to the Mississippi river and then, by raft, returned to the Gulf and to Mexico in 1543. They had lost over half of their men, 300-350 had survived. They were wearing animal skins for clothes, and most were in poor health, De Soto himself died and was buried on the Mississippi River.

The immediate results of this monstrous trek through totally unknown lands were paramount. Some of the horses that escaped or were stolen helped establish the first populations of mustangs in North America. The pigs De Soto brought along with them introduced wild hogs into the south. De Soto was instrumental in forming the aggressive and hostile relationship between the indigenous tribes and Europeans along the entire North Gulf coast. On several occasions they encountered aggressive indigenous groups in the new lands, but more often than not, his expedition instigated the violence. More devastating than the battles, however, were the diseases carried by the members of the expedition. Several areas that the expedition crossed were de-populated after their passing. Many of the natives fled the more densely populated areas that were being affected by the strange new illnesses, escaping towards the surrounding hills and swamps. The social structures of the indigenous population at the time were fundamentally changed by the De Soto expedition and its aftermath of de-population.

Of note, 15 clerics lost their lives with the expeditions of Narvaez and De Soto. Their purpose in going on the exploratory expeditions was to have a chance to minister to the indigenous people before the onset of the suffering and dying that appeared soon after Native Americans were contacted in so many previous engagements. One objective of these trips was to begin new settlements. The secular church clerics also wanted to minister in these towns that would be springing up during the expeditions. There is no way to know either the fruits of their labors with the members of the expeditions, or with the indigenous peoples that they encountered. The fact is that none of the clerics that went with the expeditions ever survived the trips.[102]

Lucas Vasquez de Ayllon had come to the Indies with de Ovando in 1502. He did well with a sugar plantation and was appointed a member of the Superior Council in San Domingo. In 1521, he sent an expedition to Florida under Francisco Gordillo in a quest to find the Northwest Passage. The expedition landed near Cape Fear in North Carolina. De Ayllon followed the Gordillo expedition three years later and discovered Chesapeake Bay and the James River. After reporting to King Charles V of his discoveries, De Ayllon was granted the land he had discovered, so in 1526, de Ayllon led a new expedition of two ships and 600 colonists and founded San Miguel de Guandape[103] (near the future site of Jamestown). This site was abandoned after one year due to a very hard winter and attacks by the indigenous people.[104]

As late as 1600, Spain's power over what is now southeastern USA was unquestioned. From the perspective of evangelism and building the Roman Catholic Church of New Spain, this narrative of exploration and conquest in the first Epoch must be interrupted to examine what was happening to the indigenous peoples of the Caribbean and its mainland coastal areas that had survived the first of the terrible plagues after contact was made with Europeans.

After the smallpox epidemic came the first great measles epidemic in 1531-34.[105] This was another virus totally unknown to the Americas, and the effect on the populous greatly accelerated the demise of the indigenous Caribbean people. Smallpox and influenza along with the measles continued to show up regularly decimating what was left of indigenous groups. But the death plagues still were not finished with Florida and the Caribbean.

Colonial Slavery

As the explorers made contact and opened up new areas, general knowledge of the Caribbean area expanded exponentially. During these first 30 years of initial contact, wars, enslavement, and especially disease had ravaged the Taino and Carib populations moving them towards extinction. Enterprising colonists, looking for their path to prosperity, saw the great profits to be made in slave trade; conveniently, the original explorers had determined where the indigenous people were to be found. Written history concerning the slave raids—the principle parties involved, how they accomplished their sordid deeds—is very scarce. Inference in some records, a few historical statements, the obvious results of coastal de-population and the availability of indigenous slaves to the Greater Antilles are the only clues that this sordid industry in human trafficking took place.

Pope Paul III, in 1537, had stated in his Sublimis Deus, "American Indians must never be treated as 'dumb brutes for our service' for they too were part of mankind, by no means to be deprived of their liberty, or the possession of their property, even though they may be outside the faith, nor should they in any way be enslaved."[106] Obviously, not all Spanish Roman Catholics chose to obey the inspired, infallible words of the Pope. "Slaving expeditions date from the early years of Spanish occupation in the Antilles . . . The first two expeditions sent to Yucatan . . . had [as] important objectives the taking of slaves to work the settled islands."[107] As early as the administration of Ovando in Hispaniola ". . . kidnapping expeditions to the Bahamas became in his time a regular practice."[108] In reference to slavery on the isthmus, William Sherman states that "five or six vessels were engaged in the slave trade out of Nicaragua for six or seven years between 1523-1533."[109] Again he states, ". . . although one reads that in August 1533 there were as many as twenty ships engaged only in slave trade . . . Other Indians had been transferred from Nicaragua to Panama in the number of twenty-five thousands . . ."

Due to their proximity to the Indies, both Nicaragua and Honduras were the principal sources for slaves. Nicaragua was estimated to have had about 600,000 indigenous people at the time of the Spanish invasion. According to one earlier settler, the original population of Nicaragua had been diminished by 80%, more than a third of the Indians enslaved. "It is estimated that Nicaragua alone lost over 200,000 indigenous inhabitants to this massive slave trade as the Spanish attempted to prop up the declining Caribbean populations."[110] The rest of the population, the difference between the one third and the 80% total, can safely be assumed to have died from the epidemics that passed through from the beginning of contact with Spanish explorers. The slavers kept inserting the Native Americans who were without immunity to the epidemics into the caldrons of disease where they just kept dying almost as fast as they could be shipped.

Florida was also very close to the Indies and susceptible to raids. Although with a very small, scattered population in comparison to the Central American area, Florida commanded interest in proportion to its population. Slave raiders prowled the coast lines but the information about slave raids on southern Florida, such as the indigenous Tequesta and Calusa areas, is very sketchy. There are statements of cultural disintegration of villages due to disease and *slave raids*.[111] Ponce de Leon sailed into the Bahamas headed toward Florida which was considered to be an island by *slave hunters*.[112] Vasquez de Ayllon, *a merchant in search of Indian slaves* for Caribbean mines, mapped the Carolina coast.[113] Weak evidence indicates that slave raiding was also going on at the times of the voyages of discovery all along the Florida coastline.

Therefore, during the first generation after Columbus stumbled upon the Florida-Caribbean area, the one thing that most affected the indigenous people who were to be evangelized with the gospel and converted into Roman Catholic Spanish citizens was the incredibly swift de-population of the Caribbean area. Causes for the severe decline were many:

- First, lethal diseases rapidly spread once they were introduced by the Spanish explorers.
- Second, the wars of conquest and enslavement brought about the immediate deaths of thousands of Native Americans causing cultural disintegration for those who happened to survive the mayhem of conquest.
- Third, enslavement and the *encomienda* system forced the confinement of hunter-gatherers into close-quartered, unhealthy, and unsanitary living, which greatly accelerated the spread of infectious, killer diseases.
- Fourth, the slave trade itself that began with raids on villages—the murder, rape, and mayhem involved in the capturing of marketable human beings—left the unmarketable souls to die in a then, nonfunctional society and a ravished environment.

- After capture came the sorting of slaves, breaking up of families, physically breaking the wills of any resistant individuals, branding, chaining, and getting them to market before starvation or disease destroyed their market value.
- The final step in this process was the utter humiliation of being sold into a life of servitude until death came as a release from the horror of labor in the mines, construction, and cane fields.

In approximately one generation, the indigenous population of the Caribbean was gone. They were lost spiritually from the perspective of the Roman Catholic Church in that the vast majority died without ever having seen a priest or having received any form of evangelism or baptism. And they were lost as a race of people. They no longer existed.

It also needs to be noted that the colonists and the clerics were totally at odds with one another during this epoch because of the decisions of the Roman Catholic Church concerning the Guanches. Following the pattern of the Canary Islands, indigenous people who were baptized could not be sold into slavery. It was therefore the assumed responsibility of the slavers and the colonists to see that none of the indigenous people came into contact with a cleric lest they become Christians and legally could not be enslaved. Even *encomienda* holders "protected" their natives from the clerics to avoid the hassle of what to do with a Christian Native American once they were baptized.[114] This was the obvious flaw in the whole *encomienda* system—the *encomendero* was the person responsible for the Christianization of the indigenous people under his authority in the absence of any clerics.

Of interest, most of the written histories[115] declare the extermination, the annihilation, or the extinction of the Caribbean Taino and Carib groups, yet, one does not need to look far to see that *they* are here with us today. There are Web pages on the Carib people on the Internet,[116] there are villages in eastern Cuba that claim to be indigenous Taino, and there are reservations of Calusa and Tequesta people in Florida.[117]

Considering the history of these indigenous peoples, one wonders how anyone could say today that they are the descendents of one particular indigenous group. That history includes the conquest and immediate mixing of Spanish and American blood, the importation of many continental indigenous people to the Caribbean and their mixing with the indigenous and Spanish, the mixing of the island people themselves in defense against the Spanish. And all that was done over decades, hundreds of years ago with no written records. Ideologies, race, and indigeneity today have both political and economic ramifications which raises the question of motive for all indigenousness claims.

The Roman Catholic secular church continued to expand into the new population centers of the Antilles and coastal areas of the mainland, building new bishoprics and establishing the hierarchy of the secular church. The Mercedarians built the first convent in Santo Domingo and then founded the first Convent on the continent in Panama (1522); it would become the starting point of Spanish expansion into South America. In 1528, the Mercedarian Francisco headed for Nicaragua where, with four religious assistants, he established a Mercedarian convent in the new city of Leon. Mercedarians were the first religious to arrive in Guatemala in 1535, where Juan de Zambrana founded a convent in the old city of Santiago de Guatemala.[118] It should be remembered that this is the era when tens of thousands of indigenous freemen, by the Pope's definition, were being abducted as slaves and sent to the Caribbean and Peru. Yet it seems the secular church did nothing in protest but simply ministered to one another in their installations and to the European population of the area as if life about them was normal.

Of the great mendicant orders—Franciscan, Carmelites,[119] Dominicans, and Augustinians—the Franciscans arrived first, then the Dominicans who labored in this first epoch. The approaches and methods of these two orders were very distinct. The Franciscans, in their rule of poverty, were really the only clerics actually to live among the Taino people of the Greater Antilles and attempt to evangelize them, as seen in the example of the lay brothers that accompanied the Ovando party to Hispaniola. In general terms, the Franciscans' defense of the indigenous people followed the course of charity and compassion. Franciscans were the only order with experience in evangelizing the native people in the Canary Islands. This previous model did not wholly apply because they were not sure the Taino were completely human. They felt it was necessary first to transform them into men and afterward to labor to make them Christians.[120]

Franciscans built the convent at La Vega and later others throughout the islands. Those convents had to have been built with indigenous labor and it can only be assumed that at least the men and women assigned in *encomiendas* to the Franciscans were evangelized and probably baptized.[121] Encomiendas meant a captive audience, and probably some type of instruction was given to the native people under Franciscan care and employ. Still the Taino were dying off so fast it left few to evangelize, convert, or acculturate. Very few indigenous congregations were ever started, and none continued for long.

The Dominicans' approach was more characteristic of their order's emphasis on the theoretical and judicial route: teaching, church law, and inquisition.[122] It was the Dominicans that looked at what the explorers and colonists were doing to the "free" natives and were sickened by what they were seeing. Dominicans were the only order that did not participate in the encomienda system but vehemently attacked the system. When Las Casas rebelled at the excesses of the conquest of Cuba and decided to do something about it, he joined the Dominicans. Las Casas would go on to champion the cause of the indigenous people from the Caribbean to Mexico and on to the courts of the Crown of Spain. It was what Las Casas saw in the Caribbean that would cause him to lead the fight resulting in the Laws of Burgos, the New Laws, and eventually change the course of history for the indigenous people of New Spain in the epochs following the Florida-Caribbean conquest.

From most perspectives, the first epoch of Spanish-American encounter was a total disaster. The feathered, painted, naked beings the Spaniards encountered in America had confounded the entire Spanish nation as they read the strange reports. The missiology of the Canary Islands could not be made to apply, primarily because the indigenous Americans were dying off too fast to apply any workable methodology of evangelism. The Tridentine Roman Catholic Church had the major missiological purposes of saving souls and extending the church. One soul that is brought into a relationship with Jesus Christ is significant; however, a few souls out of hundreds of thousands cannot be seen as anything but failure in the objective of making Roman Catholic Christians of the Tainos and Caribs of the Caribbean. As far as making Spanish citizens of the indigenous Americans, again the conclusion is total failure: they were not Spanish citizens; they were dead.

Analysis of the Spanish Imperial Missiology for the First Epoch

What is needed to analyze what was accomplished in the area of evangelism, conversion, and teaching Spanish citizenship in each of these epochs of conquest is some kind of missiological framework that can give uniformity to the discussion for each succeeding epoch. The fundamental issues of missiology have been discussed for almost 2,000 years, because the church has always been aware to some degree of its duty to be missional. Arthur Glasser summarized the major areas of apostolic missions as[123]

1. *Apostolic practice*—this area concerns how to express evangelistic practice as commissioned by Christ[124] and as it is taught in the New Testament, both individually and corporately as the church, to bring about obedience in all that Christ taught us.
2. *Church and Mission Structure*—this area deals with the structure of the church and it's ecclesiastical authorities, the expressions of the same church in other geographical areas, and the relationship of the institutional church with other symbiotic structures historically found in the church.
3. *The Gospel and Religions*—this area deals with the Christian response to encounters with other religions that do not acknowledge the Lordship of Jesus Christ.
4. *Salvation and the non-Christians*—this area deals with the destiny of those who have never heard the gospel of Jesus Christ, the efficaciousness of the redemptive work of Christ, of God the Father who is not willing that any should perish, and the testimony of creation that leaves each man "without excuse."[125]
5. *Christianity and culture*—this area deals with the validity of each separate culture as a creation of God, but corrupted by sinful nature, and the usability of elements of culture to worship and glorify God.

These five major areas of missiology will serve as the framework of discussion for each epoch of conquest in this study.

The Apostolic Practice of the clerics as understood by the Spanish Roman Catholic traditions during this first epoch will be presented in two parts: doctrines for the salvation of souls, and the methodology or forms of evangelism used by the clerics to teach those doctrines. Yet even before these doctrines and methods we must note the one great area of obedience demonstrated by the friars: they went *to the ends of the earth* of their own free will, following their Lord's command to go and make disciples. They responded to the Pope's plea and the invitation of the King of Spain to reach the heathen with the gospel according to Rome—the only gospel known to them. They went in good faith and many gave up their lives in their zeal to be found faithful. Whatever else may be said, they left the comfort and safety of convents and churches to strike out into the unknown because their Lord called them to go.

Concerning the salvation doctrines that the clerics brought to the Florida-Caribbean epoch, what little there was can be classified as Tridentine in nature: the apostolic exhortation included the Christological command to be baptized, usually to the total exclusion of all other aspects of the salvation message. The concept was nearly universal that it is better to have the indigenous people baptized, even by force, if necessary,[126] and have entrance to an eventual destiny with God, than to have a free-will refusal and eternal damnation. Hence, whenever possible, indigenous people were baptized. Unfortunately it was usually those on their deathbeds, children of those already dead, and the *encomienda* laborers of the clerics that actually ever had an opportunity to be baptized in this first epoch.

The other six sacraments of the Roman Church were not practiced for the Tainos and Caribs because of two basic concerns: the high view of the sacraments held by the clerics prevented sacraments from being applied to natives, and because there was a fear that the indigenous people were not capable of understanding the significance or true meaning of the sacraments.[127] It should be remembered that, in the eyes of the Spanish, it was not yet determined if indeed these feathered, naked, totally immoral (by European standards), incomprehensibly pathetic, indigenous Americans were really human.

For the Spanish, there was only one true religion—the Roman Catholic Pontifical system. As seen in the last chapter, all others were heretical or of the devil. To the Spanish, there was ample evidence that the religion of the Taino and Carib people were fabricated in the pit of hell itself—nudity, barbarism, immorality, sodomy, incest, cannibalism, and finally the evidence of the judgment of God himself pouring out all the lethal diseases on these people because of their wicked ways. For the friars, there could be no dialogue with the native shamans, only a complete repudiation of their demonic powers, false icons, and a prohibition of their rituals.

The evidence suggests that there was really very little *Apostolic Practice* going on during this Epoch. What was being practiced was so limited in scope and content that it would have indeed been a miracle of God for any of the Florida-Caribbean indigenous people to have come into a saving knowledge of Jesus Christ the Redeemer. The invasion of the Canary Islands—with the military conquest of an inoffensive native people, an imposed Spanish cultural dominance, and forced Roman Catholic conversions—was the missiological pattern of *apostolic practice* brought to the Caribbean, but the American natives died too fast for it to be implemented. The church that was being established was basically of and for the Europeans with the Tainos and the Caribs barely able to receive the crumbs that fell off the European tables.

Literature often notes the religious nature of the conquistadores and the colonials that came to New Spain. Under this heading of *apostolic practice* must also be highlighted the *lack* of genuine apostolic practice during this epoch. As has been noted, there seems to have been a decided lack of Christian morality on the part of both colonials and clerics as they dealt with the Caribbean people. It is true that the nearly all male European population at the time of conquest, in the presence of a nearly all naked indigenous population, was an already out of control situation from the start. Vainly one searches for any attempt by the few clergy to bring a semblance of control to the situation. The bastard sons and daughters of the colonials were regarded as indigenous American, not Spanish, the fruit of their wombs being raised by their mothers, usually not knowing their fathers, giving rise to a whole new category of cast in New Spain—one that one day would *be* the people of New Spain, the Mestizo, and also, in the absence of fathers, giving birth to the matriarchal society of *La Raza*. However, for this epoch, the mixed blood decedents were just *Indios* and treated like Tainos or Caribs. This new mixed race would account for most of the few Indios to survive this epoch.

The other area of a glaring lack of *apostolic practice* was in the slave trade. Even though the leader of the Roman Catholic Church had declared the indigenous Americans free men, there are few instances in world history of such a prolific and disastrous slave trade as was conducted by the Spanish colonists during this epoch. Later the condemnation would come both by Spanish law and Roman Catholic Church law, but not in time for the tens of thousands of souls lost to this terrible, illegal practice. Not only did the early clerics fail to condemn the slave trade or attempt to stop it, but most clerics participated in it through the *encomienda* system.

Church and Mission Structure during this Florida-Caribbean Epoch must be viewed as totally European. When the first church structures were built, they were extensions of the church organization in the Canary Islands. The first bishoprics continued to be under the direct jurisdiction of the Archdiocese of Seville.[128] The secular church of New Spain was from the beginning an extension of the Church of Rome, the only true church, and simply an extension of its hierarchal structure. Among the mendicant orders there was no thought of an indigenous clergy; if the successful model of indigenous clergy of the Canary Islands was remembered, there was no time to implement it among the rapidly declining Taino population. There appears to be no record of indigenous students or novices being admitted into any convent for spiritual training for the time under study. The church was a totally foreign institution, and really only for the benefit of Europeans in New Spain during this first epoch of conquest. The few indigenous people who were baptized were not brought into full communion as brothers and sisters in Christ Jesus as seen in the absence of all other sacraments other than baptism.

In the area of *The Gospel and Other Religions* the Friars were severely constricted by the Spanish Crown's concept of Roman Catholicism being the one true church, and all other expressions were deemed false and of the devil. All of New Spain must be as Spain itself—with one true religion and none others tolerated. This meant a totally intolerant attitude towards the religion of the "pagan" Tainos and Caribs of the Caribbean. Once the Spanish were in control militarily, all practice of indigenous religion had to cease. Shamans were not permitted to practice their rites forcing the indigenous religion underground for the duration of their very short simultaneous existence with Roman

Catholicism. The history of this epoch does not reveal any attempt at dialogue between the clerics and native Shamans concerning an understanding or interface between the two religious expressions. There could only be one religious expression—Roman Catholicism. However, as an underground religious expression, many of the pagan ways and world views did continue as a folk Catholicism among the new Mestizo class of indigenous people.

The area of *Salvation and Non-Christians* was also severely limited in practice by Trent. Baptismal regeneration and mercy compelled the Spanish to baptize, often against the wills of the indigenous people. Baptism was seen as salvation. Therefore all non-Christians were to be baptized without will or understanding if necessary. The only other option was eternal hell, assuming these savages were human enough to be destined for hell without baptism, or just oblivion as the other animals.

The last area of missiological concern, *Christianity and culture,* deals with the concept that God is the God of culture, that our core traits of beliefs, feelings, and values were originally created in humanity by God for his own glory.[129] All three of these areas were corrupted by the sinful human nature caused by the condemnation in the fall from grace, but elements of all cultures of the earth can still reflect this divine heritage. The surface traits of culture are explicit: those from inside the cultural context can tell another person from outside the culture something of those beliefs, feelings, and values. This diversity of culture, as seen in the surface traits in the context of the indigenous people offers the points of intersection where foreign-cultural concepts interact with the indigenous concepts to be rejected, accepted, or synthesized into a new syncretic practice.

The ethnocentric Spanish were suffering from something far worse than just their sin-nature: the sin of Satan himself—their prideful superiority complex. With their confidence in superior technological achievements and arrogance in their societies' political and artistic achievements, it appears that it did not enter the Spanish mindset that there was anything of value in the indigenous cultures they were destroying. In their eyes nothing could serve as a bridge to comprehension of the gospel message, no points of intersection where foreign cultural concepts interact with the indigenous concepts to bring mutual understanding. The Spanish attached no validity to the indigenous cultures and made no attempt to understand the indigenous perspectives of what was happening to their world.

Summary

In summary, for the Florida-Caribbean Epoch of Spanish conquest, the Spanish expression of what would become Tridentine Roman Catholicism became one element of a barrier that prohibited any true missiological cross-cultural witness of Christianity to take place before the indigenous populations of the Indies had ceased to exist as distinct peoples. Other barriers to cross-cultural ministry were epidemics of European disease causing the rapid decline of the indigenous populations, the ruthless and savage killing by the conquistadores in initial conquests, and the terrible baseness of human nature as revealed in the uncontrolled behavior of the Spanish colonists in exploiting the indigenous people, enslaving them in direct and consistent violation of the Roman Church's prohibition to do so. Then finally, the pride and arrogance of the Spanish blinded them to any value the indigenous cultures may have had. The religious workers were far too few and far too late in coming to have had any real affect on the outcome of evangelism in this first epoch.

CHAPTER V

SECOND EPOCH: THE HIGH CENTRAL VALLEYS

Epoch Two Introduction

We have already been briefly introduced to the second epoch of conquest, the *Central Valleys* of New Spain, by the advances of Cortéz and his valiant crew as they cruised up the coast of Veracruz and established their small settlement of Villa Rica. They expected to find people and towns in the coastal planes, but what they learned from La Malinche[1] was that the mighty empire they sought had its capital just over the eastern corridor of mountains. La Malinche spoke Nahuatl (Aztec) and Maya, was baptized Marina, and evidently became a beloved mistress, interpreter, secretary, and then mother of the son of Cortéz.[2] First, Jerónimo de Aguilar—a former Mayan captive—translated from Spanish to Maya, then Marina from Maya to Nahuatl, the market language of the Aztec Empire. Far more than just translate, she could give Cortéz the insight in conferences as to whether emissaries were speaking the truth; she could guide him through cultural barriers and explain more deeply what he was trying to communicate to the Aztec leadership. Cortéz himself said, "After God, we owe this conquest of New Spain to Doña Marina."[3]

At the time when Cortéz was preparing to march inland, his knowledge of New Spain was still quite sketchy. He had a fairly accurate understanding of most of the coast of the Gulf of Mexico and the Greater and Lesser Antilles. Of the continent to the north he knew almost nothing—the mythical edge of the world could have been just north of the Veracruz coastline and it would have changed nothing for this small party of conquerors. The only concept that Cortéz had of the people, the jungle and mountain geography, the heat and humidity or cold and ice-capped mountains, was what La Malinche could communicate to him through Aguilar, their translator. In the Valley of Mexico, Cortéz—with just 616[4] men and a woman—was about to attack a mighty, warlike empire in excess of 20 million people who controlled an area even more vast than that Spain itself.

Cortéz had no idea at the time that he was just the latest in a long series of conquerors. New civilizations had been emerging over centuries as conquerors who built upon the ruins of previous cultures formed new empires to take their place in a continuous history of more than 3,000 years. Nor could he know that while his North African Carthaginian ancestors were just beginning to penetrate and settle the Iberian Peninsula,[5] the Olmec, whose historical lands he was marching through to get to the eastern corridor of mountains, was one of the most advanced civilizations on earth. Because the Olmec and their contemporary civilizations—the classic period of Teotihuacan,[6] the Toltec master builders of Cholula,[7] Monte Alban on its mountain top,[8] and the great Maya centers[9]—all are well studied, there is no need to revisit them here. Lesser known civilizations from the classic period to the Spanish invasion were the people of La Quemada in the state of Zacatecas, the Totonác people of El Tajín on the central Veracruz coast, the Huasteco people centered on the Pánuco River, and the Zapoteco and Mixteco of the Sierra Madres del Sur mountainous regions. Cortéz had no idea what an amazing history he was so rashly plunging into and altering forever.

Of interest to this study are the contemporary empires of the conquest which are the Aztec and the Tarascan Empires and their interaction with the Spanish from 1519 to 1571, the *Golden Age of Missions*[10] in Mexico. These two empires simultaneously held the entire region south of the Altiplano deserts of central Mexico to the jungles and swamps of the Tabasco isthmus which separated the Maya from the Aztec. The Western third of this area was held by the Purépecha people, called Tarascan by the Spanish, and included all of the present-day state of Michoacán, as well as pieces of Jalisco and Guanajuato.

The Tarascan (Purépecha) People

Their empire had lasted since the end of the classic period, about 1100 AD[11] to 1530 AD, when subjugated by the Spanish. The center of the Tarascan Empire was their capital city of Tzintzuntzan. From this religious and administrative center, the Tarascans consistently and effectively defended their territory against their constant enemies, the Aztecs of Tenochtitlan. The Aztecs had attempted several times to conquer the Tarascans but had never succeeded. This left them with a major rival on their Western border. In combat they repeatedly suffered losses to the strategies of the Tarascan generals. In 1478, the ruling Aztec lord, Axayacatl, marched against the Tarascan Empire. He found his army of 24,000 warriors confronted by an opposing force of more than 40,000 Tarascan warriors. The ferocious battle went on all day. Many of the Aztec warriors fell and others were forced, back badly wounded by arrows, stones, spears, and sword thrusts. The following day, the Aztec army retreated, having suffered the loss of more than half of their elite fighters.[12]

At the time of the Spanish conquest, the Tarascans had no written language at all to administer their intricate economic and political network. This differentiated them from the other higher civilizations of Mexican history and has made a study of their history difficult. Evidence from archaeology is intriguing but still fairly sparse. Another unique fact is that the Purépecha language is unrelated to any other known Mesoamerican language—its closest cognates are the Zuni of New Mexico, and the Quechua (Incas) of South America.[13] Tarascans used bronze for their weapons which allowed a sharp edge that copper alone could not be made to do. They used gold plating, another technique not used by any other group in Mesoamerica.[14] Their famous lacquer work was only known there, and in China.

But it was their skill in management and communication, not just their military technology that won the wars and kept their territory intact. Their expansion came about primarily, if not exclusively, through the use of warfare against neighboring populations for the sole purpose of expansion of their religion—like the Spanish they practiced evangelism by warfare. The Tarascans succeeded through both conquest and intimidation using traditional weapons that included the bow and arrow, lances, the *atlatl*, as well as some use of maces and slingshots.

Weapon points were made of metal, obsidian, or a combination of both materials. Defense against the enemy's weapons came from shields and cotton armor. Allied soldiers from assimilated tribes were encouraged to use their traditional weapons and did so with great effect: the Chichimecas from the Northern provinces were skilled archers, and the Otomí from the mountains were experts with the *macana,* slings, and hand-to-hand combat.[15]

Underlying the social, political, and economic structures of the Tarascan Empire was its state religion. Their expressions probably assumed their final forms within the last 150 years before the Spanish conquest. They centered on adoration of the god Curicaueri, who was identified with the sun. There were a great many other deities as well: gods of the heavens, of the earth, and of the underworld, each with a system of temples and sacred locations throughout the Lake Pátzcuaro Basin. Human sacrifices were made with the usual victims being prisoners of war. They were given enough strong drink to almost knock them out, and then taken to the stone of sacrifice, where their hearts were cut out and offered to the sun.[16]

The Cazonci, which could best be translated *king,* had the duty to conquer new lands for the god Curicaueri. Thus, it is not surprising to find that religion and warfare were intimately linked as well. The king's role was all-encompassing. He functioned in the priestly hierarchy and as a representative of the gods. He was also war chief and supreme judge of the nation, and he was the absolute ruler of the city of Tzintzuntzan.[17]

Aztec People

The Aztec empire is probably the best known and understood of all pre-Columbian indigenous civilizations. For this reason only factors that affect this study will be considered along with the extreme reaction of the Spanish when the two cultures came into contact. The Aztec had conquered and subjugated all lands between the Tarascan and Mayas: the Totonác, the Otomí, the many expressions of Zapotec and Mixtec of Oaxaca and Guerrero, the Tlapanec and many minor groups of the Rio Balsas basin. The Aztec conquered and ruled the indigenous nations through terror and trade. The basis of their terrorism was a perverted expression of a nearly universal Mesoamerican religion adapted from the previous civilizations,[18] an extreme expression that focused on human sacrifice primarily of captured warriors. This demanded constant warfare for the securing of captives and a military that was an integral part of their society—all men were part of the militia and on call for war. Most of the indigenous societies of what is today southern Mexico were tribute nations and chaffed under the domination of the hated Aztec at the time of the Spanish conquest.

The religion was typically pantheistic with worship of the sun god Huitzilopochtli, represented by the green hummingbird figure, at the center. He was a god of war—constantly fighting the night, the stars, and the moon with bolts of sunlight to bring on the day.[19] There were gods of the cardinal directions, personal gods, plant gods, and gods for merchants, gods for warriors, gods for farmers, and the gods of conquered nations that were captured, taken to Tenochtitlan, and incorporated into the Aztec pantheon of deities.

The Aztec nation was a theocracy with elaborate cult rituals that were taught in schools along with crafts, hieroglyphic writing and interpretation, mathematics and astronomy, chanting of the historical narratives, and understanding the symbolism of architecture and the calendar that regulated every aspect of Aztec life. The calendar encompassed a 52-year cycle. The Aztec priests had to calculate cultic ritual by knowing the precise interconnection between each particular god and their celebration days as dictated by the calendar, and how to propitiate the right god at the right time. The distinction between "high religion" involving ancient wisdom, scientific knowledge as taught by the Aztec priests and that of the common man was very similar to the Roman Catholic attitudes towards distinctions between the instructed theologian and the everyday worshiper that just did what he was told.[20] Catholicism with its hierarchy of Christian saints, its implicit recognition of position and authority, and multitudes of holy places and icons approaches closely the perspective with which the Aztec peoples regarded their gods.

The Aztec thought of his gods as having strong material powers: therefore their spiritual aspects counted little with the common man. In practice, "the priests gave guidance and prescribed the ceremonies, and the worshippers gave heed to those special divinities upon whose patronage their life directly depended, much as a devout Catholic selects certain saints for veneration above the list of those whose days are recorded on the calendar."[21] Sahagún's descriptions set forth the elaborate rituals with their emphasis on timing, preparations, and costume and needn't be repeated here.[22] The application of human sacrifice to the most mundane ceremonial acts brought to the Aztec worshiper a satisfaction of giving that which is most precious to their gods—the gift of a life (but for the Aztec nearly always somebody else's life).

As repulsive as it might prove to be, the priesthood of the Aztec must be examined for it is at the heart of this study. It was an all male association responsible for the details of religion in a theistic society. As such, they were the custodians of knowledge: Aztec history, mathematics, astronomy, medicine, agronomy, and most importantly Aztec theology, the chronology, and the practice of religion in conformity with the calendar and the heavenly bodies. In some areas of the physical sciences they were ahead of Europe at the time of conquest. In some areas of theology and religion, they were about as debased as members of the human race may become.

Young boys were given to the priesthood where the practice of sodomy was the norm; no contact with women was allowed. Cortés described their regulations as being so strict that the conduct of Roman Catholic clergy would be an offence to the Aztec, the way the clergy violated their own rules. The food of the temple priests were the arms and legs of the sacrificial victims.[23] Their daily ministering consisted of slicing apart sacrificial victims and ripping out their hearts. Díaz said that all the walls of that shrine were so splashed and caked with blood that they and the floor too, were black. Indeed, the whole place stank abominably. The immediate reaction of the Spanish was horror at this repulsive shrine to Tezcatlipoca, the god of hell, covered with layers of blood, and five human hearts on the brazier in front of the idol. This was the work of the Aztec priests. The Spanish concluded it was a religion straight out of the pit of hell.

The Conquest

The classical narrative of Bernal Diaz will serve as guide for a journey with Cortez and his army in an attempt to understand both the religious nature of the conquest, the ingrained hatred for Montezuma and the Aztec by the other indigenous groups, and the reaction of the indigenous populations to Roman Catholicism. When the Spanish arrived in Cempoala (today Zempoala, Veracruz), the Totonác capital and the largest city on the Gulf of Mexico with a population of about 30,000 at that time, Cortéz had a discourse with the cacique who Díaz called the *fat chief*. Cortéz explained that human sacrifices must stop, and he explained many things concerning the holy religion. On hearing all this, the fat Cacique heaved a deep sigh and broke into bitter complaints against the great Montezuma and his governors saying that they had taken away all his golden jewelry and so grievously oppressed him and his people that they had to obey, since Montezuma was Lord over many cities and countries and ruler over countless vassals and armies of warriors. Cortéz had made his first indigenous ally.

The much larger party marched on the next day with over 400 indigenous porters, each able to carry up to 50 pounds on his back and to march 15 miles per day. It was the custom of caciques to provide porters for important officials, but this was an ordinary provision most welcomed by the Spanish. At the town of Quiahuitzlan, a fortified settlement located on the lower slopes of a volcanic mountain on the gulf coast of Veracruz, they were well received, but at the same time the town was visited by five Mexicans, tax collectors of Montezuma. The caciques there turned pale and trembled with fear at the news of the arrival of Aztec officials. The royal tax collectors reproached the caciques for receiving the Spanish; for the offence they demanded 20 male and female citizens of Quiahuitzlan for sacrifice as peace offerings to their gods for the wrong that had been done. Cortéz immediately had the five arrested and ordered the local caciques not to pay taxes any longer to Montezuma. The act of arresting the representatives of Montezuma so astonished the local leaders that they began to call the Spaniards *Teules*, gods or demons depending on how it is translated.[24] By one act, Cortéz had thrown off the tyranny of the Mexicans and joined forces with the Totonác; at that point in the campaign, more than 20 Totonác towns had thrown in with the Spanish conquerors.

Later at Cempoala, after hearing Cortéz' customary exposition of the holy faith, and his injunctions to give up human sacrifice and robbery and the foul practice of sodomy and to cease worshipping their accursed idols these people then swore obedience to His Majesty. With much controversy the men of Cortéz' band then threw down and destroyed the idols from the top of the pyramid. The priests of the temple were outraged but could do nothing despite their fierce appearance. They wore black robes with hoods, waist length hair so clotted and matted with blood that it could not be pulled apart. Their ears were cut to pieces as a sacrifice and they smelt of decaying flesh.

(The following acts of worship and cultural practices taught to the Totonác will be italicized.) After the pyramid was cleaned of all blood and debris, an altar was then set up with an *image of Our Lady* and *a cross placed up on top of the pyramid*. Four *priests of the temple were chosen;* they were bathed, their hair was cut, and *white robes were given to them*. They were ordered to *put fresh flowers on the alter everyday* and *keep the whole area clean*. They were taught how to make candles from local wax and, *always to keep one on the alter burning*. Mass was then said by Fray Bartolomé de Olmedo, *eight girls were baptized*, and then given to different soldiers.[25]

On the march to Mexico, the Cortéz army, now with 20 caciques and their thousands of warriors, passed through Jalapa and Socochima where they "... *proclaimed the truths of Our Holy Religion*, and of King Charles who had sent them to put an end to human sacrifices and robbery ... and other things that needed to be said. *A cross was erected in each town and its meaning explained*, and they were told to *treat it with great reverence*."[26] They crossed the high passes and descended into the region of Tlaxcala where they and their allies fought a bitter campaign until the Tlaxcalans surrendered to them, submitting their warriors to join in the conquest of Tenochtitlan of the Aztec. Díaz and Prescott both provide details of the campaign against the city-on-the-lake. After the campaign there was nothing left of the magnificent city except piles of rubble and piles of bodies—mostly indigenous from both armies. In the end it was smallpox that killed more throughout the valley than the weapons of war. With Tenochtitlan destroyed and the Aztec empire decapitated, the reigns of rule were taken over by Spanish conquistadores.

Wherever the Spanish went, European disease soon followed or often even preceded them. From the previous chapter, the period of 1519-21, saw the first smallpox epidemic devastate the Caribbean area. The virus then advanced with the Europeans onto the mainland, first de-populating the Huasteco region, afterward proceeding over the eastern corridor of mountains with the party of Cortéz and attacking

Tenochtitlan simultaneously with the allied armies. The indigenous allies of Cortéz were not immune and suffered proportionate losses. Without smallpox Cortéz most likely would have been delayed considerably in overthrowing Tenochtitlan. Then in 1531-34, epidemics of measles and influenza struck the Central Valleys of Mexico joining up with the continuing waves of smallpox; the results were devastating to the indigenous populations. In 1545, epidemics of typhus and a pulmonary plague swept through the high Valleys, and in 1550 an epidemic of mumps further reduced the population. All these together, plus nine more repeated epidemics within the first 100 years, would reduce the indigenous population of the Valley of Mexico from more than 20 million at the time of the conquest to approximately one and a half million by 1619.[27]

The Missionary Friars

In this second Epoch of conquest the religious workers, both secular and monastic, were much better prepared to face the challenges before them, for none could look back at the Caribbean area without feeling a sense of utter failure. The church was established there, but hundreds of thousands of indigenous Caribbean natives had perished without hearing the name of Jesus Christ. Faced with many millions of high cultured indigenous people in the central valleys of New Spain, the friars creatively devised new methods to affect mass baptisms before the native population again perished without the administration of this sacrament. The one overriding element was to allow no one to die without baptism. Knowledge of the gospel or other sacraments was of lesser importance. The utter chaos caused in the Caribbean by the barbarous colonists without any effective, official administration, and then the massive slave trade that preceded any kind of European civilization or Christian evangelization of the coastal mainland could not be allowed to happen again. Experienced clerics were coming as soon as the end of hostilities made it safe to travel, missionaries would precede secular church officials, and they were coming in large numbers knowing that the task before them was impossibly huge.

When Cortés stepped ashore in 1521, two Roman Catholic friars accompanied him—Juan Diaz and Bartolomé de Olmedo. The pair accompanied the invaders and baptized those who were willing during the long trek to Mexico, helped set up altars and crosses, led in the Mass before battles and in the prayers of thanksgiving after battles as well as the priestly functions concerning the dead. More than two thirds of that valiant little band of soldiers, sailors, and adventurers died during the long trek, the siege, and destruction of the Aztec capital. Few primary records can be found concerning Juan Diaz; apparently he served as the assistant to Bartolomé de Olmedo, for Olmedo would become known as the *First Apostle of New Spain*.[28] Apparently it was Olmedo who led the first of the cultic practices during the penetration from the coast to Tenochtitlan.

Cortéz realized the need for missionaries. In his fourth letter to Charles V, Cortés "asks for monks rather than bishops or prelates for, if bishops and prelates come there would be the same wasting of funds in pomp and vices or in legacies to their children or relatives . . . and the [natives] should see them practicing the vices and profanations such as in our time they are accustomed to practice in Spain, it would bring discredit upon our faith . . . The damage would be so great that no amount of preaching could overcome it."[29] The orders under rule had undergone great spiritual transformation in the fifteenth century while the secular church had resisted reformation and transformation; this was obviously common knowledge to the people of Spain at the time of the conquest. Cortés wanted missionaries who could do the work of ministry, who would have the respect of the indigenous Americans, but above all, who were spiritual and able to communicate their spirituality. "In the early days of New Spain missionaries had been called upon to do the work of the inadequate secular clergy . . . thus the big part of the religious organization of the country fell into the power of regular orders and was more or less free from control by the government."[30]

Three Flemish Franciscan friars—Juan de Tecto, Juan de Aora, and Pedro de Gante—were the first to reach Tlaxcala in 1523.[31] Gante, who in the past was the confessor to Emperor Charles V, quickly learned the native language (Nahuatl) and established a school for native children in Texcoco. Because he believed that education and religion should be natural parts of everyday life, Gante learned the native culture, then taught reading, catechism, and native arts in both Spanish and the local dialect. Three years later he founded a similar school in Mexico City. His *Doctrina Cristiana en la Lengua Mexicana* was published in

Antwerp in 1528 and in Mexico in 1553. Pedro de Gante came to be known in Mexican history as the "Father of Mexican Education."[32] His ministries and life revealed something of the quality of the missionaries responding to the call of missions in New Spain.

These three friars were followed by the legendary *12 apostles* the following year. Fray Martín de Valencia was chosen to head a band of 12 Franciscans who were to labor for the conversion of the Mexican natives. Upon their arrival in May, 1524, to the amazement of the Aztec chiefs, they were received with the most profound veneration by Hernando Cortéz.[33] On the second of July, 1524, Fray Martín—as apostolic delegate under the direct authority of the Pope—presided at the first ecclesiastical synod in the New World.[34]

Another of the first band of Franciscans who sailed for Mexico with Fray Martín was Fray Toribio de Benavente *Motolinía*, who survived all his companions. As he and the other brothers passed through Tlaxcala on their way to the City of Mexico the Aztec saw the humble demure and ragged habits of the Franciscans and kept repeating to each other the word *Motolinía*. Fray Toribio, having asked the meaning of this word and learning that it was the Aztec word for *poor*, is reputed to have said, "It is the first word I have learned in this language, and, that I may not forget it, it shall henceforth be my name."[35] Bernal Díaz Del Castillo, an eyewitness of the arrival of the first friars, singles Motolinía out from the others, saying of him, "Whatever was given him he gave to the [natives], and sometimes was left without food. He wore very torn clothing and went barefoot, and the [natives] loved him much, because he was a holy person."[36]

Motolinía would later make a journey to Guatemala where he ministered for a time before passing on to Nicaragua. Returning to Mexico, he was appointed *Guardian* successively at Texcoco and Tlaxcala. He, along with Frey Toribio, when it was decided to found the settlement of Puebla, was one of the two commissioners chosen to carry out the task. They worked with the indigenous laborers to build the city. Not only did Motolinía say the first Mass there on April 16, 1530, but with his companions, he made all the allotments of land for settlers, while choosing for the convent the site upon which it is still to be seen—the beautiful church of San Francisco.[37]

After the 12, greater numbers of friars began to come and they came more frequently. The Franciscans began in 1524, the Dominicans in 1526, and the Augustinians in 1533. By 1559 there were 380 Franciscans, 210 Dominicans, and 212 Augustinians ministering in New Spain. As can be seen in the example of Valencia and Motolinía, the friars filled all the functions of the secular church during this period. By the time the Jesuits came in 1571, New Spain's ecclesiology had reached such a point of organization that the ecclesiastical authority of the orders and the presence of the mendicant friars was seen as an offense to the secular church. As a result, the *sodalities* (the missional orders) and the *modalities* (the institutional church) began at this time to exchange their roles of domination of the New Spain church.

The Franciscans were formally invited into Tzintzuntzan, Purépecha territory in 1525; the Augustinians were assigned to the area by Viceroy Mendoza in 1537. These first friars focused on the densely populated areas around Lake Pátzcuaro. They preached against polygamous marriages and ritual drunkenness, both customs quite acceptable to the Purépecha. Much of their time was spent in destroying public symbols and images of Purépecha gods, and in tearing down the magnificent stone temples. The first two attempts by Franciscans at establishing themselves in Purépecha territory were complete failures indicating the difficulty of evangelizing in a region that had not been militarily defeated. For the Purépecha people the Cazonci of Tzintzuntzan was god, he was the supreme leader of worship and by that standard, the friars just did not measure up; and the hatred stirred up by Nuño Guzman, soon to be discussed, was still most difficult to overcome.

The friars persisted and by 1583, the Franciscan province had 47 convents, 21 in Michoacán and 26 in Jalisco. By 1602, the Augustinians had 20 houses of prayer in Michoacán.[38] With the arrival of Bishop Vasco de Quiroga the secular priesthood was initiated for the Purépecha region.

Political Aspects of the Conquest of the Central Valleys

A bit of intrigue opened this second epoch. Velázquez, as conqueror of Cuba, sent his lieutenant Cortéz to found a colony on the mainland coast in the Maya area discovered by Grijalva. There Cortéz fought with the Mayans and subdued them, receiving the gift of 20 female slaves, one of whom was La Malinche. Learning of the mighty Aztec empire and confirming Grijalva's discovery, and using the information from La Malinche, Cortéz seized the opportunity for his own gold and glory. Leaving his area of colonization in Tabasco and proceeding up the coast of Veracruz, he founded Villa Rica and began the subjugation of the local indigenous population. Velázquez, fearing that the highly competent and ambitious Cortéz would exceed his orders, sent another lieutenant, Narvaez, to arrest Cortéz and bring him back to Cuba. Cortéz, learning of this, reversed his campaign into the Aztec empire, surprised Narvaez, capturing and arresting him. The men following Narvaez when they learned of this new campaign for riches and glory, decided to join forces with Cortéz in his assault on the Aztec empire.

Another political trail that must be followed is that of Nuño Beltrán de Guzmán,[39] called by some the *Himmler of New Spain*.[40] As the governor of Pánuco, his application of tyranny was complete and deplorable beyond understanding; Cortéz described his government as violent, arbitrary, and exploitative of the indigenous people. From his beginning in New Spain, the ambitious Guzmán was determined to undermine and replace Cortés. He envied the conqueror of Mexico and initiated a campaign of defamation against Cortés, sending reports back to the Spanish court that Cortés had murdered his wife and was planning to set up an independent kingdom in Mexico.[41]

After completing his Honduran campaign and returning to Mexico City, Cortés found some officials from Spain waiting to relieve him of his command and to send him back to Spain to clear his name of the damage done by Guzmán. Soon two of the three members of the official Spanish delegation that replaced the leadership of Cortéz died under suspicious circumstances. The survivor of the three, Alonzo de Estrada, both incompetent and cruel, was soon replaced by a four-man *Audiencia* (a new judicial and administrative body authorized to rule New Spain) that included Guzmán and the new bishop Juan de Zumárraga. When the other two members died mysteriously, this left Zumárraga, who had no military or political office, and the newly appointed head of the *Audiencia*, Nuño de Guzmán, to rule New Spain. Guzmán's maneuverings and intrigue had paid off for a time, and Cortéz was not able to return to his previous positions of leadership.

Cortéz, himself a master of intrigue, seems to have met his match in Guzmán who now ruled all of New Spain with an iron hand. Zumárraga, in peril of his own life, confronted Guzmán whose administration was one of the most disastrous periods ever faced for the indigenous people in New Spain history. Zumárraga, with only his spiritual authority, was incapable of controlling the diabolical Guzmán who began a reign of terror against the indigenous people and all the loyal followers of Cortéz. Guzmán sold natives into slavery, seized the estates of his political enemies, and did everything he could to undermine and destroy the colonists loyal to Cortés. Guzmán's cruelty was exceeded only by his greediness, even confiscating the saddle mule of Pedro de Alvarado, because he had been Cortés's right hand man during the Conquest.[42]

Cortéz succeeded in clearing his name and was then appointed *Marqués del Valle de Oaxaca,* but the Crown did not return him to power in New Spain; that power would stay in the hands of the *Audiencia,* or as was the case, with Guzmán. But Zumárraga had finally succeeded in smuggling reports out of New Spain as to the nature and acts of Guzmán, so a new *Audiencia* was appointed and on its way to dispose of Guzmán.

When Guzmán heard of the intensions to replace him, he chose to defend his rule by extending the subjugated borders of New Spain. Announcing that he planned a new conquest, he looted the treasury, gathered together an army of 300 discontented colonists who felt they had not received their share of spoils, and 6,000 indigenous allies who were more than willing to attack their old enemies the Purépecha. On Dec. 21, 1529, he set out west to conquer lands and peoples who till now had resisted the conquest.[43] The Purépecha had already been subjugated and were a tribute nation, but that did not matter to Guzmán.

In that previous subjugation the Purépecha (Tarascan) nation had already become a refuge for Aztecs who fled the initial domination by the Spanish. There were Aztec groups called *Tecos* (ancient Mexicans) who had been dominated by the Purépechas expansion who gladly received the new immigrants. So the current *Cazonci* (King) of the Purépechas was well aware of the contest going on east of the mountains which had always separated the two empires. The Cazonci had, in fact, refused to answer the delegation of Aztecs that had come pleading for help and had those ambassadors executed. Upon hearing that the Spanish were on their way to conquer him, the Cazonci simply gave up the ghost; it was said he died of fright. When Cristobal de Olid,

Cortez's trusted lieutenant, crossed the mountains in 1522 with an invasion force, the son of the Cazonci—newly installed after vicious infighting among the royal heirs which had cost the empire many of their key leaders—fled the presence of the Spanish but was captured and returned to Tzintzuntzan.[44]

Due to the civil war throughout the region in the establishment of the heir of the throne of the Cazonci (now held by the son Tangaxoan), many of the towns were without caciques, without leadership or authorities in place. When Olid captured the Cazonci, he established the king's submission and conversion, then baptized him and set up a puppet government in the capital of Tzintzuntzan. Afterwards it was only a matter of appointing a new cacique for each township (a geographic division equal to a county, or in New Spain a *municipio*), and the Spanish, with their puppet leadership in place, simply took over the reins of power in the Purépecha nation, something the Aztec had repeatedly tried and had repeatedly failed to do. The caciques were ordered to supply *encomienda* workers for each of the colonists as they received grants of land, Francisco de Villegas being the first *encomendero* in 1524. With Juan de Ortega subjugating the caciques that resisted the *encomenderos*, the subjugation without conquest proceeded quite smoothly.

Then in 1529, Guzmán came on the scene with his impromptu army fleeing the coming New Spain administration. King Tangaxoan, now a Purépecha governor of the Tarascan realm for the Spanish, received messengers sent from Guzmán demanding gold. In the interest of placating Guzmán, Tangaxoan made the fatal mistake of sending him silver and gold. This unwise act only served to whet the appetite of the tyrant. When his expedition arrived in Michoacán, he seized the king and demanded a huge amount of gold. Of course Tangaxoan couldn't produce it. So Guzmán had him dragged through town behind a horse, then burned alive. Ever the pious hypocrite, Guzmán explained later that he ordered Tangaxoan's execution because the king had abandoned Christianity and lapsed back into paganism.[45] Guzmán took his army of Tlaxcalans and Aztecs, greatly enhanced by Purépecha warriors who had been forced to join his campaign, and proceeded west into what is today the Mexican states of Michoacán, Jalisco, Zacatecas, Nayarit, and Sinaloa.

Guzman continued his unsavory destruction and murder in these Western and Northern Mexican states for seven years. Typically, the savage bands attacked an indigenous village, stole all the food stores of maize, vegetables and small animals, then razed and burned the dwellings. Often the native leaders of these villages were tortured to gather any information about mines, other towns, or other peoples in the area. His violent expeditions into the southern Chichimec lands were a main cause of the Mixtón rebellion and the hostility of the Chichimec tribes for many decades to come. His army penetrated to the middle of what is today the state of Sinaloa where Guzmán founded the town of Culiacán. A combined army of 30,000 Cáhita speaking people (a Uto-Aztecan language group) in a great battle near the site of Culiacán finally stopped this advance. Although the battle was won by the invaders, both armies were defeated by the diseases Europeans had been spreading throughout the new lands. Ravaged by a measles epidemic from 1530-34, an estimated 130,000 indigenous people died in the Valley of Culiacan. Guzmán saw his indigenous army of conquerors decimated by the vary diseases they had introduced.[46]

With the campaign finished and his army gone, Guzmán divided up the conquered lands among his surviving followers giving generous plots of land and large *encomiendas* of captured slaves to each. Culiacán was established as an administrative center for one district and Tepic for another. Guadalajara was founded on three different sites; Purificación and Compostela were established. The territories Guzmán conquered became known as *Nueva Galacia;* the whole area later was brought into the administration of *Nueva Vizcaya*. Spain did recognize these territories as a separate entity from the *Audiencia* in Mexico City, hopefully putting Guzmán out of reach of the central authorities looking for him. It did not work. Guzmán was arrested in 1536, and a year later he was sent to Spain in chains. He died a prisoner in the Castle of Torrejón in 1544, ". . . the detestable governor of Pánuco and perhaps the most depraved man ever to set foot in New Spain."[47]

This narrative has carried us beyond the Central Valleys and the second epoch of conquest. However, it was necessary to understand the political and social context in which the newly arriving friars had to fulfill their missionary obligations to God and country. In half a generation this tremendously vast area with its many millions of inhabitants was added to the responsibilities of the small groups of recently arrived friars. The Caribbean practice of *encomienda* had crystallized into a firm institution by the time the conquistadores went forth from the Caribbean to the mainland. Grave abuses were already drawing the scathing condemnations of the friars who had made themselves the champions of the rights of the indigenous Americans.[48]

In summary the Spanish administration of this epoch had made some policy decisions that would prove to be problematic for New Spain: they destroyed rather than upgrading the civilizations they encountered, imposing their own viceroys and bureaucrats in place of indigenous leadership. The Crown displayed its ownership by attempting to run New Spain from its European base. The result was that laws made in Spain mattered little in New Spain because the colonists continued to impose the encomienda system of exploitation, recreating a European style medieval feudal system for New Spain. This disenfranchised and excluded the native born from participation in self-government, bogged down the whole decision making process, and complicated the enforcement of laws. In the midst of all this the mendicants were reaching out to these indigenous multitudes with the gospel of Jesus the Christ as defined by the Council of Trent.

Apostolic Methods of the Second Epoch of Conquest

A great deal can be said of the methodologies in the work of the first mendicants of this epoch. The Flemish Gante learned the Nahuatl language of the Aztec and immediately plunged into the development of schools to teach the children of noble, indigenous families and became known as the Father of Education in Mexico. The 12 Franciscan Apostles engaged in a highly public debate with the religious leaders of the Aztec religion, according to Sahagún, and through the debate we are told that the Aztec priests, being convinced, were baptized, and "we wonder at the great multitudes of [Aztec] that legitimately lost all confidence [in the old ways] and immediately accepted the new God."[49] Sahagún also states that "the [natives] wasted no time in displaying their desire for Christianization[50] by immediately constructing churches with the very rocks of the pre-Hispanic temples."[51] Temples were being torn down as fast as the Franciscans, with the aid of soldiers and native laborers of the encomiendas could do it.[52] Three approaches to outreach arose in the new context for missions: education focusing on children that have the potential to become leaders, intellectual debate between mature leaders of both cultures in a public forum, and utter destruction of all symbols of the previous religion to prove the superiority of the Spanish faith.

It is important to grasp the context of the conquest from the point of view of the people of the Aztec Empire. First, remember that the Aztecs were neither monolithic nor homogeneous, and that it included tribes that were chafing in anger as conquered people, tribes in outright rebellion, and others that were never completely conquered. They were like bugs caught in a giant spider web—part of the whole, but always struggling to find a way out of the mess they were in. Second, although the majority of these conquered indigenous nations all had their separate gods, the cultic practices were of a recognizable pattern throughout the empire. The pyramids, or *cue* as Díaz called them, were the center of worship and sacrifice, and though of different styles and forms, they all generally served the same purposes. Carved stone images represented their gods; various symbols, sacred places, family alters, and well-defined celebration days throughout the year all centered on the pyramid.

A third point to remember is that there was always both a high expression of religion concerning the major gods and their cultic practices, and there was a common expression of religion as found in personal gods, favorite gods, family altars, and local sacred places that were recognized in or near each village and town. Of importance to note was the celebration of the calendar events for each high god which was an intricate, magnificent, social activity with the majority of the population participating in the various activities, nearly always including human sacrifice as well as many other types of offerings to the gods. The Aztec cultures placed a high premium on the society as a whole and much less emphasis on the individual of the society as did the medieval Spanish conquerors.[53]

When the Spanish entered the picture, they first decapitated the society by utterly destroying Tenochtitlan. Then they decapitated the practice of high religion by throwing down the temples, outlawing the priesthood, outlawing human sacrifice, prohibiting warfare (other than their own of course), and smashing all the gods they could find.

Overnight, required practice of religion had ceased, and for the masses, there was nothing yet presented to take the places of former gods, either intellectually or politically, which in a theocracy are inseparable from religion. The Spanish had created a huge leadership vacuum that needed to be filled as quickly as possible.

The Franciscan friars entered and from the start held a nearly monopolistic situation over the people of New Spain.[54] In addition to their European frame of mind, they were all well aware of their utter failure in the Caribbean, both of making religious converts and of making Spanish citizens. The indigenous of the Caribbean had died too fast to do much of anything. Now in the highlands of the Valleys of Mexico, smallpox had already struck and hundreds of thousands had already died. It looked like mass extermination by disease was going to repeat itself. But there was a solution to the problem of salvation according to the doctrines of Trent. The mass baptisms of the Jewish *Marranos*, the mass baptisms of the Muslims (even against their will), and the mass baptisms of the Guanches of the Canary Islands all had been accepted as necessary and approved by the hierarchy of the church. The concept of baptism without prior instruction was acceptable evangelism according to the Tridentine doctrines. The course was then set: as many Aztecs as was humanly possible needed to be baptized as quickly as possible *before they all died too.*

Therefore the friars set about baptizing the people of the Aztec Empire. Ceremonial cleansing was part of the cultic practice of most Americans and baptism fit right into that definition as an initiation rite. Accepting a new religion was not a novel thing in the eyes of the Aztec. Those that had been defeated by the Aztec armies had to accept Aztec faith and cultic practice. The gods of the conquered people were hauled to Tenochtitlan and set up in a lesser pavilion as being subservient to the more powerful Aztec gods. Syncretism was the religious philosophy of the Aztec, for it could only produce a religious synergy when different faiths were added together. If these new Spanish conquerors had a more powerful God that defeated all the Aztec gods put together, then it was only natural to accept their cultic practice and join the party. With such a receptive public, the friars began their evangelistic ministries with gusto.

Pedro de Gante is said to have baptized as many as 10,000 in a day. Toribio de Benavente claimed he had baptized over 300,000

Aztec. Torquemada bore witness to the fact that Motolinía personally had baptized over 400,000 in his ministries. In 1531, the first bishop Zumárraga wrote that 1.5 million indigenous Americans had been baptized in less than ten years after his arrival. In 1536, five years later, it was claimed that 4 million had received this Roman Catholic sacrament of initiation.[55] It is true that the Aztec were pledging ritual allegiance to the conquering powers, something people in their area of the New World had always done; yet, these are still remarkable numbers considering how few mendicants were present in New Spain at this early stage.

The friars had also learned their lesson about the need to evangelize using the native tongue of the people they were sent to transform into Roman Catholic Christians. As the friars arrived in New Spain, their first one to two years were spent in learning one of the major indigenous languages. Soon they were able to preach the "good news" in Nahuatl, Otomí, and Purépecha, allowing them to relate culturally to the people and to better understand their spiritual needs. This led directly to the friars' use of drama in evangelism.

The Franciscan missionaries found themselves in the midst of several new cultural expressions; the cultic practices were intimately and inseparably related to spectacles and processions of drama that conveyed the deeper meaning of their religious beliefs. This was one of many strikingly similar traits of Tridentine Roman Catholicism and Aztec religious expressions.[56] The Aztec societies were accustomed to seeing their religion acted out in a public forum. The friars responded with an evangelical theater that was a restructuring of an already existing system of visual and theological indoctrination with its accompanying theatrical techniques: dramas, comedies, pantomimes, living pictures, *autos religiosos tradicionales* (inquisitions),[57] and processions created with the deliberate intension of teaching the dogmas of the Roman Catholic Church. Rather than formal theatrical types meant for entertainment, they were intended to be an instrument to demonstrate and convince the audience of Christian truth.[58] From its very conception, the evangelical theater in New Spain was a mixture of elements from both Old Spain and the indigenous New Spain cultures.

The drama used for evangelism formulated by the Spanish friars for the purposes of conversion of the native peoples of New Spain mixed the ritual performance techniques of the indigenous people with

Catholic doctrine in ways which reflected the friar's own biases for both the culture of the indigenous people and their religious practices. The friars edited biblical stories to prevent a return to sinful practices, and women were not allowed to perform. Many of their theatrical works mocked what they considered to be indigenous vices.

When brought down to the essentials of an organized society, for both the political realm and religion, which are the same in a theocracy, the characteristics of semi-feudal Spanish practices and native expressions for the same purposes, were quite comparable. "The Spanish recognized native institutions which were similar to their own . . . and the Native Americans on their part realized that certain institutions which the Spaniards established among them were basically like those they themselves had evolved."[59] These parallels of the Spanish and Native American societies greatly facilitated the Spanish takeover of the reins of power in the decapitated Aztec empire and the implantation of Roman Catholicism in place of the pantheism of the Aztec.

The Franciscan missionary strategy for this second epoch was well conceived, and planned out, having learned from their previous experience in the Indies. Their strategies were then taught in the new convents and seminaries that were being established in New Spain and refined over time as their encounters with the Aztec, Otomí, and Purépecha people forced modification of their procedures. Christopher Vecsey outlined these missionary procedures:[60]

1. *Entrada*—the friars sought to overwhelm natives with showy vestments, music, painting, statuary of sacred images and ceremonies. They gave gifts to win confidences.
2. After the entrada, the friars sought to move themselves into the center of indigenous social life, build a church and friary.
3. From these centers, the friars began their [visitations] around the periphery of their territory, in time [an outlying mission] could become a center with its own priest.
4. The friar tried to win the confidence and loyalty of the [indigenous] leadership, while baptizing and making the children their own.

5. The friars undermined the indigenous social order by becoming both civil authorities and by controlling the means of production, as well as being the source of goods from without.

In the second epoch of conquest, this missionary strategy was not nearly as well thought out or applied, as Vecsey indicates in the above procedures, but the friars did make great strides in these directions for ministry. The institution that was already being implemented and established before the friars could begin their own strategies was the *encomienda*. The presence of huge geographic areas under the control of *encomenderos,* invariably the best lands available, greatly hindered the development of a workable missionary strategy—exactly the opposite of the intended purpose of the *encomienda*. A closer inspection reveals how profoundly it affected the evangelism of most of the indigenous people. The *encomendero*, or owner of the rights to indigenous labor, was given the requirement to evangelize, build a church, and see that Roman Catholic worship was properly conducted and everything pertaining to their local church building was maintained, as a condition for receiving the land grant and its quota of laborers.[61]

The following are John Brannon's definitions of the Spanish *encomienda* terms which have no equivalent in the English language. *Repartimiento* was the division or distribution of the native villages and towns, giving them to the colonists and conquistadores for the purposes of unpaid labor. The *encomienda* then, was the commission or charge for the care of the individuals that passed under the authority of the *encomendero*, or the colonist, with the grant of land and the natives that resided on the land or those that were given into his care.[62] The beginnings of the concept of *encomienda* were seen on Hispaniola when the colonists took or purchased slaves for labor in the mines and plantations. Since there was always a need for more labor the colonists took free men (and women and children) and forced them to work without pay. Then governor Ovando took over the right to bestow indigenous labor and *to divide* (the Spanish verb is *repartir*) these "free" people among the colonists; in so doing he established the *repartimiento* as a legal institution. It was this *encomienda* system that was transported to the mainland and was rapidly being instituted by the conquistadores. On mainland New Spain it was primarily the captain of the conquistadores that gave the encomienda to his lieutenants and other worthy recipients of land grants once subjugation was complete.

As was the case with slave holders in almost any era, the way indigenous Americans were used and treated by the *encomenderos* depended entirely upon the nature of the man with the authority. At the beginning of this second epoch, the *encomendero* could fix a tribute, require personal services, demand labor of any type, and rule without oversight or accountability within the *encomienda*. Such authority without accountability led to great abuses and worked such great hardships on the natives that change in the laws was demanded. Laws were established that, in addition to the Christianization of the Native Americans mentioned above, the *encomendero* was legally obligated to protect and see to the welfare of all the indigenous people under his charge.[63]

The lands that were controlled by indigenous towns within the *encomienda* remained in the possession of the villagers themselves, whether as individuals or as a corporate body. This was carefully safeguarded by the Crown as the *encomienda* system evolved.[64] It was also made very clear that the *encomendero* had no judicial or political authority over the people in his care. The *encomendero* was, in fact, expected to be a lay missionary, a clerk for the civil administration collecting tribute, as well as a town elder or overlord for the people under his care. Upon receiving this grant of *encomienda* and at his own expense, the *encomendero* was legally obligated to protect and to Christianize the natives assigned to him. The *encomendero* was required by law to maintain arms and horses in readiness to take the field at a moment's notice against all enemies who might attack the colonies from without, or rebel against lawful authority from within. This provided a permanent militia with excellent combat value and was, for a long time, the basis of the only functional military system in New Spain. Often the *encomendero* included the best of the indigenous warriors in his complement of militia, all fully outfitted by the *encomendero*.

From the standpoint of the friars who had to depend upon this system of *encomienda* for evangelism of the masses, the system was an abject failure in respect to Christianization. There was just no way that the few friars could evangelize the millions of indigenous people scattered over such vast territories. Where Roman Catholic *encomenderos* acted like

Christian men, there was some degree of success in evangelization, in building of chapels, and in respect to worship and celebrations. Yet even when these efforts were successful, the usually unschooled *encomendero* was in no position to teach, to preach, or even explain a reason for the Christian hope that was within him. Far too few of *encomenderos* actually tried to complete their obligations to the church. Without adequate instruction, and a poor substitute for the high expressions of Roman Catholicism, the majority of the indigenous people simply completed the new requirement of baptism and attended worship in the chapel, but continued with their most useful or favorite gods and family altars while at home and in their villages. In the majority of the *encomiendas*, there was little or no attempt to evangelize. The indigenous peons continued in their old worship patterns, often doing this in the small chapel, if the *encomendero* had bothered to build one.

It was during this second Epoch of conquest that intellectual battles were raging in New Spain and in the courts of the Spanish empire. The philosophical questions of the right one nation had to make war on another, or how to justify war were hotly debated. Many were now saying that the Spanish had changed places with the Moor and were now the invaders and oppressors of native people. Another intensely passionate debate concerned whether or not the indigenous Americans were fully human considering their utterly pagan nudity, immoral life styles, and sickeningly base behavior, at least by European standards. Also, the Dominicans had taken the battle against *encomiendas* and slavery to the Crown itself, with the writings of friars like Las Casas being published and spread throughout Europe and New Spain. These debates and their results were to produce new concepts of international law[65] and formed a precedent for the development of that whole field of judicial practice.

Out of these debates came the Laws of Burgos of 1512. They were the first set of laws governing the behavior of the colonists in New Spain where Spanish common law did not apply, and, in particular, in regard to how they interacted with the natives of America. The Laws prohibited the mistreatment of indigenous people; they encouraged evangelism, but further codified, authorized, and legalized the colonial practice of encomiendas. However, in doing so the Laws limited the number of people who could be allotted to each colonist, as well as regulating the work, the pay, provisions, living quarters, and hygiene of the laborers.

Pregnant women were exempt from work. The Laws prohibited the use of any form of punishment by *encomenderos* and established officials in each town for that purpose. Chiefs and other nobles were exempt from the ordinary labor and could retain servants.[66]

As stated earlier, Spain was many thousands of miles away and communications were very poor. Colonists raised such a protest when they did hear of the Laws that they forced reconsideration and no real enforcement of the Laws of Burgos ever took place. The Dominicans continued their fight against the encomienda system, and finally 30 years later, in 1542, the New Laws of Burgos were issued, this time with the elimination of the encomienda system. The backlash from the colonists was so extreme that it was feared a rebellion would erupt.[67] So the clause retracting the encomienda system was removed. Bannon states that "We do know that the New Laws provoked the greatest battle of the century, indeed of the whole colonial period . . . and that important ecclesiastical and lay figures felt that the enforcement of the laws could mean the ruin of the New World."[68] After all was said and done, the New Laws changed nothing, and the original Laws of Burgos never were strictly enforced. In reality the laws were so poorly regarded in New Spain that they appeared as a legalization of the previous untenable situation and in practice did very little for the situation indigenous people faced.

Although Cortéz had called for monks and the mendicants had responded in ever increasing numbers, some among them were commissioned to fill the roles of leadership in the secular church. Juan de Zumárraga in his controversies with Guzmán is one example. He was a Spanish Franciscan prelate recommended by Charles V for the post of the first bishop of New Spain in 1527. Without having been consecrated and with only the title of bishop-elect and the descriptive title of *Protector of the Indians*, accompanied by Andrés de Olmos, he left Spain with the first of the civil officials being sent to New Spain. After the deaths of two of the new auditors and a tremendously stressful interlude with the new auditors of the first *Audiencia* (ruling committee), new auditors were appointed, among them Sebastián Ramírez de Fuenleal—Bishop of Santo Domingo—and the lawyer Vasco de Quiroga, who later became the first bishop of Michoacán. With the arrival of the first Viceroy, Antonio de Mendoza, the rule of the *Audiencia* in New Spain ended.

At the insistence of the Emperor, Pope Paul III separated the See of Mexico from the metropolitan See of Seville and erected the Archdiocese of New Spain, appointing Bishop Zumárraga first archbishop and designating the dioceses of Oaxaca, Michoacán, Tlaxcala, Guatemala, and Ciudad Real de Chiapas as suffrages. Thus the Roman Catholic Secular Church structure of New Spain came into being. The vast majority of clerics were the mendicant friars of various orders, but there still existed a mutual respect at this point between the secular church and apostolic mission expressions of the Roman Catholic Church.

As the first Roman Catholic bishop in New Spain, Zumárraga faced a number of difficult problems in his administration of the secular church. One was the multitude of indigenous people who asked for baptism which forced the missionaries to adopt special forms for administering this sacrament. In one method the recipients were placed in groups with children in front. Prayers were offered for all. Then with a cedar branch water was then flung out over the whole group, or water was then poured on the head of each by assistants running though the crowd. Hundreds at a time could be baptized with this practice. It faced no opposition while the Franciscans alone were in charge, but as soon as other religious orders arrived, doubt began to be cast upon the validity of this form of baptism. Bishop Zumárraga submitted the case to Rome which declared that the friars had not sinned using this form, but decreed that it should not be thus administered in this manner except in cases of urgent need. The need was urgent. Tens of thousands of indigenous people were dying of diseases before they could be baptized.

Another major problem arose regarding indigenous American marriages. The pre-Columbian religions had allowed the practice of polygamy and the additional taking of concubines. When natives were baptized Roman Catholic, the question arose as to which were legitimate wives, which were concubines, and whether any indigenous marriages were valid at all. According to the Council of Trent, only marriages done by priests in the Roman Catholic Church were valid. The question was whether to respect the customs of the past, due to Old Testament principles, or enforce Spanish customs based upon the New Testament. Bishop Zumárraga took part in these debates and the case was submitted to the Holy See. It was resolved that the converted natives should keep the first woman wed as their wife and let the others go. There is little discussion as to what became of wives and concubines thus released from the family relationships or of their children who were then made illegitimate.[69]

Among the secular ministries of Zumárraga was the school for indigenous girls (the famous Colegio de Santa Cruz in Tlatelolco), the introduction of the first printing press into New Spain, the foundation of several hospitals—especially of Mexico City and Veracruz. Additionally, he encouraged industry, agriculture, and manufacturing for which he brought trained mechanics and journeymen from Spain, and the printing of many books. When the first Viceroy, Mendoza, was appointed to New Spain to end the brutal exploitation of natives, Zumárraga worked with him to strengthen the Spanish hold on the mainland through education, to implement the New Laws, and to further exploration. Mendoza also gave grants of encomienda and land to principal conquerors and to churchmen to extend the secular church.[70]

Bernardino de Sahagún, another of the early Franciscan missionaries, made a great impact on the church's understanding of the Aztec as a people. Sahagún has often been called *The Father of Modern Ethnography* because of his methods which included using native informants to elicit information on Aztec culture from the Aztec point of view before the fall of Tenochtitlan. He is best known for compiling the Florentine Codex, also known as *Historia General de Las Cosas de Nueva España*, written first in Aztec and then translated into Latin. The 12 volume set is still the best source for understanding the people of the preconquest Aztec empire. Sahagún said that the purpose of his work was to bring to light all the words of the Nahuatl language with their exact and metaphorical meanings, and all their ways of speaking, and most of their practices, good and evil.[71]

Among the Purépecha, en entirely new method of social organization and evangelism was being perfected. Vasco de Quiroga came to New Spain late in life; he would have been in his early sixties. Trained as a lawyer, he was late in taking holy orders, but the church recognized his ability and promotion came rapidly. During the years of 1547-1554, Quiroga was back in Europe to attend the Council of Trent (1545-1563). He missed the first phase of the Council but was able to participate and soon returned to his post in Michoacán where he served as bishop from 1537 until his death in 1565.[72] Quiroga remains a controversial figure in Mexican history. He was a renaissance humanist, a theological conservative, a social liberal, a political reformer, progenitor of the Mexican social security system,[73] and a crusader for the rights of indigenous peoples.

Quiroga served on the commission that sent Guzmán back to Spain in chains, knew firsthand the destruction Guzman's army had done in Michoacán, and as bishop was determined to undo the terrible damage Guzmán had inflicted upon the Purépecha people. In addition to war, epidemics resulted in a 30% demographic decline among the native population of Michoacán.[74] Appointed both bishop and judge for Michoacán, Quiroga was then free to put his dream of an ideal community into practice. Using Thomas Moore's epic work that was available in 1516, Quiroga had as models his Christian understanding of Eden and Plato's concept of the republic as a perfect commonwealth governed by intellectuals.[75] Quiroga believed that applying these organizational models among the local Purépecha population would be a perfect way to counteract the horrendous depredations of Guzmán.[76]

Quiroga's plan, which he implemented with outstanding success, was to create communities in the vicinity of Lake Pátzcuaro, the heart of the Purépecha country, where the native people would not only receive religious instruction, but also receive instruction in arts and crafts and in the fundamentals of self-government. In this land so brutally ravaged by Guzmán, the people slowly came to realize that the kindly Bishop was also a representative of the European race, as was the sadistic, brutal *conquistador;* there was hope for a life worth living.[77]

This was a totally new twist to the concept of *reductions* or *congregations* that were being applied elsewhere to congregate the natives in Spanish style pueblos. Quiroga was highly successful in reaching his goals in both political and economic development, though the Purépecha had little say in the leadership or organization with these new Spanish intellectuals. "The skills he implanted among [Purépecha] of the Pátzcuaro region have been passed down to their descendants, who [today] are considered among the most skilled craftsmen in Mexico."[78] Quiroga's ambitious plans extended his territorial jurisdiction, which brought him into direct conflict with the Spanish *encomenderos*[79] to the north, especially with Juan Infante who was quite involved in a full-blown war with the Chichimecas and had little concern for intellectual experiments. Indeed the Chichimeca wars had completely overshadowed the utopian experiment with the Purépecha, and by the wars' end, the experiment had also ended.

In Quiroga's Christian utopian plan, each community was to be centered on a plaza with a church for worship, all citizens were to be baptized, and all sacraments and Roman Catholic priestly functions were regularly carried out. It was to be mans' best shot at creating a utopia in New Spain. However, it differed little in spiritual results from the other congregations and reductions. The indigenous people were gathered into Spanish style villages, they were baptized, and a convent or chapel built for their worship needs. Where Quiroga succeeded was in both the economic sphere and the political sphere for local government. They were converted into a shallow expression of Roman Catholicism and made into dependable, prosperous, tax-paying citizens of New Spain.

Spanish Roman Catholic Missiology in the Second Epoch: Central Valleys

Applying the missiological frame work of the five major areas of analysis for apostolic missions to this second epoch of conquest, it can be seen that impressive strides were made towards a more effective evangelism by the mendicants. The first area is that of *Apostolic Practice* in doctrine, in methodology, and in cultural consciousness. Salvation doctrines in practice at first were a carryover from the first epoch, which was baptizing the pagans, almost to the exclusion of any other doctrines and sacraments of the church. The very excess of *exclusively baptize* is what called into question this anemic doctrine of salvation. Just baptize was already noted to be a logical conclusion of the doctrine of baptismal regeneration when used in conjunction with the extra biblical concept of purgatory. Most Roman Catholic theologians would reject this interpretation, but we still see in this epoch literally millions of Aztecs being baptized *en mass*, if we can accept the testimonies of the first Franciscans on the scene.

Las Casas was one of the contemporary clerics who questioned this practice of mass baptisms.[80] It was Zumárraga who brought the debate to a head, taking it to the Pope with the result that the practice of mass baptism was excused, those that participated it were exonerated, and the practice was only to be used in the future when absolutely necessary. Whenever possible, baptism was to be performed in conjunction with teaching through memorization of catechisms so that theological understanding of what was supposed to be occurring could be received along with the rite. This response from the Pope did not forbid mass baptisms, and it did not *require* teaching. It just indicated a better route to go when possible. The underlying concept that regeneration by baptism eventually will be sufficient has continued until the present day.

The immediate result of the controversy was that catechisms began to appear very early in the penetration of the indigenous nations by the clerics in this epoch. In 1539, the first book to be published in America was a bilingual catechism in Spanish and Nahuatl, soon followed by Fray Alonso Rangel who translated Christian doctrine into Otomí. In 1559, Maturino Gilberti produced the first Purépecha grammar and dictionary. Convents became schools for children. By 1559, the Franciscans had established 80 convents or monasteries; the Dominicans had 40 convents for teaching, while the Augustinians had a similar number. Children learned faster and were more moldable; adults were far more difficult to indoctrinate, so most of the cleric's efforts were aimed at educating the children of noble families who would eventually have more influence over the community of Aztecs or Purépecha.

The exception to this new rule for baptism was, of course, the children. By right of conquest the Spanish claimed that all children had to be baptized.[81] This was not a problem for most, adding more gods was normal for the Aztec. Yet baptism of masses of adults and ignorant children all living apart from a Roman Catholic context—and living daily life within an Aztec or Purépecha religious context, was the start of a long path toward a syncretic New Spain religion that bore much of both theologies and both expressions. It was a fusion of religions—the sheer numbers baptized without training guaranteed a congealing of the mixture of both faiths and a distinct expression from Roman Catholicism, something totally of New Spain, distinct from most Biblical principles yet rife with both of their cultural expressions.

Sahagún used the term *mestizada*.[82] Used in this manner, the term, with a root meaning *hybrid* or *cross-breeding of races*,[83] specifically of Spanish and Native American in this case, refers to a cross-breeding of the religions, still with the name Catholicism borrowed from the European side of the mix, but with so many new forms and meanings that it is in fact a new religion, just as *La Raza* has been considered a new breed by Mexicans in the anthropological sense. The history of the spiritual conquest explains why this new religion retained the name Roman Catholic, just as anthropologically, resistance to the foreign Spanish cultural imperialism explains why the new *La Raza* kept the name *Mexican* derived from the indigenous side of the mix. The Criollos[84] always distanced themselves from the Mestizo and Native American, considering both the working classes, and seeing themselves as still truly Spanish, still truly of the Roman Catholic religion, and truly superior to the pure Native American and Mestizo. "By the apparent contradiction, this unusual conversion of masses of natives fed upon the phenomena of ethnic resistance; the ancient customs continued, in truth, within the equivalent forms of Catholic worship."[85] By explaining these phenomena in such detail, Sahagún doomed his manuscript, prepared in 1521, to obscurity.[86]

Then there is a carryover of the big question regarding the *humanism* of indigenous Americans whose debate was started in the Indies. This concept of the indigenous Americans was expressed more in the term "childlike" as used by the colonists. Not many conquistadores who had to fight them ever regarded the Aztecs as childlike. But in Spain it was part of the argument of Sepulveda, using the logic of Aristotle, to prove the Native Americans inferior to Europeans.[87] Few of the sacraments were administered to the Aztec for fear that, due to their lack of knowledge, the sacrament itself would be defiled. After baptism, the only sacraments that the Aztec would experience were perhaps confirmation, confession, and maybe communion. Later in this epoch, marriage began to be added to this list. All of these depended upon a priest being nearby, which was not too common.

In *methodology of indoctrination* the use of Christian drama built upon the foundation of the Aztecs' use of both drama and processions became major evangelistic tools and were well received by the indigenous population. As Christian celebration took the place of all the major Aztec feast days, worship of the Godhead, Mary the mother of Jesus, the saints, crosses, and many other "holy" paintings and symbols that were put in place of Aztec paintings and symbols, the Aztec pantheon underwent an extreme makeover. Seldom was there sufficient instruction to really clarify as to why one god or object replaced the other. Obedience to the new Great God and to his mother was required. That could be justified in the eyes of the Aztec, but it was always difficult to get enough information to understand all the other "gods" the Spanish seemed to worship. Therefore it was better to stay with the favored gods they always used, though it was best to do that in secret when the Spanish were around.

These thoughts touch on the concept of an apparition of Mary, the mother of Jesus, at Tepeyac. The story is based upon several supposed appearances to an Aztec, Juan Diego, in December of 1531. The details are so well known they need not be repeated here. As well as the story is known, it simply has no historical basis. It just appeared full-blown in 1648, when Miguel Sanchez published his account in Spanish. In 1649, with a native audience in mind, an account was published in Nahuatl under the name of *Nican Mopohua* by Luis Laso de la Vega.[88] For the 117 years before these two publications, there is absolutely nothing of historical significance to collaborate the stories. Zumárraga, who is a key player in the story, does not mention such a significant happening in his histories and Zumárraga's biographer, who was criticized for leaving out the story, had to claim as a historian there was nothing there to write about.[89]

In all probability, the story originated as a Franciscan evangelistic drama—possibly based upon a similar story from Spain—a devotional play that was repeated until the story was common knowledge, and after five generations of evolution, was finally written down by a Spanish author. The Nahuatl tongue was still the common language of Mexico and seeing the need for a translation, the story was composed again in Aztec. As touching the name, *Virgin of Guadalupe*, Tlapoyawa quotes Torquemada saying, "Our first Priests at Tepeyac built a church dedicated to the Mother of God *as she appeared in Spain*: the virgin of Christopher Columbus and Hernán Cortéz, our Lady of Guadalupe"[90] (the emphasis is mine). The whole story attributed to the mythical Juan Diego was brought with the conquistadores from Spain.

Though historically the story has no foundation in New Spain whatsoever, that still does not mean it is without significance today. "Sanchez's account was responsible for the popularization and spread of the devotion among the Criollos of Mexico City who saw themselves as marginalized, disdained by the peninsulares and excluded from all positions of power in government and church. The result was a strong sense of regional or group identity that rallied around the [New Spain] brown virgin."[91] There is a Virgin of Guadalupe in Spain which predates that of Mexico by centuries. Both the Spanish and the Mexican Virgins of Guadalupe are dark-skinned, and the stories are similar. In Spain the Virgin was said to appear to a poor Spanish Charro [cowboy], in Mexico to a poor Aztec, Juan Diego. The art work and symbolism are very similar and there is little question they are depicting the same thing. The influence of the brown virgin was almost exclusively among the Criollos and had very little bearing on the evangelism of the indigenous Americans until the nineteenth century, although the story supposedly originates in this timeframe of the second epoch of conquest. There is no doubt that eventually the Saint Juan Diego will have to go the route of Saint Christopher: they both are based upon fictitious characters and local folklore.

The area of *cultural consciousness* demonstrates the greatest missiological advances from the first epoch. It is obvious that coming from the Caribbean to the highland valleys of Mexico, the friars went from dealing with a hunter-gatherer, moderately organized society, to a very highly developed society; and from scattered tens of thousands, to concentrated millions of individuals. These facts alone force a respect for the societal development, the governmental system, and the scientific achievements: roads, bridges, irrigation systems, fresh water systems, agricultural development that fed millions, and aesthetic beauty in their architecture, city planning, and murals.

The war of conquest with the Aztec had destroyed the jewel of Aztec culture: Tenochtitlan lay in rubble piles. The tenacity of the defenders had forced the invaders to tear the city apart house by house to retain the advances made each day by the conquerors. Nearly all of the political leadership and noble families had been killed in the siege or by smallpox.[92] The empire was indeed decapitated, but the lower echelons of bureaucracy and administrative structure of government lay at the disposal of the Spanish conquerors. As the Franciscans entered into debate publicly with intellectuals, and evangelists tried to reason with the people, the Spanish took over the reins of government using Nahuatl as the market language for a time period exceeding the next hundred years.[93] What was missing was the development of a native clergy—the one thing that might have permitted a clear understanding of the subtleties of religion and might have avoided the creation of a new syncretistic expression derived from both of the religions.

As already noted, the drama and processionals were adapted, modified, and used to communicate what they always had for the Aztec—the meaning of the principles of religion. Convents and schools were set up to replace the training centers of the Aztec priests, often the former with the rubble of the latter. Spanish agriculturalists learned the meaning of the Aztec calendar and symbolism of the pyramids in relation to preparing the ground, planting, growing, and harvesting of the various food crops, especially the corn.[94] In general, there was a new and honest cultural sensitivity and seeking of how to best express the principles of Roman Catholic Christianity as defined by the Tridentine model in this new cultural context. The weakness was in the transplanting of the theological concepts of Christianity during the formative transition period for the Aztec. This approached utter impossibility for so few mendicants. The high expressions of Christianity did replace the high expressions of Aztec religion for the educated few. But the low or common expression of Christianity simply mixed with those of the Aztec common practices, resulting in new practices and a whole new religious expression still called Roman Catholic, but in many ways a Native American or a new *mestizada* religion, to borrow Sahagún term.

This second epoch evangelistic effort of *Apostolic Practice* was somewhat less than half accomplished for the indigenous population that was in fact evangelized; far too many of course, were not. Complete evangelism should not permit any defective or incomplete definition of the spiritual nature of man. The object of evangelism is to come into Christ through regeneration, putting aside the old nature, and entering into a personal relationship with God through the finished work of Christ as we put on the new spiritual nature so that the spiritual man is in constant communion with God. The Christian, or *Christ-like* new man is not perfect, but he is moving toward being all he can be in God through a process called sanctification while living in obedience to the revealed will of God for all mankind.

Using this standard as a measure, the evangelistic effort saw very limited success in this second epoch. The missionary has to be an incarnate messenger to the target culture showing forth Jesus Christ in understandable terms to that people during the encounter. In this context the missionary must proclaim the gospel of Jesus Christ. The friars made valiant efforts to introduce the Tridentine Roman Catholicism into the indigenous cultural expressions; by their lifestyle, dress, and actions, the friars lived what they were attempting to communicate. There were always exceptions, but this focus is on the majority. They preached, administered the sacrament(s), and attempted to orientate the people to a new cosmology.

By their fruits you will know them say the Scriptures.[95] There was far more Mariology and Saints in folk Roman Catholicism than there was of the death, burial, resurrection, and glorification of Jesus Christ, the coming King, which causes one to wonder just what was preached. Tridentine Roman Catholicism does dictate Mariology and the use of artistic means to depict the particular Spanish expression of medieval Christianity rather than focusing on the redemptive work of Christ. Of the seven sacraments, only four were known by the indigenous people, and only one was consistently practiced—baptism by water. The exception to this was that of Quiroga in Michoacán where the philosophical structure and organization did produce an indigenous population that was more trusted to understand the sacraments, and in turn received more of them. Of orientation to the new Roman Catholic cosmology for the Aztec, it is best stated that the two cosmologies were married rather than one replacing the other.

In the area of discipleship, the catechisms were printed and distributed with the use of the new printing press, children of Aztec nobles were taught in an attempt to prepare new Christian leadership for the next generation, and drama was used to indoctrinate the adults and teach Christian practice. Yet moving up to another level of spirituality, the transformation of the inner man, no evidence exists of change in the daily practice of the indigenous people, but only a regurgitation of memorized statements and an exchange of new symbols for old. Internal spiritual disciplines for each friar were traditionally learned in the monastery by the monks, but the Aztecs were not brought into the monasteries as fellow monks.

The penetration of the gospel into the native cultural expressions was limited to the external dramas, processions, and feast celebrations, which really had degenerated into drunken orgies, as they still are today for the most part. Examples of a changed life, a *Christ-like* man or woman living according to the Christian moral code in obedience to the gospel message, was not that common in this epoch. In *Apostolic Practice*, much progress had been made, but there was still a great deal to be learned, corrected, and adjusted to be considered a fulfilling of the Great Commission statement: "teach them all things that I have commanded you."[96]

The second area of missiological evaluation is that of *Church Structure and Mission*. After a number of bishoprics had been organized in New Spain, Zumárraga, a Franciscan, was appointed the first archbishop, although he did not live to take the position. At the time New Spain had five bishoprics. When the archbishop position of New Spain was created, America was separated from the Archdiocese of Seville, and New Spain finally had its own Archdiocese. However, the secular church was still basically European and for the European residents of New Spain in spite of the millions of baptized indigenous people. The natives were still basically the responsibility of the orders.

Nearly all clerics were from Europe. Convents were being built and staffed, but they were for the induction of European missionaries, for giving friars from Spain a chance to learn the indigenous languages and ways to teach Aztec children the catechisms.[97] The convent was also a refuge for missionaries coming back from their service in the mission fields. The personnel of the orders were sent and had their salaries paid by the Crown of Spain. The secular church had to live off the tithes and offerings of the local church. This was a source of much resentment by the secular clergy for the men of the orders. It gave rise to the saying that the secular priests had to work for a living; the friars of the orders did not have to work, but had their way paid. Being as the Criollos received the primary benefits of the secular church, it was they who had to pay for the services of the priests and functions of the church to keep it economically viable. Still, in this second epoch, the structure of the secular church was gradually being established, and growing slowly throughout this period. It was growing in the number of churches, in the number of priests serving, and in establishing its ministries in the cities and towns of New Spain.

In the area of the *Gospel and Other Religions* and *Salvation and the Non-Christian* there was still no tolerance, no room for dialogue or exceptions. The Spanish ran into their first real challenge to high expressions of religion in this epoch, and they responded in true Tridentine form. They sought with all their power to annihilate the

Aztec religion. By the end of the conquest of Tenochtitlan, the major temples were piles of rubble. "From the start the Spanish friars began systematically to destroy [Aztec] temples and idols throughout New Spain. The aim was always to replace the old religion with the new."[98] The temples were centers for science and learning; their functions had to cease immediately. Sahagún makes the debate with Aztec priests sound like a voluntary submission on the part of the Aztec intellectuals, yet it is difficult to believe that an entire people would so readily give up their lifetime beliefs and pursuits based upon one debate with a few violent foreigners. All friars were seen as one with the conquistadores. Perhaps what the Aztec priests were really trying to preserve by their submission was their lives.

All Aztec religion and its accompanying worship were forbidden. Soon Zumárraga was appointed Inquisitor and quickly the Aztec learned that to be caught not participating in the Roman Catholic expressions was bad. "With the urging of the Franciscan community, the bishop used his inquisitional authority to hold 19 trials for religious crimes against mostly Aztec leaders living in and around the Valley of Mexico—a phenomenon called the Indian Inquisition."[99] The Aztec suffered a range of punishments from flogging and lengthy jailing to banishment and, in the case of one indigenous leader, burning at the stake.[100] Any non-Roman Catholic form of worship was forbidden. When William Orr described the *Auto de Fe* witnessed by Friar Ilarione da Bergamo in Mexico, there was included in the condemned, "a heretical blasphemer, an unyielding Calvinist, an idolatrous Indian woman, a witch, a bigamist, and a secular cleric . . . who had celebrated some unauthorized masses, and an unbending Jew.[101] There was no religious toleration in New Spain—only Tridentine Roman Catholicism; all other religious practices were against the law of the land. As far as the *Salvation and the Non-Christian* area of missiology was concerned, there was no salvation apart from Roman Catholicism. All others were of the devil, they were heresy, and they had to be eliminated. The one area of obedience was the simple fact that the Great Commission was recognized and was being fulfilled with their understanding of the gospel by the Roman Catholic Orders.

The area of *Christianity and Culture* deals with being respectful of diversity while being faithful to critical theological principles and values, yet still open to new expression of biblical principles within the native context. Sahagún, in explaining the great debate of the 12 with the Aztec intellectuals, stated that ". . . this was the beginning of understanding the indigenous values . . . they developed an apostolic precedent based upon their respect for the indigenous cultures."[102] Perhaps that was the beginning, but in reality if it was, it did not last very long. The Spanish saw the entire theocratic empire as being an expression of demonic worship; the political leadership were dead and gone and now the religious leadership had to go. The gods were destroyed; the libraries and all historical, scientific, and intellectual writing were collected and burned.[103] The temples—centers for learning—were torn down; symbols were smashed, defaced, or covered with Christian symbols. The indigenous priests were homosexuals who practiced human sacrifice for the nation with cannibalism being a common practice; all of this was immediately put to an end with reason. Nowhere was respect, or even any attempt at toleration offered for indigenous cultures in all this.

As much as the Spanish would have liked to prevent it, the one area in which there was a complete syncretism of the two cultures was in the religion of the common people. In this area there was complete identification of the people with many of the new Spanish gods as they understood them. Roman Catholic practices were readily accepted and applied to the old gods still being worshiped in homes, fields, at road intersections, and on top of many nearby hills. It was like the proverbial tar baby—the clerics would strike a blow against paganism and all they would get for it was a fist full of tar, their hand getting stuck, and becoming a living part of the tar baby. Therefore the Aztec culture and worship practices of the common man became part of Roman Catholicism in New Spain as the Roman Catholic expressions were incorporated into Aztec practice.[104] All this was being done along side of the high Roman Catholic practice of religion guarded by the Criollos and the secular church among the Europeans.

Summary

The second epoch of conquest represents one of the greatest in our study and in the history of conquests. From the perspective of New Spain's spiritual conquest, great strides were made in the mandate of the mendicant friars to implant Tridentine Roman Catholicism and to make Spanish citizens of the indigenous inhabitants. Because of the huge number of Aztecs, 20 million in the high valleys alone, the population though decimated by disease and conquest could still be counted in millions several generations later when natural immunity to many of the diseases began to take root in the populace. By then the majority of the indigenous population of the Central Valleys would count themselves part of New Spain, or Roman Catholic Spanish citizens.

Within the religious demographics of New Spain a major division began to take place between formal Tridentine Roman Catholicism, practiced in the cities and led by secular priests with the Criollo population, and the *mestizada* expression of Roman Catholicism as expressed by the indigenous population and the new, troublesome half-breed race that was being fathered by Criollos but raised by indigenous mothers, creating a new race and a new matriarchal class of New Spain society. The formal church had become organized with its own Archdiocese, five bishoprics, and a growing secular priesthood, but with a growing animosity for the mendicant friars and their authority over the indigenous populations. The Roman Catholic Church had experienced a nearly complete domination of the Aztec high religion but failed to replace the religion of the common people. They actually saw the formation, a syncretic marriage of the cosmologies, of both religions producing what came to be known as *Folk Catholicism*. They were partially evangelized with the product of the evangelistic efforts externally conforming to some aspects of Roman Catholicism while internally becoming something new that represented elements of both religions.

CHAPTER VI

THIRD EPOCH:
THE YUCATAN REGION

Epoch Three Introduction

The Maya and the Yucatan Peninsula were mysteries to the Spanish. They were first discovered by Columbus on his fourth voyage of discovery when he happened upon a huge trading canoe "as long as a galley" with 25 naked paddlers mastered by richly clad men with their families under an awning. It was evidence that, indeed, a rich civilization existed somewhere about, although Columbus never was able to find it.

Later, in 1517, a small privately funded exploration and slave hunting venture from Cuba, sailing under Francisco Hernandez de Córdoba, sighted a long, low coast on the horizon, the northeast coast of the Yucatan. Though still far out to sea due to the very shallow beach, they could see an indigenous city of white pyramids. The next day a party of ten huge canoes came swooping out to meet them, showing no signs of fear. They were well clad men, living in towns, and displaying a high cultural appearance. The Spanish were invited ashore, but lured into a trap. The ambush wounded 13 men with two eventually dying. Notice had been served that the Maya would be a formidable enemy.

These explorers had several more skirmishes as they searched for drinking water along the coast; fresh water was scarce on the Yucatan Peninsula and each source of fresh water seemed to have a large indigenous town nearby. At Campeche over 50 men along with their water barrels were lost in an attempt to secure water. Córdoba had suffered a major defeat at the hands of those he had envisioned exploiting and enslaving. The decision was made to turn back. One ship was abandoned, there only being enough able bodied men to sail two of the ships. After making port in Cuba Córdoba died of his wounds suffered in battle with the Maya.

In 1518, Juan de Grijalva was sent by Governor Velázquez of Cuba with 240 men to explore and map out the coastline that Córdoba had sighted. They explored from the island of Cozumel the entire coastline to the great river named for Grijalva in the modern state of Tabasco. It was here while trading with the Maya that Grijalva learned of the source of Maya gold. It was to the west, a place called Mexico, the land of the México (Mé-shi-ka), ruled by the great lord Moctezuma, an empire that governed all the lands to the west. Grijalva immediately sent one ship back to Cuba with the news. And upon its arrival, Velázquez began preparing an expedition to establish a foothold on the mainland. To lead this next expedition he chose another young lieutenant, Hernán Cortéz. As this news of a great empire to the west spread, the Yucatán with its militant Maya was nearly forgotten.

Yet, before launching these plans, a surprising twist added intrigue to the discovery, conquest, and evangelization of the Yucatan. As Cortéz followed the path of Grijalva, stopping first at the Island of Cozumel, he learned of the presence on the peninsula of two Spanish survivors of a shipwreck. Finding and using local emissaries, one of the men was located—Gerónimo de Aguilar. This man served as the translator for Cortéz for the conquest of Mexico. But of the other Spaniard the shocking news was that he refused to be rescued. He had taken a respectable Maya wife, had children, and was recognized as a war captain by the Maya. It was he, Gonzalo Guerrero the Maya warrior, that had organized the attack on the Cordoba party at Campeche. A fighting man that knew Spanish tactics, weapons, and purposes of conquest was firmly in the enemies' camp.

Guerrero's motivation is unknown and his story very sketchy, but what is known is that he was responsible for leading many attacks against the Spanish, for advising Mayan chiefs and warlords of Spanish tactics, and that he was finally killed leading an attack on the Spanish many years later. That the Maya apparently converted one of the Spanish Christians to pagan ways was a total embarrassment to the Spanish.[1] It is difficult to conceive how profoundly this news shocked the senses of the Spanish that *knew* they were chosen by God to bring salvation and culture to these inferior savages.

Two other historical events happened during this same time frame. The Council of Trent was constructing and codifying the doctrines that all Roman Catholics must believe and all indigenous Americans must be taught. Secondly, Bernardino de Sahagún was writing his analysis of the religion and society of the Aztecs.[2] "Many in the order were fearful of too close an examination of what was after all the devil's kingdom."[3] But Sahagún had noted that there was much pagan continuity in supposedly Christian observances. It was becoming quite clear to any observer who dared to speak that the so-called conversions of the millions in earlier days were no conversions at all. He felt that the Franciscans had been dangerously casual in their pre-baptismal instruction and all too complacent in their later supervision of their charges. Such statements were seen as a betrayal of the order and a violation of the Franciscan code of conduct. The reader will recall that the inquisition impounded Sahagún's books and banished them to obscurity for hundreds of years. But a warning had been served; and that was to the Franciscans in particular, that indigenous conversion without instruction in spiritual things was inherently dangerous and inevitably led to syncretism of belief systems.

The Maya of the Yucatán

Few ancient civilizations can boast of a history like the 4,000 years of the Maya. To facilitate understanding of this American indigenous society, archeologists have divided Maya history into three periods: the Preclassic, from 2500 BC to about 200 AD—that huge timeframe is also divided into Early, Middle, and Late Preclassic. The Classic period that witnessed the peak of large-scale construction and urbanism, particularly in the southern lowland regions, ranged from about 200 to 900 AD. Then the Postclassic period which saw the continuing development of the northern lowlands in the Yucatán during the years of 900 to 1500 AD.[4] The ending of the Postclassic period is debatable due to the duration of the Spanish wars of conquest which took approximately 170 years. Some would say that the Yucatán never was completely conquered.[5]

In fact, the Maya empire was probably conquered, but it was hundreds of years before the Spanish came on the scene. In the seventh century Nahuatl speaking people from 800 miles to the west, the Toltec, brought with them a new religious cult and new beliefs, like the feather-serpent god Quetzalcoatl-Kukulcan that began to be included in the architecture of pyramids after the arrival of the Toltecs. Their militaristic attitudes sociologically influenced the Maya art as warrior-cults flourished. The peaceful theocracy of the Classic period was apparently eradicated. The writings of hieroglyphic texts also seem to have ceased. For about two centuries the Toltec seem to have influenced every aspect of Maya society as they themselves were being heavily influenced by the Maya culture.[6]

The Toltec influence apparently ended with Hunac Ceel (also known as Cauich) who gained Maya rule, but he ruled in a changed Maya warrior-centered autocracy. The new leadership controlled Mayan life for the next two and a half centuries with types of Toltec style sacrifices serving as an indication of a changed value systems. The new leadership lasted until about 1450, which marks the end of central Mayan government. The Maya Empire of the Yucatán broke into 16 provinces or regional powers, very similar to the ancient Greek city-states in political structure, setting the stage for intensive, petty warfare that could be the chief cause of their demise as a great empire. Endemic war and slave raiding did not seem to be for geographical domination, because there were family connections between lineages and a mutual respect for the legitimacy of authority. Generations passed during this cultural decline, especially noticed in the north of the Yucatán peninsula where Postclassic architecture is most prominent. Religious influence was at a new low and regional powers were exhausted when the Spanish began their invasion in 1524.

Some historians feel that the long decline and chaos of the last few centuries of the Maya can be explained by environmental change, exhaustion of agricultural potential, or the hunting of edible species to extinction. There are indications of a 200-year drought that might have been a cause, or that simply expedited the above with further complication. The northern Yucatán Peninsula is a harsh, barren, flat limestone shelf with no rivers, no streams, and no drinkable surface water at all. Only where the limestone shelf is broken is there access to subterranean water which naturally led to settlement in that particular place. The vegetation is malicious; nearly all of it pricks, stings, scratches, and hurts the unwary. Insects bite, sting, infect, and poison the unprotected. The whole land can very quickly turn against its human inhabitants.

Culturally the Maya have been credited as the first people to use the number zero in their mathematics. Their calendar was more accurate than any other in use at the time due to their detailed understanding of astronomy. They used an elaborate hieroglyphic writing system to both record history and foretell the future. This was a combination of phonetic symbols and logograms in which syllabic signs play a significant role. It was the only writing system in the pre-Columbian world known to completely represent the spoken language. There were approximately 1000 different glyphs, though at any one time no more than 500 were in use.

The religion of the Maya was based upon a believed cyclical nature of time. The rituals and ceremonies were closely associated with celestial and terrestrial cycles which were observed and recorded as separate calendars. The Maya priests were charged with knowing, and understanding the intricacies of these calendars and advising the people as to times and events that required attention. Worship and celebration required sacrifices, often of children because they were believed pure. Their cosmos had three major planes as in most of the indigenous American religious systems: the sky, the earth, and the underworld, which was reached through caves and holes in the ground making them holy places.

The Conquest of the Maya

The conquest of the Maya was both a long and dangerous series of campaigns in a difficult terrain that hindered the use of horse and limited the effectiveness of long-range weapons. The Maya were well trained in war and excellent close quarter fighters. There was no political center to conquer as with the Aztec, no political unity, only many regional centers that might fight with the Spanish once, and then against them in the next battle. They occasionally fought with each other, but when faced with invaders from outside the peninsula the Maya would normally unite, for they saw themselves as a distinct people. The Maya knew what had happened to the Aztec and would not repeat their mistakes. They knew what awaited them if they lost—brutal servitude in *encomiendas* or death. The Maya quickly learned, probably through Gonzalo Guerrero that to stand and fight the Spanish way would give all the advantages to the invaders. Therefore, utilizing their knowledge of terrain, food, and water sources, hit and run guerrilla fighting became their best strategy. The Yucatán was a featureless, dry, barren plane into which they could strike, retreat, and disappear with ease. Often the Europeans would capture a city, which to them meant domination and a victory won, only to find themselves isolated, besieged, incapable of holding the city, and thus suffered humiliation and retreat.

The Spanish had one ally they could count upon—European disease. During the Caribbean Epoch an influenza epidemic, probably swine flu, spread throughout the region in 1493.[7] It probably penetrated the mainland coastal areas through the trade routes. Later some unidentified, highly contagious sickness struck down nearly a third of all the Europeans in the Caribbean and untold thousands of islanders. It is most likely that this plague penetrated the Yucatán also. We do know that the smallpox pandemic of 1519-23 was far-reaching accounting for a fall in demographics throughout the Caribbean and the coastal areas of the Gulf including the Yucatan Peninsula, and it was the primary killer during the assault on Tenochtitlan for both armies. The Maya had no idea from whence it came—nothing like smallpox had ever been seen before. "We know almost nothing of how the Maya responded to the epidemic, to the shrinkage of their trade world, or to the steady movement of the foreign ships across their horizons."[8] But another Spanish fleet was preparing to come and conquer the socially demoralized, divided, and disease weakened Maya of the Yucatán.

The city-states would have to be conquered one by one, as most of them fiercely resisted the Spanish invaders with assistance from allied cities.[9] Francisco de Montejo, a veteran of Grijalva and Cortéz expeditions, petitioned the Crown for the right to conquer the Yucatán. On his first attempt, he arrived at Cozumel in 1527. With an agreement of submission from two east coast towns, Xelha and Xcaret, he left 65 men there and proceeded with 125 men to explore and subdue the northeast corner of the peninsula. They wintered at Ecab on the extreme northeast corner and then proceeded west where they found most towns in their path deserted. Then at Aké they fought a pitched battle losing about half their small army but killing about 1,200 Maya warriors. They retreated under harassment and attack to their landing site only to find most of the 65 men left there were dead from disease or murdered. Xelha and Xcaret had changed their minds about submission.[10] Montejo set up a small fort on the coast at Xamanha in 1528 and then returned to "civilized" New Spain to recruit a larger army.

Three clerics had accompanied this first expedition—two secular priests and one Carmelite. Of their work, if any missionary work was done, we know nothing. They most certainly ministered to the men of the expedition, especially to the wounded and dying, and they must have had some exposure to the Maya of Xelha and Xcaret.

On his second attempt to conquer the Maya in 1531, Montejo took the Maya port city of Canpech (Campeche), set up a fortress, and made it his base of operations. For two years, his lieutenant d'Avila waged campaigns[11] to the south subduing the Southwestern coast of the Yucatán. Montejo sent his son, Francisco Montejo Jr., inland with an army capturing Chechen Itza and also received pledges from a number of city-states as allies. Itza was declared the capital of Spanish Yucatán (Ciudad Real), and Francisco proceeded to set up *encomiendas* dividing the local towns and their indigenous Americans into parcels given to his soldiers. The Maya considered this and after a few months the people rebelled, forcing Montejo Jr. to flee back to his father in Honduras while under constant attack. There were rumors that Gonzalo Guerrero was a leader of the victorious Maya forces. Montejo Jr. joined up with Montejo at Dzilám, and they returned to Campeche and on to Veracruz. I have found no record of any clerics or spiritual work being done during this campaign.

Montejo, now in his late 60s and captain-general of Honduras, which included all of Guatemala, Honduras, Salvador, Campeche, Tabasco, and today's Yucatan Peninsula, returned to Tabasco where his son governed. He turned over to his son the royal permission to conquer the Yucatán. Montejo Jr. then proceeded to raise an army to finish the conquest of the peninsula. Headquartered in Campeche and with about 400 soldiers, Montejo summoned the Maya lords, mostly Xiu chieftains who had submitted to Spanish rule and had become valuable allies in the fighting. The Ah Canules resisted and were defeated by Montejo's men at Chakan. In 1542, he established himself at the city of Tiho, renaming it Merida. This is where the ruler Tutul Xiu, the most powerful Maya province in the northwest corner of Yucatán, submitted to the Spanish.[12] The eastern Maya city-states, chafing under the heavy hand of Spanish rule and the encomienda system, rebelled and joined together for a great battle against the Spanish and their Xiu allies. With the defeat of the eastern chiefdoms in 1546, the conquest of the Yucatán was assured. Only the Itzá around Lake Petén remained independent and would continue to fight until their defeat in 1697.[13] The eastern Maya provinces held very little interest for the Spanish and continued with a certain degree of independence until much later when the coast began to be populated. The Yucatán was still considered the northern province of Guatemala at that time.

The military conquest of the Yucatán was declared over in 1546, but disease had not finished its terrible work among the Maya. It was after the arrival of the second of Columbus' voyages that an unidentified sickness ran its course throughout the Caribbean depopulating the islands to an alarming degree. In 1575-77, a terrible mysterious disease swept over the Yucatán taking with it tens of thousands of lives.[14] This was the fourth and most deadly appearance of this strange sickness, only identified by the Maya word, *matlalzahuatl*. War, famine, disease, and oppression worked their terrible tolls on human life in the Yucatán, although the vast areas and great distances between the centers of population and the spacious widely separated layouts of Maya cities helped to stay the hand of these deadly epidemics. The Maya did fare better than most indigenous groups in surviving plagues of disease and Spanish imperialism.

The Franciscans in the Yucatán

Even though three clerics accompanied Montejo on his first expedition, there was little interest in others coming along until the Maya were subdued. Ten years after the first expedition, by special order, five Franciscans were sent to the established town of Campeche. The Maya there were friendly towards them and came with their children to be instructed and baptized. But as in the Caribbean, the colonist and a few renegades, always desperate to carve out their fortunes any way they could, caused such outrages, that the Xiu Maya became hostile and the friars had to be withdrawn.[15]

Then in 1545 nine more Franciscans arrived[16] directly from Spain. Landing at Campeche, the governor explained their purpose to the chiefs, and the friars set about building their first convent on the present site of the St. Francis church in Campeche. The first convert to be baptized was the chief of the Xiu at Campeche. He learned Spanish and served as interpreter for the friars lending his authority to their message.[17] The Franciscan leader, Luis de Villalpando, set out on foot for Mani in the mountains to the south where soon over two thousand converts were engaged in building a convent and church building. However, when the friars preached against the cruelties of the chiefs on their vassals and slaves, the chiefs organized and resolved to burn all the friars alive on their own altars. The mob arrived to find the two friars praying before an altar where they spent the whole night in prayer causing the Maya to pause. The following morning a detachment of soldiers happened by and rescued the friars. The leaders of the mob were arrested, and 27 of them were condemned to death. But intervention by Villalpando saved their lives.

In 1548-49, fifteen more Franciscan missionaries arrived strengthening established missions and starting new ones. The Franciscans labored on the part of the Maya against the cruelties of the encomienda system already in place, but constant warfare allowed the Spanish to make new slaves of the captured warriors. Then in 1551, a royal edict liberated the slaves throughout New Spain. Within a very short time the mission station at Campeche had over a thousand converts including several chiefs.[18] In 1561 the Yucatán was made a diocese with the bishop residing at Merida, and ten more Franciscans arrived. By 1562, 12 convents had been established—six in permanent, stone structures. Over 200 villages had local churches, a school, and a mission-trained Maya schoolmaster. The achievements of these early friars were truly remarkable. But few spoke Maya and dependence upon the Maya schoolmasters was wide-ranging. What was actually being taught in most schools and village churches was, in fact, a very syncretic form of the Christianity from what the friars thought was being taught.

In some places chiefs and lords persisted in calling the people away together in hidden places to preach and teach their rites and ancient ceremonies. The Spanish, of course, prohibited these gatherings, condemning them for their drunkenness and disorderly conduct. The friars prohibited going out at night after the final bells of the church had sounded. But secret Maya "churches" were being set up where the Maya continued to marry, to baptize, and divorce with disregard for the Spanish friar's monopoly on these spiritual rites. The rumor was spread that baptism of infants would eventually kill them, so parents sometimes hid their infant children from the friars. An abundance of rules appeared to hold in check all these nonconforming and strange behaviors on the part of the baptized Maya but only in appearance. The indigenous people conformed by putting their own understanding to the rules and rites. The Maya did what the priest said to do outwardly while he was with them; afterwards, they adapted their own meaning to the forms of the new rites. On the surface it appeared as though all was well until two boys stumbled onto some idols and human skulls in a cave.

The Franciscan Inquisition

It was 1562, Franciscan Diego de Landa, who had arrived as Provincial head of the Franciscans of the Yucatán, became aware that many of the baptized Mayans were secretly practicing their ancient rites. The friars were horrified. What they thought was their showpiece of evangelism and conversion was actually a sham. As the friars questioned the Maya commoners around them, they found that nearly all were still practicing idolatry in their homes, their fields, and in sacred caves. It must be remembered that the native population was, in fact, exempt from the jurisdiction of the Holy Office of Inquisition. Notwithstanding, the Franciscans arrested the Mayans in large numbers and subjected them to torture, known as *garrucha,* whereby the wrists are tied with chords over their heads and then the person was suspended in the air. If they did not confess their sins, heavy rocks were suspended from their feet; at times, flogging was added to the suspended person until they finally confessed to idolatry. This was not Spanish Inquisition, though it was called that. There was no tribunal. Mayans were tortured after their confessions were taken. There was no secular authority involved that was charged with carrying out any punishment ordered by a Tribunal of Inquisition. The entire process of questioning was illegal, the torture was illegal, and the thrashings handed out later, up to 200 lashes per person, were also illegal by Spanish and by Church law.

The worse the torture became, the more the Mayans "confessed" to idolatry. Landa organized his own court system and in the course of three months over 4,500 Mayans were tortured into giving confessions of idolatry. During the course of these investigations at least 158 Mayans died as a direct result of the interrogations. Clendinnen says that "The unashamed violence of the Franciscan inquisition is at once the best evidence for the political domination they had achieved in the peninsula, their anger at [Mayan] betrayal, and their sense of the desperate urgency of the situation." [19] Those who confessed to idolatry under torture were let down and then had to find idols or invent them, or they were tortured again. In this manner, confessions were made to all forms of idolatry, even human sacrifice. However, at later inquiries, most Mayans declared that they were speaking the truth when questioned as to whether they had idols; but, when torture was ordered, they agreed together that they had to confess to something to stop the torture, and so they invented stories to satisfy the friars.

The proceedings were stopped by order of the bishop of Mexico. Landa had forced the revelation of the whereabouts of every conceivable type and size of idol, real or imagined all historical and religious writings, and locations of paintings and hieroglyphics. However by the time of the intervention, there had been destroyed, it is said, approximately two million hieroglyphic manuscripts and sacred images—practically the whole of the indigenous Maya literature.[20] Even as late as 1586, by royal edict for the suppression of idolatry—any idols, native manuscripts, or Maya images found were still being destroyed. Absolute authority without accountability had again raised its ugly head and obliterated the recorded history of a Native American people—and the loss again is ours as well as the Mayas.

Franciscan Ministries

The cruelty of the Franciscan questioning draws attention away from the great work that many of the same Franciscans were doing at this time. They used the encomienda system to build their convents and churches, to teach agriculture and animal husbandry. They produced dictionaries, grammars, catechisms, sermons, prayer and confessional manuals as tools for their evangelism and teaching efforts. What the friars taught, and what the Maya actually learned, modified, adapted, and accepted were often very different concepts, it is true. Baptism with teaching was part of the Franciscan evangelism, though obviously it was still insufficient for spiritual understanding. The Franciscan notion of conversion was seen as a gradual one, not a transforming, individual experience with God, such as the evangelical model of conversion, but a slow, cumulative, collective process by which whole communities based upon baptism as a beginning, would grow into learning the Roman Catholic observances. The Tridentine concept of *community liberty*, rather than individual liberty, was again coming to the forefront.

Maya cities and towns already existed, so the friars built their centers in the midst of Maya population centers. Attendance of children at teaching sessions was required. Natives in authority were compelled to accept baptism. Sons of lords were required to be sequestered in schools attached to monasteries, drilled in the catechisms, taught Spanish culture, and to have contempt for their father's ways. Graduates were then used as schoolmasters to teach in the rural areas. Though a number of smaller towns and pueblos were depopulated and some were moved for encomienda labor reasons, this type of consolidation or *reduction* was usually not necessary for religious reasons but for political reasons and at the convenience of the Spanish.

Teaching, as used to describe what went on in the convents, was really a focus on training in correct external behavior[21] rather than a transfer of knowledge of Christian theology or biblical practices. The training was on correct bowing the head, kneeling, when to respond and when to keep silence or be piously still. Four main prayers had to be memorized, though the meaningless foreign sounds held no spiritual insight whatsoever. Such a meager portion of Christianity was all the friars could give in their nearly impossible schedules trying to reach the multitudes before them. Mendieta attempted to describe the work of the friar in his *História*:

It happened everyday that one lone friar would count the people in the morning, then preach to them and sing Mass, and after that baptize both children and adults, confess the sick no matter how many, and then bury any dead there might be. And so it was for 30 or 40 years and in some places so it is still. There were some (and I knew them) who preached three sermons in different languages, one after the other, and then sang Mass, and did everything else that had to be done, all before having anything to eat.

The thatched huts, which were the first monasteries, normally housed two friars. One of them was usually doing the circuit of evangelism to surrounding villages and towns. The Maya spoke only one language, though regional dialects had to be grasped, it was not like the remnants of the Aztec empire with its multitude of languages. Evangelistic assistance from the encomienda colonist was required by law but not forth coming in the Yucatán. The friars were seen as indigenous representatives; constant complaints to the Crown confirmed this. Therefore the Franciscans could only count on animosity from the colonists that saw evangelism of the Maya as counterproductive to labor needs. The wars of conquest had given the colonists a large number of slaves and all that labor would be lost should they become Christian.

Roman Catholic Missiology in the Third Epoch

The first area of consideration in missiology is that of *Apostolic Practice.* In this third epoch, which follows immediately on the heels of the conquest of the Central Valleys, we find very little change in evangelistic practice. Although the Franciscan friars did seem to have responded to criticisms of their lack of teaching in the second epoch by implementing the training of schoolmasters who could teach in Maya and thus do a better job of preparing catechists, the deep rooted flaw of not monitoring what was being taught and learned would come back to haunt them later. Part of the problem in *apostolic practice* for the Yucatán was the lack of competition and accountability. The Franciscans had a monopoly on evangelism in the Yucatán. With no other orders, no secular church, weak civil leadership, and strong Franciscan leadership, the stage was set for a Franciscan imperialism that led directly to an intense spiritual oppression by the Franciscans. The Franciscan Inquisition of the Maya never could have happened if Dominicans had been present.

The methodology of training up young leadership and using them as schoolmasters was an advancement built upon Franciscan experience in the Central Valleys. The concept greatly multiplied the effectiveness of the always too few missionaries, but there was insufficient oversight and control of what the indigenous teachers were actually teaching. The learning of proper forms, memorized catechisms, and correct behavior, without understanding the theology or reasons for the practices, had to lead to syncretic understanding of the symbols. Again, without accountability, there was arrogance in the friar's complacency, thinking that by doing the best they could in practice of outward function, that inward understanding was also taking place. It was a most rude awakening for the friars to find that by teaching a few young people forms they did not understand, that it would change an established religion thousands of years old that had weathered previous invasions until the invaders themselves were absorbed.

Native leadership was excluded from the evangelistic process with but a few notable exceptions such as the chief of the Xiu. Most chiefs and lords were forced to be baptized and outwardly accept Roman Catholicism to retain their leadership positions. These lords and chiefs were the very ones who assumed leadership and priestly functions when the new religion proved to be inadequate to meet the religious needs of the Maya people. This inadequacy could have been directly provoked by a lack of understanding of the theology behind the forms and symbols. Symbols without understanding cannot take the place of established functions in a literate, high civilization such as the Maya city-states.

During the wars of conquest all the Maya priests, who could be, were killed; they were specifically targeted by the Spanish as trouble makers. Those that survived were forced to be baptized. It is always very dangerous in cultural transformation to leave previously established leadership with a people who know them as leaders, while failing to fill the leadership void with any other competent replacements. The inevitable result was the continuance of Maya rituals being as the need for their existence continued and Roman Catholicism failed to fill the void created by the suspension of openly practicing the previous cultic forms.

This led directly to one of the most repulsive developments in Franciscan history, although it was the Maya who were going to have to pay the price for such Franciscan arrogance. As terrible as the inquisition was as an institution, it did have rules and procedures that were followed to the letter in both Spain and New Spain. Such a powerful control mechanism had to be firmly controlled itself and used very wisely to be effective, which it was for the most part. In the Franciscan Inquisition of the Yucatán those controls and rules were ignored. Anger and arrogance took the place of logical control, and the result was one of the more shameful chapters in the New Spain conquests. The humble brothers, who were sent to be the salt and light of the gospel, became the apostolic bearers of torture and death for thousands of the very souls they came to save.

This is another innate result of the Tridentine philosophy teaching that the Roman Catholic version of Christianity is the only true version of the Church of Jesus Christ on earth; that baptism without teaching can save; and if eventually saved with baptism and purgatory, souls were better off dead now than continuing in a life of sinful behavior. It was the philosophy of Trent and the practice of Spanish sovereigns that put spiritual authority above legal authority and the civil laws of the land. Finally this arrogance of believing that there can only be *One True Church*—or expression of the church—with all other expressions of faith false, that substantiates the belief that one man can harm another in the Name of God and for the lasting benefit of that individual so tortured and persecuted.

Also under the category of *Apostolic Practice* is the total lack of cultural consciousness on the part of the friars. They were dealing with a very highly developed, established cultural expression much older than their own that had survived other conquests and invasions. The friars came in as conquerors with the inherent pride and self-confidence that they were better than the Maya people. This cultural arrogance blinded the friars to the existence of those valid and truthful factors within the Maya culture that guided their thinking, molded their practices, and produced the Maya's own rituals and ceremonies. To put it simply, the Franciscans were answering questions the Maya were not asking and ignoring the questions the Maya were asking. To put it another way, the friars were taking away the high expression of faith from the Maya and replacing it with Roman Catholic low or common expressions of faith that held no meaning for the Maya. Therefore the Maya native leaders were forced to complete in secret their world view explanations reconciling ancient understanding with the new Roman Catholic practices.

Though the illegal Franciscan Inquisition did almost completely eradicate the idols and images from the Maya people, and many would feel that was good, it did also erase the written history of the Maya people confounding us to this day. Obviously Landa was following the example of Juan de Zumárraga, who had the Aztec codices burned. Zumárraga was also just following the example of the Cardinal Ximenes, the Archbishop of Toledo, who burned all the Muslim literature in Spain. With this act of book-burning Landa overshadowed and regulated to obscurity all the great work that the Franciscans did in the Yucatán peninsula. The Spanish, in the name of Roman Catholicism, have probably destroyed more priceless historical documents than any other people in recorded history.

In the Yucatán, the friars established many convents and local churches. Evangelism did not go beyond the minimum of previous epochs, still shackled by the Tridentine concepts of baptismal regeneration and the Spanish superiority complex that denied the Maya most of the sacraments. The secular church that began to take over the work of the friars continued to minister to the Europeans and the groups of Maya that chose to draw near to the Roman Catholic Church. But for continuing generations the Maya obstinately continued to call their people together for secret meetings or under cover of night to worship their idols and perform their celebrations and recall their histories. To this day the Maya continue to straddle the two worlds of the Maya and the Spanish.

Summary

The Franciscans, using methods that seemed to work in the Central Valleys, were given an exclusive franchise to convert the Maya people. They began as before with baptisms, training of young leaders, and then using the Maya graduates to teach in the village schools. These schoolmasters actually did most of the work of ministry in a syncretic world of Roman Catholicism procedures, but they never abandoned their Maya worldviews. As a result the indigenous religion of the Maya continued strongly under the guise of European religion.

When the existence of the Maya religion's undercover ministries were found out, a great persecution of the Maya resulted, in what is now called the Franciscan Inquisition, with thousands of Maya being tortured and many dying. Through this time of suffering, in a real sense, the Maya achieved an unofficial compromise with Roman Catholicism in that both the Roman Catholic and the indigenous Maya religions continue to co-exist in the same regions.[22]

CHAPTER VII

FOURTH EPOCH: THE GRAN CHICHIMECA

Epoch Four Introduction

The roots of what was to take place in the Chichimeca regions are again found in the second epoch with the exploits of Guzmán and his indigenous army of conquerors. Due to the extreme violence of his campaign, many indigenous groups were not only hostile towards the Spanish, but also knowledgeable in ways to fight them. A number of refugees from the Mixtón rebellion in modern day Jalisco had fled into the Gran Chichimeca region bringing notices of the cruelty, the diseases, the new methods of fighting using steel weapons, armor, war dogs and horses, and how the Spanish always fought with the assistance of their indigenous American allies that were the natural enemies of the high desert warriors.

The Gran Chichimeca consisted of the inland desert valleys between the two corridors of mountains—the East and the West Sierra Madres—and all the lands of this area north of the Bajío, the lower fertile planes roughly between today's Queretaro and Guadalajara. The Chichimeca area originally crossed over the highest ridges of the Eastern Sierra Madres to include the large Pame groups and then continued in the eastern direction until they encountered the Huastecos of the coastal areas. This was the territory of the tribes known as Chichimecas. They ranged throughout this great land as nomadic and seminomadic clans and groups. When the wars officially began, in approximately 1550, the various Chichimeca tribes were the Caxcane, the Tecuexe, the Guachichile, the Guamare, the Pame, and the Zacatecos.

The name Chichimeca is a derogatory term (chichi = dog, mecatl = rope or line, a descendant of the dog)[1] used by the more sedentary people to the south of the Gran Chichimeca for all the nomadic tribes to the north. These northern tribes were raiders, cunning warriors who were deadly with the bow and arrow, and natural guerrilla fighters using hit and run strategies. Because of their reputation as fierce fighters, and the relatively uselessness of their lands to the Spanish, there was little reason for the Spanish to venture into the Gran Chichimeca areas. That is, until the moment those huge deposits of silver ore were discovered there.

People of the Gran Chichimeca

Most of the seminomadic Zacatecas people shared a primitive hunting-collecting culture, based on the gathering of mesquite seed-pods, nopales and tunas (the fleshy cactus leaves and its fruit the cactus apple), and wild onions. Some of them also lived off of acorns, roots, seeds, and some wild fruits. In some areas, they even cultivated maize, squash, and a great variety of herbs, chilies, and tomatoes. From the mesquite seeds they made white bread and a type of beer. Many Chichimeca tribes utilized the juice of the agave as a substitute for water when the latter was in short supply. It also served for making pulque, a strong, sweet beer still enjoyed today (which when distilled becomes tequila).

The Zacatecos occupied much of what is now northern Zacatecas and northeastern Durango at the time of the Spanish invasion. Their lands bordered with those of the Tepehuanes on the northwest and the Guachichiles on the southeast. Most likely they were the descendants of an ancient civilization of this region known today as La Quemada. More than a hundred ruin sites in the State of Zacatecas bear witness of a great civilization along the eastern slopes of the Western Sierra Madres between 200 A.D. to 1250 A.D. These ruins present the imposing appearance of wide streets, massive fortifications, ceremonial sites with terraces, causeways, and their gigantic pillars speak of a great people in the distant past.[2] But what the Spanish encountered in the Zacatecos were bands of proud, brave, and bellicose warriors who were excellent marksmen with their arrows.

From the forested areas of the Sierras the Zacatecos made a solid, one room dwelling of adobe and wood. They slept on the floor, and usually had a fireplace in the middle of the floor made of rocks for warmth and cooking. Their diet included rabbit, deer, clacuaches (similar to the raccoon), snake, and other edible creatures such as the frog and rats,[3] as well as worms—a good source of protein (most people today are familiar with the white worm in the bottle of mescal). Men wore breechcloths, while women wore short petticoats of skins or woven maguey fiber. Both sexes wore their hair long, usually to the waist and practiced monogamy. They smeared their bodies with clay of various colors and painted themselves with the forms of reptiles. This mud and paint helped shield them from the sun's rays and also kept biting and stinging vermin off their skin.[4]

The Guachichiles had a similar life style to the Zacatecos, but more adapted to the great, high desert valleys. As part of the Uto-Aztecan linguistic family, they were distant cousins to the Aztec and the most recent newcomers to the high desert valleys. Some of the Guachichiles groups were reputed to eat the flesh of their enemies in rituals, often amidst their torture, perhaps also a connection to their Aztec cousins. Nomadic, they depended upon hunting, gathering, and raiding for their basic needs more than dependency on any form of agriculture. They preferred raiding for their basic needs. Their name comes from the Aztec word for *red head* due to the painting of their bodies, coloration of their hair, and head decorations. "In the development of tribal alliances, the Guachichiles were considered the most advanced of the Chichimec tribes. They were a major catalyst in provoking the other tribes to resist the Spanish [invasion] and the exploitation of [Chichimeca] lands . . . The Spanish frontiersmen and contemporary writers referred to the Guachichiles 'as being the most ferocious, the most valiant, and the most elusive' of all their indigenous adversaries." The friars found their language difficult to learn because of the many sharply variant dialects found among the wondering clans and groups. The conversion of this indigenous people to Christianity would require a high price to be paid.

The Cazcane indigenous group was seminomadic, occupying today's states of southern Zacatecas and northern Jalisco areas. Occupying territory to the west of the Guamares and Tecuexes and south of the Zacatecos Indians, they were a partly nomadic people but with four principal religious and population centers. They were the primary activists in the Mixtón rebellion and they received the greatest reprisals as a result. After their subjugation the Cazcanes began serving as auxiliaries to the northward Spanish advance and soon began to suffer reprisal raids from the Zacatecos for aiding the invaders.

The seminomadic Pames constituted a very divergent branch of the extensive Oto-Manguean linguistic family in the mountainous southeast of the Gran Chichimeca. It has been stated that there is no archaeological evidence concerning the Pame, yet Powell quoting Kirchhoff says, "they used temples on hill tops with stairways up to them and with religious sentinels." It would seem the Pame did have established ceremonial sites for observing celebrations, plantings, and harvests, perhaps due to the influence of their neighbors the Otomí. However, most of what is known about their history has been written since the conquest. The Pame lived in dispersed groups in the mountains and deserts where the Spanish found it both difficult and undesirable to conquer people living in a land of such rough terrain. The missionaries attempted to move the Pame into centralized towns of the larger valleys where missions could be established. However, in most cases, the Pame returned to their own homes and the missionary attempts to establish communities in which to socialize and evangelize the Pame failed.

At first contact with the Spanish, bands of the Pame together with Guachichiles and Guamares waged a fierce guerilla war against the Spanish and the Christian Otomí that fought with them invading the Chichimeca territories. But the futility of fighting the Spanish became obvious and the Pame remained relatively uninvolved in the Chichimeca war. It is difficult to tell if this was because the lands they inhabited were marginal and thus not so greatly threatened, or if the Pame simply learned their lesson and sought to stay out of the war. In any case, the Pame, unlike many of the neighboring tribes, were not destroyed. Throughout their history, the Pame's ability to live on the periphery of more densely populated Mesoamerica has enabled them to continue to exist while at the same time limiting Pame ability to succeed economically within the dominant community.

The Chichimeca peoples are not known to have built temples, with the possible exception of the Pame, as the ancient peoples of this area did. Their only known deities were the sun, moon, and certain stars or star formations. Only the Pame are known to have idols, "among others, the mother of the sun."[5] They rendered to their gods worship with flowers, weeds, aromatic herbs, and a service of dancing. There was no known sacrificial system involving human lives. Central religious figures were a type of priest, the *curanderos*, or healers who taught that some illnesses were caused by natural conditions, but most were caused by supernatural spirits in an animistic type of religious expression.

The Fourth Epoch of Conquest: The Gran Chichimeca

The first Viceroy of New Spain, Antonio de Mendoza, was an activist whose enlightened policies caused New Spain to thrive. He soon commissioned explorations that included that of Coronado to the northern interior of the country to find the rumored Seven Cities of Cibola, which turned out to be the Pueblo indigenous towns of the upper Rio Grande area. Next Mendoza sent out Cabrillo to attempt to locate and explore Upper California in 1542. Continuing the policy of *repartimientos*, he strengthened the Bajío area with grants of encomiendas of land and indigenous people for labor to principle conquerors. Two of these became men of renown as frontier defenders in the mountains of northern Guanajuato on the Chichimeca southern border. They established peace with the Otomí chiefdoms in the area and would become leaders of critical defensive points in the Chichimeca wars.

This was the beginning of the fortified ranch. In previous times, the Spanish built defensive castles, as in the Canaries, or strong houses with palisades around them as in the Caribbean Islands or the first settlements on the mainland. But when in the Second and Third Epochs of conquest the Spanish were invading higher sedentary cultures with cities and societal infrastructure already in place, there was no need for a fort, but only to take the city. As colonists followed the bloody trail left by Guzmán and his dissolute army, they found themselves establishing ranches and haciendas in the midst of nomadic or seminomadic bands and tribes very hostile towards the Spanish invaders. With constant vigilance they always had to be ready to defend themselves often against overwhelming numerical superiority. They had to win, or they died.

The *encomendero* colonists had colleagues and indigenous Christians given in *repartimiento*, but other than that, they stood alone in self-defense. This meant that *encomienda* natives had to defend themselves and their families also; therefore, they had to be armed with modern weapons and taught how to use them correctly. All structures had to be built in such a way to offer covering small arms fire to each other. Often an adobe or rock wall was built to surround the whole of the settlement providing an outlying defense and protection for the animals as well as keeping sources of both food and water safe. The social gap between the Christian native, the Mestizo, and the Criollo leader became much narrower in the Bajío along the New Spain northern frontier with the Chichimeca. Survival was a matter of trust and dependence upon one another.

The Augustín friars established contact with groups of Pame in the mountains of Hidalgo in the late 1530s where they founded a convent at the edge of the large Pame group. By the late 1540s they had founded another in Xilitla, now in the State of San Luis Potosi. Although sporadic Pame raiding on the ranches of encomenderos continued to be a problem, an advance outpost was established in Valles near the north coast of the province of Pánuco by Andrés de Olmos, the Franciscan grammarian and ethno-historian. On a map these locations were the beginnings of an encirclement of the southern and eastern edges of the vast, unknown Gran Chichimeca region as the Spanish encroached into the interior plateau of northern New Spain during the 1540s.

Spanish encomenderos with their fortified ranches drove the Guamares, Pames and Guachichiles out of the valleys and grasslands of the Bajío. Resistance of the indigenous people was fierce but never organized or consistent. The Otomí joined the ranchers and greatly benefited through gifts of livestock and Spanish merchandise. Cattle, goat, and hog rising took over the prairies or *llanos*—huge valleys divided by low mountain ridges. "The territory proved ideal for raising the strong, dark, longhorn cattle that are ancestors to the modern Spanish fighting bull. Moreover, the land supported the hardy merino sheep, which were an excellent source of meat and wool."[6] The grasslands of the Bajío spawned a new identity for the mixed blood Mestizo, the *vaqueros*, or the first North American cowboys. The livestock, of course, gave more reason for raiding cultures of the Chichimeca to attack the less vigilant ranches. As far as the Spanish were concerned something was going to have to be done about the Chichimeca trouble makers.

From strong points along the southern Chichimeca border parties of militia and frontiersmen were making occasional excursions to explore and bring retribution against the indigenous groups for raids on the ranches of the Bajío. On September 8, a Basque nobleman, Juan de Tolosa, met up with a small group of Zacatecos at the foot of a high bluff. The militia cavalry men tried to show themselves as friendly and in turn the Zacatecos showed the Spanish some nearby mineral outcroppings. They understood that the Spaniards were greatly interested in special kinds of rocks from the ground. Once it was officially determined that the mineral samples from this site were a very rich silver ore, a small mining settlement was established at what was to be the future site of the city of Zacatecas.[7]

Very soon, silver fever brought a multitude of prospectors, entrepreneurs, and laborers streaming into the Gran Chichimeca from all parts of New Spain as rumors of the rich discovery spread. Indigenous field laborers from the south of New Spain, eager to earn the higher wages offered by mine owners, flooded into the region. In the next two decades, rich mineral-bearing deposits were discovered farther north in San Martín (1556), Chalchihuites (1556), Avino (1558), Sombrerete (1558), Fresnillo (1566), Mazapil (1568), and Nieves (1574).[8]

Many of the Zacatecas and Cazcanes, who had participated in the Mixtón rebellion near Guadalajara, escaped the crushing Spanish retaliation with its resulting slavery by fleeing to the Chichimecas. These refugees warned of the dangers of these Spanish invaders who brought diseases more deadly than their weapons. The indigenous refugees wanted retaliation; the rest of the Chichimeca tribes wanted these invaders off of their lands. The Guachichiles wanted to kill them all because that was their custom for all invaders. They never were an organized army—they would fight as they always had using the incredible vastness of their land, hit-and-run guerrilla warfare tactics, ambushes, traps in mountain passes, and by overwhelming the smaller parties with lightening speed, efficient killing, and quick withdrawal.

As the mining camps developed the need for indigenous labor, the needs greatly exceeded demand, even with the outrageously high wages that were being paid to anyone with mining experience. Soon raids were being conducted to capture slaves from the nearby native camps. Food was scarce but high prices were paid in silver, therefore food stores of the indigenous people were prime targets for the Spanish scavenging parties.[9] Only healthy adults in their prime could be sold at a good price to work the mines so all others were left dead or with certain death by starvation without food as their camps were looted and then destroyed. The indigenous people responded with a fierceness never experienced before by the Spanish who had always relied on shock, fear, and utter terror to carry the day of battle against Native Americans. These Chichimeca struck back with even more creative and gruesome intimidation tactics and beat the Spanish at their own game. The invaders soon came realized they were at the end of a totally unprotected supply line stretching 320 kilometers to the south—a two week journey in the best of conditions. All that silver was going to prove to be very costly indeed.

Soon the small mining town of Zacatecas found itself under siege. No one could venture forth without well armed guards. The intensity of the attacks continually increased with each year until in 1554, the worst disaster of all occurred. A train of 60 wagons with an armed escort was attacked by the Chichimecas in the Ojuelos Pass. In addition to inflicting great loss of life with hundreds dead, the Chichimecas carried off food supplies, animals, clothing, tools, and weapons.

It was rare for the Spanish of these caravans to escape with their lives. The Chichimecas ambushed them at any point along the two week journey. They used hit and run tactics against the columns until they were too weak to repel a frontal attack, then hit and destroyed the remnants. Anyone taken that escaped immediate death faced humiliation, torture and suffering beyond description in the hands of the Chichimeca. Often the failure of supplies to arrive at the silver mining camps would be the cause of great hardship, starvation, and even the abandonment of some mines. Neither persuasion nor punishment by officials would appease these desert warriors—there was just too much hatred and self justification on both sides.

Indigenous Christians, the allies of the Spanish, were singled out for special treatment when captured by the high desert warriors because those people had submitted to the hated Spanish and turned traitor to their own people. There was also a special hatred for the friars and their helpers, a grim reminder of the hostilities held against the clerics of Roman Catholicism since the Mixtón rebellion which was caused (in the eyes of the indigenous people) by this new religion being forced upon them.

Without their native allies, the Spanish would never have suppressed these seminomadic, high desert warriors. Because the Purépecha, Aztec, Otomí, and Cazcanes hated their ancestral enemies as much as the Spanish did, they were more than willing to fight, and especially to capture and enslave the Chichimeca peoples. These native allies received a salary of food and supplies, gifts, and other privileges such as being permitted to mount war horses, and using Spanish fire arms and armor. By the late 1580s, many thousands had died on both sides and a general depopulation of the Zacatecas mining camps became a matter of concern for the Spanish authorities.[10]

The Spanish military tactics of conquest had worked well for civilizations with central authority such as chiefs or emperors. Against the Chichimeca it seemed there was nothing they could do to stop these fierce desert warriors. With no king, and no population centers, they had no structures that could be attacked. They were like ghosts who appeared out of the barren desert, struck with incredible violence, and then just melted back into the desert without even leaving a trail to follow.

For over 35 years the war continued with a frightening annual toll. Though the Dominicans questioned the morality of the Spanish invasion of Chichimeca territory and often registered their complaints, the economics of the silver mines always won the argument of justification for the constant warfare against the "naked painted warriors" and their families.[11] "For a generation and more, from roughly 1550 to 1585, most Spanish frontiersmen so abhorred the Chichimecas that they could think of no alternative to enslavement or annihilation."[12] The turning point came with the appointment of Alonso Manrique de Zuñiga, the seventh viceroy of New Spain. As viceroy, he developed the basic policies to guarantee a sound pacification of the northern frontier. He evaluated the deteriorating situation, consulted expert advice, and started by reversing many of the practices of the past.[13]

He discovered that many Spanish militias had begun raiding peaceful indigenous villages for the purpose of enslavement to be sold to the mines. Infuriated by this practice, the new viceroy prohibited further enslavement of all captured natives and freed or placed under religious care those who had already been captured. He also appointed

Antonio de Monroy to conduct investigations into this conduct and to punish the Spaniards involved in the slave trade.[14] Over several years a real fighting force was organized using available man power from presidios reinforced with experienced military personnel, residents from fortified homesteads, men from towns who were contracted to provide a fighting force for designated periods of time, and conscripted indigenous work forces, mostly of Otomí descent.

Miguel Caldera, a captain of Spanish and Chichimeca (Mestizo) descent that grew up in the town of Zacatecas during the war, led this efficient fighting force that began seeking out and confronting the individual Chichimeca tribes.[15] The new face-saving plan for both sides became known as *Peace with Purchase*. The Spanish agreed to amnesty for all fighting parties. Food, clothing, good farm land would be given to the Chichimeca groups to establish themselves in a sedentary way with all the agricultural implements necessary to raise crops and practice animal husbandry. Peace was guaranteed with protection of their rights as a people. The captains sought out the various tribes and individual groups, and one by one they agreed to peace. After 40 years of fighting, both sides were tired, resources spent, and everyone involved just wanted the hostilities to end. In 1590, Mexquitic and Tequisquiapan sold themselves into the peace plan officially ending the Chichimeca war.[16]

Apostolic Methods of the Fourth Epoch of Conquest

In the beginning of this epoch the encirclement of the Gran Chichimeca brought more and more contact with the Chichimeca tribes and pressure was felt on both sides. The huge frontier ranches with their *encomiendas* of Otomí and Pame laborers were driving the nomadic indigenous peoples out of the Bajío. The Mixtón revolt in Jalisco had been put down with great violence forcing many Cazcanes into slavery with the encomiendas that were appearing throughout the Bajío and also providing many more Chichimeca enemies as the Tecuexes and Cazcanes fled the Spanish and joined the more northern bands of Chichimecas. The Zacatecas mines spurred a thrust into the heart of Chichimeca territory with new highways cutting deep into Chichimeca lands connecting the northern outposts with the Bajío. Where Spanish colonizers went, friars and clerics went with them, often ahead of them into these enemy held territories. Friars had also come with the Spanish militia of Guzmán forcing their Roman Catholic religion on the native people as one of the root causes of the Mixtón rebellion, along with the slave trade. As a result, friars were singled out for retribution in Chichimeca raids as one of the sources of all this foreign evil.

In this fourth epoch of conquest, four basic strategies emerged for the evangelization of the Chichimecas, the establishment of the Roman Catholic Church, and the extension of New Spain's government over the area. First was the establishment of the Spanish town or pueblo using *encomienda* labor, which included two types: the convent centered town and the fortified-inn centered town. The second was the private *encomienda*, which was also expressed in two types: the frontier ranch and the frontier plantation, both of which were the forerunners of the great haciendas. The third was the Christian encomienda which was led by a missionary with Christian natives who came for the purpose of teaching the local indigenous people the new Spanish way of life. The fourth strategy was the Presidio, or military camp, for the purposes of safety and protection along the *Silver Highway*. They all had as a common purpose the creation of a Roman Catholic Christian entity in the midst of a foreign culture, whether friendly or hostile, for the purpose of evangelizing and changing the indigenous culture by example, by pedagogy, and/or by force if necessary, to accomplish the goals of the Spanish invaders.

As mentioned earlier in the initial penetration of Pame regions the Augustinian friars made contact on the northeast fringes of the Otomí areas deep in the eastern corridor of Sierra Madre Mountains. It must be remembered that New Spain was an extension of the Kingdom of Castile; the viceroy was the King's official representative. Nobody did anything in New Spain without official orders and permission directly from the King, or from his viceroy. Once the permission was granted Augustinians still had to secure labor to build their convents and chapels. The viceroy, at this point, was the only authority that could grant an *encomienda* for labor drafts. So with these permissions secured, in 1537, Antonio de la Rosa entered the high Eastern Sierra Madres, and founded the convent at Meztitlán. In 1553, he built the convent near the ancient Pame town of Xilitla that would serve as a fort also. By then he spoke the language and knew more of the nature of the Pame, and the need for defensive construction. Xilitla was attacked by Pame in 1569, and again in 1587, probably inspired by reports of the Chichimeca war that was raging on the other side of the Sierra Madres.

Built for the purposes of *reduction* or *congregation*, these convents were the focal point of bringing seminomadic people together where they could be indoctrinated and brought under Spanish administration. They were the foundation of Christian towns, in which the convent, the church, homes, and then economic development would follow, as the friars taught animal husbandry, town planning, new agricultural techniques, and new technologies in general. Soon the convent grew to a village, then the village into a town. These two Augustinian Christian towns served as the base for sending new friars out to surrounding areas to repeat the process. This model of evangelism developed the twofold purposes of the friars: to build the Roman Catholic Church and to make Spanish citizens of the indigenous people. Throughout the colonial period this pattern was repeated.

Until this epoch the towns that had been started were begun for the purposes and benefit of the Spanish settlers, often they would be built next to an indigenous settlement of their *encomienda*. In the second epoch of conquest the hamlet or town was basically already there; the Spanish simply took over the administration and made it their town or city, or the Spanish chose to leave them indigenous towns. Meztitlán and Xilitla were settled in Pame areas and were further developed by the friars to evangelize natives and launch future evangelism once they became prosperous as *indigenous* Christian towns.

Another town established in this manner was San Miguel de Las Chichimecas (Now: San Miguel de Allende). The village was founded in 1542 by the Franciscan monk Juan de San Miguel, who established a convent to evangelize the Pame that were being displaced and also to teach European weaving and agricultural techniques to the native people. The settlement prospered, becoming the local market center for surrounding haciendas trading in cattle and textiles. The Roman Catholic Pame and Otomí of Juan's encomienda became skilled tradesmen, weavers, and *vaqueros* (cowboys). The Augustinians centered their activity in Yuriria, where they founded a monastery in 1550 and set about establishing Christian *congregations* in that area.

Another type of *encomienda* that was used for evangelism and starting a town was the fortified inn, a type of Spanish frontier lodging, offering provisions and a secure stronghold for times of trouble. These were established in the lower crescent at the southern edge of the Chichimeca region, but the best examples of these were the villages that were established along the Silver Highway between Mexico City and Zacatecas. The fortified inn rescued many travelers off this dangerous highway by providing a refuge and defensive center against Chichimeca attacks. Controlled by license, they provisioned travelers, provided rooms and livery, served meals, and sold produce and livestock, all at set prices fixed by a pricelist from the government. These fortified inns—constructed by repartimiento (the provision of a specific number of impressed indigenous laborers by the government) were built and run by both the religious and private enterprises for their own particular motives. When built by the friars, the purpose was specifically to evangelize, provide for Roman Catholic religious worship, and establish a Christian presence in the midst of the indigenous people.

The privately owned encomienda was the second type of evangelistic model that resulted in the great haciendas. A number of famous names in the Bajío area opened the gateways to the Chichimeca regions. Men such as Hernán Peres de Bocanegra y Cordoba of the Acambaro region, Juan Infante of the Comanja region, Juan de Villaseñor established the frontier settlements of Puruandiro and Penjamo, and Juan de Tovar in the Yuriria area.[17] These *encomiendas* were granted as rewards for service to the Crown usually to men in the military, conquistadores, and of course to the friars who needed the labor for construction. Keep in mind that a fundamental requirement of the *encomendero* was, "In return for the grant of a *repartimiento* or *encomienda* the *encomendero* was legally obligated to protect, and at his own expense to Christianize the natives assigned to him, and he was required by law to maintain arms and a horse in readiness to take to the field at a moment's notice, whether against Indians, Spaniards who might rise up in rebellion, or European enemies who might attack the colonies."[18] As yet there was no other military in New Spain. In the fortified ranches of the Bajío, *encomenderos* actually built up a small army for their own protection and for the forays against the Chichimeca enemy.

As part of their obligation to Christianize the natives at their disposal, most of these "ranchero" owners had a small chapel built, often at their own expense, and employed a cleric, usually the services of a traveling friar, to visit regularly and minister through baptizing, teaching, and leading in mass. The fortified ranch was usually the private dwelling of the owner and his family, so eventually an additional chapel had to be built in the indigenous village for the basic needs of the native people. If there were a number of villages in the *encomienda*, they each would have to have a chapel as the indigenous people were baptized.

The plantation with its *casa fuerte* followed the same pattern with the exception that farming was much more labor intensive than ranching. Greater numbers of laborers were needed on a fairly continuous basis to keep a very large, un-mechanized agricultural program going. As these agribusinesses developed, they became the foundation of larger population centers. Larger churches and permanent staff were necessary to meet the needs of the plantation and all the native workers who may have been slaves, *encomienda* residents, *encomienda* indentured peons nearby, or paid labor from the towns nearby.

A third strategy for evangelism and Spanish dominance in this epoch was a type of *encomienda* that could be called the Christian Community. Friars entered an area with intentions of building a convent or strong-house with an *encomienda* of Christian indigenous workers from outside of the area who were brought to the unevangelized area for the purpose of using the community of Christian natives as a witnessing model. The imported Christians evangelized and taught as a Christian community in the midst of the pagans.[19]

An example of this occurred after the pacification of the Guachichiles through *Peace with Purchase* in the mining area of Charcas. Devoid of population because of constant raids which shut down the mining operations, some friars with a group of more than a 120 Christian Tlaxcaltecas arrived in 1591, and with permission of the viceroy began to clean up, rebuild, and reestablish a convent. After purchasing favor with the Guachichiles in the area, the Tlaxcaltecans began to implement a program of evangelism and acculturation that brought in the nomadic tribesmen and established them in the community. This model of native evangelists in community was very successful in bringing in the most hated and despised of the Chichimeca groups.

As the Chichimeca mixed and intermarried with the Tlaxcaltecas the stigmatism and identity of the hated Chichimecas was lost.

The fourth strategic model for evangelism and acculturation was the Presidio. Until this point in time there had not been a professional military presence in New Spain.[20] The local militias were always the backbone of any punitive raids, and defensive actions. Conquistadores comprised volunteer armies financed by the leader who had been appointed by the Crown and promised specific rewards if successful—often governorships and titles. Captains and successful conquistadores received first choice of encomiendas and rights to exploit mineral deposits found, understanding that all land was property of the King and their part was the remuneration by the King for developing the King's property. It was the utter violence and longevity of the Chichimeca war, balanced against the fantastic riches of the silver mines that forced the Crown to create the first professional military in New Spain. The Silver Highway had to be kept open. Yet the Chichimeca were steadily gaining the upper hand in the war, now using Spanish guns, Spanish horses, learning Spanish tactics, and using them more efficiently than the Spanish themselves. Only the tremendous number of casualties balanced against the very limited population of the scattered groups of Chichimecas kept them from fully dominating the Spanish. Still, it was only after two full decades of war with the Chichimecas that the concept of stationing troops and forts at intervals along these highways with military escorts for wagon trains actually began to be carried out. Finally in the 1570s the strategy of presidios and fortified towns became the foundation of Spanish military strategy in the Gran Chichimeca war.[21] The most dangerous stretch of highway lay between San Felipe and Zacatecas where the road followed the edge of Guachichile territory. The first two presidios using paid troops taken from the escorts of the Audiencia were set up at Ojuelos and Potezuelo (near Ocampo today) as natural, one day travel stops going north from San Felipe where the heaviest raiding was taking place at the time. Three more frontier forts were built between Ojuelos and Zacatecas. Others were built later as new silver mines opened and had to be protected. To supplement these five forts, a garrison of presidio soldiers was established at San Felipe. They were also garrisoned in the towns of Celaya and Guanajuato as supply camps.

In summation, this presidio system of forts did contribute to the stability of *Silver Highway* travel and probably lent moral support to the other efforts. Philip Powell calls attention to the fact that "the number of soldiers needed for such a system, combined with the dearth of quality in both captains and soldiers meant irritating and harmful behavior by this soldiery, with attendant increase of Chichimeca hostility toward the invaders."[22] He concludes that this type of military force was not the best way to achieve peace on the Chichimeca frontier. Some of these presidios were near established towns such as Ojuelos and Aguascalientes. Others stood alone at strategic military locations. When the presidios closed down in the 1590s, there was no reason to maintain the sites; therefore, their sites and actual locations were lost to posterity. Because they contributed to the safety and ministry of the convents and chapels in the small towns, they facilitated the missionary effort. This model was to be used much more effectively in the future Epochs of conquest and would be copied by the English as they moved west hundreds of years later.

To these four new strategies for the penetrate-and-occupy type evangelism must be added the secular church model. The great silver tycoons of this period, Cristóbal de Oñate, Diego de Ibarra, and Juan de Tolosa, were counted among the richest men in New Spain. They were quite generous with their new wealth, building lavishly decorated churches furnished with the best that was available. They financed the clergy necessary to provide full Roman Catholic services in these new churches, and, in general, kept the secular church growing at the same pace that new towns were coming into being. This, in part, was an impetus to growth that allowed the secular church to become an equal to the missionary church of the mendicant friars and to question their supremacy in New Spain as the religious leaders. In this Epoch, the Secular Roman Catholic Church through fortified inns, encomiendas, and presidio towns, kept an equal pace in growth with the mendicant Roman Catholic Church, and even challenged the mendicants to move beyond to more remote, unevangelized areas.

Analysis of Spanish Missiology
in the Fourth Epoch: Gran Chichimeca

The missiological framework with the five major areas of analysis for apostolic missions can now be applied to this fourth epoch. For the area of *Apostolic Practice* we are looking at the means to evangelism or the way the great commission was expressed in context of actual ministry to the indigenous people. The one new and all encompassing factor in this epoch was war. Unlike the other epochs, there was no period of conquest and subjugation followed by evangelism and church building while reforming indigenous people into Spanish citizens. The Chichimeca war just continued on and on unabated, getting more fierce, more destructive, and taking a tremendous toll in lives and property on both sides. The entire enterprise for work, life, societal development, and ministry had to go on at the same time, with a tool in one hand and a gun in the other. Thus the concept of the frontiersmen came into being in this epoch.

The frontiersmen could be man or woman, indigenous or Spanish, but more often was a person of mixed race. The *Mestizo*, as the common man of New Spain, came into his own self-identity on the Chichimeca frontier. Previous class distinctions mattered not at all where the pressures of life and survival itself depended on the person fighting at your side, all genetics and history aside. The Native American was still the lowest man on the totem pole with his humility and lack of understanding of his own situation; the Hidalgo still on the top with his no-work-with-hands ethic and superiority complex. That left the Mestizo to rise to the occasion with his ethic of hard work, his acceptability to both the other groupings, and his ability to both submit to authority and to persist on his own volition in the absence of authority.

This epoch also saw the foundation of many cities and towns where only cactus and small groups of seminomadic indigenous people had existed. By 1600, Zacatecas rivaled Puebla as the second most important Spanish town in New Spain.[23] Other cities founded at this time were Querétaro, Celaya, Guanajuato, San Miguel, San Fernando, Morelia, Guadalajara, Culiacán, San Luis Potosí, and Zacatecas. The secular church was growing with these new cities, while the mendicant friars continued to develop the indigenous *ranchos* of the countryside.

The territory subjugated and controlled by New Spain had doubled in size during this epoch but at a very high price in human life and resources on both sides.

The primary method of evangelism for this epoch was the formation of a defensive settlement in the midst of the hostile territory: the presidio for defensive purposes only; the fortified inn and the *encomienda* strong-house for economic reasons only; or the indigenous pueblo, the convent, and the utopia Christian settlement for primarily evangelistic purposes. All of these strategies for penetrate-and-hold settlements would eventually result in convents, chapels, larger churches being built, and the *encomienda* and slave or free indigenous people being baptized and accepted into the realm of Spanish dominance.

In the beginning of the penetration into the Gran Chichimeca with the fortified convent and the strong-house *encomienda*, the profundity of evangelism was comparable to the level in epoch two of the Central Valleys. The responsibility of the *encomendero*/evangelist ended after baptism and the building of a small chapel for the itinerant friars to use when present. Syncretic practices were highest in these areas of little or no teaching with Christian education being not much more than observing the life of the Spanish *vaqueros* and, to a degree, copying them—not the best of Christian models. Minimal administration of the sacraments other than baptism coexisted with the continued practices of the previous religion under the guise of Roman Catholic processions, rituals, and symbols with each area developing its own unique version of Christopaganism.

As the Chichimeca wars progressed, native pueblos were started, foundations of cities were built, and the formal clergy of the secular church began to establish themselves as well, evidenced in the more formal expressions of worship and more complete forms of evangelism utilizing all of the sacraments of the Roman Catholic Church. After the war was settled, convents and cathedrals were built or finally could be finished,[24] and clergy training was established, including lay brothers from among the indigenous people. While there was still an official prohibition to the establishment of a Native American clergy, lay brothers could be trained and sent to work with the friars in missionary outreach. The two areas where evangelism reached its' highest expression was in the major secular Roman Catholic centers such as Zacatecas, where hierarchal clerical teams were complete and resident to the area, and also in the utopian pueblos of the Purépechas, where the governmental organizations maintained both church and society in detailed structure.

However, due to the Tridentine limits placed upon the Roman Church, the Christology that was taught by the friars was either very weak or nonexistent. Jesus the Christ was a baby in the arms of Mary in most symbolism; he was the suffering, crucified man in the passion plays, or he was lying in the coffin at the side of the entrance to a cathedral.[25] Very seldom if ever was the resurrected, glorified Jesus Christ the coming King ever portrayed in processions, in drama, or in art. In place of a complete Christology, Mariology has been substituted to a point that the doctrine of the Trinity, the three persons of the Godhead, was a vague or unknown doctrine.[26] Eschatology was reduced to the extra-biblical concept of purgatory, and the costs to the surviving family and friends to get the deceased out of there more quickly.

The doctrine of salvation through the vicarious sufferings of the Christ was still reduced to the physical act of baptism as in previous epochs. Very little doctrinal teaching graced this fourth epoch but as it progresses there was the addition of teaching the catechisms. The more common usage of the complete list of sacraments in several areas of the Gran Chichimeca could be interpreted as a more complete salvation message, but unfortunately that was primarily for the Europeans of the cities and towns. The concept of teaching the finished work of the Christ and salvation as a gift of God by grace through faith[27] was also greatly hindered by the Tridentine doctrine of man participating in his own salvation by works of obedience. The *obedience* part of this doctrine became the emphasis that was taught, not the *grace* through faith part.

Therefore, in the area of *Apostolic Practices,* evangelism was still greatly constrained by the Tridentine doctrines, leaving most of the rudiments of Christology, eschatology, and soteriology, untaught and unknown to most of the baptized community of Native Americans. Ecclesiology was becoming much more organized, with fairly large segments of native religion incorporated into the practice of Roman Catholic Christianity. The only discipleship of new believers that took place was in the convents of the Augustinians and Franciscans, where the training of a few lay brothers for the purposes of assisting the evangelistic friars was pursued to some degree. If the memorization of catechisms could be considered discipleship, then there was a level of discipleship-teaching taking place among the Pame and other Chichimeca groups as translations progressed and catechisms became available for use. Using the biblical model of Jesus with his disciples it was only in the convents with lay brothers where actual discipleship took place.

In the area of *Church Structure and Mission* for this Epoch a change took place in the institutional authority between the two major branches of Roman Catholicism—the monastic and the secular church structures. Cortéz didn't even want secular church clerics in New Spain because of his concern that their poor Christian testimony and pompous life styles would be an offense to the natives who were far more disciplined in their paganism than Roman Catholic clerics were in their Christianity. But during previous epochs continuing reformation and wise selection of bishops for New Spain, often taking them from the orders, had promoted the development of a strong, Tridentine Roman Catholic expression in New Spain which, combined with the inquisition, maintained that expression among the Criollos or European descendents. The indigenous people were still regarded as mentally incapable of high religious concepts and, therefore, could not be held responsible as were the *gente de razón* (reasonable people). In this epoch it was accepted that the indigenous and half-breeds were not going to come up to the level of the high expressions of Roman Catholicism; they were *Indios* and that was to be expected—but they were still counted as Roman Catholic.

In this fourth epoch the secular church undertook a large part in the expansion of the church through the encomiendas, the fortified inns, and the establishment of churches and cathedrals in the new cities and towns. It was recognized that the mendicants were necessary for the untamed indigenous areas; however, the need for their services in the domesticated areas was now being questioned. The poor mendicant mentality did not fit in the now often prosperous, even rich, new cities and towns of the Gran Chichimeca. The mendicants were in fact an offence to the other classes of New Spain society being as they both lived like natives and defended them against the colonists, especially in their attacks against the *encomienda* slavery and exploitation of the free, indentured laborers or *peons*.

The leaders of the mendicant societies had the authority of a bishop derived directly from the Pope and their position was sanctioned by the King. They were financed by the Crown and responsible to the Crown, not to the leadership of the New Spain secular church. These two systems in the same geographical location eventually had to clash. Jesuits, the Society of Jesus, who did not consider themselves mendicants, arrived in New Spain further strengthening the secular church. They were highly educated, very worldly in their emphasis on education and paying their own way by profitable economic development and business practices. They were the vanguard of the Roman Catholic renewal efforts and the counter attacks against the evangelical reformation movements that refused to submit to the Tridentine doctrines of the Roman Catholics.[28] Together, the militant Jesuits and the solid Roman Catholic secular bishops were changing the spiritual landscape of New Spain, establishing the secular church on solid Tridentine foundations.

Therefore this epoch marked a new chapter in the overall development of the Roman Catholic Church in New Spain, with the arrival of the Society of Jesus and with the secular church beginning to exert its dominance. The mendicant church began to fall into disfavor when it failed to move on once the local churches were established in the proximity of secular church authority. The friars were criticized due to a few examples of abuse, debauchery, and laziness in the mendicant ranks, and thus a poor reputation of their spirituality was being given to all the mendicant friars' efforts. They were also faulted for failure to continue to open new areas for evangelism. The concept that missionaries, the orders, were to work where there was no church and not pastor their own established churches was becoming accepted ideology for the Secular Roman Catholic Church. The *One True Church* was finding it most difficult to deal with two separate authority structures in one geographic location.[29] They still do.

In the areas of the *Gospel and Other Religions*, and *Salvation and the Non-Christians* there was no difference, no improvement, no growth in understanding as to the relationship of Tridentine Roman Catholicism and all other religions of the world, including other Christian expressions. This is still seen as good by many even today: Dark Age, European (Spanish) expressions of Christianity are still thought by some to be the only valid religion, the only way to God, all others are of the devil. In this Fourth epoch, there still was simply no missiology involved in this position; it is ethnocentric, imperialistic, cultural dominance with no thought for the indigenous values that were being shattered. After over a hundred years of experience in apostolic practice with the indigenous Americans, these two areas of missiology still had not been birthed. This represents an inherent blindness to the cage that Tridentine theology put around the New Spain apostolic movement. The Tridentine gospel was understood to be the only true gospel, and there was no salvation apart from Roman Catholic baptism.

In the area of *Christianity and Culture,* the validity of other cultural expressions is being considered. As corrupt as the elements of a society may be by sin nature and the cursed, fallen world, the basic nature of culture is still a product of God's creative hand and will contain elements that can be used to glorify God and be used to communicate the gospel message. In this approach missiology is looking for ways to use the target culture to communicate critical theological principles while respecting diversity in the expression of those Christian principles in the new socio-cultural context of the target society.

In Quiroga's experiments in sociology an honest attempt to accomplish a new cultural expression by the indigenous people is evident. He was not attempting to make the natives culturally Spanish; he was trying to make them culturally *perfect* (which was Spanish in the eyes of many contemporaries). Had the *intellectual leaders* been Purépecha the experiment might have achieved better results, but having foreign *intellectuals* (Quiroga and his Spanish priests) doomed the experiment to failure. It would have taken leaders from inside the culture of the Purépecha acting as change agents to succeed in such a complicated undertaking. The results were a hybrid of the *reduction,* the system of congregating seminomadic natives into pueblos where they could be trained in the new religion and learn the Spanish social structure. Many very worthy goals were accomplished, but the end result was still a rape of the Purépecha culture, while superimposing what was thought to be the perfect Spanish cultural expressions of society.

As far as the Chichimeca cultures were concerned, there was so much hatred and violence involved on both sides for over a 40-year period that it was utterly impossible to imagine value in one another's cultural expressions. Never before in New Spain had the Spanish been repaid in kind to such an extent for their cruelties to the indigenous people. Even after peace with purchase was established and the war itself was ended, it was the Christian Tlaxcaltecans from the Central Valleys who sought out the Guachichiles with the intent of evangelism. Following the Spanish example, not even the indigenous allies of the Spanish had any desire to evangelize their ancient enemies, the Chichimecas. Today most of the Chichimeca cultures are extinct. There is a remnant of two dialects of Pame, or Xi'iuy as they call themselves, in the mountainous regions of eastern San Luis Potosi. Of course, there was no silver or gold in those areas.

Summary

In this fourth Epoch of conquest Roman Catholic missiology changed and adapted due to constraints forced upon the friars and clerics during the 40 years of the Chichimeca war. The great silver deposits in the Gran Chichimeca were both the cause of the invasion of Native American territory and the financing for the invasion of the lands of the seminomadic peoples. A primary objective of the friars was always to bring the indigenous people under Spanish domination and remake them into Spanish citizens. This was accomplished to a large degree by the friars, the secular church, and private enterprise exploiting the land through *encomiendas* and the silver mines. The most common method of subjugation was penetration into hostile territory by fortified convents, inns, and ranches, strong-houses built for defense, and the presidios near indigenous pueblos. When the Chichimeca could not be beaten, the Spanish sued for *peace with purchase*—buying the peace that war failed to achieve. But this did result in indigenous villages being formed, nomadic people becoming sedentary peoples, and all becoming citizens of a Spanish style society. They were Spanish citizens because they were baptized by Roman Catholic priests.

In the evangelistic area less than half of the essential doctrines of salvation were being taught or practiced, leaving the new baptized believers with a deficient and very rudimentary understanding of basic Christianity. This cemented the marriage of Christianity and paganism resulting in a new *mestizaje* religion, another syncretic religion which is now being called Christopaganism.[30] The gulf between the high expressions of Roman Catholicism as practiced in the European segments of New Spain society in the cities and that of the common man, the indigenous and the Mestizo people, was recognized and accepted as deficient but still a legitimate expression of New Spain Roman Catholicism. The animosity long held between the mendicant orders and the secular church became a wall of hostility with the secular church emerging as the dominant force in New Spain Roman Catholicism. There was still an intolerance that bordered on fanatical in the areas of non-Roman Catholic religions and other cultural expressions of religion, whether Christian or pagan. No culture or religion besides the Dark-Age, Roman Catholicism was recognized as valid in New Spain, although Christopaganism with Roman Catholic baptism was tolerated.

CHAPTER VIII

FIFTH EPOCH:
THE NUEVA VIZCAYA

Epoch Five Introduction

Following the pattern for previous epochs, the beginnings of Spanish contact in the Nueva Vizcaya region began in the fourth epoch with the Chichimeca wars. Often, a definition used for Nueva Vizcaya is, "everything north of Zacatecas." The region encompasses the current states of Baja California, Sinaloa, Sonora, Durango, Chihuahua, and parts of Texas, Nuevo Leon, and Zacatecas. The time for this epoch under study will be limited to essentially the seventeenth and eighteenth centuries, although the indigenous resistance and hot wars covered a period of more than 300 years.[1]

There were three events that influenced the knowledge of the Spanish for this region before intentional penetration and conquest began. The first event was the penetration of Guzmán and his indigenous army of Tlaxcalans, Aztecas and Tarascans into what is now Sinaloa in 1529-31. They were met by an army of 30,000 indigenous warriors. Guzmán decisively defeated them while disease wreaked havoc on both armies and ravaged the area. After establishing the town of San Miguel de Culiacán, in what is now the capital and geographic center of Sinaloa, Guzmán retreated to the south leaving enough of his slave raiders to continue supplying his labor needs. The Chichimeca wars were just beginning and the great silver rush to Zacatecas was attracting most of the frontiersmen. The province of Culiacán was a small island of Spanish power hundreds of miles from Spanish civilization through dangerous and difficult terrain and angry, highly capable warriors that hated the Spanish and their deadly diseases.

The second major influence on the Spanish knowledge of the north came from the remnants of the Pánfilo de Narváez expedition. Four men who had survived the storms, ship wrecks, captivity, and slavery escaped and then wondered for years as foreign shamans (healers). They had landed on the coast of Florida, explored the coast, shipwrecked on the Texas coast, and escaped inland wandering over Texas, New Mexico, Chihuahua, Sonora, and into Sinaloa. Safely back in Mexico City in 1536, Cabeza de Vaca drew maps and told his tales of Native American nations and cities, but most of all, the immensity of the land to the north.

The third influence on Spanish knowledge was the expedition sent by Viceroy Antonio Mendoza to investigate this preposterous tale by finding and recording the northern cities, to explore the northern coast, and to report on the land route, the people, minerals, and their economy. As head of the expedition, Mendoza chose a priest of good reputation, Marcos de Niza, who would travel with a group of native allies and an intriguing guide—none other than Estevan, the Moor, who had already survived seven years of wandering in the northern area. Niza left Mexico City in the fall of 1538 with the new governor of the province around Culiacán, Francisco Vasquez de Coronado, who had become governor after the arrest of Guzmán. Leaving Coronado in Culiacán and following the trail that the four survivors had left coming in from the north, Niza accomplished his mission and filed his reports.[2]

In 1540, with a new commission by the Viceroy and funded by many investors, Coronado marched north from Compostela, in modern day Nayarit, with a huge army, to conquer the Seven Cities of Cibola confirmed the year before by Niza. They found the cities, but no wealth. Coronado sent side parties out in several directions that discovered the Grand Canyon and the mouth of the Colorado River. After Coronado subjugated Cibola (The Pueblo people), he occupied other Pueblos in New Mexico and marched as far as Kansas but never found gold.[3] For the investors, the expedition was regarded as a failure.

Because the *encomienda* system of labor advanced with the Spanish conquistadores and their *repartimientos* continued as rewards for service, the *reducciones* used by the friars to create indigenous towns was usually in the background of all advancement made by the Spanish. The peace-by-purchase program brought this system to the forefront in the latter stages of the Chichimeca war. The *reduction* system was perfected by the second Viceroy of Peru in 1572-80.[4] This system called for a town plan with a church in the center, a school and convent for the living quarters of the priest, and then workshops, stables, and dwellings for the indigenous people. The only major difference between the Franciscan and the Jesuit *reductions* was that the former put the church in the middle of the square which separated the church from the living quarters and school while the Jesuits would usually put the church to one side of the square with the services and school beside the church. In both cases a system of rectangular blocks would be laid out from the square with uniform living quarters for the indigenous people that made it possible to maintain surveillance in any direction from the plaza.[5]

The Chichimeca war was raging to the south. But in 1563-65, Francisco de Ibarra, a wealthy silver mine owner, traveled through parts of Nueva Vizcaya, constructing settlements of a permanent nature. Ibarra gave this area its name after his home province of Vizcaya in Spain. He founded the first capital of the province, Durango in 1563, which was named for his birthplace. Francisco de Ibarra's expedition was responsible for some of the first European observations on the Acaxee, Xixime, and Tepehuán indigenous groups of the north.[6] He brought with him on these expeditions miners and colonists opening up mining centers in Zacatecas, Chihuahua, Durango, and Sinaloa. Wherever Ibarra encountered indigenous resistance, he would put it down with force.

The Indigenous People of the North

Traveling to the north from Zacatecas, the desert valleys between the Sierra Madre mountain ranges dropped lower in altitude, the daily temperatures rose higher, the land became more astonishing in its' grandeur, and the population of indigenous people became more sparse. Yet down the inside of the western corridor of mountains, the higher mesas and canyons provided water, pasture, and shelter against the extremes of the elements providing very fertile ground for corn, squash, beans, chilies, tomatoes, and fruit trees. The groups of indigenous peoples of the north were referred to as ranchería people.

They lived in villages which were usually scattered over a large area with each family's dwellings separated from the next by the lands they cultivated. This contrasted greatly with the villages and cities of the southern groups that lived in towns and went out to their fields of labor. In the north the scattered, extended family settlements were not very conducive to providing a ready labor market for the mines that were being discovered and developed. Therefore the Spanish felt that the native population had to be brought together near mining areas for the *encomienda* labor system to work.

Typical in the life of these indigenous Americans was a religion that was animistic with the sun, the moon, the planet Venus, the eagle, and the deer being the most commonly venerated objects and creatures. The *ranchería* people held special rituals at the time of sowing, when beginning a hunt or fishing, and when going to war.[7] They utilized the multipurpose, wild, maguey plant for their mild alcoholic drinks used in fiestas and rituals as well as for fiber to make cloth, bags, rope, etc. Both men and women wore their hair long and adorned with feathers and colored stones. They built homes out of wood, stone, and adobe, well designed to protect from heat and cold as seasons changed. Most of the northern tribes participated in a long distance ball game running between villages.[8] They hunted deer, rabbit, wild turkey, pheasant, and possum. Government of the rancho was in the hands of a chief and a council of elders.[9]

In comparison with other Epochs, Nueva Vizcaya saw little resistance to the Spanish invaders at first. Both conquest, and later rebellions, were not particularly challenging to the Spanish dominance. This belied the warrior culture of the northern tribes which was as essential to their cultural survival as that of the Aztec to their south. Warfare was a part of life and critical to the advancement to leadership positions in their societies. Early Spanish observers described acts such as the eating of an enemy's heart, consultation of oracles to determine battles, and ritual dances which all contributed to the cohesiveness of indigenous society and unity against all external enemies. Warfare usually took the form of raids which were fought over boundaries, resources (especially water), and women. Warfare was a means by which junior males acquired social status and demonstrated leadership ability. Friars noted that in time of war the most courageous of warriors become captains and other warriors freely chose whether to follow them.[10] When the Jesuits forbid internal warfare, the means to become a leader were denied. By inserting missionaries into leadership status and positions, the chiefs, warriors, and shamans were all effectively demoted.

The Society of Jesus, Missionaries

The Society of Jesus was first called "The Company of Jesus" due to its' military type of organization and soldier spirit. The founder, Ignatius Loyola, was a veteran military man who had served with distinction. The Society was formed as an order of clerks regular, that is, a body of *priests* organized for apostolic work that followed a *religious rule* but relied on their own labors as well as alms for their support. As an order the Jesuits added some new twists. They were all well educated, ordained priests in the secular church, and with an understood calling to educate. They were more comfortable in relationship with the secular church than with the other mendicant orders. Their corporate task was, "to carry out whatever the present and future Roman pontiffs may order which pertains to the progress of souls and the propagation of the faith; and to go without subterfuge or excuse . . . to whatsoever provinces they may choose to send us."[11] *Jesuit* was a 15th century derogatory term for one that used the name of Jesus too much, or used it in place of his own name, revealing how the Jesuits were received by the other orders. The nickname stuck and was born with pride.

Coming late to the missionary movement in the Americas, the Jesuits had some catching up to do. They first set their sights on La Florida where no one seemed to be working. However, the Jesuits were not well received by many of the tribes in La Florida. Already ravished by European disease, preyed upon by slave raiders from the Caribbean, the Native Americans already knew no good would come from these black robed foreigners. But this new breed of friars did do well with the Timucuan people in the San Augustín area. In 1566, one year after its founding, San Augustín became the Jesuit base for all other evangelistic efforts.[12] They expanded up the East Coast founding a mission in 1571 in Chesapeake Bay in what would become Virginia. One year later all eight clerics were martyred. About that same time their two superiors further south died of sickness. Leaderless and discouraged, the remaining Jesuits retreated to the population centers of Mexico where they returned to their first and most common ministry—education.[13]

The Jesuits had conflicts with the natives who resisted their presence and proselytizing in La Florida; they had conflicts with the Spanish authorities over jurisdiction and their degree of spiritual authority—they were priests but organized as an order. But most of the Jesuit conflicts were internal, among themselves due to their own lack of vision or an established mission strategy, as well as reeling from the failure of the La Florida missions. A new General was elected in 1572 and stated that the principle goal of the Jesuit mission in New Spain was the conversion of the unfaithful. To this end he insisted that the Jesuits establish schools for the natives, those already baptized, and that the Jesuits learn Native American languages. These schools were to be located where the natives had already undergone conquest and were partially acculturated. They would work with domesticated indigenous elites to control and further acculturate the indigenous populations. This strategy was based upon the work of the early Franciscans who had much success in the Second Epoch of conquest.[14]

Armed with a clear missionary vision and a strategy in hand, the Jesuits started a school at Tepotzotlán among the Otomí in 1518, and then another at Pátzcuaro. Two schools to educate Aztec children of nobles were started in Mexico City in 1584 and 1586. These were church schools designed to train young indigenous elite to be Christian civil leaders of their communities, but not for the priesthood or other ministries which had already been forbidden Native Americans by law in 1555. These schools were not convents or missions; they were boarding schools designed to separate young men from their families and the influence of their parents and to divorce them from their indigenous culture. The idea was to make them into agents of cultural change. A stated goal was to educate the children *so that they did not appear to be sons of natives*. The curriculum of the Jesuit schools for indigenous children gave no consideration to preserving any aspect of indigenous culture—the purpose was to replace indigenous culture with Spanish, Roman Catholic culture. This was the background of the Jesuits in New Spain when the Viceroy called upon them to penetrate and evangelize the Nueva Vizcaya region. In 1591 the Chichimeca war was over, the north was wide open for the Spanish to step in and possess the land.[15]

Peace-by-purchase brought an end to the terrible 40 years of war. As a new strategy for conquest, peace-by-purchase completely replaced the conquistador concept of scorched earth terror; still fresh were the terrible memories of how that strategy had been turned back on the Spanish with a vengeance. However, there had to be a medium for implementation and the Jesuit Order seem ideally suited for the job. By nature and strategy the peace-by-purchase program and the Jesuit Society seemed designed for each other. In Nueva Vizcaya the Society of Jesus abandoned the pedagogical strategy developed further south to pursue a system of mission districts called *Doctrinas*. This fit more closely the frontier goals for pacification. Two missionaries circulated within the *Doctrina*, preaching, teaching the catechism and baptizing those who requested it. As the missionary structure evolved, it became very hierarchal, as the militaristic Society of Jesus was inclined to be. The mission centers were where the missionaries resided. The *visitas*, today they would be called mission churches, were visited regularly from these centers. When a sufficient number of mission churches were organized in a new area, a new mission center would be organized with new missionaries and the whole process repeated.[16]

Part of this strategy was the peace-by-purchase commitment to provide, not only organization into communities, but also economic help, as well as spiritual teaching. It was the responsibility of the Viceroy to provide the implements for agricultural improvement, livestock for animal husbandry, seeds or seedlings for orchards, and cloth for clothing. The Jesuit brothers had to distribute to those who would best use them, teach the use of the tools, the crafts, and the care of the European stock which had never been seen by indigenous people before the Spanish came.

It appeared that the whole system was working for a time. The Franciscans, who were the first to go north, appeared left out and became jealous of the position of the Society of Jesus. Jesuits had material help and the authority of the Viceroy behind them when European financing for the Orders and North American missions was getting scarcer. In 1557, Spain had declared the first sovereign bankruptcy in recorded history. Spain was engaged in war on several fronts: with the French and also with the Netherlands which had been going on for 80 years, additionally the Anglo-Spanish war was being fought on both sides of the Atlantic. Therefore missionary effort in New Spain was low on Spain's list of financial commitments greatly curbing the Franciscan and Dominican efforts. The Franciscan friars also resented what they perceived to be an invasion of their territory by the Jesuits who seemed to be teamed up with the secular church of New Spain against the "real" mendicant orders.

There was usually conflict brewing between the Society of Jesus, the colonists, and the mine owners over the question of indigenous laborers. The whole economic system was based upon exploitation of the indigenous people. The first mines and haciendas were established in 1575 and quickly became the primary industries and they had to have workers. Sometimes the indigenous people worked out of choice or for perceived personal benefit, yet many were coerced or forced, and many were treated as slaves.

Indigenous slavery had been outlawed by the Crown in 1550, but the many laws contradicted themselves. The *New Laws* to protect the natives against exploitation were implemented in 1542, although the clause 35 of the *Laws* that removed the encomienda system was stricken from the *New Laws* in 1545. In 1549, the required personal service to Spanish *encomenderos* by indigenous people on their land· was prohibited. Still, the colonists and miners needed labor, so civil officials, using the military if necessary, collaborated with them to secure that labor, regardless of the law. When compulsory wage labor was instigated by law in 1550, contradicting the indigenous freedoms gained by the previous New Laws, the Jesuits were caught in the middle of all the legal ambiguity and contradictions in practice regardless of the laws.

In practice, Jesuits had to compete with civil officials who sent native peoples to work for Spanish settlers through *repartimiento* labor drafts. Spanish hacienda and mine owners enticed natives from the Jesuit missions with wage earning jobs that were attractive to some natives who chafed under Jesuit authority. With these competing interests, the Jesuits could not keep indigenous people living in the mission villages for long and did not have the force or support of local civil and militia officials to do so. The missions were becoming way-stations for indigenous people on their way to the job market—civil officials always knew where to look for semicivilized indigenous people. The natives found themselves at the bottom rung of society as usual, and at the bottom of the food chain in economic terms. At times the natives viewed the Jesuits only as preparing the way for exploitation through labor drafts. Moreover, there was encroachment of mission lands on native land and on the water resources so important in an arid region. Only the colonists were benefiting from the confused situation and it was to the colonists' advantage to keep the situation confused.

Society of Jesus Methodologies

The methodologies of the Jesuits reflected both their military mentality and their pedagogical models. The Jesuit mission system was meant to take the place of the military presidio which did close to nothing to accomplish Spanish objectives with the native people for pacification during the Chichimeca war. As administrators of the peace-by-purchase program for *reductions,* which was the gathering of scattered rancho families into Christian pueblos to concentrate a labor pool and re-orientate them to Spanish administration, there was necessarily a very close cooperation expected with the civil authorities ·and *encomenderos* in these joint areas of responsibility.

The methodology of the Society of Jesus is revealed in this condensation of Gradie's account of the pacification of an Acaxee rancho area: The Jesuit missionary and the *encomendero* chose sites for new villages and ordered the Acaxee to leave their traditional settlements for the new ones. The intent was to reduce the number of smaller settlements in inaccessible places originally chosen for defense, and to replace these with larger villages built where the missionaries could visit more easily. At each new village site, the missionary and the encomendero oversaw the construction of a temporary church and the priest celebrated mass and baptized all the young children. The missionary erected a cross and, after first showing the natives how, demanded that all genuflect before it. The priest then taught the assembled natives some prayers that he had transcribed into the Acaxee language beforehand. The males were forced to cut their long hair, and the entire assembly was given a lecture on the advantages of wearing the clothes the Captain distributed. The missionary then gave a name, always a Spanish one, to the new village. In some places indigenous leaders considered sufficiently Hispanicize were appointed as assistants who would remain in the new village to teach the other adults the catechism so that they would be ready for baptism when the missionary returned.

The fact is that the spacious, very scattered small settlements of the natives were their best protection against the often fatal diseases brought by the Europeans. These *reductions* forced the concentration of indigenous people for Spanish purposes and deprived the indigenous of this excellent natural defense which greatly accelerated the spread of epidemics that came with the colonists and Jesuits. Throughout the province of Nueva Vizcaya these new *reductions* were being devastated by the most common killers that ravaged the south: influenza, smallpox, and measles. The natives, particularly the Tepehuán and Tarahumara rightly faulted all the Europeans for the dreadful plagues.

Susan Deeds explained how the captain of the security detail instructed the Acaxees in the correct behavior towards the missionary. She said whenever a missionary arrived at the village the Acaxees were to kneel and kiss his hands and were told to obey the missionary in all things. It was the work of the military representatives to see that at each new village some food, salt, knives, material for clothing, and tools were left, but with the threat that if the Acaxees did not obey the missionary, strict punishment and no gifts would be the result. Physical punishment was always administered in public by civil authorities to humiliate indigenous leaders and teach correct discipline. The missionary oversaw this but never participated directly. An objective was always to break down the generational lines of indigenous authority and to position the missionary as the new leader, but not without risk, for that also made the missionary responsible for all that was happening to the indigenous cultures.

The Xiximes of Sinaloa are another example of how the *reductions* were completely altering the indigenous way of life and replacing local Native American leadership with Jesuit priests in their places. First contact with the Xiximes was made by elements of Guzmán's army, most likely on slave raids into Xiximes territory, but they found the Xiximes so inhospitable that they soon retreated and left the Xiximes alone.[17] In 1565, Ibarra marched into their area and subdued them. The Xiximes revolted in 1610, and a large force of 200 Spanish and 1,100 native warriors put down the revolt.[18] The Jesuits were then brought in to restore order after the rebellion was put down, and the Xiximes were *reduced* from 65 fortified, defensive indigenous villages to five new Spanish settlements with ready access by the missionaries. The missionaries brought with them tools, seeds, clothing and livestock, all distributed while following their standard procedures for establishing a new Spanish village.[19]

For this epoch the previous strategy of education, taking in the sons of chiefs and great warriors was not completely abandoned. The University of Durango dates its founding from the Jesuit school for native children. Jesuit mission centers trained native youth in the basics of reading, writing, mathematics, music, and humanities. And as the frontiers moved northward, Jesuits were there to open missions and schools from Culiacán to Chihuahua. Many of the great institutions of higher learning in Mexico today owe their humble beginnings to the educational emphasis of the Society of Jesus.

Much of the history and tradition for this epoch focuses on the individual priests of the Society of Jesus. There was always an emphasis on learning the language of the people and something of their customs—if for no other reason than to destroy them. But not all priests had a gift for learning new languages. In those cases, which were many, the native language translator became the key to effective communication, to gather up the women and children for their catechism lessons and baptisms. The indigenous translator also served as an informant that allowed the priest to understand somewhat the responses to his teaching, the needs of the people, and the areas of cultural conflict.

Without the translator the Jesuit priest was often helpless, unable to communicate or understand.[20] Yet most of these translators are seldom even mentioned, less often named, or still less is credit given to them for their ministries of service to both priest and their communities. Often they are called catechists, for they did the actual teaching, but far too often they are not remembered by either documentation or narrative. As Christ said to the disciples, "Without me you can do nothing." Even so the priest was indebted to the native language catechist without whom he could do nothing.

The Society of Jesus in Baja California

The lower Baja peninsula is included in this Nueva Vizcaya epoch because it coincided with the mainland movement, because all missionary work was done by the Jesuits, and because the methodologies used for evangelism and *reductions* were basically the same as those used on the mainland. The major contrast to the other areas was that the Baja is a peninsula. It is a desert surrounded by ocean with very little to support life apart from modern technology which neither the Jesuits nor the Native Americans had access to during this epoch.

The first attempt at settlement on the Baja peninsula was by the men of Cortéz at the current site of La Paz in 1535. The attempt to establish a pearl fishing center on what was thought to be the island of California was a failure due to the harsh climate of the Vizcaíno desert and its surroundings. One of his three ships was lost and 23 men died from starvation while waiting for supplies. Cortéz left never to return. The peninsula is 700 miles of flint-like land in mountain ranges, peaks, and barren plateaus cut by sharp ravines and arroyos, all strewn with lava-studded sweeps. From this baking ground sprouts a variety of cacti that would fill a book with names. The Jesuit Miguel Venegas called it the most unfortunate, ungrateful, and most miserable land in all the world. He was accurate in his assessment. Perhaps even more miserable were the tribes of indigenous people that somehow managed to survive on this nearly uninhabitable peninsula.

Sebastían Vizcaino, a captain of the Manila trade, secured permission to establish a colony at La Paz and subdue the indigenous people. He established a colony but they found out very quickly that no European could survive on what the natives ate. Supplies ran low, the indigenous people were hostile, and Vizcaino decided he had better things to do. This pattern was followed by many others. Lured by pearls but faced with the realities of the Baja, they quickly retreated from its hostile shores, sudden violent storms, and murderous pirates. The pirates were opportunists like Francis Drake, Thomas Cavendish, and the lawless Dutch that hid in the many fine harbors of the Baja waiting for Spanish galleons returning from the orient.[21] The New Spain leadership wanted safe ports on the Baja to protect its vital Pacific shipping lanes. They turned to the Jesuits to establish a colony and subdue the poor, unruly indigenous people. Some of the previous ventures in the Baja were hosts to Jesuits that were exploring the possibilities of opening a work in that barren land. The Jesuits were well informed of the difficulties that must be faced, and overcome, to establish a series of lasting settlements on the Baja Peninsula.

It is estimated that the total population of indigenous people on the Baja Peninsula ranged between 40,000 and 50,000 at the time of the Cortéz encounter. They were divided into three distinct ethno-linguistic groups: the Guaycura from La Paz to the south of Loreto, the Pericú in the south, closely related to the Guaycuros between Cabo San Lucas and La Paz, and the Cochimí who occupied an extensive area throughout the middle of the peninsula. It is said that these Baja natives were sprawled along the lowest levels of the cultural scale of development, but that they could survive at all in that majestic wasteland speaks of a harmony with nature unrecognized and unrepeatable by the Spanish. Another Jesuit described these people saying, "What a nation this is, miserable and indescribable beyond compare." Some of the refinements of the Jesuits were to get these indigenous folks to stop eating insects, snakes, worms, and parts of their own feces.

The cultural and material expressions of all the peninsular peoples were quite similar. These indigenous groups harvested fish and shell fish from the abundant sea, and fruit in its season from the cactus, as well as wild berries, roots, the agave, and small game. They were a nomadic people who built small shelters when necessary, wandering to where the food could be found in the different seasons. The men went naked, the women with only woven mat coverings suspended from their waists by a cord. The men decked themselves out with strings of small shells, pearls, dried berries, and mother of pearl as necklaces, bracelets, and armlets. There was no marriage as such, but a simple cohabitation (without habitat!) and a universal promiscuity; in fact, the Guaycura language had no word for husband. The Guaycuros tribesmen seemed to have no idea of a supreme being or of any future existence after death with reward or punishment.[22] Other recorded details of habits and of life among the Baja people are best left to one's imagination. There was no room for any concept of a noble savage in the Baja; by almost any form of measurement, the indigenous people of the Baja were at the very bottom of the scale.

By the start of 1697, the Jesuits were well established on the mainland working with the coastal tribes of northern Sinaloa. After a number unsuccessful ventures in Baja, the government of New Spain and the Spanish crown were reluctant to finance any further attempts to domesticate that wasteland, but the Jesuits were economically self-sufficient enough to proceed on their own. The party organized by Eusébio Francisco Kino, under an agreement with the leader of the order, set out from the swamps at the mouth of the Yaqui River in Sonora. Because a rebellion in Sonora required his presence, Kino stayed behind and Juan Maria de Salvatierra led the penetration of the Baja founding the Loreto mission. Loreto eventually became the seat of government, a military presidio, the distribution center for all of Baja, and finally a town. During this epoch the Jesuits had an arrangement whereby the military and civil governments were under the control of the missionaries and administered from the mission in Loreto. Crosby says that for half a century missionaries dominated most religious, military, economic, and social endeavors of the Baja.

In March, 1699, encouraged by more favorable growing conditions in other locations, the Jesuits set about extending their missions. They founded San Xavier, second of the California missions, and later that year the third mission was founded in the midst of many trials for the Jesuit priests. These trials included the loss of a ship with its supplies, the deaths of friends in extreme hardship, lack of essential resources for survival, indifference in New Spain to their plight causing periods of depression, even when, more than once, the padres and their companions were reduced to subsisting, like the savages had previously, upon wild berries, roots, and the fruit of several species of cactus. Also the Jesuits faced attacks from natives and insubordination among the soldiery sent to protect them causing desperate situations. But in spite of it all, in 1705, the missions San Juan Bautista and Santa Rosalia were founded, and then in 1708, the San Jose mission was firmly established.

The Jesuits were following their well established plan of *reductions*. With incentives, primarily offering a steady supply of food, and offering physical protection to entice the wandering natives to come in. Indigenous pueblos were established with a mission church and adobe housing. As usual, the Jesuits demanded hard work in the fields and in the construction of the mission infrastructure. In this process the natives were taught crafts and trades, with food and education given to them. But the land was harsh and unresponsive to European methods of agriculture. When crops failed, or when a supply ship failed to arrive, it was necessary to send the mission natives back to the wild and resume their traditional food-gathering techniques for survival. Unfortunately this was not always successful, as dependent living in the indigenous pueblo had taken away their skills of subsisting from the creatures and plants native to the peninsula.

Weber observes that "In an unusual gesture, the Crown had granted the Jesuits nearly absolute control over Baja California, and the missionaries, hoping to keep Indians insulated from moral contamination, had restricted immigration to soldiers and their families who worked directly for the missions. Yet even with a virtual monopoly, the Jesuits could not create flourishing missions in such an arid, inhospitable land."[23] By contrast, the same methodologies applied just across the Bay of Cortéz were yielding solid movements to Christianity in several very diverse indigenous groups. Perhaps with more time the Baja cultures could have reintegrated along more European lines, but there was to be no more time for the Baja cultures.

In 1709, the first of the epidemic disasters struck the indigenous people of the Baja. "The Indians were newly exposed to smallpox, typhus, measles, and syphilis. As they had no immunity to these diseases, the population decreased with alarming rapidity. The spread of disease was exacerbated by the [physical] closeness of mission life."[24] As mission natives died off, other wandering families were brought in and the cycle repeated. By the time that the Jesuits were expulsed from New Spain in 1767, the last census taken by the Jesuits indicated an indigenous population that was left in the Baja at about 7,000 people. Within another century there were no Pericú, Guaycura, or Cochimí in the southern two thirds of the peninsula. Vernon stated the overwhelming tragedy of the Baja California missions was that imported diseases so decimated the indigenous population there were virtually no survivors to carry on life in the rural village style envisioned by the padres.

By 1750, the missions of Baja were producing grain, fruit, livestock and other staples, almost sufficient for their own consumption, and were no longer in straits of necessity. The policy of trade with the mainland and ships that sailed the west coast trade route returning from the Philippines was also modified. Trade was measurably encouraged, and pearl fishing was again allowed. Much discontent was expressed against the Jesuits by the New Spain authorities due to their tight controls and the limited access to the Baja. The Jesuits were accused of concealing resources, self-interest, economic exploitation, and smuggling.[25] Jealousy and infighting among the orders and lack of trust by the secular church was about to bring one of the most effective Roman Catholic mission agencies to a complete halt in New Spain.

Disease was killing off the indigenous people of the Baja and they rightly blamed the Europeans. The tremendous change in culture and lifestyle required by the padres, particularly the ban on polygamy, infuriated the natives. They finally revolted in 1734, raiding the four southern missions. They sacked the compounds killing two Jesuit priests. Disease, psychological disorientation, or what missiologists call cultural disintegration, had set into the Baja. By the time the Franciscans took over the Jesuit work in 1768, the fate of the Baja California tribes was already sealed. Immediately following the expulsion, the military took over the administration of the missions. The system that was already reeling from loss of converts due to disease suffered drastically from the incompetent and corrupt rule of the soldiers who were appointed to operate the missions until the arrival of the priests from the Franciscan order. By that time, mission orchards and fields were untended, religious articles were missing, lost, or stolen, and many natives had deserted. A number of the Baja missions were never occupied again after the Jesuit expulsion.

During this Fifth Epoch of conquest in New Spain, international forces were beginning to change the way the Roman Catholic Church did missions. The Jesuit Jose de Acosta is best known for his treatise *De Natura Novi Orbis Libri Duo*, also produced what may be regarded as the preliminary draft of his celebrated *Historia Natural y Moral de Las Indias* (Seville, 1590). He was a theologian who spent 16 years as a missionary in Peru. The latter title was translated into the six major languages of Europe.[26] He is known as one of the fathers of modern Roman Catholic missiology. Then came the ministry of Thomas de Jesus, 1564-1627, one of the last great apostles in the vanguard of the Italian Congregation's expansion throughout Europe. He developed the *Desert Houses* of prayer and community service. In 1607, he broke from the superiors in Spain and dedicated himself to missionary projects throughout Europe. He founded new congregations dedicated exclusively for the purpose of providing a support team for missionaries being sent out. This was all incorporated into the Italian Congregation and the ministries continued.[27] Many of the missionaries sent out from Europe were the result of the apostolic vision of Thomas de Jesus. The concept of the missionary *support team*, organized for economic and prayer support of specific missionaries, had come into being. Built upon the foundation of these two men, the whole field of missions, or *missiology*, as a distinct area of theology and ministry practice came into being.

Revolts in Nueva Vizcaya

The pacification of Nueva Vizcaya was not what it seemed. It was subjugation, a foreign occupation, an experiment in cultural imperialism by the Spanish. But strong undercurrents were building under the surface threatening the domination of the Spanish. Disenfranchised indigenous leadership were observing, learning and planning their return to power. The rape of their cultures and the imposition of a foreign religion with utter disdain for the ancient religious expressions were causing a seething hatred for the Spanish, but especially the Jesuits, the black robes that had displaced the indigenous leaders, undermined their authority, and ridiculed their beliefs. More than 40 years had passed since the penetration of Ibarra into their lands changing their lives completely.

Since the Europeans came, the area had been racked with sickness and disease. The following is a list of the known major outbreaks that affected northwest New Spain:[28]

1530-34	Epidemic of measles valley of Culiacan
1535-36	Epidemic of smallpox valley of Culiacan
1545	Epidemics of typhus, pulmonary plague
1550	Epidemic of mumps
1559-63	Epidemics of measles, influenza, mumps, diphtheria

1576-80	Epidemics of typhus, smallpox, measles, mumps
1595	Epidemic of measles
1601-02	Epidemics of smallpox, measles, typhus
1606-07	Epidemics of smallpox, measles
1612-15	Epidemic of typhus
1616-17	Epidemics of measles, smallpox
1623-25	Epidemics of smallpox, typhus, pneumonia
1636-41	Epidemics of smallpox and the plague
1645-47	Epidemic of malaria

Very likely these continuous waves of sickness and disease were the catalyst that finally pushed the Native Americans into rebellion. Most rebellions coincided with one of these major outbreaks. The God of the Jesuits could not save the indigenous people from the terrible deaths that these sicknesses caused. Indigenous leadership claimed that going back to the old gods and the old ways would heal them, and in going back to the old ways the chiefs and shamans would be the rulers once again. Entire societies of natives were under explosive stress: young warriors could not advance without war, old leaders were not respected, foreign gods did not work, and the new taskmasters were excessively hard and cruel. The Xiximes were the first to revolt in 1601.

The Xiximes were not reacting to the Jesuits or the Christian God. They had been subjugated by Ibarra, but essentially left alone after that. Referred to as the *wild people of the mountains* by those having dealings with them, they had been accused of being cannibals, at least more so than other indigenous peoples, but with no substantiation, or contemporary collaborating testimony as to their culinary delights.[29] The 1601 revolt was short-lived, but a second revolt in 1610 was well planned. Seeing the Spanish as the likely source of the diseases plaguing their communities, the Xiximes stockpiled stores, collected arrows, and built up stone fortifications. They attempted an alliance with the Acaxees and the Tepehuanes, but these ancient enemies of the Xiximes could not be persuaded. However, the rebellion was put down and this time the Jesuits were brought in to *reduce* them into controllable villages.[30] Still the other indigenous peoples were watching and learning how the Spanish dealt with rebellion.

The more serious challenge to the Jesuit and the Spanish system was by the Tepehuanes in 1616-20, again coinciding with epidemics of smallpox and measles. Seeing that the Christian God could not or would not help them and seeing their whole way of life being eliminated by the Spanish, this revolt had the purpose of killing and destroying everybody and everything foreign. Most of all they wanted to eliminate the black robes. With this accomplished the indigenous leaders could take back their rightful places and return to their old religions.[31] The rebellion was well planned and took the Spanish by complete surprise. On November 16, 1616, entering Atotonilco, the Tepehuanes martyred ten priests, *because they were Jesuits*, and killed an additional 300 Spanish colonists. They succeeded in convincing both Acaxees and Xiximes to attack Spanish mines and small settlements. By the end of that year, the province was described as destroyed and devastated, almost depopulated of Spaniards.[32]

The rebellion continued into 1620 with a huge loss of property and lives. It is estimated that about 1,000 allied Indians died and about 4,000 Tepehuanes died. It was one of the bloodiest rebellions in northwest New Spain.[33] Afterwards many of the Tepehuanes fled to the other mountain tribes to escape retaliation, especially to the Tarahumara who were as yet not subject to the Spanish. The Jesuits returned after the pacification to reestablish their missions. The Tepehuanes who remained were reorganized into mission communities with native governors and mayors, but under close supervision of the Jesuits. Many more indigenous rebellions would continue to occur, but this was the last large-scale resistance to the Spanish and Jesuit presence in the Northwest New Spain provinces.

In the Sinaloa-Sonora coastal areas indigenous resistance made first encounters difficult for the Jesuits, but it would become one of the more fruitful areas of ministry for them. In 1533, Diego de Guzmán advanced to the north from Culiacán and encountered the Yaquis in the river valley of that name. He succeeded in dispersing the Yaquis but withdrew, impressed with the fighting ability of the Yaquis warriors. Thirty years later Sinaloa was included in the newly organized province of Nueva Vizcaya. The Jesuits began their ministries in the central areas of the current state of Sinaloa, assisting the *encomenderos* to *reduce* the natives who had survived the plagues and diseases to that point. They organized indigenous Christian pueblos on the *encomiendas* for the purposes of evangelism and supplying a labor pool for the plantation economy that was rapidly developing.

The Jesuits pushed into the frontier areas to the north in 1591; then eight years later Diego Martinez de Hurdaide fortified San Felipe and used it as a base camp to conquer the surrounding areas.[34] He subjugated the La Fuerte river groups—the Sinaloas, Tehuecos, Zuaques, and Ahomes indigenous peoples. The Mayo people, who lived between the Mayo and La Fuerte river systems, numbered about 15 towns. As early as 1601, they showed a curious interest in the Jesuit missions of the Culiacan Valley and sent delegations to inspect the churches being built.

The Mayo military leaders signed a treaty of peace with Captain Martinez and invited the Jesuits to come and evangelize the Mayos. In exchange, the Mayo began to aid the Spanish against the Yaqui, their hereditary enemies. "In 1613 . . . the first mission was established in [Mayo] territory by the Jesuit Father Pedro Mendez, who had visited them some years before, [with] over 3,000 persons receiving baptism within 15 days in a population estimated at 20,000. The Jesuits quickly implemented their program of *reducciones* and all the Mayo were congregated into seven indigenous pueblos where mission churches were built"[35] By 1620, all the Mayo and most of the other smaller tribes of the area were baptized totaling nearly 30,000 new Roman Catholics.[36]

The Yaqui group was not quite as welcoming as the Mayo. Occupying approximately 80 autonomous communities in the southern Sonora area on the Yaqui river system, they had fought Guzmán, but welcomed Ibarra who had come in peace in 1565. In 1608, and again in 1610, the Spanish attacked the Yaqui area, but in both cases the Spanish and their native allies were soundly defeated. The Yaqui had a defensive system allowing them to assemble a force of up to 7,000 warriors in a matter of hours; they knew their own territory and fought very well as a unit.[37] They had been badly mauled when they fought Guzmán's army, but since then they had developed ways to fight effectively against the Spanish military tactics.

The Yaqui evidently impressed with what they saw the Jesuits doing among the Mayo, utilized the services of Mayo intermediaries and asked the Society of Jesus to enter Yaqui areas to do missionary work. They were very interested in economic development through the peace-by-purchase program.[38] Though the Jesuits normally did not go in among unpacified indigenous groups, their success with the Mayo by invitation had given them confidence. The invitation was accepted.

The Jesuits came and began their *reducciones* program, congregating the more than 80 Yaqui settlements, about 60,000 people, into eight "sacred" towns or Yaqui indigenous pueblos where churches were built in the center of the new communities. The Yaquis learned the Spanish ways that were of value to them, but steadfastly protected their Yaqui customs and integrity as a nation—much like the Purépecha, another undefeated nation. When silver was discovered in the Yaqui River valley and the Spanish civilians invaded taking land and Yaquis for labor, the Yaqui allied with the Mayo, their ancient enemies, and for the next 190 years the Yaqui people continued to fight the Spanish and then the Mexicans after they separated from Spain.[39] Amazingly through it all they never gave up their expression of the Roman Catholic faith.

Analysis of Spanish Missiology in the Nueva Vizcaya Epoch

The missiological framework with the five major areas of analysis for apostolic missions will now be applied to this Fifth Epoch of conquest. A major shift took place in this epoch as the Society of Jesus entered into the cutting edge of missions with both resources and vision. It was a time when the other mendicant orders that had led the way in indigenous evangelism were experiencing both the displeasure of a maturing secular church in New Spain and had experienced the eroding of their Imperial financial and material support due to European wars and constant attacks on their vital Atlantic shipping lanes. The Franciscans and the Augustinians had their place in the penetration and subjugation of the Native American nations of Nueva Vizcaya, but the leadership of the missionary outreach had passed to the Society of Jesus. Baja California was exclusively the mission field of the Jesuits as well as most of Nueva Vizcaya.

Apostolic Practice: The purpose of the Society of Jesus, as they began work in continental New Spain after losing more than half their numbers in La Florida, was not to focus on evangelism, but to make good disciples out of the new Roman Catholic natives by properly training and mentoring the children of elite indigenous families. Education through boarding schools became their methodology. This strategy worked very well to make good Spanish citizens and stronger Roman Catholics in the well developed cultures of the Central Valley regions. With the conclusion of the Chichimeca wars and the new peace-by-purchase strategy for conquest in the north, the viceroy wanted missionaries to administer the program because he knew the history of uncontrolled Spanish civilians. He wanted friars to be the go-between for the natives and the civil authorities. The well organized, efficient Society of Jesus fit the job description very well.

This new ministry would entail a foundational shift in the missiological thinking of the Society of Jesus in New Spain. They came under the twofold commission, *for the progress of souls and the propagation of the faith*. In La Florida the propagation of the faith did not go so well. In the Central Valleys the progress of souls through education was going very well. Now they were being asked to return to the propagation of the faith, but through socio-cultural change. "While change agents may have a positive effect in the development of communities . . . the primary objective of . . . cross-cultural ministry is to help people come to know Christ and thereby to become his disciples."[40] Propagation of the faith implies dissemination of the gospel message of Jesus Christ. The missionary then becomes God's agent in the transformation of the individual, and then is responsible to disciple that transformed individual to live a changed life within the community thus exerting a positive effect on the wider culture in which they are found. The Jesuits realized they were being called not only to be socio-cultural change agents for the viceroy, but also that the position could provide opportunity to be spiritual transformation agents of God in the process.

Peace-by-purchase was a program of pacification in the place of military conquest. By placing the priest in charge of the program at the local village level, Roman Catholic Christianity became inseparable from the pacification, domestication, and Spanish acculturation processes. Thus the Jesuit priest came to represent all three. This was a great strategic advantage for the evangelization of the indigenous people. The priest had the authority to gather the scattered small communities into indigenous pueblos taking the leadership away from the social and military leaders of the natives and putting himself in their place of leadership. As the one chief/judge/priest, the Jesuit could organize, punish, preach, baptize, and teach, as well as establish local leadership and village structure, set laws, administer the labor force, oversee construction projects, and rural development projects. What made the priests' great powers tolerable for the subjugated people was the "purchase" part of the deal—the priest supplied the food, clothing, tools, plants, and animals that made the whole settlement self-sufficient and, in most cases, even prosper.

The one major disadvantage for the priest-evangelist was that he became the object of all the discontent of the disenfranchised former indigenous chiefs, judges, shamans, and warriors who formerly gained their prestige in battle, war that was now outlawed by the Spanish. The failure to use the indigenous leadership and the undermining or destroying of their positions and functions within the community was the primary weakness of the Jesuit application of the peace-by-purchase system. This failure would eventually cost many of the Jesuit priests their lives.

Apostolic Practice: In the area of evangelism, once the actual Christian evangelism practice was separated from the social development and political reorganization, very little changed from the previous epoch. Evangelism was still essentially preaching to enjoin adults to reject their gods and accept the worship of the Roman Catholic God, but the Jesuits presented many different images and symbols that contradicted the concept of one God. Water baptism was enforced for all children as well as adults if they wanted to participate in the new Spanish pueblo social and economic structure, and most of them did. Therefore indigenous motives for conversion had little to do with religion. Discipleship was still just memorizing some catechisms and reciting some rudimentary prayers by memory. The forms and symbols of respect for the priest as the new political/spiritual leaders were being taught, but these really did not fit the pattern Christ himself taught in the servant-leader model. However, the new forms were appropriate for the Tridentine Roman Catholic model that taught behavior and ritual, but did not affect beliefs or world views of the converts.

Though the Society of Jesus took their very name from the Lord Jesus Christ, there does not seem to be much more emphasis given to preaching Christ than in previous epochs. In the churches they founded, there was still more emphasis given to Mariology, crosses, and saints, than to the resurrected, glorified, Savior. In the schools being founded, the student bodies quickly became more European and Mestizo, or *mestizada* natives, rather than those that were culturally indigenous. This was a major a goal of the Jesuits that was being accomplished. But that did not necessarily make them Christian. The schools were not an important factor in evangelism, but they did make the community *appear* to be a Spanish community.

In the area of ecclesiology, the expression of the church within the indigenous culture, the same pattern of constructing purely European expressions of architecture and adornments with Tridentine Roman Catholic high forms of religion were practiced in the worship services. Without indigenous leaders the natives were attending the services but they were not really participating in them. Roman Catholic fiestas were being taught and select ones celebrated but less emphasis was being placed on drama compared to the earlier epochs. Dance, processions, and drinking seemed to fit much better with the culture of the northern tribes for worship, but those forms were usually practiced outside of the church buildings and apart from the priests.

The result was that much Roman Catholic tradition and European culture was being taught by the Jesuits, rather than biblical doctrine with the consequence that much of the salvation message was not known, nor was it being taught to the indigenous people. The Jesuits were doing an excellent job of teaching Tridentine Roman Catholicism which was being incorporated into the native religious systems along with their previous understandings of the spiritual world around them.

It should be noted that the missionary as an incarnate messenger to the indigenous culture showing forth the love of God in an unthreatening, intercultural dialogue, was not the Jesuit method of evangelism in this epoch. They were very threatening, culturally quite insensitive, and to the indigenous leadership they were arrogant and derogatory. The cultural blindness of the Jesuits rendered them unable to see themselves as the indigenous people saw them; therefore, they were totally surprised at the violence of the rebellions directed towards them.

Church structure and mission: There seem to be no records of the formal transfer of church jurisdictions from the Jesuit structure to the secular church during the period of Jesuit missionary activity. To their credit the Jesuits did have the best working relationship with the secular church of all the orders at the beginning of their ministries. However, as the order became both economically and politically more powerful, the secular church more and more saw them as a threat to their authority both within the church and without. When the Society of Jesus was expelled from all New Spain in 1767, all properties under their jurisdictions came under the direct authority of the Viceroy as civil head of the church under the Royal Patronage given by the Pope to the Spanish Crown.

Under the Viceroy's supervision social planners attempted to move all the Native American pueblos from frontier mission status into secular parish church status. However, few secular priests wanted to live in the native pueblos. Secular clergy did not feel they could minister and survive where semi heathen parishioners still called drunken dancing *worship* and paid their offerings in eggs and squash, if at all.[41]

The viceroy decided that there was still a need for missionaries and the Franciscans were the only other ones willing and available. They were more than happy to take over what they felt was their rightful ministry all along, but found themselves very hard pressed to come up with enough personnel to supply friars for all the vacancies left by the Jesuits. The larger towns and pueblos with more settled populations became part of the closest parish to it while most of the small former Jesuit missions continued under mission status and had to suffice with a visit now and then by a cleric. This had the effect of strengthening the syncretic indigenous aspects of worship practice while blunting the impact of Roman Catholic practices.

In most rural areas there was a Roman Catholic Church where pre-Columbian beliefs were exercised under the symbolism and artifacts of the Roman Catholic ritual. The gulf between common belief and practice and high Roman Catholic Church worship just continued to expand. As indigenous populations died off and Mestizo populations grew up in their place, visits from priests became less and less frequent until eventually the installations in many rural areas were nearly abandoned by the clergy, but maintained by local residents for their own forms of religious service and worship.

In the missiological area of the *Gospel and Other Religions* there was still a total inability to recognize any religious expressions other than Roman Catholic, whether pagan or Christian, as being valid. There was an expanded ability to recognize pagan elements that had been incorporated into worship in the indigenous areas as neo-Roman Catholic. Although the inquisition was still in effect to deal with heretics and blasphemers, rarely was it exercised at all, principally because the law forbids applying the inquisition to the Native Americans.

The more specific area of *Salvation and Non-Christians* was still understood in the broadest sense that pagan were lost and had to have the gospel preached to them. The primary impetus of this great missionary endeavor was still the clear understanding that only the vicarious suffering of Christ can save. Therefore the un-baptized were lost. It was still imperative that the natives in paganism be baptized somehow. The basic Tridentine doctrines of salvation were still only understood in terms of water baptism and purgatory, the doctrine that says those that are baptized, with or without understanding, shall somehow get through purgatory and be saved eventually.

The fifth missiological area for analysis is that of *Christianity and Culture*. In none of the preceding epochs has there been such a complete rape and destruction of the indigenous culture as here in the Northern Province under the Society of Jesus who took very seriously the mandate to make Spanish Roman Catholics and culturally Spanish citizens of the indigenous tribes of the Northwest. The Society of Jesus, with their collective choleric personality, and with both the civil and religious powers entrusted to them, were literally unstoppable as they totally dismantled the native societies and reassembled them into the Spanish Roman Catholic pattern. Externally a new, seemingly successful social-hierarchal pyramid was built with the Jesuits at the top while internally the Jesuits were building an active volcano that trembled under the stress of social pressures without release until the day came when it blew up in rebellion.

The most serious flaw in the Jesuit missionary endeavor in New Spain was the rejection of cultural leaders within the northern tribes as the peace-by-purchase program of social engineering was implemented. They were faithful to the theological principles as dictated by the

Council of Trent, installing their icons and symbols, but the teaching through catechisms did not impart sufficient understanding to avoid the syncretism that was being accepted as common Roman Catholic religion among the indigenous peoples. In doing so the Jesuits had left the door wide open for indigenous revitalization movements. The people were standing with one foot in each cultural world. The natural leadership, those who had the most to gain, were still in place to make the revitalization of indigenous culture and religions happen. All that was lacking was a spark to set off the explosions; the epidemics of disease provided those sparks.

Summary

In this fifth Epoch of conquest, the Society of Jesus had come into its own as a mission force in New Spain. Their methodology was strongly shaped by their commission from the viceroy to be the instruments of administration for the peace-by-purchase system of indigenous subjugation for the northern tribes. Their Tridentine Theology and close relationship with the secular church constrained their practice to *reductions* and baptism of children and consenting adults. Discipleship was still simply learning the catechisms, European culture and traditional Roman Catholic expressions of worship. The Jesuits were still exclusive and inflexible in their treatment of other religions. Their failings were in the areas of not recognizing the validity of non-Roman Catholic cultures, not identifying with another culture, and not allowing critical Christian principles to be expressed in another cultural context. Failure to recognize and utilize native leadership and incorporate that leadership into the new pueblos proved to be their greatest barrier to success. It would take several years of warfare with the resulting dispersion of their people through utter defeat before the Tepehuanes would again submit to being called Roman Catholics.

CHAPTER IX

SIXTH EPOCH:
THE NUEVO MEXICO

Epoch Six Introduction

As seen before, the first contact with the indigenous groups of New Mexico began in the two previous epochs of conquest. The first was the long march of the four survivors of the Narváez expedition and the tales they told. Then came the Mendoza expeditions, first the one by Niza, then in 1540, the conclusive Coronado expedition that determined there were no cities of gold, but there were indeed cities and very good land for colonization by the Spanish. Coronado had attacked the Zuni, made peace, and then set up base camp for exploration. He sent teams as far west as the mouth of the Colorado River and as far northwest as the Grand Canyon; then he sent the Alvarado company east to a great river and off into the great plains with the indescribably huge herds of wild cattle-looking beasts. With a thorough understanding of the area and leaving the Zuni and Pueblo with a thorough understanding of who the Spanish were, what they were like, and what they intended, Coronado returned to the south.

With a more factual understanding of what lay to the far north, the administration of New Spain, the colonists, and the adventurers pondered the next step for themselves, the King, and God—probably in that order. First the Chichimeca war had to be successfully concluded and Nueva Vizcaya had to be occupied and stabilized. After the Chichimeca wars, with the wealth of the silver mines to back him and with orders from Felipe II of Spain who decreed the pacification of New Mexico *without* expending funds from the treasury,[1] Juan de Oñate was chosen to lead an expedition to the New Mexico on the other side of the northern deserts, to pacify and colonize it in the name of the Crown. In 1598, as Governor, Captain-General and Adelantado, Oñate—with 130 families, 270 single men, 83 wagons and carts, 7,000 cattle herded by drovers, and 11 Franciscan friars—crossed the Rio del Norte (Rio Grande) at El Paso del Norte where the mighty river passes through the mountains and took possession of the province of New Mexico.[2] These were not the first of the Friars to tread upon the sands of the Pueblo nations.

The Pueblo People

New Mexico apparently received its name from the Spanish who had crossed the vast wastelands from the high civilizations of the Mexicans of New Spain, and then came upon the cities of the Pueblo people and felt that they were seeing another high civilization like Mexico of the Aztec, at least compared to the hunter-gatherers of the Chichimeca and Nueva Vizcaya regions—therefore the name: *New* Mexico. Obviously the people of the Pueblos were descendants of the cliff dwellers of the Pajarito Plateau. Late thirteenth and early fourteenth century cliff dwellers abandoned their cliff cities for no discernible reason yet discovered and migrated to the upper river valleys of the Rio Grande. They replaced or melded with the pit-house dwellers then occupying the region, but maintained the same social patterns that linked them directly to the people of the cliff towns.

In the centuries before the Spanish came, the individual Pueblos had forged a way of life, an indigenous culture that was highly religious in nature. Religion organized the whole environment and all of pueblo life. Worship was everywhere because the spirit was everywhere. Their faith helped create a life of order, moderation, and unanimity from a combined and voluntary consent of the whole people of each town. There seem to be no political leaders or chiefs as they are distinguished today. Their economy was enhanced by well developed trade routes that brought products from East Texas the Great Plains and as far away as the Purépecha Empire of southern Mexico. It was the traders that brought news of the strange, bearded white men that captured whole nations making them slaves and who spread terrible sicknesses that killed in a most grotesque manner.

Everybody together in the Pueblo owned all the land, all the ritual places for worship, and all the sacred relics of the Pueblo. Assignment of usage was by a council of elders who represented one aspect of their governing structure. Land use was allocated to heads of families according to need. Rooms or apartments of the Pueblo city were a permanent possession of individual families for as long as the family existed. More rooms could be added to them as the family expanded, but when the family died off, the apartment was abandon. Families owned personal objects and items in their apartment and they owned the fruit or produce of their plot of ground which included corn, beans, squash, pumpkins, gourds, and cotton. Their technology included systems of canals for irrigation of crops, and looms for weaving cotton and maguey fiber cloth for clothing. Each town had a number of internal organizations, each with particular functions or jobs to do, including secret societies with inherited memberships.

Most authors use the term *cacique* for the apparent leader of the Pueblo. However, the Spanish word has a very different meaning than the functions allocated to a Pueblo leader. The Spanish applied the name *cacique* (an hacienda administrator or supervisor that governed in place of the owner) and the term *Pueblo* (small town) quite erroneously, but both have continued to be used giving the wrong connotation to the particular place or person. In the American English vocabulary, a *senior pastor* or a minister of religion better describes what was called the Pueblo cacique. The residents of his town or district were his congregation. As in Islam the civil and religious laws were the same thing for the Pueblo, bringing further consternation to the Spanish who only knew a clear division of King and Pope. The Pueblo leader was chosen by members of his secret society and served for life. In his duties he was first and foremost a holy man; he blessed, approved, and often presided at worship ceremonies, and his personal duties included a great deal of fastings and prayers. He appointed men to a type of priesthood for a stipulated time of service. In general he was the fountain head of all spiritual belief and practice for his pueblo or town.

Another whole order of cultic practice was the Kachina worship structures. There were usually several Kachina cults in each Pueblo; each had a head similar to a priest in his duties. The cultic celebration was the medium by which people of that cultic group could formally take part in the religious life of the Pueblo, just as parishioners attend a church service. The head of the cult held custody of the Kachina masks which were used in the great community Kachina prayer dances, and oversaw the care of the Kachina carvings. Only mature, married men of good standing could wear the Kachina mask as it was believed that he actually became part of, or one with, the Kachina who was an ancestor spirit that interceded for the Pueblo.

In the creation story, according to the theology of the Pueblos, people emerged from the underworld along with the spirit that is in all things. Some of the spirit was good, some bad. Father sun walked the sky by day and then descended into the underworld at night. The lesser moon was placed in the sky in the absence of the sun, but his weakness was assisted by the stars that are always there. Clouds were dead ancestors; all were spirits that came back to bless the people. The Pueblos believed that man must be in harmony with spirit which is in all things. Prayer and observance were part of daily life taking many forms but always visible forms such as turkey feathers or corn meal, the stuff of life that carried prayers, even pollen from flowers served the same purpose. The prayer stick was about eight inches, carved and painted, and could be used locally or left in strategic places to maintain the prayers longer. Group prayer, in which the whole community participated, took the form of fiestas with sacred drums, music, and dance. Often a *koshare* (sacred clown), a masked dancer, intermingled to mock the participants and the spirits as he moved among the people.

Much of this theology was represented in the Kachina worship patterns. The dolls represented the ancestor spirits in the clouds and thus became instruments of prayer like the prayer sticks and the turkey feathers that materially bore the prayers and maintained them constantly before the gods. These Kachina spirits spent half a year with the Pueblos and half a year back in the underworld. Large elaborate masks also were used in the major celebrations, in particular the calling of the Kachina from the underworld at the appropriate time each year to do their ministries for the people. Scholars[3] have noted the coincidence of the appearance of the Kachina religion with the marked difference in the construction of the Anastasia towns, as well as a climatic change to a dryer, drought-prone time. This religion, introduced about 700 years ago still organizes the Puebloan life today.

This general description of the indigenous people of the Pueblo world could be misleading. *Pueblo* was the Spanish name given to them, but they called themselves the Hopis in the far west, the Zunis to the west also, and the Tiwas to the north. In the center of the Pueblo area were the Towas, the Tewas, and the Tanos. More to the south, still along the Rio del Norte, were the Southern Tiwas. Still further south were the Tompiros and the Piros. These were the major areas or concentrations of the more than 60 *pueblos* or living compounds recorded by the Chamuscado-Rodriguez party. These loose confederacies in turn allied and fought, but in general lived together in mutual acceptance of one another.[4]

Other indigenous groups in the New Mexico region were the nomadic plains dwellers who traded with the Pueblos primarily through the great Pecos Pueblo to the east at the edge of the Great Plains, though neither group ever really trusted the other. Two groups of Apaches—the Lipans and the Mescaleros—were nomadic and lived almost completely off the buffalo within the confines of west Texas, but there were also groups of desert Apaches to the west of the Pueblos. "The social unit of the Lipan and Mescalero Apaches was the extended family. Several extended families generally stayed together and were led by their most prominent member, who acted as chief advisor and director of group affairs."[5] A number of these groups lived in close proximity to one another and could unite their warriors for defensive or offensive purposes or for social or ceremonial occasions. The leader of the combined groups was the band leader. The Lipans had no formal organization larger than the band. They dressed in buffalo skins and lived in tents made of tanned and greased hides, which they loaded onto pack dogs when they moved with the buffalo herds.[6]

The Apaches were the first of the plains Native Americans to adapt to the horse. Learning to care for, and ride with runaways, traded, or captured animals, the Apaches quickly adapted to their use of horses and the great advantages they provided for mobility and war. Formerly peaceful trade relationships between Apaches and the Pueblos deteriorated as the Spanish-dominated Pueblos were discouraged by the Europeans to trade with the Apaches and were forced by the Spanish to work the farms and ranches. When the Pueblos became unwilling or unable to trade with the Apaches, these nomadic plains people turned their new equestrian skills to raiding. Within a generation after their arrival Spanish settlers and the Pueblos of New Mexico were suffering from almost continuous Apache raids.[7]

The Jumano were another indigenous group, evidently related to the Pueblo people. They occupied the Rio Grande valley from the El Paso area and on south to the Rio Conchos area. In the upper Rio Grande they were sedentary much like the Pueblo people. Surviving testimony says that they grew corn, beans, and squash for food, made pottery to store the food and seeds, and wove cotton cloth for clothes and blankets. They went naked most of the time but used clothing and blankets in the winter. They tattooed themselves over most of their bodies; the men shaved their heads except for one spot at the top of their heads where feathers were attached to the long hair.

The plains Jumano occupied the region of north Texas, between the two great sedentary people the Pueblos and the East Texas Caddos. They hunted buffalo and moved with the herds, lived in teepees as did the other nomadic plains people. As the Apache, they used dogs to carry much of their belongings while migrating. They were traders and often trafficked goods as they wondered the plains between the two great indigenous groups east and west. The great annual indigenous market at the springs of the Comal River in Texas, now New Braunfels, was the principle gathering place for an exchange of goods as the Pecos Pueblo was to the west side of the plains.

The Conquest of New Mexico

With the possible exception of Upper California, this epoch of conquest of New Mexico is probably better documented, studied, and archeologically explored, than any other epoch. Because of this, with one exception, I will only recommend a number of books from the bibliography for any reader who would like to delve into this in more detail. The evangelism of the Pueblos is the main focus of this study and I will proceed with that emphasis, noting the political and social events as they relate directly to evangelism. Recommended readings:

Paul Horgan, *Great River*
Elizabeth John, *Storms Brewed in Other Men's Worlds*

John Kessell, *Kiva, Cross, and Crown,* and also, *Spain in the Southwest*

Robert Preucel, *Archaeologies of the Pueblo Revolt*

David Roberts, *The Pueblo Revolt*

Christopher Vecsey, *On the Padres' Trail*

David Weber, *The Spanish Frontier in North America*

The one exception we must note because of its' effect on evangelism was the so called Acoma revolt and its aftermath. Acoma, built on top of a high bluff for defensive purposes, an undefeated stronghold for many centuries, submitted to Spanish dominance. But in the early period of pacification an incident occurred that even today influences the mentality of Pueblo people. It is a story of cultural conflict, of an outsider's inability to understand cultural symbols and meanings. It is a story of disaster resulting from a group of people acting without knowing the precise meaning another people give to apparently insignificant issues within their own culture.

Thirty soldiers under Oñate's nephew Juan de Zaldivar stopped at Ácoma to barter and pay for supplies needed for their travels. During the exchange one soldier got into an argument with a woman over a turkey. A shout arose, and the Pueblo people arose. The soldiers attempted to form a defensive circle within the Pueblo and then tried to beat off the ensuing attack. In the three hour ruckus that followed, 11 soldiers and two native servants died, including the nephew of Oñate. The rest of the soldiers fled.[8]

Oñate organized his army for vengeance and attacked the stronghold. With a clever deception the fortress city was taken; 500 Ácoma warriors had died, 300 women and children died during the battle in the defense of their homes.[9] Many had actually committed suicide jumping off the cliffs rather than be taken prisoners by the Spanish. The Spanish claimed an illusion of St. James had appeared—only two Spanish soldiers had perished in the battle. About 80 Pueblo men and over 500 women and children were taken captive.[10] All the captive children under 12 years of age were declared innocent, taken from their families and given over to the Franciscans for care and nurture as indentured servants. All captives between 12 and 25 were sentenced to 25 years of servitude. All other male captives, only about 24 left,[11] had their right foot severed and in addition sentenced to 25 years of servitude. It would be two generations before the decedents of the Ácomas would return and rebuild their Pueblo city.

Over the next few years, the Spanish would learn that, to the Pueblos, the turkey was not primarily meant for food, for the turkey feathers bore the prayers of the people and were thus sacred to them. When the soldier attempted to buy or take the turkey from the Ácoma woman simply to eat it, the woman, horrified at losing her means of prayer and being treated so crudely by the foreigner, resisted him by calling others to her aid. This misunderstanding triggered the entire rebellion of the Ácoma. The turkey cost the Spanish 13 lives, the entire city of Ácoma lost its population to death and slavery, all its children were carried off by strangers into servitude, and the Spanish were dreaded and accursed for nearly three generations, eventually resulting in the great Pueblo revolt of 1680 in which every Spanish citizen and their indigenous converts were killed or chased clear out of the province of New Mexico.[12] When the Spanish come to understand the significance of the turkey to the Pueblo people, a whole new understanding of the significance of Ácoma developed.

A bronze statue of Oñate stands at a visitor's center near Española, N.M. On the 400th anniversary of the conquest of New Mexico a celebration was held. Within days the right foot of the statue was cut off by the *Brothers of Ácoma*.[13] The tragedy of Ácoma has not been forgotten by the Pueblo people over 400 years later.

Oñate was under orders to pacify New Mexico by *Peace with Purchase*, not to conquer them as in previous epochs of conquest. Not only had he used *fire and sword* against the inhabitants of the land, but he had violated his own commission in doing so. The friars came thinking they were to evangelize pacified indigenous Americans but instead found themselves dealing with the conquered, walking wounded, a people subjugated by force. The Pueblo people fled their towns when they saw Spanish coming; the few Puebloans that the friars could gather cowered from them and feared their very presence. The Ácoma "fire and sword" conquest would be a major deterrent to Christianity, and the Ácoma battle would become a primary reason for recalling Oñate.

The Franciscan Missionaries

The Franciscans had taken on the responsibility to evangelize the newest Northern Province. By the end of the Chichimeca wars, most of the previous works of the Franciscans had been secularized and incorporated into dioceses of the secular church. In 1572, the Crown of Spain had ordered the Jesuit *doctrinas* incorporated into dioceses under the control of bishops as a cost-saving measure.[14] The secular church was telling the Franciscans to go find other pagans to evangelize, and many friars were anxious to do just that. Fray Marcos de Niza had gone with Coronado's expedition to serve as his guide and counselor. However, Coronado found the friar's descriptions of the land and cities wanting, actually calling him a liar, and sent him packing back to Mexico. This left one priest, two lay brothers, and two native helpers who continued with Coronado.

Of the five friars who remained with the Pueblo when the Coronado expedition returned to Old Mexico, Luis de Escalona went to the Pecos Pueblo and Juan de la Cruz to the Tiguex Pueblo. A number of the Tlaxcalan expeditionary forces, all baptized Roman Catholics, chose to remain with the Zuni and were eagerly welcomed into that Pueblo district. Juan de Padilla who had accompanied the search team to the east returned to work with the natives of the Missouri river valley. All five of these friars were never heard from again and presumed to have died. Of the first six Franciscan missionaries to New Mexico, five died the martyr's death, and one returned to Mexico City in disgrace. It was not a very impressive start for the Tridentine Roman Catholic Church. However, some Franciscan missionaries could not forget that many native souls awaited conversion in the Pueblo towns and that the work begun by Franciscan martyrs cried for completion.

In 1573, laws were passed that stated the penetration to the north be by pacification, not conquest, and by missionaries with only token military escorts as Spain's agents of discovery, as well as for the conversion of indigenous people. Therefore in 1581, a trio of friars with an escort of 8 Spaniards and 19 Tlaxcalan aids, known as the Rodriguez-Chamuscado expedition, drove a large contingent of livestock with them as they traveled through the land of the Pueblo, studying them, visiting Pueblos and bringing a message of peace. When Juan de Santa Maria decided to leave the expedition and return to Mexico to report on all they had found to that point, the alarmed Puebloans, believing he would bring more people back with him, decided to kill him. As he lay sleeping local natives dropped a big rock on his head, crushing him in the manner they reserved for a man with an evil spirit. The rest of the party who had ventured out on to the Great Plains encountered Apaches who were appeased by the shooting of about 40 buffalo. Upon returning to the Pueblo area and learning of the death of friar Santa Maria, the eight soldiers decided to withdraw to the south. The two remaining friars determined to stay and evangelize the Pueblo, and all 19 Tlaxcalan helpers agreed to stay with them. The whole party that stayed was soon to join the other martyrs of New Mexico—only two of the helpers escaped the Pueblos to bring news of what had happened to the friars and their Tlaxcalan helpers to the silver mining town of Santa Barbara in the south.

Antonio de Espejo led a small party back to the Pueblo to confirm or rescue the friars, bringing with him two more friars. Espejo took the Rio Conchos route, then up the Rio Grande spending time with the Jumano pueblos at the river intersections, naming it La Junta. He confirmed the deaths of the friars but continued on up the Rio Grande as far as the Keres Pueblos. The friars returned to Santa Barbara with their sad news confirmed. History records some Franciscans who tried to introduce the Christian faith at Ácoma, Zuni, and Hopi Pueblos, where the Espejo expedition had visited, but Espejo's conclusion was that Christianization of these areas would require military conquest.

The brutal governor of Nuevo León had followed Guzmán's path to riches through the illegal slave trade, preying on the Jumano and Tamaulipans of the lower Rio Grande. The Viceroy had him arrested, but his henchman Lieutenant Governor Gaspar Castaño de Sosa with a gang of 60 frontiersmen, called by the Viceroy outlaws, criminals, and murderers, rebels against God and king, and all the riffraff left over from the war against the Chichimecas escaped to the north following the Pecos River to New Mexico, capturing indigenous people for slaves as they went. Castaño de Sosa subdued a number of Pueblo towns, and erected crosses in each town to give his poorly concealed motives a religious flavor. Meanwhile, the Viceroy had sent Captain Morlete with 40 soldiers in pursuit of Castaño de Sosa and his band. On the way they met returning frontiersmen and traders with captured native slaves on the trail. These men were promptly arrested and the native captives set free to return to their homes. Castaño was caught at the Santo Domingo Pueblo, arrested, and returned to Mexico in chains.[15] It does not appear that any friars were involved in either one of these two penetrations into New Mexico, which was out of character with official conquest policy, but understandable in a context of rebellion.

It seems strange that 15 years passed between the Coronado conquest of New Mexico and Oñate's pacification campaign. The reasons for the delay were external to the expansion of New Spain. In the last 15 years of the sixteenth century, the English pirate Thomas Cavendish was raiding Spanish settlements all along the coasts of the Americas, stealing, burning, and murdering as he went. In 1588, the Spanish Armada was being destroyed by the English fleet of Francis Drake, another gruesome pirate who had pillaged and destroyed peaceful Spanish settlements throughout the Caribbean. But Drake's fleet had essentially only destroyed armed merchantmen in that famous sea battle, while the core of the Spanish Armada, the galleons of the Atlantic fleet, survived their voyage home. Few of Drake's vessels had dared to challenge a Spanish Galleon. Then a year later, the English Armada was rebuffed by the Spanish off the coast of Spain. The Spanish Crown had to default on its debt repayments in 1596, throwing the Spanish empire into economic confusion, which greatly affected the colonies. But the failure of the English Armada was a turning point in that Spanish-English war ended in the peace of 1604. Spain was also fighting both France and the United Provinces of the low country at the same time. These pressures on the Spanish empire and on its finances were the reasons penetration to the north was put on the back burner of priorities, delaying Oñate's expedition for over five years.

The population of the New Mexico Pueblos was estimated at approximately 80,000 at the time of Spanish penetration. There were 11 friars with Oñate's pacification expedition. This was double the number he had asked for in his contract which had specified that only friars from the Franciscan order be sent to avoid competition between orders. Even at this point the secular church was still challenging the mendicant orders. On the eve of Oñate's departure, the bishop of Guadalajara challenged the exclusion of *all others* interpreting this to mean the exclusion of secular clerics. He demanded that the churches founded in New Mexico belong to his diocese only[16] but the challenge failed.

All the previous clerics along with their indigenous helpers who had stayed in New Mexico had perished. This did not phase the small band of Franciscan missionaries. Oñate, once he felt established, decided it was time to begin the conversion of souls, the exaltation of the Holy Roman Catholic Church, and the preaching of the Holy Gospel. The Father President addressed a gathering of 31 Pueblo leaders and explained the salvation message to them. He asked if they would like to be saved at that time and the response was no. First, they desired to be instructed in all that was being proposed to them as necessary for this salvation. Then if they liked what was being taught, they would gladly respond in a positive way. But if they did not like what was being taught, it would not do well to force anyone to follow this new teaching that the Spanish proposed.

The Father President of the small group then divided up the friars into individual responsibilities of perishes over which they would preside. To Father Francisco de Miguel was given the province of Pecos beyond the eastern mountains including 40 towns and the nomadic people of the plains—one man for the people of Eastern New Mexico and all of West Texas! To Father Juan Claros was given all the towns of the Tigua language group to the south along the Rio Grande River; Father Juan de Rosas the province of the Keres language on the Rio Grande River and everything north from there; Father Cristóbal de Salazar the Tewa towns to the north; Francisco de Zamora the province of the Picuries and Taos and river towns to the north together with the Apaches north and east of the snowy mountains; Father Alonzo de Lugo the Jemez province of nine towns and all the Apaches west of the river; Father Andrés Corchado the city of Ácoma on its rock, the Zuni and Hopi far to the west, and the Sia province. Each was to go alone to his perish, some up to weeks away walking. Remember these are Franciscan friars in their brown robes, rope belt, and barefoot or with sandals, men of faith and little else as they followed to their destination the Puebloan leaders who had come to hear the governor and agreed to listen to the teaching of the friars.

A wagon train of supplies arrived around Christmas time and with it six more friars. Nearly every supply train in the future would bring a few more friars, and, as quickly as they arrived, they were spread out among the various mission works in progress or sent to start new works. By 1625, there were 50 churches built and 26 friars ministering through the mission system. In 1629, Estevan de Perea led a group of 30 friars with 36 heavily loaded oxcarts into Santa Fe. Eventually over 200 Franciscan friars would make the pilgrimage north to the Pueblo towns to preach the Roman Catholic Apostolic message and the gospel according to Trent to the Pueblo people.

From the beginning it was the purpose of the friars to destroy the religion of the Pueblo people and replace it with Roman Catholic Christianity as in all previous epochs of conquest. Without understanding the deeper meanings of the indigenous faith, such as the prayer dances, the prayer sticks, and everything related to the Kachina expressions, or the deep religious nature of the Pueblo people as touching everything around them, the friars set about systematically to eliminate all Pueblo religious symbols. The practices of the Kachina expressions were expressly forbidden. The "false idols" were destroyed when possible, "the padres burned thousands of religious objects, storming the kivas periodically and confiscating masks and statuary . . . Pueblo ceremonialism was suffused with sexual expression, including displays of homosexuality and bestiality, and the padres were determined to wipe it out."[17] This had the effect of forcing the Kachina worship underground where it thrived under the guise of Roman Catholic forms of worship or in syncretic Roman Catholic expressions.

Punishment for continuing to practice the Puebloan religion was designed to exterminate the practices. The Hopi were particularly resistant. Individuals were shamed with public whippings for their intransigence. One Hopi who was unrepentant received 200 lashes and was paraded publicly before being sold into servitude at auction. But even this type of punishment did not break the Hopi, most of who resisted the missionary inroads and killed the evangelists whenever they could.

In the power struggle between the civil government and the Franciscans, the government officials, including the governor himself, would often encourage expressions of indigenous religion and protect their religious practices if for no other reason than to oppose the political power of the Franciscans. Therefore the Franciscans used the legal charges and methods of inquisition against the Spanish civil leaders. But inquisition disciplines depended upon civil authorities for execution of justice and, therefore, were limited to excommunication for extreme cases. The Puebloans, sensing the discord between the temporal and spiritual authorities, would often play one against the other for their own self preservation and to continue their indigenous way of life.

By the 1650s there were as many as 20,000 baptized Puebloans but never more than 30 to 40 Franciscans at any one time. Their period of service was normally ten years on the field, upon which they could retreat to a monastery and enter a time of rest, meditation, and study. However, constant tension persisted between the Kachina and Roman Catholic religious systems. The indigenous religion was ingrained and had not been repudiated in any practical way. New diseases had come with the new God and his representatives and neither religious system served to stop the epidemics that just kept coming.

Both systems had an almanac of ceremonialism, and the Pueblo people loved fiestas and pageants. Both systems had their ritual places like the kivas and the plazas for the Puebloans, and the churches with their plazas in front where the fiestas and celebrations took place according to the theology they were expressing. Both systems had much religious paraphernalia. The Puebloans had the Kachina fetishes, the prayer sticks, masks, and tobacco with sacred pipes; the Roman Catholics had crosses, rosaries, statues, medals, holy water and incense for their rituals. The Pueblos had their initiations into secret societies, rites of passage, and name giving. The Roman Catholics had baptisms with name giving, confirmations, and membership, with exclusive rights for members such as communion, installations, and ordinations.

The Puebloans held to their high theology of the underworld, the Great Spirit, the spirits of ancestors, and holy places. They expressed their common worship through the Kachina ceremonies, while each had their own familiar or favorite Kachinas for daily communion and for which they maintained personal alters. The Roman Catholics had their monotheistic dogmas, catechisms, and songs, but prayed to the mother of God who had no mother, to crosses and pictures, and to a huge number of saints that really seemed to be doing the same things as Kachinas but now with new, foreign names. Compliance with the correct rituals of these holy powers had positive benefits, according to both religions, although what those powers supposedly were differed from one to the other.

The Franciscans regarded the Pueblo religion as devil worship and the Kachina rituals as idolatry. The Pueblo priests were regarded as satanic priest and dangerous enemies of the Franciscans. To the friars the sky-world of heaven was the direct opposite of the Puebloan underworld which to the friars obviously was hell. Franciscans felt the Pueblo reverence for nature was worshiping the creation rather than the Creator. These differences should have been more obvious, but in spite of all the new church buildings, and the great multitude of baptisms registered, the two systems seemed to co-exist in constant tension while flowing along together. When the fullness of incompatibility finally dawned in 1680, for the first and only time in New Spain history, an indigenous nation threw out the Spanish.

Franciscan Methodologies in New Mexico

In previous epochs of conquest a pattern in the methodologies of the Franciscans evolved as they adapted to a variety of cultures in different geographic areas. This pattern can be expressed in five strategic areas[18] and can be used to evaluate the application of Franciscan strategy with the New Mexico Pueblos. According to Christopher Vecsey, the first step was the *entrance* by which the friars penetrated into the new mission field. But in the case of the Pueblo, this was not done according to the pattern defined by Vecsey primarily because the entrance was marred by several failed attempts before actually gaining entrance with the Coronado expedition. For reasons we shall never know the testimony of the first Franciscan friars was rejected and they were killed. Solitary figures without backing and without protection, they gave their lives for their faith and the Roman Catholic Church.

The 11 friars accompanying the Coronado expedition were not equipped with finery, music, and ceremony. They divided up the land into provinces and each priest went off alone with little but their spiritual authority as an asset and faith in the calling of their God. As wagon trains came, usually at least one per year, they would bring more friars, more supplies, tools, nails, hinges, seeds, seedlings, animals for breeding, and always more supplies for the necessary religious functions of the church. With these gifts for the peace-by-purchase program, the friars could require labor from the Pueblos for the necessary structures of the mission. As the mission complex grew, so did the number of Puebloans that became dependent upon the mission complex for their subsistence.

During his initiation time the priest learned the language, the customs, and developed leadership among the Pueblos for the different tasks at hand. The friars taught how to make adobe bricks that could be substantial enough for the large edifices of the mission compound, while learning indigenous methods for similar tasks. He taught the use of tools and wood craft and taught how to plant the new seeds and seedlings while learning the indigenous methods of planting and the ceremonies that were necessary for a productive harvest from their understanding. He taught animal husbandry, horticulture, and a number of home industries while he was learning how to adapt the indigenous technologies if they better served the purpose at hand.

While the priest was learning the language there were usually indigenous men from Old Mexico, or those that had already learned sufficient Spanish from among the Puebloans to act as rudimentary translators. The friar could teach by example doing for the Puebloans and then doing with the Puebloans all that he was trying to teach. Children are quick to learn, and they are the best conversational language teachers for new learners. They were the focus of the novice friar's energies during the initial entrance stage. The adults were eager to learn the new plants, new techniques, and new technologies the Spanish had to offer. Those combined with their own methodologies increased the variety and supply of food stuffs which is always a blessing to any agrarian people. Yet it was the livestock that would change their lives and living on a much larger scale. The upper Rio Grande is a tough, unforgiving landscape for any people to scratch out a living. To continue their existence, the Puebloans learned all they could from these strange invaders from the south.

Secondly, after the entrance, the Franciscans attempted to move themselves into the center of native life, especially the spiritual life of the people. The center piece of that control was the church and friary in the population center. The problem with this strategic point was that the Pueblos were already there, and there was no place in the city master plans for a church. In most cases, the Pueblo people did not want the church in their city. Therefore the majority of these first churches were built *beside* the Pueblo. This gave the church compound adequate space for construction, for expansion, and to have a patio or grounds for enclosing all the mission's animals and specialty work areas.

The drawback was that it left the Puebloan worship areas intact. The time-honored custom of the Franciscans of building their churches in the former worship areas as both a symbol of dominance over the old religion, and to keep an uninterrupted flow of people to that "holy" area, could not be implemented with the Pueblo. It also permitted the Puebloans to continue with their old ways of worship and celebration under the noses of the Spanish, much to their chagrin. This was a cause of unending conflict between the Franciscan and the indigenous Pueblo priests of the societies responsible for the Kachina rituals. However, it did provide the Christian congregation a relatively safe haven from the external attacks, whether physical or verbal.

Thirdly, this safe-haven mission complex allowed the friars to begin their visits around the periphery of their assigned territory, knowing they always had a base to which they could return. In some provinces these visitation areas meant walking up to several weeks. Often the friar was accompanied by a number of indigenous helpers brought from Old Mexico, or acquired from among the Puebloans. Their objective was to developed another congregation, build another mission complex, and eventually send a full-time friar who could make that into a base of operations for himself. The new friars who were coming to New Mexico would be mentored by the more experienced friars until they were able to minister on their own in the new locations.

Fourthly, the next strategic step was to win the confidence and loyalty of the Pueblo leadership. The congregation of Pueblo leaders at the beginning with Oñate had said they would like to be taught, and then they would decide whether they wanted to be Roman Catholic or not. It was the friar's principle objective to win these leaders. In this objective with the Puebloans, the friar usually failed. The Spanish were slow to grasp that they were up against a highly developed, ancient religion that worked for centuries for these people and, in a great many ways, was the religious equal of Roman Catholicism. They called the leader of the Pueblo a cacique, but he was far more than a civil administrator, he was the indigenous bishop, the spiritual head of the opposition party to the Franciscans. He knew his position as protector of his people and their ways, and he was not all that interested in changing.

The friar baptized the children, which mattered little to anyone but the friar. He taught them his ways and explained the catechism, but as long as they were learning the Pueblo ways in their homes, and the young men were following their fathers in the all important spiritual matters—becoming members of the inherited secret societies—the Kachina worship expressions continued among the Puebloans. The Roman Catholic mission compound actually unwittingly became a symbol of the Pueblos' duel religious life. Just as their respective compounds existed side by side, so the people struggled to complete the obligations to both, their loyalties to both, for the special benefits that each had to offer. For hundreds of new converts there was no doubt that religious proselytism had taken place; they were Roman Catholics in heart and practice. But for thousands, Roman Catholicism was a necessary practice to inherit the benefits of the foreign invaders, but their hearts were still with the ancient ways of the Pueblo.

The fifth of the strategic methods of the Franciscans was to undermine the indigenous social order by becoming the authorities, controlling the means of production, and controlling the sources of goods from the outside. In this strategic objective the Franciscans again had their hands tied; the old social order was entrenched, was in operation, and was very effectively doing its job of running the Pueblo. The Franciscans could not take over the Puebloan leadership because the Pueblo was self-sufficient and had no need of the Franciscans. The Puebloans had wants, they had desires, they could use the new technologies, but none of these were of sufficient value to give up their leadership positions in order to obtain them, and the traditional ministry of the Pueblo leadership was to *maintain* their social order.

The authority of the foreign priest with his foreign religion was in no way superior to the authority of the Kachina priest with the vested interest he had in maintaining the Pueblo religious practices. The contest was like another Mount Carmel experience with both sides calling upon God to prove that theirs was the right way, but none of the gods were answering with fire, and the people just kept trying to make the best they could of the two opinions. The massive church/ convent edifice gave the Spanish a bit of an advantage in sheer size, as it dwarfed most Pueblo structures and could be seen for miles around. Indigenous helpers did facilitate the burden of the few friars, but there never were enough friars to establish any real orthodoxy.

The combination of weak and disinterested Spanish civil leadership was also a constant source of frustration for the Franciscans. Civil leadership, during this colonial period as a rule, undermined and contradicted the leadership of the Franciscan order. In their weakness and insecurity, the civil leadership fought for jurisdiction and authority rather than supporting and reinforcing the cause of evangelism and the building of churches. Juan de Eulate, the governor in Santa Fe, openly encouraged the Puebloans to continue in their pagan ways; he protected and favored ceremonial leaders and told baptized natives they did not have to give up their idols, concubines, or their Kachina worship.[19] Civil government at this time paid no heed to indigenous rights; they condoned forced labor, slavery, and exploitation of captured children, while charging the friars with these crimes.

That the governor assigned *encomiendas* to his friends should not have been a surprise. The entire colony was a cauldron of poor leadership, animosity, hostility, and no one in authority really seemed to care that much—with the exception of the Puebloans who were watching it all. Governors' repeatedly described the Pueblos as meek, well-mannered, and tractable; they did not take into account that they themselves were not. The Pueblos were fed up with Spanish contemptuous manners, and they were ready to do something about it. They were less than a quarter of their former numbers due to diseases introduced by the Spanish, disenfranchised in their own nation, and loosing the spiritual battle as the Roman Catholic Church very slowly but steadily grew stronger through their *Peace with Purchas* programs. The arrogant Spanish friars could strike at the Pueblo priest and Kachina worship, but the Puebloans had to endure it in silence as retaliation against the Spanish religion brought reprisals from the Spanish militia.

After the removal of the liberal governor Bernardo Lopez de Mendizábal by the inquisition for encouraging indigenous religion in 1661, the friars launched a great effort to stomp out Kachina worship. The militancy of the friars had the opposite effect of driving many professed Roman Catholic believers back to defend their Pueblo priests. The harvest of 1667 was inadequate, precipitating five years of drought with little or no harvest for many. In 1671, a smallpox epidemic struck and the Roman Catholic God seemingly did nothing to help the sick and dying.[20] The Puebloans were becoming even more disillusioned with these foreign gods and powerless expressions of Christianity.

The weakening of the Pueblo societal structure and the incompetence of the Spanish civil government left many of the outlying Pueblos in indefensible situations. Ancient enemies took advantage as Apaches, Navajos, and Comanches began raiding, striking deeply into the heart of the Pueblos using horses and guns captured or traded from the Spanish. To counter them, the Spanish trained Puebloans to fight side by side with them as during the Chichimeca wars, but not with harquebus or horses. Still, the Pueblo war captains learned Spanish war tactics and observed the use of war horse and firearms.[21] They would put all this to good use against the Spanish during the coming revolt.

One more deciding factor for the Pueblos was the arrest by Governor Juan Francisco Treviño, in 1675, of 47 Kachina priests, mostly from the Tewa Pueblos. Three of these priests were hanged as examples, one hanged himself to deny the Spanish the privilege, and the remaining 43 were brutally flogged and imprisoned.[22] The Tewa marched on Santa Fe in a show of force that caught the governor off guard. He ceded to their demands and released the prisoners. One of those Kachina priests was an unknown entity to the Spanish. Brooding on his public beating and imprisonment, Don Popé of the San Juan pueblo moved to Taos and consulted the Kachina ancestral spirits as to what he must do. Planning and organizing his steps well over the next five years, for he must succeed completely or fail in all, he used the ancient Puebloan communication technique of the knotted chord. The revolt was set to begin. On August 9, 1680, young Pueblo runners set out with their instructions, jogging from Pueblo to Pueblo and into destiny; the utter destruction of Spanish New Mexico was underway.

The runners carried the message to destroy all the Spanish in their own Pueblo and then proceed to Santa Fe to join together for the destruction of the capital and the Spanish leaders.[23] The Spanish had been warned on many occasions about a possible uprising. Many Puebloans had kinship ties with the Spanish, eight decades of living side by side had cemented economic and friendship relationships. But few Spanish really believe it could happen, even after it did. Some runners were intercepted by the Spanish and the rumors were confirmed, but it only precipitated the rebellion a bit prematurely. Every Pueblo north of Isleta in the far south erupted. Not a single Spaniard survived in the far away Acoma, Zuni, and Hopi Pueblos. In Taos, only two soldiers managed to fight their way out after their families had been killed. All the surviving Spanish with their loyal Puebloan Christians gathered at Santa Fe which was blockaded by Tano warriors until Pueblo reinforcements arrived.

Nearly a thousand refugees had gathered in Santa Fe, but only about 100 were men who could fight. Within a week over 2,500 warriors surrounded Santa Fe. The firearms captured in outlying areas were now used to good effect against the Spanish. Their only hope was to escape Santa Fe. They broke out and headed south, but surprisingly the Puebloans did not give chase, content to see them going. The motley crew held few priests—most of them were already dead. Special punishment was reserved for all priests captured. The pent-up hatreds of the Puebloans for the Roman Catholic religion, for their persecution of the Puebloan worship and their Kachina priests were poured out on the Franciscans.

At Sandia the Puebloans defecated on the mission altars and hacked in pieces the crucifixes and statues of saints. They threw the chalices and other holy instruments into manure piles. The friar, Juan de Jesus was stripped naked, mounted on a pig, and whipped as the pig ran about until the missionary died of his wounds. At Acoma the Puebloans stripped and tied two friars together, dragged them through the Pueblo and then stoned them to death. These dreadful scenes were being repeated throughout New Mexico. Few of the Franciscans escaped the pent up wrath and, as one Spanish official said, "The hatred of the barbarians for our holy faith."[24]

The long and terrible retreat to El Paso continued on down the Rio Grande River. Mournfully they passed from one deserted town to another, passed burned out haciendas littered with gruesome corpses of families well known to all the solemn marchers. Mounted Puebloans followed and watched their retreat, more anxious to capture and hold all the livestock that they could, rather than to bother with the sad, retreating column. The column came to the faithful town of Isleta, but found that town deserted also. Spanish and natives alike had fled south to escape the slaughter, having heard that all the Spanish of the northern Pueblos were already dead. Approximately 40 miles below Socorro the two groups joined up, and then continued south to El Paso. Arriving at El Paso, discussion was held about a counter attack, but only 155 fighting men could be mustered, and only 471 horses fit to travel were found. The vast majority of the 2,500 refugees were women and children who had to be protected also.

Re-conquest would have to wait. The Puebloans now had horses, guns, knew Spanish military tactics, held the land, and hated the Spanish. Any Puebloan with sympathies for the Spanish had died with them or fled with them. As the Spanish were retreating, Don Popé consolidated his gains by eliminating every trace of Spanish Roman Catholicism in the Pueblos. Rites of purification were conducted to spiritually cleanse the former Roman Catholic areas. Baptized Puebloans had to wash in the streams and scrub themselves with yucca root to purge themselves of Christian baptism. Churches were pulled down and the rubble scattered. New kivas were built and Kachina paraphernalia brought out of hiding for an intensive round of rituals to restore the old harmonies between the Puebloans and the spirit that permeated all. Christian marriage was repudiated and the former style of marriage with multiple wives was reestablished.

But the Puebloans would not, could not, unlearn the new skills and understanding brought by the Spanish, nor divest themselves of the technology that had bettered their lives and made them more productive. With the looting after the Spanish left, many had acquired the tools and equipment that would make them even more self-sufficient, and these things they would not give up. Two problems were left unsolvable: the European diseases were still in the land, and the rains still had not come—the drought continued. But the Spanish were gone and would not return for another decade.

Analysis of Franciscan Missiology in the Sixth Epoch of Conquest

In this sixth epoch of conquest and evangelism little is different from standard Franciscan practice of former epochs. Indeed less is accomplished and little is done that could be considered advancement of the missiological field; the practice of missiological principals is stagnated for the most part. It is obvious the Franciscans did adapt some Jesuit methodologies that seemed to be effective in the application of the peace-with-purchase program. In evaluating the *apostolic practice*, the stuttering start of the Spanish penetration seems to be symbolic of the same stuttering evangelistic effort by the Franciscans. In the previous penetrations of the New Mexico Pueblo region before Coronado, the Spanish were offensive and arrogant to the indigenous people. News from the long-distance trade routes for nearly a century had indicated that the Spanish were dangerous, exploitative slavers who carried with them terrible diseases never before seen. The common understanding was that the invaders should be avoided if at all possible and repulsed if they came. Yet knowing these attitudes of the Puebloans, time and again the Franciscans elected to strike out on their own without supply or protection. And they died.

It was only after Oñate, in violation of the Viceroy's orders and the King's principles of pacification, applied the conquistadors' terror tactics of *fire and sword* at Ácoma, that it was safe for the friars to move about unprotected. The friars were accepted by the Puebloans as equals, men to be listened to, but the respect given the friars was a respect born of the Puebloans own integrity; the Franciscans still had to earn that respect. Yet they continually acted as if the Puebloans were a conquered people. After Ácoma, there was also a fear of retaliation by the vicious Spanish civil authorities if the Franciscans were not treated fairly. This still did not make the Puebloans a subjugated people in attitude or in their free will to decide for themselves if they wanted Roman Catholicism or not.

Two other factors greatly influenced the imposition of Christianity in practice. First, the Puebloan priestly hierarchy remained intact. This allowed the free exercise of the indigenous religion and its practices alongside that of the Roman Catholicism which provided a continuing alternative and a constant comparison as to which was better for any given situation. The second was the inability of the priests to construct their houses of worship within the town complexes of the Pueblos. The common practice of decapitating the leadership of the indigenous religion and the destruction of their worship centers was not possible. Now it was the Roman Catholic Church that was outside the gate, or along side, with the kivas inside the city, thus making Roman Catholicism symbolically a foreign religion, not of the people.

This was the first time in New Spain that the Roman Catholic friars had to minister and coexist with direct competition; they had to face-off, head to head on level ground with another highly traditional religion. Converts had to be persuaded and convinced of the new religion to be baptized, and after baptism the new religion had to keep proving itself better than the former religion to keep its membership. There were evidently a great number of baptisms as Puebloans tried to experience the new religion, often for the benefits of material goods, new technologies, and livestock. But the healthy continuing worship patterns of the Kachina cults indicate that the friars were not succeeding in this direct competition with a functioning indigenous worship system.

What this competition did mean was that preaching, teaching the catechisms, answering questions with relevant explanations, and reasoning with Puebloans who sought understanding was required of the friars. No longer could regurgitation of memorized facts suffice as discipleship. If there was no heart understanding, the next worship service would probably be with the Kachina priest where counter explanations would be offered. Therefore a true and more complete evangelism was taking place in this Sixth Epoch of conquest with some converts who accepted the new teachings in heart and head, as well as in outward appearance. The three basics of Christology, ecclesiology, and eschatology had to be taught in a relevant format. The elements of salvation, especially the sacraments of the church were not withheld as so often occurred in the past. Though an indigenous Catholic priesthood was forbidden by law, there are examples of up to 20 trained native leaders participating in the worship services[25] and carrying out the functions of the friar, while under a friar's supervision.

There were a large number of Puebloans that through persecution, revolution, and flight, remained loyal and firm in their confession of faith. They were converts to the new religion. Yet, there were far more who kept their feet in both camps of religion, the Kachina and the Roman Catholic as many do to this day. After the rebellion and victory, a large number of these Puebloans washed off their baptism and reverted completely to the Kachina worship. These joined the others violently debasing Roman Catholicism, rejecting the new teaching they had received, torturing and murdering the priests, and displaying a profound hatred for all things Roman Catholic. There were many possible contributing factors for the welling up of the revolt, but there is no doubt that the Franciscans bore the brunt of the anger of the Puebloans, as did the Jesuits in the Nueva Vizcaya rebellion.

The Franciscan was the priest in charge of the new religion, and he was there beside the Pueblo, living with the people. He represented the Spanish society as a whole. What could also account for the extreme animosity could have been the comparison of the two priesthoods in operation together. The Puebloan priest was one of them; all the friars were foreigners. The indigenous priest ruled by spiritual authority, the friar by corporal punishment. The Kachina priests practiced their rituals in the kivas and patios of the Pueblo in spite of ill-mannered, hostile interference and destruction of Kachina paraphernalia by the friars. The friar practiced his religion outside the Pueblo, away from the people, and never did the Kachina priest attack or violate the sacred place of the Roman Catholics—until the rebellion. The Pueblo secret society chose their senior priest for his qualifications and ability to lead; the friar was thrust upon them from the outside and no one really knew what manner of man he was. The Kachina priest was forced into hiding and to practice in secret; the friar attacked, persecuted, even had arrested and, in some cases, killed Kachina priests using civil authorities because Roman Catholicism was not overcoming the Kachina religion in fair head-to-head competition. At least, not fast enough for the Franciscans.

In the area of *Church Structure and Mission* there was no interaction in New Mexico. The Franciscans were given exclusive jurisdiction for the evangelization of the Pueblo people. The secular church was prohibited from entering, even when the bishop of Guadalajara demanded jurisdiction over the area. The missiological implications were good by casual observation but very shaky by inspection. It could be said that the missiological situation was ideal; with neither competition from secular church nor other missionary orders, all energies could be focused on the one priority of evangelism and then building up the church. But seldom are monopolies good for the people, as was seen in the Yucatán. The Franciscans brought to New Mexico an older strategy that had worked with others in another time and place, but there seemed to be no consideration as to whether it was the correct strategy for the Pueblos. Nomadic and seminomadic indigenous tribes of the Chichimeca and the northern desert valleys responded well to the Peace-by-Purchase strategy. That in itself should have said that the highly developed sedentary society of the Puebloans with a religious system that permeated every aspect of their being would require a different approach for evangelism and discipleship. But due to the Franciscan monopoly, for the Puebloans there was no other choice.

Once again what became obvious are the weakest areas of missiology for Tridentine Roman Catholicism, the *Gospel and Other Religions*, and *Salvation and the Non-Christian*. The friars still understood the command to go and they knew there could not be any salvation apart from the gospel of Christ. Yet in New Mexico the Franciscans encountered a very complete religious expression that adequately reflected the worldview of a people who had built their entire societies around the worshipful expression of their understanding of the spirit that encompasses all. The priesthood of this religious expression was also the highest form of their theocratic civil government in each respective Pueblo. What the Spanish called the *cacique* was an exalted position within the Pueblo society but very different from what the Spanish supposed. The Franciscans simply dismissed this high-ranking religious leader as a witch, a worshiper of the devil. The Spanish insensitivity and their total lack of understanding of who the *caciques* really were doomed the possibility of ever incorporating the indigenous leadership into the Roman Catholic or civil leadership.

The Franciscans made the same mistake that the Jesuits were in the process of making in Nueva Vizcaya: alienating and circumventing the indigenous leaders while leaving them intact where they would eventually do the most harm to the Roman Catholic cause. Tridentine doctrines did not permit the possibility of considering there being any merit to the Pueblo religious expression, and Tridentine doctrine required the overthrow and annihilation of that expression. This can be described as insensitivity and cultural blindness on the part of the Franciscans that lead to hostile responses and alienation of the Pueblo leadership. It is true that the biblical command to go and preach the gospel to all nations was being obeyed, but their gospel tool box had very few and very old tools.

In the area of salvation through the efficaciousness of the redemptive work of Christ, the Tridentine doctrine of baptismal regeneration was still seen as the only essential aspect of evangelism. A great many of the Pueblos were baptized and many of them received instruction, more than has been found in any other epochs of conquest. Yet in the aftermath of the Pueblo revolt, a record falling away occurred exceeding anything seen to this point in the New Spain conquests. For a person to be *in Christ* and to become a *new man* in the Spirit obviously required more than water baptism alone could provide. A great many Pueblos were baptized, but this situation is a clear demonstration that they were not children of God through that sacrament alone. Sahagún's observation again comes back to haunt the missiologists: why was it not being understood that the whole methodology being used by the friars was not making Roman Catholics out of the vast majority of people within the indigenous nations? They were counted as Roman Catholics, but they were not spiritually regenerated Christians. Obviously a number of indigenous Puebloan individuals came into the Roman Catholic understanding of Christianity through this Tridentine process, but only because the Spirit of God did His baptismal work in their hearts, as only the Holy Spirit can do, in addition to the friar's work with water on their heads.

It was observed that a significant number of Puebloans did seem to make a complete break with their former religion and accept Roman Catholicism. This seems to be attributable to the more in-depth teaching and reasoning of the friars, a more complete utilization of the sacraments, and a willingness to debate publically the merits of Roman Catholicism. For their sincere profession of faith many of them died a martyr's death, or were forced to flee for their lives with the Spanish survivors of the rebellion. This seems to indicate the most complete preaching of the gospel message encountered in any epoch to date. Circumstances had forced the friars out of their comfort zones and into a more theological preaching of the biblical message along with all the paraphernalia of tridentinism.

The last area of missiology to be considered is that of *Christianity and Culture*. There was much to be learned and profitably used in the Puebloan culture which was completely overlooked because the Spanish could see no validity in the indigenous cultural expressions. There was no respect for the accomplishments of the Pueblo society and no attempt to identify with the Puebloans in their world. In forcing the Kachina religious expressions underground, the Franciscans, in a sense, contributed to the preservation of pure forms of Kachina religious practice which had to be maintained completely separate from the new Roman Catholic expression being programmed into their society.

Many of the Puebloans were developing split personalities to function in both religious worlds but not permitting the two to meet within themselves. They had one foot in each, but could remove either one of their feet and still function religiously quite well. Christianity must penetrate culture before it can modify cultural behavior. By keeping both religious worlds completely separate, Roman Catholicism could not touch the Pueblo culture.

Summary

After a slow, stuttering beginning the Puebloans were offended and distrusted the Spanish who confirmed their fears with the terrible destruction of Ácoma and the conquering subjugation of the Pueblo people by force, rather than through pacification by *Peace with Purchase*. This resulted in three major obstacles for the Franciscan friars in evangelism:

1. The pueblo leadership was promised that they would be allowed a free-will decision on accepting or rejecting the new religion;
2. The Puebloan priestly hierarchy was left completely intact and functioning;
3. Most Roman Catholic Churches were outside the Pueblo towns while the Kivas were inside the towns.

This meant that for the first time in New Spain, the Roman Catholic Church had direct competition, and had to convert by persuasion, teaching, and convincing through a much more effective evangelism. The result was two religious systems side by side, and many of the Puebloans had one foot in each. This was not a syncretism but more like a split personality when it came to worship.

The Franciscans had exclusive right to evangelize in New Mexico with the other orders and the secular church excluded to avoid competition between them. This actually resulted in a sort of dictatorship by the Franciscan Father President with no real accountability. The Franciscans alienated the indigenous leadership calling them witches and devil worshipers, forcing the Puebloan Kachina worship underground totally intact and functioning. The two competing religions with the majority of Puebloans following both of them resulted in the majority reverting to Kachina worship patterns after the Pueblo revolt and disassociating from the Roman Catholic faith. Salvation by water baptism which was supposed to provide spiritual regeneration for the majority of Puebloans only meant corporate apostasy once the Spanish were thrown out.

CHAPTER X

SEVENTH EPOCH:
THE RIO GRANDE VALLEY

Epoch Seven Introduction

In 1579, Luis de Carvajál returned to Spain making contract with the
Crown to conquer and settle 600 square leagues of land in the northern
frontier of New Spain with the name of *Nuevo Reino de León,* one of
the first geographic areas to be discovered by the Spanish and one of
the last to be invaded and subjugated. From surviving documents it is
a bit difficult to determine just what was designated *Nuevo Leon.* To
call it the Lower Rio Grande valley would be within parameters, but
that does not define the geographical area when the coastal plains of
the Gulf Coast and many other river drainage systems flow through
what geologically is the Rio Grande plain. The area can be visualized
as everything east of the eastern Sierra Madres Mountains and north
of the Pánuco River. Coming from the north, everything south of the
Balcones Scarp line which defines the southeastern edge of the Edwards
Plateau (the Hill Country of Texas) would fall in this area of study, as
well as the western valley area where the Rio Grande emerges from
the Big Bend country and flows east including the whole Rio Grande
valley that then begins to take shape. The ruggedness of the Big Bend
geography also serves as a separation for Jumano people of the southern
Great Plains northwest of the Big Bend area from the Coahuiltecans
of the Rio Grande Plain. The mountains of Mexico's State of Nuevo
Leon and the shores of the Gulf of Mexico complete the encirclement
of this area. Today this is the valley region of Texas and the northern
portions of four Mexican states: Chihuahua, Nuevo Leon, Coahuila,

and Tamaulipas. The name Nuevo Leon is used simply because it is the first named Spanish settlement contract for this vast area.

A harsh and very difficult area to subdue, the extreme western portion starts as part of the Chihuahua desert; indeed, most of the Rio Grande Plain appears to be desert without the irrigation that has made the valley area so productive. The wind seldom ceases to blow—very hot in the summer, often below freezing in the winter months, except where the temperatures are moderated by the proximity of the ocean. Cold fronts roaring through can cause rapid and extreme temperature changes within hours. For this epoch, mosquito infested swamps dotted the area and flash floods were common. But the Valley had good soil, plenty of water, and a long growing season which interested the Spanish settlers.

Historically, the coastline of the Gulf was mapped out in the sixteenth century. There is confusion about which explorers first saw and named this river alternately called Rio de Las Palmas, the Rio Bravo, the Rio del Norte, or the Rio Grande at different times and in different places. Guzmán was appointed governor of Pánuco in 1526, and as seen in the first epoch of conquest, he proceeded to build up a large slave trading company that raided deeply into the surrounding areas. He probably did not enter the Rio Grande basin, but his reputation and the European diseases the soldiers brought with them did, instilling a fear and hatred of the Spanish long before any Spanish were ever seen. The remnants of the Narváez expedition saw the river and crossed it several times in 1528-36. Cabeza de Vaca's report provided much knowledge of the land and its people—though the seven cities of Cibola never did materialize as they were described by explorers. The remnants of the de Soto expedition had to cross the Rio Grande to get back to Mexico City in 1543, having explored the whole north coast of the Gulf of Mexico from the west coast of Florida to the Mississippi River; they sailed down the Mississippi and along the Gulf Coast and back to Mexico. The Spanish explorers and fleets sailed along the Gulf Coast of Tamaulipas and Texas for about 150 years before it was decided to occupy the land for Spain, before the English or French did it first. Spain's possession of the entire Gulf Coast and eastern Florida were unquestioned at the time based upon discovery, conquest, and very sketchy possession. However, the land was just too big to be occupied by Spanish settlers alone—especially if there was no gold, silver, pearls, or trade to justify the expenses of settlement. Keep in mind the administrative nightmare a new settlement represented from the King on down to recruiting colonists and financing them. Someone besides the Crown of Spain had to bear the cost of indigenous wars and settlement and the devastation inflicted by indigenous people who contested the Spanish invasions.

Still, the Spanish were beginning to penetrate this great river plain. The Spaniard José Luis de Carvajál's first administrative position in New Spain had been the Alcalde (Mayor) of Tampico, and as such, in the fall of 1568, Alcalde Carvajál rounded up 77 English sailors marooned on the Gulf coast by John Hawkins.[1] The buccaneer had lost some of his ships in a tangle with the Spanish fleet in Veracruz harbor; in fact, over 100 sailors from the very crowded *Minion* had been put on shore to make their way to French ports in the north. Later, commissioned as captain, Carvajál was sent to chastise hostile native bands at the mouth of the Rio Grande. He claimed to have punished the people responsible for the massacre of 400 castaways from three ships wrecked on the coast en route to Spain.[2] During that campaign, he crossed the lower Rio Grande into what is now Texas.

During the Chichimeca wars Captain Carvajál, by orders of the fourth Viceroy (Martin de Almanza),[3] attacked the Chichimecas of the frontier mountains (now Nuevo Leon) in an attempt to stop the devastating raids on the silver mining settlements in the high plains of central Mexico. His travels took him north and then east where he again entered the familiar Rio Grande plain, but from the opposite direction as before. In 1577, Carvajál founded the town of Saltillo and discovered the silver mines of San Gregorio. In 1579, Carvajál returned to Spain and obtained permission and a land grant of 7,350 square miles (600 square leagues) in the Rio Grande Plain, well north of where the vicious Chichimeca war was still ragging. Back in New Spain, and with about 200 men from Saltillo, he found a site where he established the new settlement of Leon (now Cerralvo) in 1582, which became the capital of the Northern Province for about 150 years. Cerralvo received the title of an organized town in 1630 under the name of Pueblo de San Gregorio de Cerralvo.

It is difficult to establish exactly when the town of Monterrey was founded. The most probable story deduced from available data was that around 1587, Montemayor with 12 comrades, some with their families from Cerralvo and Saltillo, established the village of Monterrey in the valley of *Nueva Extremadura*, naming it for the current Viceroy, perhaps to secure his favor for doing it without permission. Presenting himself as the successor of Carvajál, Montemayor named himself governor, a position that was legally established in 1599. Waldo Cortés was a secular priest who was brought in with the original group. The first Franciscans who entered the valley with Carvajál were the friar Lorenzo de Gavira in 1582, followed by Martin de Altamira in 1603. In spite of much unreliable and conflicting data, it is obvious that the Spanish were well established in the southern-most parts of the Rio Grande Plain by 1600.

In 1681-82, the French explorer, Robert Cavelier de la Salle, sailed down the Mississippi from Canada to the Gulf of Mexico.[4] This was about 140 years after the De Soto expedition had camped on the Mississippi and buried their leader there, and yet there was still no Spanish presence anywhere along the Mississippi. De la Salle took possession, in the name of King Louis XIV, of a territory three times larger than France and declared: "I name thee Louisiana."[5] He must have known it had already been claimed by the Spanish, but since none of them were around to contest his bold claim, French settlements were established at New Orleans and Mobile. The Spanish had settled Pensacola, which stopped the French advance to the East.

Early in 1686, the Marquis de Laguna, then Viceroy of Mexico, learned of the French intrusion due to the capture of a prize French ship taken by the Spaniards from a French expedition; however, the ship's destination was unknown. It is probable that in La Salle's first expedition into the interior of Texas, the Comanche Indians obtained knowledge of his location and communicated it to the Spaniards through their trade routes across the Rio Grande. Therefore, the count of Monclova, who entered on the duties of the Viceroyalty in 1686, finally had accurate information about the French penetration into territory claimed by the Spanish. A military post and settlement was established at Monclova and Captain Alonzo de Leon was appointed to the command under the title of governor of Coahuila. Captain de Leon, dispatched a military force of 100 men, scoured the country and hunted out the French. He found two Frenchmen who had been shipwrecked among the coastal Cenis, took them prisoner, and returned to Mexico with a good report of the hospitality of the Cenis of East Texas and the need to establish missions among them.[6]

In 1691, Domingo Terán, appointed the governor of Coahuila and Tejas, proceeded with 50 soldiers and 7 lay friars to establish missions and military posts. His party took cattle, seeds for planting, and established settlements on the waters of the Red, the Neches, and the Guadalupe Rivers. Soon these infant colonies, as well as that at Fort St. Louis, failed due to hostile natives, failed seed crops, and cattle that contracted diseases and died. In 1693, all these settlements were abandoned. This situation had to be communicated to the king. He was informed of the great expense trying to start up the colonies, of the problems with the indigenous people, and that it was recommended the settlement of the province be postponed to a time when circumstances would offer more hopes of success.[7]

Tejas was once again without European settlers, and few of the Spanish had any interest in continuing colonization efforts. The abandonment was eventually approved by the Viceroy of New Spain in 1694. However, events were already in motion to force a continued Spanish presence in Tejas and to establish permanent settlements there.

About the same time that the San Francisco mission was established, another mission was started on the north side of the Rio Grande called San Juan Bautista. With the failure of the East Tejas missions and withdrawal of the presidio garrisons, the San Juan mission became a Spanish observation post, as well as continuing as a trading post between the tribes to the north and the Spanish to the south of the great river. When travel became more frequent between Mexico and Tejas, San Juan became known as the beginning of what would later be called the San Antonio road.

In 1716, a French party led by St. Denis left Mobile and made their way to the Spanish Presidio/Mission among the Cenis Indians of East Tejas. In doing so, St. Denis blazed a road along a trail first traveled two years previously that came to be known as the San Antonio road, the only road through Tejas for the next 140 years. Since trade outside of the Spanish colonies was strictly prohibited by the Spanish Crown, this blatant violation by the French for trade purposes alarmed the Spanish as they realized the need for a more secure frontier against the French[8]

War was declared between the French and Spanish in Europe and, as often was the case, it spilled over into their North American colonies. The French reinforced Natchitoches in Louisiana, attacked the Spanish missions of East Tejas, and drove the Spanish out, all the way to Bexar (Today: San Antonio). The Spanish counterattacked with 500 cavalry and drove the French back to Louisiana. They then established a presidio at Adaes and the San Miguel de Linares mission in 1717, just 15 miles west of the French Fort St. Jean Baptiste of Natchitoches.[9] Los Adaes (in Louisiana today) was then named the capital of the province of Tejas. In 1720, a force of Spanish attempted to establish a presidio on the Mississippi but encountered a large group of Missouri who were allies of the French. By deception the Missouris presented themselves as friends and then fell upon the Spanish who thought they were Osage. The entire Spanish force was annihilated, including the Spanish priest who was singled out for special torture. There were no more attempts to extend Spanish territory to the northeast from Tejas. The Los Adaes mission and ministry to the Adaes Indians was declared a failure and abandon in 1772.

This entire affair served as a wake-up call to the Spanish Crown. If they were to hold the French in check, Tejas had to be settled by the Spanish. "The king of Spain, having information of these proceedings, issued his orders for the pacification and reduction of Tejas as he considered it of great importance to the security of his dominions in New Mexico."[10] It is said that the year 1715 may be considered the year of the beginning of missions in Texas. From this time may be dated permanent occupancy by Spain.[11] But neither the French nor the Spanish were the first to occupy the Rio Grande Plain. Although called by the invading Spanish at different times: Nuevo Leon, Nuevas Filipinas, Las Tekas, and Tejas, and even though the Nueces River and the Rio Grande at times would become the boundaries separating the land of *Texas* from Tamaulipas, Nuevo Leon, Coahuila, and Chihuahua, the indigenous people knew of no such divisions.

The Indigenous People of Nuevo Leon

The New Mexico epoch introduced some of the indigenous people of this area. Among them were the Apaches—seminomadic, seasonal farmers who followed the buffalo during the off seasons of agriculture. But according to the Pueblo people, they were newcomers to the plains. The attitude of the Puebloans is revealed in the word *Apache*, meaning enemy in the Zuni language. The Apache were one of the first of the Texas native groups to have their lives revolutionize by the introduction of the horse. Although they were not indigenous to this epoch of study at the beginning, as the Comanche tribes swept into the Great Plains from the north, the Apache were forced down into the Nuevo Leon areas displacing many of the native Coahuiltecan people of the Rio Grande Plain. The Spanish were not the only invaders during this epoch of conquest.

The first indigenous nation under study that occupied the eastern regions of Nuevo Leon is that of the Tonkawa people. Their historical territory was along the Balcones Escarpment northeast of present day San Antonio. At the time of the first Spanish contact, the Tonkawa had a large territory that included parts of the Edwards Plateau region west of Austin and San Antonio. The Apache, around 1600, and the Comanche, around 1750, moved into the region and pushed the Tonkawa to the east of the Edwards Plateau. This is where they were in most of the Spanish subjugation period pertinent to this study, just to the east, and along the Balcones Escarpment. They were friendly with the Karankawa and shared the lands with them and the Coahuiltecan people merging from the south. The Tonkawa resisted Spanish colonization and played a leading role in the destruction of the Santa Cruz de San Sabá Mission. In 1784, the Spanish killed El Mocho, the leading war chief of the Tonkawas, ushering in a time of uneasy peace.[12]

As in many other indigenous groups and tribes, the Tonkawa practiced levirate, which required a brother or another male from the same clan if a brother no longer existed, to marry the deceased brother's wife. The same kinship relation carried over to the female side of the family where sororate, a younger sister married her dead sister's husband, was practiced. Following this same pattern, when a man died his personal property was distributed among his siblings' children rather than to his own in order that the property might stay within his clan. Orphans became wards of the mother's clan. This social system insured that widows and orphans had provision and care.[13]

Today, very little is known of the Tonkawa life cycle. Shortly after birth, a piece of wood was tied to the baby's head to flatten it. The sparse knowledge of Tonkawa marriage customs seems to indicate a lack of emphasis on the actual ceremony. Death rites received more attention in existing records. When a person neared death, his friends would gather and form concentric rings around the dying, chanting and swaying until the individual passed on. The deceased was then buried along with his prized possessions. The band mourned for three days and then carried out a smoking ceremony that was meant to purify those contaminated by contact with the dead. This ceremony also allowed the society to realign and reintegrate itself following the loss of a member.[14] Similarities with the other two indigenous nations of the Rio Grande Plain seem to indicate that many cultural details were duplicated.

Another indigenous nation of the Nuevo Leon area would be the Karankawa on the upper east coast of the Gulf from Galveston bay down the coast to the Nueces River and up to about 100 miles inland. There were several distinct bands, perhaps with even a tribal organization.[15] Much of the history of the Karankawa is lost—no ethnographic friars or historians lived among these people. They were good fighters and European settlers feared them. Many of the Karankawa warriors were over six feet tall. They had bows almost as tall as they were and shot long arrows made from slender shoots of cane. It is said they would appear suddenly in their canoes, attack, and then disappear into the swamps and woods where Europeans had a hard time following.[16] Spanish slave traders cruised the coast of Texas, kidnapping Karankawas for the Caribbean slave trade. Later, the French, under the explorer LaSalle, attempted a colony in Karankawa territory. The French stole two canoes, and when the Karankawa questioned the French, a shooting war started with nearly all the French being wiped out. There is apparently no record as to how European disease introduced by the Spanish and French might have affected the Karankawa after these contacts.

The religious beliefs of the Karankawa have been discerned from descriptions of their celebrations and what is known of their life cycle practices. When a child died, the entire group mourned; at dawn, noon, and sunset, they performed their mourning rites. If a son or brother died, the family would mourn for a month and remain in seclusion, refusing to obtain food. The *mitote*, a ceremony that was performed during a full moon after a great victory in battle, a successful hunt, or fishing expedition, included the consumption of an enemy, roasting and eating pieces of his flesh while the victim looked on. These acts of cannibalism were presumably to prevent the victim from having a second or third life. The Karankawa believed that it transferred the fortitude, courage, and fighting skills of the victim to whomever consumed him. This was also the ultimate revenge, to devour an enemy's flesh while he watched. Cannibalism was ritual with the Karankawa, as with many North American tribes, not part of the daily diet as with the Caribs or the Aztec.

Marriage among the Karankawa Tribes was usually arranged between the man and the parents of the woman he desired. The suitor presented gifts to the parents of the woman and if accepted, the woman would be given over. The newlyweds would then start their own family. For a time the husband would give all that he brought back from the hunt to his bride, who would in turn give it over to her father, who would give back just enough for the couple to survive. After a time the husband and his bride would officially join his own band, ending the couple's association with his wife's father and mother.[17]

The Coahuiltecan, the third indigenous nation inhabiting this region, occupied the lowlands of the Rio Grande Plain on both sides of the river up to the mountains to the south, to the north until they encountered the Edwards Plateau, and the regions of the previously named indigenous peoples to the northeast. The name can be taken as a geographic catchall that could also be defined as the folks that lived in south Texas and northeastern Mexico. They extended down the coastal plain to the region of the Tenek, or Huasteco nation, historically centered on the Pánuco River. They were the least organized of the indigenous people of the Rio Grande Plain. They had hundreds of small, autonomous, distinctively named groups living primarily by hunting and gathering. The lifestyle of these Coahuiltecan groups and bands reflects the harshness of their habitat; as hunter-gatherers they had to keep moving and could only sustain small groups, very similar to the indigenous groups of the Baja California area which was the most difficult habitat in New Spain.

The Spaniards had little interest in describing the natives, who appeared to them as little better off than the animals they hunted. There were no ethnologists or anthropologist among the friars that first came into the region and no one seems to have noticed anything distinct about these nomadic residents of the Rio Grande plane. Of their religious beliefs and practices we know almost nothing. Religion was apparently similar to many tribes of North America where they believed in a spirit world expressed in many ways. In parts of Nuevo León some Spanish observers did link Coahuiltecan populations by cultural peculiarities such as hairstyle and body decoration, which all taken together contributes very little to an understanding of the Coahuiltecans.

Being as the Rio Grande Plain is very hot, the Coahuiltecan wore little clothing: breech cloths, fiber sandals, and in bad weather, the Coahuiltecan wore cloaks made out of rabbit, coyote, or any other hides that were available. Women wore knee length skirts with no tops and the children went naked. Some experts believe that the Coahuiltecan groups spoke related languages and shared the same basic indigenous culture.[18] One article indicates that there were probably seven languages and dialects spoken in this region, and the Spanish friars had attempted to put their catechisms into these different dialects.[19]

Life for the Coahuiltecans was tough, but there was food if one knew where to look for it. A wide range in soils fostered a variety of life sustaining wild plants such as mesquite beans, maguey crowns, nopales (the edible cactus leaves), prickly pear fruit, pecans, acorns, various roots, and tubers. Deer were widespread and available as large game animal, and bison also roamed the Texas/Coahuila region. Other game animals included the peccary and armadillo, rabbits, rats, various birds, snakes, iguana, frogs, and snails. Fish were abundant in perennial streams and the bays, and shellfish could always be found in the saline waters of the Gulf.[20] Although the Coahuiltecan area was one of the poorest regions of native habitat in North America, small groups, moving with the food availability of the different seasons and natural harvests, taking game as they went, could live adequately in this harsh, semi-desert, land.

There are references to the *little ice age* as a period of several hundred years in which the zone of this epoch had a cooler average temperature and received a higher annual rainfall.[21] There are descriptions of shipwrecked survivors having to build rafts to cross rivers that are easily fordable streams today.[22] This could mean that more areas were covered with forest, and that the climate was cooler and much less harsh when the Spanish first came to the Rio Grande Plain, and possibly that groups, clans, and tribes were larger, healthier, and better organized than the indigenous people of the second Spanish entrance. This could indicate that the fall of indigenous demographics was even more severe than what is suspected. No data exists for a determination of conditions previous to this seventh epoch in the Rio Grande Plain.

This history and the descriptions of the indigenous inhabitants have been summed up as the context of the first Spanish entrance into the Rio Grande Plain. This area and East Texas in general were great buffer zones invaded and claimed by both Spain and France with undermanned, underfunded, poorly supplied attempts to create European settlements by which claims could be established. War in Europe meant war in New Spain and Louisiana for no conceivable reason except that it was an excuse to try to adjust the borders of European claims to territory.

Between the hostilities of the European powers lay the indigenous people, still fighting their traditional enemies, fighting the invasion of French on one side, Spanish from the other, and fighting the Apache being forced into the Rio Grande Plain from the west by the Comanche. They were attempting to survive the terrible diseases that would appear without warning, taking warriors, women, and children at a frightful rate. Indigenous societies were falling apart as their cultures crumbled under the stress. Europeans armed and turned indigenous people against each other for the invader's own benefit, while disease decimated tribes, clans, and groups. Many old ways were lost by the indigenous people in desperate attempts for survival at any cost. This was the indigenous situation encountered by the Spanish in their second entrance into the Rio Grande Plain.

Colonization by Design

Most of what was discussed in the previous section was long ago history when New Spain was served the wake-up call by the French from Louisiana, and also by the brutal, merciless English and Dutch heretic pirates on the open seas. There had to be safe harbors along the Gulf Coast for the Spanish fleets to survive. There had to be towns in the Rio Grande Plain and East Texas if the French were to be contained in

Louisiana. However, there was no gold or silver, or much of anything else of value in all that territory to help finance and make a colony productive. The colonies of Nuevo Leon on the southern fringes of the valley had started with silver mines but survived on the product of haciendas and ranches. Established colonies in Texas could survive on agriculture and ranching—the land was good for that. But agrarian settlements require long-term investment and securing funding from the Crown of Spain for colonization or evangelization was no longer a viable option for this epoch of study.

Preceding the colonization of this second entrance by the Spanish, much had been learned about Texas. In 1683-84, Mendoza crossed the midsection of Texas from the Pecos to the Colorado River, and then down the Colorado and back to the Pecos, mapping and gathering information on natives and geography.[23] During the years of 1685-90, a number of expeditions explored and mapped the Rio Bravo (Grande) to the north and east.[24] For nearly a hundred years the mining towns and the increasing number of haciendas of Nuevo Leon had been expanding north towards the great river, exploring their territory and penetrating the northern frontier for various reasons and of course, just curiosity.

Colonists knew that the Coahuiltecan had been paying a terrible price for their contact with the Spanish. In the area around Monterrey, "Chapa tells us that 161 bands that used to live in the area around Monterey . . . simply disappeared because they got sick and died. He went on to tell that the 95 surviving bands had lost 80-90% of their members."[25] To this should be added that the encomienda system of forced paid labor allowed the colonists to take the Coahuiltecan at will and require them to work in the mines—the life expectancy of the unskilled miners was very short. Those who fled the Spanish towards the north were overcome by the Apache who were fleeing south from the Comanche coming down from still further north.

It must be noted again that the indigenous population had severely declined before this second entrance of the Spanish into the Rio Grande Plain. A number of nationwide epidemics had ravaged Mexico and the Caribbean, as mentioned in the earlier epochs. In 1519-22, the smallpox epidemic not only had raced through the Caribbean and then on to the mainland helping Cortéz to defeat the Aztec, but had also depopulated the Huasteco region, most likely moving north through lower Texas by the trade routes. In 1550, a mumps epidemic moved throughout New Spain. In 1559-63, measles, influenza, mumps, and diphtheria spread rapidly through all of New Spain. In 1576-80, typhus, smallpox, measles, and mumps again ravaged New Spain and the Caribbean. With no resistance, these terrible plagues could easily account for the more than 90% population loss in the Rio Grande Plain during the 150 years between the settlement of the Monterrey area and when the second wave of colonization penetrated Texas. Only the fact that these microscopic invaders were so fatal that the indigenous people died too quickly for the diseases to spread very far kept the various groups and tribes from immediate extinction.

After the initial ravages of these epidemic waves entire groups and clans were no longer viable. Survivors combined with others who remained alive resulting in intermixing of cultures. Atmospheric warming trends after the *little ice age* forced adaptations to the changing weather conditions further complicating survival. Invading Apache from the north caused further dislocation forcing changes to the local cultures. Remnants of the once established and dominant cultures that had suffered and survived five to six generations of sickness, fatal disease, attacks, and cultural disintegration, could account for the strange circumstance of listless, vegetable-soup mixtures of unmotivated groups, poorly defined cultures, and intermixed languages of the Nuevo Leon basin.

Having been in existence now for about 250 years, New Spain had a great deal of experience in dealing with the indigenous people ranging from sedentary, high society cultures to the fierce, nomadic, desert warriors. They had fought and won, or fought to a standstill, all indigenous peoples encountered, and they had encountered an incredibly divers number of cultures in their North American history. For this Seventh Epoch of conquest excellent leadership would draw upon this experience to accomplish their best planned and executed colonization period, which also greatly affected the missiology during this region's subjugation.

This Seventh Epoch was also distinguished by the fact that neither military nor church leaders lead the way. Well organized and well financed colonists brought European settlement to the Rio Grande Plain. Extensive survey work determined the best locations for both agriculture and ranching centers, and then well administrated pueblos or towns were established. Sufficient numbers of colonists were assigned to each location to maintain the new colony until it was well rooted and able to stand on its own. Franciscans and Jesuits did come at the same time to establish indigenous pueblos near or simultaneously with the Spanish pueblos, both as labor pools and under the guise of *Reductions*. Though some of these native pueblos were temporary in nature, or were soon assimilated through interaction with the Spanish pueblo, some endured and eventually became Mexican towns.

José de Escandón was a key figure in the colonization of the Rio Grande Plain. He was chosen to receive a Spanish land grant for his settlement plan called *Nuevo Santander*. Two of his informal titles describe the man: the *Father of the lower Rio Grande Valley* and the *Exterminator of the Pames of Querétaro*, ostensibly for leading the assaults on the Pame uprisings in Guanajuato and Celaya in 1727.[26] Later in his career, to reward him for his services, the Spanish Crown granted him the title of *Conde de Sierra Gorda*, (Count of the Mountains) making him a nobleman and free from having to pay taxes.[27] He was considered one of the greatest statesmen of New Spain in the eighteenth century.

Escandón, as a military leader, was appointed to map the Rio Grande Plain and submit a proposal for the subjugation of the indigenous people. He accomplished this by sending seven groups from seven different locations (Tampico, Valles, Queretaro, Linares, Cerralvo, Monclova, and La Bahia), all to meet at the mouth of the Rio Grande. For two years, Escandón advertised before leaving Queretaro in 1748 with 750 soldiers and 2,500 colonizers. While passing through San Luis Potosí and Tula, he added more colonists, animals, and equipment. Colonists, from established families of the region, knew their trades in agriculture and ranching. Induced to come with promises of land and other concessions, they especially looked forward to freedom from Spanish officialdom in the semi-isolated Rio Grande Plain.[28] The soldiers, not conscripts, were chosen as family men who would build their own homesteads while responding to the demands of crisis and soldiery.

The long wagon trains of household goods going north, along with their herds of livestock bring to mind the great wagon trains of the American West which would come 200 years later. Over the next seven years Escandón with his well motivated colonists founded 23 Spanish and indigenous Pueblos,[29] mostly in the Rio Grande

Plain, including Laredo (TX), San Fernando (MX), Reynosa (MX), Dolores (TX), Victoria (MX), and Juamave (MX).[30] A few settlements such as Juamave were already illegally in existence before this great colonization of Nuevo Santander started; therefore, Escandón simply adopted them and made them legal. There were other settlements like the ranches along the Nueces watershed and additional *ranchos* north of the Rio Grande which accounts for the state lines of Tamaulipas and Nuevo Leon originally being on the Nueces River, not the Rio Grande. Escandón was responsible for the administration of the Nuevo Santander colonies up to the San Antonio River for 22 years.

Though some towns, such as Reynosa had grown into a regional center with 15,000 inhabitants by 1765, most of the population of the Rio Grande Plain was rural, the typical community being the ranch or ranching village. The basic social structure was the family or clan as generations were added in these relatively isolated communities.

In the Rio Grande Plain, the original land grant holder, and later his descendants, lived and worked on the ranch. There was little gap between the owner and the cowhand, with the democratizing influence of the horse culture and self-defense having worked its magic on the Spanish and the absorbed indigenous people alike. Roundups and brandings were community projects, as well as levee building and irrigation projects.

Allegedly Escandón had two enemies, the Jesuits and the secular priests. These, of course, were the other two local geographical authorities who sought to dominate the colonists. The Jesuits, because of their idea of *reductions,* had to have the pueblos their way or they could not function. They were thrown out of all the Spanish empire in 1767, their lack of respect of the other institutions of the Roman Church appearing as arrogance to their contemporaries. The secular priests reviled Escandón because they saw themselves as in charge of all souls within their geographic dominion. Also, when Escandón used Franciscan friars to establish indigenous pueblos, the secular priests were offended. In this epoch one of the novelties was that the orders and the secular church were entering to minister in the same area at the same time and rather than cooperate, found themselves in competition with one another.

The Friars and Priests

By the 1750s, much had change in New Spain. The terrible Chichimeca wars were just a frightful memory, now two generations back in time. Silver mining brought a standard of wealth unheard of before to the entire region, indeed in all of Europe. The great silver rushes provided very productive, steady employment, although the indigenous American was still the common laborer and on the lowest rung of the social ladder. While New Spain was growing stronger and wealthier, Old Spain was growing weaker, both politically and economically. The Jesuits had brought a whole new methodology to frontier missions in the interior of New Spain. New cities were coming into being and sedentary, indigenous populations were established in pueblos throughout the region. The vigor shown by the reformation movement within the orders had long since waned. Missions that should have been turned over to the secular church were still being pastored by the members of mendicant orders. Few Franciscans were venturing out into unknown lands. Of the mendicants it was said: "At the period of which we write, the clergy of New Spain were inferior to that class in Europe, in both morality and intelligence. With the exception of the Jesuits . . . the entire clergy of Mexico were not only destitute of the virtues necessary to their station, but were in every respect profligate. Some of them, disregarding their vows of poverty, turned merchants; others, forgetting their oaths of chastity, indulged in the grossest licentiousness."[31]

Many Franciscans and in particular one young friar Antonio Linaz de Jesus Maria noticed the deterioration of his order's calling. He preached the gospel to the seminomadic Pame of the valley of Rio Verde and the mountainous regions of San Luis Potosí and Queretaro. The sedentary peoples of the south and central portions of New Spain had received the Roman Catholic gospel, but the northern frontier mountainous areas were virtually abandoned, or never subjugated due to the difficulty of reaching them both culturally and geographically. Linaz, who was sent to Europe as a representative of his order, pondered during the long voyage the problems of the Franciscan Order in New Spain, and sought solutions to get the apostolic order back into the forefront of missionary work which had been yielded to the Jesuits. While in Europe, he presented a solution to the General of his order, and with his approval, to Rome. He recruited 23 Franciscan friars and returned with Papal authority to establish a special institution for the training of missionaries before sending them out to their respective fields.[32]

The first school, *El Colegio Apostólico de Misioneros Franciscanos para la Propagación de la Fe*, (The Apostolic College of Franciscan Missionaries for the Propagation of the Faith) was established in the old convent of the Holy Cross in Querétaro (La Santa Cruz de Querétaro).[33] This new concept—missionary *pre-field* preparation to equip those called to be missionaries for the highly specialized demands of cross-cultural evangelistic ministries—also provided a place for missionaries to return after their apostolic service for a time of debriefing, rest, and spiritual renewal. The idea of preparing missionaries in practical as well as philosophical and theological ways became a requirement for candidates resulting in more than 30 of these special mission schools for the *Propagation of the Faith*, the last one organized being San Luis Rey of the California missions.[34] For this Seventh Epoch of study, the school in Queretaro and the San Francisco convent in Zacatecas prepared most of the friars who would be working in the Rio Grande Plain, Nuevo Leon, Nuevo Santander, and Texas.

In essence, the new methods taught in these missionary schools were a summation of the effective methodologies of evangelism learned in indigenous areas of New Spain to that date. First, the preaching had to be adjusted to the ability and cultural understanding of the indigenous people—that is, presented in a way that truly brought understanding of the gospel of Jesus Christ according to Trent. Second, the friars had to understand more deeply what it meant spiritually to be a missionary, to take their apostolic calling seriously. Thirdly, the friars had to understand that they were preaching a holistic gospel—their work was to develop the whole man spiritually, physically, and economically so that he could participate in the whole of Spanish society.

These were the first developmental strides the Franciscans had made in missiology since their initial entrance into the New Spain mainland in the second epoch. This educational philosophy dictated that the spiritual always had to go hand in hand with the material development of the indigenous people. Undoubtedly many of the ideas came from observing the Jesuits in Nueva Vizcaya, and Quiroga's social experiments with the Tarascan nation. Friars no longer baptized and then figured out how to feed and clothe the natives while teaching them to be Spanish culturally. Under this new philosophy the Franciscans aimed at making the indigenous people into *spiritual* Christians, and making them a skilled, self-supported, contributing member of their community as practiced in the Quiroga indigenous pueblos of the second epoch. Seldom were these goals completely achieved, but the expected results of ministry raised the bar considerably, as were the abilities and performance expected of the missionary.

In most all missionary work, the support structure and the pre-field preparations are of great importance; still the final results will depend almost entirely upon the man on the field following the Spirit of God—that is, the character, integrity, obedience and spirituality of the man sent. Because of the complexity of the change agent role in a cross-cultural context, especially when dealing with the conflicting spiritual concepts that inform the two different cultures, there is no way really to know how a missionary will perform in his cross-cultural ministry context until he is in it. When the friar is at the end of a communication and supply line with a time lag of weeks or months, the situation can rapidly become dangerous for both the missionary and the people of the target culture. The schools of mission founded by Linaz were an attempt to face this issue head-on by requiring a period of two years minimum of working together, praying and studying together, learning language, and attending to one another's needs. In this context of living and working together the character and personality traits could be evaluated and personal problems dealt with by experienced, spiritual leadership as skills were being learned to make the missionary more effective in his calling.

The indigenous people of the Rio Grande Plain had already suffered repeated epidemics, demographic collapse, and in some cases cultural disintegration. They were besieged by enemies and foreigners from all sides and they were losing, or had lost, their own cultural integrity. The friars were under the authority of the Viceroy who had demanded the reduction of the natives—the system that collected and confined them to villages, or new indigenous pueblos. But to do this the indigenous Americans had to unlearn all that they had previously acquired. The native's wandering, seminomadic life had to cease; he now had to have a sedentary home; he had to learn to survive on a fixed piece of land and a few domesticated animals; he had to have a fixed place of worship. From the native's perspective his passions and morality had to conform to a new standard, a new understanding of himself, and of God, or really all the new gods the Spanish were introducing. The native's habits, manners, and his entire nature had to change.[35] Yet he still was just an *Indio*, and he was still on the lowest rung of the social ladder.

The friars in these missionary schools were being prepared to attempt to take the indigenous people through this nearly impossible set of changes. The colonists and Crown of Spain would not tolerate the previous indigenous existence; the Roman Church could not tolerate their previous religion, and at this point, the indigenous people of the Seventh Epoch of conquest were utterly defenseless against the Spanish. For both protection and survival, the Rio Grande Plains native people would be assimilated very quickly into the Spanish culture.

Reductions of the Rio Grande Plain

From the conquest of Hispaniola in the Caribbean the institution of the *encomienda*—giving control of large chunks of land with the indigenous people on it—resulted in the indigenous Americans becoming slaves, or serfs at best, on their own land. This usually resulted in uprisings of the subjugated people, runaways, resistance, and an implacable hatred of the foreigners on the part of the numerous groups and tribes still retaining their freedom.[36] The concept of the *Reduction*—gathering together the nomadic or seminomadic groups in an area to found an indigenous pueblo (a Spanish style town of natives) was an attempt to avoid the *encomienda* form of slavery but achieve the same results of founding sedentary societies of the indigenous peoples patterned after the Spanish town. They all had the elements of a Spanish village: a church, school, house for the priest, workshops, and then dwellings laid out in rectangular bocks with a plaza and with the church in the center.

Two features were distinct to this epoch in the foundation of indigenous reductions. The first was that they were being established simultaneously in the proximity of the foundation of Spanish towns. One was not created to dominate the other; while colonists founded their towns, friars founded their reduction pueblos. The second feature was that, though some indigenous pueblos did continue on to become

New Spain towns, many became a type of halfway house for the indigenous North Americans who soon ended up in the Spanish towns or haciendas as a labor pool for the Spanish. Because of this population loss to the Spanish town, some mission reductions closed after only 10 or 20 years. Other reductions had such a large turnover of inhabitants it was difficult to teach them anything before they moved on to other settlements.

Both supplying a continuous flow of natives to the Friars and keeping them in the reduction pueblo once they were there was difficult. Freedom, dear to all, was the way of life of the indigenous people. To congregate them, the military had to bring them to the selected location for a mission pueblo. Not content with the fruits of persuasion and kind treatment, the native people taken, especially the very young, were trained up in the mysteries of the Roman Catholic Church, methods of agriculture, and cottage industries. This began a new mix of sedentary people around the mission reduction towns in the midst of still free, migratory groups. To add to the strength of the missions and the number of the converts, reliable *mission natives* of these pueblos were sent out among their free brethren to bring them in either by persuasion, sometimes by deception, and finally if necessary, brought in by force.

To supplement their own meager incomes, the friars had to charge for their services. In addition to the head-tax levied on all natives under the Spanish, there were the tithes, marriage fees, offerings for any petitioned service or prayers, and especially for absolution for past offences by the priest.[37]

In this epoch of conquest, the many laws designed over the years to protect the indigenous people were both published and in effect, and, for the most part they were being respected. However, much of the poor success of the missions in accomplishing their goals resulted from loopholes in the regulations of the Spanish government and incompetent officials. The soldiers that were assigned to the Rio Grande Plain after the first wave of colonists were established, were underpaid, poorly trained, badly clothed, idle, and disorderly.[38] Though the soldiers gave the friars people with whom they could work, by example the soldiers were undermining all that the friars were trying to teach. The colonists needed laborers and the indigenous people were the only source available. Since the founding of the silver mines, good wages were being paid for good workers and also by colonists, which caused a constant draining of the population of the mission pueblos.

In spite of all the problems, under the direction of the Franciscans, indigenous people built their own communities, erected stone churches, and developed stable agrarian economies. With the assistance of two or three soldiers from the nearby presidio, some of the natives were taught to use European arms, so that nearly every militia had enlisted within it a strong complement of mission native auxiliaries. In the mission pueblo the indigenous people learned loyalty to the Crown of Spain, rudiments of Spanish culture, proper Roman Catholic dogma and homage due to the local symbols of deity, along with the vocational skills needed for economic self-sufficiency.

The days were highly structured for mission natives. Before sunrise, bells called them to morning Mass and religious instruction. After worship they returned to their quarters for a morning meal. Some men would then head for the fields, orchards, gardens, or quarries. Others stayed to practice learned skills such as tanning leather, forging iron in the workshops, and different wood crafts. A few were shepherds tending livestock at the distant ranches. The women cooked, sewed, spun, weaved, gardened, fashioned candles and made pottery. Fishing and arrow making occupied the older residents, while all children over five practiced their catechisms, usually in the Spanish language. The success of vocational training was apparent in the structures the Indians built, the farms they carved out of the land, and the growing herds of horses, cattle, sheep, hogs, and goats they tended.[39]

The indigenous people who grew up in the mission pueblos were well indoctrinated in the Roman Catholic culture. Many had the same or better understanding of spiritual teachings as their Spanish town counterparts. Many Spanish men still took native wives and concubines, and their children married others of mixed race or other indigenous people resulting in many who called themselves Spanish or Roman Catholic who lived culturally as Spanish colonists, and yet by blood were more than 50% indigenous by race. Due to baptism the natives all had Spanish surnames. Therefore the indigenous people rapidly disappeared into the Mestizo culture as Roman Catholics, claiming to be culturally Spanish, while denying their indigenousness—yet they were and continue to be far more Native American than the majority of those claiming Native American descent on North American indigenous reservations today.

The Mestizo, as they were being called, had a rightful claim to both the indigenous and the Spanish cultural heritages. Often they spoke both Spanish and one or two indigenous languages. They were Roman Catholic outwardly, but a great many still honored beliefs from indigenous religions. They respected the old *holy places* even if they now had Spanish names. They used the *curanderos* (healers) when sickness, disease, or social problems required it. Therefore, the Spanish pueblo with its secular priests, or the mission pueblo with its Franciscan or Jesuit friars, both ended up becoming Mestizo, Roman Catholic, and culturally Spanish in its administration and with its Spanish upper-class families, while maintaining heavy influences of indigenous culture within its lower class families. The cast systems evolving endured for many decades but were eventually made illegal, but that did little to change the attitudes of the people. The cast divisions still can be seen today in most northern Mexican towns.

Spanish Roman Catholic Missiology for The Seventh Epoch

It is now possible to apply the framework for missiological analysis to this Seventh Epoch of conquest of the Nuevo Leon, Nuevo Santander, and what geologically can be called the Rio Grande valley with the Coastal Plain. The first area is *apostolic practice.* At the beginning of this epoch a lethargic, poorly motivated Franciscan clergy was just going through the motions of organizing native communities, usually as an appendage to a European colony. They were using the encomienda peonage labor to build and maintain facilities while baptizing and teaching children how to be good Roman Catholics. Considerable animosity existed between the Jesuits, the secular priesthood, and the Franciscans with unending jurisdiction squabbles.

This situation was a primary cause of a reform movement within the Franciscans of New Spain, led by Antonio Linaz that resulted in the formation of specialized schools for missionary training. Friars were taught that preaching had to be presented in a way that truly brought understanding of the gospel, that the friars themselves had to understand more deeply what it meant spiritually to be a missionary, and that their work was to develop the whole man spiritually, physically, and economically. Throughout this Seventh Epoch the new attitude towards their goals and purposes for the Native Americans resulted in one of the most efficient conversions of any indigenous group encountered in any epoch. Culturally the indigenous people were responding, learning and assuming their new identity and adapting to Spanish agricultural and ranching methods to such a degree that the indigenous cultures disappeared within a generation. The natives were still there, but the Tamaulipans of this vast area were culturally Mestizo within this short time frame.

Therefore the combination of a desperate, dying people and an escape into a well organized, alternative life style yielded great success in both areas: bringing the natives into the Spanish cultural sphere, and at the same time bringing them into the Roman Catholic sphere. Superior Franciscan leadership for this epoch must be credited with these results.

There were those who did not want Spanish society or religion. They fled to the mountainous areas and waged a type of guerilla warfare causing havoc among outlying haciendas and the smaller, isolated towns. They were the last of the proud, dying indigenous cultures, but the last, nonetheless. These painful exceptions marred the otherwise very successful pacification of the Coahuiltecan people groups of the Rio Grande Plain.

Apostolic Practice advanced in methodology that would continue to be a key to successful missionary work for ages to come: the specialized training of candidates planning to minister in a frontier mission field. The amount of Christology or the doctrines of salvation that were included in this new emphasis is not the issue here. The stated goals of baptizing, teaching, and cultural conversion to New Spain Spanish culture were accomplished by this new-school methodology. This area of mission theory and practice took a giant step forward in this second entrance of the Spanish to the Rio Grande plain.

In the second area of missiology, *church and mission structure*, secular and mendicant priests were entering the Rio Grande Plain in both the first and second entrances to this region. The secular priest established works in the new Spanish towns; the friars established works in the new indigenous pueblos. Though some of the pueblos became established towns, many were short lived with the newly converted and instructed neophytes quickly moving on to become part of other Spanish pueblos and towns. This would seem to indicate a more harmonious working relationship between the Franciscans and the secular clergy, but not with the Jesuits who were expelled soon after the beginning of this epoch—precisely because of their lack of cooperation with the other Roman Catholic institutions. So a symbiotic relationship did seem to function with the mission structure feeding into the secular church structure. The expressions of Roman Catholicism as taught by both mendicant and secular priests were sufficiently uniform that there seems to have been little difficulty for a person to pass from one religious authority structure to the other. We must credit the strict enforcement of tridentine theology for this uniformity.

With the expulsion of the Jesuits, there was also a movement to secularize all existing mendicant properties. This move apparently was to take the most productive lands out of the hands of the clerics who were usually the first to establish themselves on the best of the land available. This did not slow down the friars of this epoch. They just continued to expand their missionary works into the north, across the Rio Grande into what is today South Texas.

The Gospel and Religions and *Salvation and non-Christians,* two distinct and important areas of missiology today, have been combined in this analysis because Tridentine doctrine allowed for no other religions but their own, as the one true religion. Because there was no room for salvation in any other religion, or any other Christian expressions that were not in submission to the Roman Catholic traditions, the policy of the mendicants and secular priests was always to eliminate the other religions encountered and harshly deal with any other Christian expressions as heretics. The inquisition was still around for the latter, though not often invoked, and it was accepted as illegal to apply the inquisition to indigenous people of this epoch. The one exception to this Tridentine ignorance of apostolic missions was the fact that the friars and secular priests *went* in response to the Great Commission; they understood the command to go, in spite of the terribly anemic gospel message they carried.

Christianity and culture is another area greatly constricted by Tridentine theology. New Spain was Roman Catholic and Spanish culture was imposed upon all other cultures the Spanish encountered in the Americas. Even at this late date in the conquest there is no recognition of the viability of other cultures, or that God as the creator of culture could be glorified in cultural expressions other than Spanish Roman Catholic. There was still no indigenous priesthood in New Spain. The cultures the Spanish did encounter in this Rio Grande epoch were in various stages of disintegration, without cultural centers, and without a written language. The Spanish would have seen nothing there to preserve, even if they had ever bothered to look.

As has so often happened in the North American conquests, with the Spanish objective of imposing their culture and the Roman Catholic religion on all of the indigenous societies (and eventually they did succeed to a degree) it is not surprising that no matter how successful the friars were, or how poorly or how failed their attempts may have been, that the indigenous people seldom survived for more than a few generations as a people. The greatest single factor in the loss of indigenous cultures was still disease. Disease that preceded the Spanish then came with the Spanish, and when indigenous people by force were confined in pueblos at relatively close quarters, the concentration only enhanced the spread of diseases. Probably the second greatest destructive factor in the loss of indigenous cultures was the cultural disintegration, the loss of the indigenous society's compass, leaving those that survived the plagues without a viable way of life, without purpose, direction, or the will to continue living as a distinct people. Then the Spanish invasion with the wars, then slavery, encomiendas, peonage, and confinement into towns and villages took their toll on native ways of life. However, by the time the conquest had reached this point, the indigenous cultures were already doomed to utter destruction. It really did not matter to what degree the friars tried to maintain a healthy respect of the indigenous cultures, if they bothered at all. Cultural disintegration and a reintegration into a subculture of the Spanish town were inevitable.

CHAPTER XI

EIGHTH EPOCH:
THE UPPER CALIFORNIA

Epoch Eight Introduction

The discovery of the *island* of California by the mutinous men of Cortéz in 1533 was only of significance because the survivors reported pearls on the natives who had attacked and killed 20 of their men. This got the interest of Cortéz who attempted a colony at La Paz with three ships, but after two years quit the hostile shores of the Baja. It took another 162 years of failures before a permanent colony was established by the Jesuits. Not finished yet Cortéz sent Francisco Ulloa up the Bay of Cortéz. Ulloa discovered the mouth of the Colorado and established that California was not an island at all but a very long peninsula. It was in 1542 that Rodríguez Cabrillo with three ships entered San Diego harbor and claimed Alta California for Spain.

In 1565, Spain claimed the Philippines and sent Andrés de Urdaneta, an Augustinian friar, to study the western Pacific winds and currents. Discovering that the currents circled back to the coast of California, he established the trade route for the Manila galleons which hauled the riches of Asia back to the harbor of Acapulco on the west coast of New Spain, transferred them overland to Mexico City, on to Veracruz, and then up the gulf current to the Carolinas and across the Atlantic to Spain. The Pacific crossing was a horrendous feat for the galleons, often with over 50% casualties of their crews due to scurvy and beriberi. Some thought that a safe harbor on the California coast would help make shipping safer by shortening the trip for resupply of provisions.

Until 1579, the Pacific had been regarded as a Spanish ocean. Then the murderous pirate Francis Drake crossed through the Straights of Magellan, attacked Spanish settlements and shipping, then traversed the coast to as far north as San Francisco Bay. Following on his heels there was another English pirate in 1586, Thomas Cavendish, with a series of terrible raids on Spanish settlements inflicting murder and mayhem until he successfully attacked a Spanish Galleon just off Cabo San Lucas on the Baja Peninsula.[1] Deemed expedient that the Spanish create a safe harbor on the California coast, Sebastián Vizcaíno in 1602, was sent north to chart and sound the coast and harbors with specific orders not to bother the natives found in those parts. Vizcaíno entered San Miguel bay, formerly named by Cabrillo, renamed it San Diego, and continued to Monterrey Bay describing Monterrey Bay as a very good harbor. However, since threats from England seemed to subside, the pressures for a safe harbor on the coast of California were forgotten.

Time must be taken in great strides when the history of New Spain is considered. Approximately 160 years later again the threats to the California coast by England and Russia were considered. By this time the English were moving west across the continent on a line from Northern Canada to Louisiana. Little was known about the Great Plains or Rocky Mountains at that time, or the obstacles they would present to westward expansion. Russians were developing the fur trade in Alaska and rumored to be moving down the coast of California, as the whole of the west coast of North America from the Baja on was known. In 1765, José de Gálvez was appointed inspector general and sent to New Spain to report on the conditions, especially of the northern frontier areas. Analyzing the information he had gathered Gálvez concluded Russia and England were the primary threats to New Spain's California, especially the unoccupied north Pacific coastal areas.

After formulating his plans for putting down the frontier wars in Sonora and establishing military governments for administrative efficiency, Gálvez moved his headquarters to the Baja in 1767 preparing for a major effort to colonize California. He had hoped to use the missions of the Baja for a base and for supplies but was sorely disappointed upon his arrival. The year before, Gálvez himself had participated in the expulsion of the Society of Jesus delivering arrest warrants and helping to round up Jesuit priests. Only months before his arrival on the Baja all the Jesuits had been removed and the missions were already in a sad state of disrepair. Food stores were gone, orchards and plantings had been left without irrigation and had dried up, and the livestock had been slaughtered.

The Franciscans had just arrived to take the place of the Jesuits and were beginning to restore order but their plans were changed and they were now commissioned to leave the Baja and go to California with Gálvez. At the best of times the Baja had barely supported its own indigenous people; there was certainly no extra for Gálvez to furnish a California expedition. After 236 years as a Spanish possession, the Baja had a European population of about 400 military or ex-military personnel including their families, and a few hundred pitiful mission natives scattered among the remnants of 14 mission compounds throughout the lower third of Baja California. It is hard to imagine a more pathetic missionary endeavor as the Baja appeared to Gálvez.

To use the natives, Gálvez at first tried to rally those who were still left around the missions but found they could not be managed or led. He needed the missionaries. They were the only group of men experienced in managing Native Americans efficiently and were experienced at making them productive. In the age of enlightenment many Spanish officials shared Gálvez's antipathy toward the friars and their missions, but Gálvez still hoped that he could use the missionaries for his own purposes of colonization in California. At no time was there much thought given to conquering Upper California; it was already considered part of New Spain. The concern was to protect it from the English and the Russians by establishing towns and presidios along the coast up to San Francisco, which upon its discovery quickly replaced Monterrey as the key to holding California. But to do that Gálvez needed the indigenous people for labor and to populate his colonies as Spanish subjects. Fortified missions were still the key in Spanish frontier strategy for subjugation and development.

Therefore in 1769, Gálvez implemented his plan for the establishment of colonies in California. He sent two brigantines loaded with men and materials to San Diego, trusting that they would give a head start to the construction of a base camp. Gaspar de Portolá, along with Junípero Serra, led the largest land party starting northward up the Baja from La Paz. Fernando de Rivera, leaving from the more northern Santa Maria mission with 25 soldiers and 40 mission natives moved out ahead of Portola's group. They averaged about five miles a day cutting the first road up through the Baja. It was a long, hard march but as soon as the Portolá group encountered the new path being cut by the Rivera group, they were able to move along very well.

As bad as it was for the two road parties, it was much worse for the crews of the two brigantines. Spanish galleons had been sailing the Western coast from California to Acapulco from the Asian trade for many decades and knew how treacherous that stretch could be. Still, sailing against the wind and the currents at the poorest time of year for doing so, the two ships eventually made it, but 31 members of the crew died from scurvy, and another 20 died after they reach San Diego.[2] It was a disappointing reunion when the three parties came together,[3] but they still had the major objective to be accomplished. Portolá took a band of 60 healthy men to continue their march by land to find Monterrey Bay. They broke a trail along the coast until, stymied by the mountains at San Luis Obispo, they had to go over the coastal range and then follow the Salinas river valley to the coast again. They could not find the bay of their project plans, even though the Salinas River emptied into it. It just didn't fit Vizcaino's description of a great harbor, but they did find San Francisco Bay. With that, they returned to San Diego[4] to wait for the supply ship that was to come later, but the brigantine *San José* out of San Blas had disappeared, never to be seen again.

Among the indigenous people of California, there were no military alignments, no political arrangements or confederacies to pool resources in time of trouble. No diplomatic relations between indigenous groups had been created for common defense. The Spanish purchased submission of the local indigenous groups using the Peace with Purchase concepts; subjugation by force was seldom necessary. Far more often they used intimidation or just relied upon the priests to do their job of *reducing* the groups to mission compounds where they could be trained in the basics of the Spanish society. There were several rebellions, but at first sign of resistance, the rebellions were crushed with pursuit of the leaders, whippings, and executions. The relatively small Spanish forces could not afford to let the indigenous people unite or come to know their own strength in numbers.

It was a very good thing that there were no armies to conquer in California. Just taking possession was challenge enough, almost beyond the Spanish capabilities, even with the well laid plans of Gálvez. Upper California might as well have been an island over two thousand miles away from Mexico City with seemingly nothing of value except some possible harbors for Spanish shipping. Wind, currents, and storms were against any north bound coastal shipping, exacting a frightful cost in ships and lives. The worst deserts on the continent and tribes of fierce desert raiders like the Mojaves, who deeply resented anyone crossing their territory, blocked all land routes. Few of the leaders in New Spain were sure that California was really worth the cost of colonization, even for defensive purposes. But that was what missionary orders were for—to go where no one else could go and do what no one else would, for the Crown and for the Roman Catholic Church. And the friars did it willingly for God, and for the Crown they served.

The Indigenous People of California

At the time of the Spanish takeover, the population of California is estimated to have been about 310,000 people,[5] with possibly as many as a hundred distinct languages and dialects.[6] California encompassed more language diversity than any other equivalent area in the world.[7] Of the 46-native linguistic stocks recognized within the limits of the United States, 22 were found within California. Most of these languages have perished without record.[8]

The geography was nearly as varied as the languages were. The northern coastal redwood forests were nestled between snow-capped mountains and cold ocean currents. The Sierra Nevadas divided those forests from the Owens Valley farm lands, which were bordered on the other side by barren desert mountains. The Sacramento and San Joaquin Valleys approached desert conditions, but with the river systems there was abundant water for irrigation, plus thousands of square miles of rolling grass lands for livestock. At the southern part of Alta California there were near tropical conditions on the coast with warm ocean currents and then rolling desert sand dunes in the southeast corner. The Mojave Desert with its Joshua tree forests rolled right up to the pine forests of the San Bernardino Mountains. All of these diverse terrains had their small tribes of indigenous people who had adapted to their geographic conditions and lived in harmony, but somewhat isolated from one another, with whatever their piece of land had to offer. The colonists were soon to learn that plants which grew anywhere else in the world could be grown well somewhere in California.

To deal with this cultural-geographic diversity, Alta California has been divided into cultural areas where the geography forced similarities among the tribes. These areas were called Northwest, Northeast, Central, Southern, Great Basin, and the Lower Colorado. The details of each cultural area require far more attention than this study can give. California indigenous culture was essentially distinct from all tribes east of the Sierras, characterized by the absence of those features which dominated tribal life elsewhere.[9] The area of most Spanish missions, the Southern coastal areas west of the Lower Colorado deserts, will be examined here in more detail. These were the Chumash, Gabrielino, Luiseño, and Kumeyaay (or Diegueño) of the coastal areas; and the Serrano, Cupeño, and Cahuilla of the interior.

Along the coast the indigenous people were hunter-gatherers with large, sea-going plank canoes for hunting sea mammals, fishing, and the gathering of shellfish. From the land they harvested acorns which were ground and leached with water to remove the bitterness. Nuts, berries, wild rice, clover blossoms, cactus apples, and various roots were collected, while herbs were produced in small kitchen gardens. Stone carving was highly developed among the Chumash for making mortars, pestles, metates, animal effigies, and other utensils. They also made various pottery vessels for storage and domestic use. Of the domestic skills, basket weaving seemed to have been the best developed. The tribal geographic areas were generally well defined ranging from about 50 square miles for smaller tribes, up to several hundred square miles for larger groups. Boundaries of tribes were well marked, recognized, and respected between groups.

Socially both men and women wore their hair long and practiced tattooing. Men went naked except during ritual dancing, women wore short skirts trimmed with feathers. The dance was to music of rattles, flutes, and bone whistles. The Californians had no drums. Weapons were stone knives, a throwing stick to stun rabbits, wooden clubs, and the bow. Hunting was for small game only. Marriage and divorce were simple agreements; polygamy was common. Burial was by cremation in most tribes with the body and most of the possessions of the deceased burned with him, the bones later gathered and buried. The dead were never named again.[10]

The tribal headman exercised leadership in areas of production, distribution, and conservation of food and other material resources such as canoes, furs, pottery, and stone implements. Leadership was hereditary with a tribal structure of sociopolitical ranking under a chief, although he had very little authority. There was usually a process for the selection or de-selection of particular individuals for leadership. The shamans were also recognized leaders—individuals that seemed to have a rapport with spirits and bore the spiritual gifts of healing, cursing, prophecy, and they were appealed to for counsel for hunting, war, weather control, etc. These shaman usually were accompanied by a dream helper, a representative animal that came and spoke in dreams to offer counsel. This position was usually hereditary. Normally the headman and the shaman cooperated in reinforcing each other's positions of leadership.

Old people, mostly men, would tell stories by campfire to pass on wisdom, myths, and legends to succeeding generations, especially during the winter months. This was where the creation stories and basic ideas of life and the physical world were taught. Coyote, always an important figure in California mythology, could be a trickster, fool, or hero in these stories. Indigenous mythology was used to interpret or inform concerning the coming of Europeans. When Drake and his men landed on the coast, the Miwok looked upon them as the dead returning from their home at sea. When the Pomo first saw the sails of a ship on the sea, they thought it was a gigantic bird that portended the end of the world, an apparition which proved to be true for indigenous California.[11]

Common practices causing the Spanish concern, and that missionaries tried to suppress, were certain grossly obscene dances and very licentious conduct. Aged parents or those with health problems were choked to death by their own children in some tribes, usually by crushing the neck with a stick. Infanticide and abortion were so prevalent the practice was very hard to prevent, even in the mission context. With nudity and promiscuity common, the self-indulgent sealing, trading, and exploration crews who sailed the California waters had already introduced a number of European and sexually transmitted diseases forcing the indigenous demographics into swift decline by the time the Franciscans arrived on the scene.

The Franciscan Friars in California

Miguel Jose Serra entered the service of the Roman Catholic Church at the age of 16, and soon joined the Franciscan Order taking the name of Junípero. He studied philosophy and theology, received a doctorate in philosophy at the University of Luliana in La Palma, Spain, and taught at the Convent of San Francisco in La Palma. At the age of 36, Serra submitted to the encouragement of his own disciples, volunteering to serve the Franciscan missions in the new world. He left Cadiz and sailed for Vera Cruz, Mexico. His first assignment was in the Sierra Gorda in Mexico, where he served for nine years (part of the time as superior), learned the language of the Pame Indians,[12] and translated the catechism into their language. Then when the Franciscans were asked to take over the Jesuit missions in Baja California in 1767, these remote facilities became Father Serra's responsibility. In 1769, he set off on the expedition with Gaspar de Portolá where he founded missions at San Diego and Monterey, established the Roman Catholic presence in California, and converted the native Californians to Spanish New Spain culture. He spent the rest of his life in Alta California.

The local natives resented the Spanish penetration of their well-marked land boundaries. However, they were helpless against the offensive brutality of the soldiers and priests invading their land. Immediately the friars began establishing mission complexes: first San Diego in 1769, then San Carlos at Monterey in 1771, San Gabriel in 1771, San Antonio de Borromeo in 1771, San Gabriel Archangel in 1771, San Luis Obispo in 1772, San Juan Capistrano in 1776, San Francisco in 1776, Santa Clara in 1777, and San Buenaventura in 1777.[13]

When Serra founded the mission in San Diego the land belonged to tribes of the Taipei of the Kumeyaay group, and just to the north were the Ipai of the same group. They had a combined population best estimated between 6,000 to 9,000 people.[14] The California tribal groups, given multiple names by others, had their own names for themselves usually local variations; nomenclature and tribal distinctions are not well-classified.[15] Following the pattern Serra had used in the Sierra Gorda of Hidalgo, he organized the native Californian converts to teach them European agricultural techniques. Agriculture was not previously practiced in indigenous California.[16] Mission grounds became model farms that quickly began to feed both the mission population and the presidio in San Diego, per an agreement made by Serra with the Viceroy and according to Gálvez's plan of colonization. In the mission, baptized Kumeyaay were given Spanish names, dressed in blue cloth outfits, and taught to become productive farm workers. They also learned to care for livestock, most of which they had never been seen before, to tan hides, and produce candles, bricks, tiles, shoes, saddles, soap, and other necessities for themselves and the greater community.[17]

The coexistence of the mission compound and native settlements, converted and unconverted villagers, colonial cultural, political, and material practices, along with persistent indigenous practices and beliefs, defined the complex, multicultural, multilingual society of the mission period.[18] The life of the mission Kumeyaay was quite regimented and disciplined.

"The mission system had disrupted every aspect of native life . . . even so, although the Spaniards went far toward regulation [of] outward behavior by imposing regimented time in the work place and spatial confinement, in the end they were unable to eradicate all preconquest traditions, material culture, and historical, religious, and practical knowledge . . . precontact social relations persisted, not only in the countryside, but also within the mission compound itself."[19]

This regulation of behavior included physical punishment for offences, incarceration, hard labor, stocks, and/or limited rations. Indigenous flight from the missions brought on search and restoration military patrols by militia personnel who brought back not only the escapee, when possible, but often any other indigenous people stumbled upon, especially children and their mothers. The cooperation with presidios or soldiers stationed at the mission was essential to the friars' operation of the California mission system. "Missionaries might complain about the soldiers' misbehavior . . . but generally saw them as indispensable collaborators and protectors."[20] The primary work of the soldiers was to assist the friars in their assigned task of civilizing the natives and maintaining the mission's labor force for commercial production essential to all the California colonies.

As difficult as mission life was for the indigenous people, the alternatives were often less attractive. The friars built upon the felt needs of the indigenous people. Cultural disintegration, invasion and destruction of native habitat, loss of family and other relationships due to disease, all were *push* factors that caused the old ways to cease to function. Hunter-gatherer tribes found they could not survive using the old ways. Physical survival, the search for enough food, shelter, and protection brought many of the weakened, debilitated tribal survivors to the missions. Some authors point out that the concentration of indigenous populations at the mission was a primary cause of the rapid spread of disease, of the alienation of indigenous cultural patterns, and a collective depression, all resulting in an accelerated population decline. Still, especially during drought years, recruitment increased substantially as small groups of hungry, frighten people turned to the missions for survival.[21]

Other reasons for going to the mission were the opportunities to use new tools, to acquire new knowledge and techniques, especially in agriculture and animal husbandry, and to learn the use of equipment for increased production. It is hard to imagine what the introduction of the machete did for a hunter-gatherer who was accustomed only to stone implements, or how the steel knife or cooking pot change the responsibilities and possibilities of the women's chores. The introduction of new vegetables, fruit bearing trees, and grains added great possibilities to the standard diet. The introduction of domesticated animals such as the pig, sheep, goats, chicken, ducks, cattle, donkey and horse all changed forever the diet and way of life for indigenous people. Finally it should be mentioned that a very real draw to the mission, but with extremely negative results, was the opportunity to partake of distilled alcoholic drinks, greatly desired by most Native Californians who, through the effects of addiction and drunkenness, soon became problems in their own right.

Once an indigenous person was baptized, he or she became a neophyte, or new believer, a Spanish Roman Catholic member of society. While many natives were lured to join the missions for reasons mentioned above, as well as out of curiosity and a desire to participate and engage in trade, many found themselves ensnared in the mission system once they received the sacrament of baptism. To the friars, a baptized native was a student, a new beginner that had to be trained in order to participate in Spanish society. He was no longer free to move about the country, but had to learn to work with his hands and worship correctly at the mission under the strict observance of the friars and overseers, who herded them to daily masses and their assigned work. If a Native Californian did not report for duties for a period of several days, they were considered runaways and soldiers were sent after them or any other indigenous people they could find. The focus was always on women and children causing the men to eventually join them at the mission compound, and stay there for the sake of their families.

Little notice was given on the west coast of Alta California to the events occurring on the east coast of North America. The English had always been just a troublesome bunch of depraved pirates. The Spanish had little interest in the north Atlantic coast, and a strong navy patrolling their trade routes kept the English in check. However, the English colonies were proving to be even more aggressive than the English themselves, and even more depraved concerning their policies of conquest and extermination whenever the indigenous people were encountered. In 1776, the rebellious colonies threw out the English and the United States of America came into existence on the northern frontiers with New Spain. This only increased the depravations of the aggressive, upstart nation that seemed to respect no agreements, no treaties, and certainly nothing established by the Spanish of New Spain. Soon they overran Louisiana, Texas, and penetrated New Mexico, always looking west to Alta California. They did not consult the indigenous nations or the Spanish of New Spain about their concept of North American *Manifest Destiny*—the term given to stealing all the land they could take and hold by force, from Native American or Spanish alike. Events were already in motion that would soon be affecting the California missions.

An example of how the missions continued to expand all along the California coast was San Juan Capistrano. It was founded as a mission in Acágchemem territory in 1776. By 1796, nearly one thousand Acágchemem resided at the mission. The vast majority of initial converts at San Juan Capistrano were children, a common pattern in most of the missions. The children were likely brought by their parents to make alliances with the missionaries and to gain the benefits the missionaries were introducing.[22] By 1812, the mission gained control of the entire Acágchemem geographic area, changing its cultural, economic, political, and spatial order.

A total of 146 Franciscan friars, all of whom were ordained as priests, and most Spaniards by birth, served in California during the years of 1769-1845. Of that number, 67 missionaries, nearly half, died at their posts—two of them as martyrs. The remainder returned to lower New Spain, soon to be called Mexico, or to Europe due to illness, or having completed their ten-year service commitment. As the rules of the Franciscan Order forbade friars to live alone, two missionaries were assigned to each settlement and sequestered in the mission's convent. To each of these pairs of friars the governor assigned a guard of five or six soldiers under the command of a corporal, who generally acted as stewards of the mission's temporal affairs, subject to the friars' instructions.

Californios, as all non-indigenous people came to be called, established Los Angeles as a Spanish pueblo and quickly gained control of the countryside setting in motion the *Rancho Movement*, and coming into direct opposition to the friars' control of the lands claimed by the missions. Franciscan Missions that had been established on lands claimed by indigenous groups, claimed the entire well defined land of those groups as the indigenous people died out and/or became mission neophytes. Mission herds expanded to fill the lands around mission compounds. In theory, the missions were holding these indigenous lands in custody for the neophytes. But the baptized, acculturated, neophytes were rapidly moving on to opportunities with the ranchers and privatized haciendas. Retired soldiers were given rights to use lands and huge *ranchos*, as they were known in California, came into being on dispossessed indigenous lands, bringing more direct challenges to mission land claims. During this time the rural population of indigenous people was slowly being consumed by European disease and the disintegration of their cultures. Indigenous ways of life could no longer be maintained in the rapidly changing California context under European control.

In 1802, a particularly devastating measles epidemic hit the California missions, soon followed by another in 1805. The latter was catastrophic because it was accompanied by outbreaks of whooping cough and dysentery at the same time. Still later a powerful earthquake totally destroyed the mission buildings at San Juan Capistrano, killing

40 indigenous worshipers inside.[23] It appeared to the natives the Roman Catholic God was not collaborating in the friars' plans for indigenous Californians. Then in 1813, Spain passed a law for the secularization of all missions that had been established for more than ten years.[24] In 1821, the Mexican Republic came into being and quickly moved to deal with their indigenous populations. Civil colonial leadership jumped at this chance to get their hands on mission properties. In the mid-1830s, Mexican colonists sacked the missions dividing the church properties, equipment, and land among themselves.

For the mission natives who had actually made the transition to Spanish Catholic culture and who had lost connections with tribal villages and indigenous ways, returning to a natural indigenous existence was rarely successful. Limited choices meant becoming feudal laborers in colonial villages and on Mexican ranchos. It is estimated that between 1834 and 1838, nearly 15,000 of the 53,600 baptized mission Native Americans were left in this precarious condition by way of the confiscation of their properties, their stock, equipment, and other valuables.

The independence of Mexico had little impact politically on the missions of California; there were unsolvable problems much closer to home to occupy the Mexican central government. Weak and continuously changing federal governments left the outlying provinces like Texas and California essentially to survive on their own. While Mexico had granted citizenship and abolished the *casta* system for indigenous people under the *Plan of Iguala*, the plan could not stop the Spanish cultural tradition of viewing indigenous people as the lowest class of people in Mexico, still without the legal right to hold private property. Six years later Mexico initiated the expulsion of all non-Mexican born religious workers from Mexico, which included the entire hierarchy of the secular church and nearly all the friars of the various mendicant orders.[25] The remaining California indigenous groups were then faced with the utter impossibility of survival as indigenous people or maintaining their own cultural integrity. The only group who had an interest in protecting, ministering, and evangelizing the indigenous people who were still left in California were now gone at the time of the Native Californian's greatest need for refuge.

European diseases again returned with a vengeance, further reducing the indigenous demographics. Smallpox hit California again in 1833, causing major disruptions among the Pomo, Wappo, and then the Wintun in 1838, the Miwok in 1844, and the Pomos again in 1850. An unknown disease among the Wintun, Maidu, Miwok, and Yokuts in 1833, wiped out 4,500 people, ten percent of their populations. In all, diseases were estimated to have caused 60% of the population decline up to the end of the Mexican period; the California indigenous population had fallen to a total of only about 150,000 people.[26]

Then the English speaking North Americans descended upon California. In 1847, the last of the resistance of Mexican Californios' surrendered in Upper California, and the Bear Flag revolt was won. In 1848, Upper California and most of Northern New Spain were ceded to the North after the United States of America's invasion and conquest of lower Mexico. In 1849, gold was discovered in the Sacramento Valley and the rush by Anglo Americans into California spelt doom for the remaining indigenous groups in the mountains and valleys of California.

The rapid depopulation, from about 150,000 indigenous people in 1848 to about 30,000 in 1850 when California became a part of the United States of America, indicates something of the hideousness of what had happened to the indigenous populations already ravaged by European disease, cultural disintegration, dispossession of their lands, and separation from the Franciscan friars—the only people on this earth who cared anything at all about their well-being. The atrocities of the California "forty-niners" against the indigenous people, as measured by the disappearance of approximately 120,000 of them in a two-year period, is one of the more despicable chapters in California and American history that, by comparison, leaves no grounds for criticism by English settlers of the Spanish, their missionaries, or their methods.

Spanish Roman Catholic Missiology

The missiology applied in the eighth epoch of expansion into California must be viewed in the context of political control and economic development more than any other epoch to date. There was no other reason for Spain to bother with California other than to prevent other powers from doing so. European powers accustomed to crossing one or several national borders in a single day, had trouble conceiving of weeks of hard travel with very high risk of loss of property and life just to visit another province of New Spain. New Spain was still the King's own possession under his direct authority through the Viceroy in Mexico City where a two month turnaround in communications with the distant provinces was considered good. No one in California could figuratively lift a finger without direct authorization from the Viceroy in Mexico City 2,000 miles away.

When Gálvez planned the logistics of the occupation of California, he did not have to think in terms of conquest but in terms of possession, simply taking possession away from small, scattered, unorganized indigenous tribes. To do that he needed the experts in controlling the natives, the priest who had perfected entrance, domestication, teaching, and social indoctrination of the indigenous Americans in all kinds of living conditions. He could use the priest, for whom he cared very little, and he could get by with a minimum of professional military assets to protect his religious assets until domestication and colonization could be accomplished. Escandón used soldier-settlers for both protection and colonization in the Rio Grande Valley; the soldiers were also his settlers. Gálvez viewed both soldiers and priests as tools apart from colonists to accomplish his purposes of paving the way to establish self-supported colonies of settlers in Spanish Ranchos and Spanish towns.

In Baja California, for a time, the civil and military authorities were actually under the Jesuit priests in the administration of the colonies. In California, it was more of a symbiotic relationship where the mission had to supply the greater part of food and supplies for the soldiers for them to maintain a presence and, as military men, through typical Spanish audacity and frightful behavior, maintain control of the tribes. In turn, fear of the soldiers protected the priests as they went about their ministry of domestication of the natives. Soldiers kept the missions supplied with personnel for labor quotas, farming, and ranching tasks. Throughout the mission period, the dozen or so indigenous rebellions were quickly and harshly put down with the cost of only two priests receiving their martyr's crown.

The friars had their choice of the best lands for their all-important task of producing food stuffs for themselves and the presidios. Gálvez knew he could not count on a supply base 2,000 miles away; from the start, California had to be self-sufficient. This was no small factor in how quickly California would become economically independent of New Spain and Mexico. The indigenous people did not practice agriculture above private home garden plots; agriculture had to be taught by demonstration using the indigenous labor that was available. All domestic animals had to be imported and animal husbandry taught; natives had to be trained in the skills of the *vaquero* (cowboy) and the *pastor* (shepherd).

The North American native had to be taught and trained from scratch in nearly all areas of basic European culture, but that was why the priests were chosen for this task. So the institution of Roman Catholic Apostolic missions spearheaded the penetration of Upper California along with the presidio which was essential and supportive of the mission, but they were not there as a military invasion for conquest as in previous epochs. Both of these institutions paved the way for the Rancho and the Spanish Pueblo enabling colonization to become a reality. The mission and the friars were a means to a secular end, just one step in the process of the domestication of Upper California.

Noticeably absent is the subject of evangelization of the indigenous people. This obviously was foremost in the minds of the friars as they set out for California and in their plans for building mission compounds, but it was not the primary reason for which they were being sent. Evangelism would be their privilege as they accomplished the required tasks of establishing a Spanish presence, and that of logistically supporting the military presence.

Therefore in this Eighth Epoch evangelism was a tertiary objective of the colonization enterprise. The main objectives given to the friars were supporting the establishment of Spanish colonies by making culturally Spanish citizens out of the natives, and providing a labor pool. Hopefully they would see the natives baptized as they went about their other major purposes. With these goals in mind, the missiology of this Eighth Epoch of Upper California conquest and colonization can be evaluated.

Missiology of the Upper California Occupation

Apostolic Practice dropped several notches in any evaluation of the California missionary practices. The church was being used for secular purposes, and the primary objective of the California mission was to divorce the indigenous people from their own culture to make them culturally Spanish. This was always part of a twofold purpose of the missionaries, but in California, the priorities became rearranged. In geopolitical terms, the Upper California missions were a successful frontier institution for geographical expansion with minimal exertion and expense to the Crown.[27] At this time the Spanish Crown was not motivated by an interest in evangelism, not even in pretense, but in securing California from English and Russian expansion. Gálvez was not interested in evangelism but in using the friars to domesticate the natives and provide a labor pool for the colonists. Serra was compromised from the beginning of the project by agreements to provide food and supplies to the military presence through indigenous labor, agricultural development, and ranching. "The shifts in economic structure and . . . cultural change occurred not as a result of . . . ideology of the missionaries, but rather because of the needs of the colonial state."[28] In the process of colonization the priest could baptize and convert, with the soldiers there to coerce if the neophytes could not be gained through persuasion.

In this context of spearheading colonization, bringing about obedience to Christ was again short-circuited by the Tridentine concept of baptismal regeneration, by the pervasive concept of community being sufficient for edification or Christian growth, and by the tridentine use of idols and paintings as objects of worship rather than the invisible Godhead who must be worshiped in spirit and in truth. The friars could rest on the concept of evangelism through baptism being sufficient for salvation, and focus on the challenge of eliminating the indigenous cultural practices, while training the neophytes in the ways of Spanish-Europeans.

The results, as we have seen in previous epochs, were only a small portion of the whole counsel of God being taught or modeled. The attractions to the mission were numerous and many Native Californians responded voluntarily, but learning a new belief system was not one of their primary interests. A whole new life style, including manual labor, was designed to train the neophytes in European methods and culture, but the spiritual exercises taught by the friars could not replace indigenous meanings imputed by the natives to the Spanish worship patterns. To this day the worship of the surviving indigenous people of California is a mixture of the Tridentine Roman Catholic and indigenous religious practices. As seen before, there was a church building, there was a mission complex, and many thousands of indigenous people were baptized into the new Spanish colonial culture, but most evidence would indicate that very little actual *conversion to Christianity* was taking place.

An examination of the belief systems among survivors of the indigenous people today reveals very little Christology or any emphasis on substitutionary atonement and a powerful, resurrected, reigning Christ. It appears that images and symbols were preached in place of the glorified Christ; catechisms were taught in place of the Scriptures. The eschatology was limited to purgatory and how to get out of there more quickly. Sainthood, as established by the Roman Church, was superimposed in place of the sainthood of all believers while encouraging a type of pantheism expressed through Roman Catholic symbols and lingering native symbols.

In the area of *Church Structure and Mission* there was no conflict or symbiotic relationship. The Franciscans had exclusive right to ministry in Upper California and no secular clergy was involved until the secularization of the missions began, the vast majority of priests having been evicted from Mexico. By then, most of the missions were sacked or abandon with everything of value confiscated by the civil authorities or stolen by the colonists. All mission properties which were indigenous properties held in trust by the priests were then divided up among the colonists. Missions that continued to function as secular churches, such as in San Luis Obispo and in Santa Barbara, existed by renting out portions of the physical installations for secular purposes. Only the mission in Santa Barbara continued spiritual ministry uninterrupted to the present day.

In the area of the *Gospel and Religions* or *Salvation and the Non-Christian* there are again the constraints of Tridentine Roman Catholic exclusivism often observed in so many other non-biblical sects.

Seeing themselves as the one and only true church, in obedience to the command to go—they went. But the friars saw no value whatsoever in the indigenous world views, in their understanding of spiritual concepts, nor in their practices of communication with their gods. To the friars the Natives of California were devil worshipers, as all non-Roman Catholic religious expressions were considered to be. With the concept of baptismal regeneration and the act of baptism containing grace, if there was no Roman Catholic baptism, there could not be salvation. By grace are you saved through faith and that not of yourselves it is a gift of God not of works—is not part of Tridentine Roman Catholic missiology. For the friars, only Roman Catholic baptism could save and that, obviously, was not a part of any other religion.

In the area of *Christianity and Culture*, Tridentine Roman Catholic missiology had sunk to its lowest point in this Upper California Epoch. The predesigned purpose of the friars was to destroy the indigenous cultures the California groups, clans, and tribes. There was no thought to use them, to modify them, or to permit any continuing existence of any aspect of the indigenous California cultures. The friars took the children away from parents and taught them European views; they coerced the adults and forced them to labor and memorize routines that would hopefully program them to do Roman Catholic rites correctly, with or without understanding was not a matter to be considered of importance. Spanish mannerisms and methods were taught and learned, with little if any thought given to indigenous interpretations and understandings applied to them, as long as outward appearances were correctly maintained.

European tools, agriculture, animals, and land use were all sufficient of themselves to change forever the culture and manner of life of the Californians. Diseases introduced by the Spanish were sufficient of themselves to account for the entire drop in indigenous demographics of Upper California.[29] The fact that the mission friars were by design destroying the cultures of the California natives leaves them open to criticism and even hostility; yet, in reality, the strategy of cultural annihilation had very little impact on what was happening to the indigenous people simply because the Spanish were there, resident among them. Disease and cultural disintegration were well into their deadly work before the friars arrived; they were facilitated by the friars' arrival, and through the military and colonists, they were advancing at an accelerated pace completely apart from the immediate regions of mission influence. To lay fault on the friars for the destruction of indigenous cultures because that was one of their purposes and the best documented aspect of subjugation is poor historical research. Nevertheless in the area of cultural sensitivity, the friars not only failed, but were quite openly hostile to the indigenous cultures.

Summary

The California mission was post-typical representing a total shift in Spain's cultural policy in the Americas, according to mission historian Charles W. Polzer.[30] The Upper California missions were an economic enterprise with a built-in labor camp, vast enclosures in which relocated natives lived under a discipline that was semi-military, semi-monastic, and designed for cultural re-programming.[31] In the midst of this training in a foreign, surrogate culture, the mission was a tool of the state. Very little teaching in Christian doctrine took place; symbols and images were given in place of understanding, and all other religious expressions were prohibited. There was no competition from the secular clergy or other orders, but the Franciscans failed to utilize their monopoly on religion to bring a practicable form of Christianity to the Native Americans. The friars did succeed in transforming the indigenous survivors into Spanish low-caste subjects, but only portions of Roman Catholicism were adapted into the indigenous belief systems.

CHAPTER XII

THE EVOLUTION OF TRIDENTINE MISSIOLOGY THROUGH THE EPOCHS OF CONQUEST

It is now possible to summarize some of the progressive developments of the mendicant friars' practices of apostolic missions among the indigenous people of North America within the constraints of their Tridentine Roman Catholic theology. At the beginning of this study, and as each epoch of spiritual conquest was examined, some of the many factors influencing the ministries and practices of the friars were noted. Two purposes appeared consistently foremost in the friars' efforts: to civilize the Native Americans by forming them into tax-paying Spanish citizens and to evangelize them by converting them into Southern European Roman Catholic Christians. The value statement here is that the official Spanish policy was to incorporate the indigenous people into their transplanted Spanish society; a place was to be allowed for them to function in the New Spain social order. The indigenous people were at the bottom of that social order but the day would come when a Native American Zapotec indigenous leader would rule Mexico—President Benito Juarez.

The long-term legacy or fruit of the friar—Native American encounter in New Spain is best discerned in the individual epochs. Time lapses between most epochs were far too great for any consistency as generations came and went. Entire native nations passed away in the intervening time between epochs making generalizations difficult. Since the politics of Spain and/or of New Spain could change for both internal and external reasons, the policies affecting the indigenous peoples could be reversed overnight, and at times they were. Motivations for conquest, whether political, expansionist, defensive, or just lust for power, would change as New Spain would expand into unknown territories. A shuffle among the orders and their relationship to the civil government or their relationship with the secular church could also change for any given time period. But through it all, the need to accomplish the twofold purpose of Roman Catholic evangelism and the imposition of Spanish culture or, stated negatively, the elimination of indigenous culture had to go on, and these are the focus of the study.

To summarize the evangelistic practices for each epoch, a missiological framework was used to give uniformity to the discussion. For the purposes of summary this will be reframed into five basic questions for each of these five divisions of missiology. The questions are: How did the constraints of Tridentine theology affect the development of *apostolic practice,* of the *church and mission structure,* of *the gospel and religions,* of *salvation and non-Christians,* and the development of *Christianity and culture* during the invasion and conquest of New Spain?

Apostolic Practice

To answer the first question concerning *apostolic practice* what must be observe is how the friars expressed *evangelistic practice* based upon Tridentine theology, and then compare that to evangelistic practice as it is taught by Jesus Christ and modeled in the New Testament for all Christians to understand. The friar, as a Roman Catholic evangelist, was one who attempted to persuade other people to become Christian—becoming a Christian could be taken as synonymous with New Testament regeneration, which is deliverance from sin or the consequences of sin through the substitutionary atonement made by Jesus Christ on the cross. In addition to his spiritual commission the friar simultaneously functioned as a change agent to adapt indigenous cultures to Spanish culture.

In the beginning of the New Spain conquest, at the time of the Florida-Caribbean Epoch, there were three primary sources for Roman Catholic *apostolic practice* from which could be deduced their missiological understanding. The first came from the revitalization movements within the mendicant orders back in Europe. The second came from the practices that had evolved out of the hundreds of years of Iberian Peninsula re-conquest with its ethnic cleansings and cultural purifications as the Moors and the Jews were converted, killed off, or evicted. The third came from practices that had evolved during the invasion of the Canary Islands by the Spanish with a military conquest of an inoffensive native people, the Spanish cultural dominance, and the obligatory conversions of indigenous people to the Roman Catholic religion.

In the Florida-Caribbean Epoch the first European invasion of New Spain, which could not be repulsed by the indigenous people, was that of disease. Disease came with the first crew of Columbus who had been abandoned on Hispaniola, and continued long after the castaways were all dead. Seldom in all history has such an insidious enemy been unleashed on an unsuspecting people; it might be considered as the first biological terrorist attack on American soil. Not much less insidious were the explorers, mercenaries, adventurers, and colonists who soon followed in the wake of the rapidly moving mortal diseases. They came with their enslavements, cruelties, and refusal to acknowledge the Native Americans as human beings.

Very few friars came, fewer stayed, and of those who were able to establish some ministry to the natives, very little methodology has been revealed in available documents. History shows that there were a few friars and churchmen who did follow their familiar patterns of building European style church complexes. They ministered to the Europeans and to the very few indigenous people who survived the ravages of disease and slavery and were able to adapt to Spanish customs. If any apostolic ministry was attempted, most of the people died off so quickly it probably was not possible to practice with them any form of discipleship ministry. The tragedy of the Florida-Caribbean epoch was that in many places there was not time for any attempt at ministry before all of the native people were gone.

Available evidence does suggest that there really was very little *apostolic practice* going on during this first epoch of conquest. What was being practiced as evangelism was so limited in scope and content that it would be, indeed, a miracle of God for any of the Florida-Caribbean Taino or Carib natives to have come into a saving knowledge of Jesus

Christ the redeemer. *Apostolic practice* did not really even get started in this first epoch.

Therefore in this first epoch and the initiation of apostolic practice in the Americas, the only evidence of evangelism taking place was that of Roman Catholic baptism for a few indigenous people in contact with the very few friars. The Secular Roman Catholic Church was essentially for the European colonists who were enslaving, persecuting, bringing disease and killing off the indigenous population through military conquest, slavery, and frightful living conditions. The concept of bringing about obedience in *all that Christ taught* was not a factor in the thinking or in the practice during the Caribbean Epoch.

In the second epoch of the Central Valley conquest, great strides were made in the development of an *apostolic practice*. The friars looked back at nearly total failure in missions during the Caribbean Epoch in regard to reaching the hundreds of thousands of native islanders with the good news of salvation. They understood that their *apostolic practice* needed to change. The first response of the friars to that utter failure in the Caribbean was to put aside all formalities and pretense at doctrinal teaching and to baptize the indigenous people *before they all died again*, as in the Caribbean, when the epidemics ravaged the islanders. Therefore millions of indigenous people were baptized within the first few years of this Central Valley Epoch. Eventually catechisms were printed and distributed. Convents became teaching centers. Children of the elite were brought into residential schools and indoctrinated with precepts of the Roman Catholic faith and culture, and then sent back to teach their people in their own language. This worked for thousands, but millions had already been baptized without any instruction.

The historian Sahagún in his *La Conversión de Los Indios* used the term *mestizada,* referring to a cross-breeding of Catholicism and the indigenous religions producing a completely new form of religion, still with the name "Catholicism" borrowed from the European side of the mix, but with so many new forms and meanings, that it was in fact a new religion. The greatest success of *apostolic practice* during this second Epoch, the baptism of many millions of Native Americans and their children—often called the golden age of Roman Catholic missions—became their greatest liability in that it gave birth to a new religion which we now called Christopaganism. Yet the two continued under the same name of Roman Catholicism adding still further to the confusion.[1]

Roman Catholic baptism without teaching, and catechisms in place of discipleship, while maintaining both pagan and European worship rites and traditions, would be the pattern for most of the indigenous encounters for the rest of the conquest epochs. Those New Spain believers, mostly Europeans, who were theologically Roman Catholic, would bow and shake their heads when confronted with the Christopagan expressions, as they do today. However, the indigenous and Mestizo believers were still accepted as part of Roman Catholicism because of their baptism; the attitude that has prevailed in Mexico to this day is that one must understand that they are just *Indios*. Still, the further development of *apostolic practice* in this epoch could be seen in the addition of doctrinal teaching through the memorization of catechisms and prayers, as well as the use of Catholic processions, rites, and symbols for worship, although the meaning of these practices for the indigenous people were not necessarily Christian.

In the third epoch, the conquest of the Maya, which followed immediately on the heels of the conquest of the Central Valleys, little changed in *apostolic practice*. Though the Franciscan friars seem to have responded to criticisms of their lack of teaching by implementing the training of Maya schoolmasters who could teach in the indigenous language, and thus do a better job of preparing catechists, the deep-rooted flaw was not monitoring what was being learned and taught. With no other orders, no secular church, weak civil leadership, and strong Franciscan leadership, the stage was set for a Franciscan imperialism that led directly to an intense spiritual oppression of the Maya people by the Franciscans.

The methodology of training up young leadership and using them as schoolmasters was an advancement built upon Franciscan experience in the Central Valleys which demonstrated a clear respect for the Maya language and culture. The concept greatly multiplied the effectiveness of the always too few missionaries, but with insufficient oversight and control of what the indigenous teachers were actually teaching. Again the false concept of community obedience being accepted as individual submission to Christ was demonstrated. It was a most rude awakening to find that teaching a few young people forms they did not understand would not change an established religion thousands of years old.

Native leadership was excluded from the friars' evangelistic process in the Yucatán with a few notable exceptions such as the chief of the Xiu. Continuity in native leadership led to continuing clandestine Maya rituals as the need for their existence continued and Roman Catholicism failed to fill the void. This led directly to one of the uglier chapters in Franciscan history. The humble brothers who were sent to be the salt and light of the gospel became the apostolic bearers of torture and death for thousands of the very souls they came to save. It was the philosophy of Trent and the practice of Spanish sovereigns that put spiritual authority above legal authority and the civil laws of the land. Finally it was the arrogance of believing that there could only be *One True Church* on earth, or one correct religious expression with all other expressions of faith being false, that substantiated the belief that one man could harm another in the Name of God and for the lasting benefit of the individual so tortured.

In the fourth epoch of *apostolic practice*, the one new and all encompassing factor for this epoch was war. The Chichimeca war went on and on, getting more vicious, more destructive, and taking a tremendous toll in lives and property on both sides. The concept of the frontiersmen came into being in this epoch. The Mestizo as the common man of New Spain was coming into his own self-identity on the frontier where the pressures of life and survival itself depended on the man fighting beside you, all genetics and history aside.

The primary method of evangelism for this epoch was the formation of a defensive settlement in the midst of the hostile territory. This was expressed as the presidio, the fortified inn and the *encomienda* strong-house, the indigenous pueblo, the convent, and the utopian Christian settlement. All of these strategies for penetrate-and-hold settlements would eventually result in convents, chapels, and larger churches being built. These strong house settlements for defensive purposes can be considered advancement in evangelistic methodology that solidified the indigenous expressions of faith for those groups that fought with the Spanish.

In the beginning of the penetration into the Gran Chichimeca with the fortified convent and the strong-house *encomienda*, the depth of evangelism was most likely equaled that of epoch two of the Central Valleys. The responsibility of the *encomendero* as an evangelist ended after baptism and perhaps with the building of a small chapel for the itinerant friars to use when present.

Due to the Tridentine limits placed upon the Roman Church, the Christology that was taught by the friars was still very weak to nonexistent. Jesus the Christ was a baby in the arms of Mary in most symbolism; he was the suffering, crucified man in the passion plays or in the coffin at the side of the entrance to a cathedral, but very seldom if ever was the resurrected, glorified Jesus Christ, the coming King, ever portrayed in processions, in drama, or in art. Mariology had been substituted to a point that the doctrine of the Trinity, the three persons of the Godhead, was a vague or unknown doctrine. Therefore, in the area of *Apostolic Practice,* the carrying out of evangelism was still greatly constrained by the Tridentine doctrines, leaving most of the rudiments of Christology, eschatology, and salvation untaught and unknown to most of the baptized community of Native Americans.

Ecclesiology was becoming much more organized, with fairly large segments of native religion incorporated into the practice of Roman Catholic Christianity. The only discipleship of believers that took place was in the convents of the Augustinians and Franciscans, where the training of a few lay brothers for the purposes of assisting the evangelistic friars was pursued to some degree.

During the fifth Epoch the *apostolic practice* was dominated by the Peace-by-Purchase methodology, a program of pacification in place of military conquest that was developed during the Chichimeca wars. The Society of Jesus was doing most of the evangelism. By placing the priest in charge of the Peace-by-Purchase program at the village level, Roman Catholic Christianity became inseparable from the pacification and domestication processes. The Jesuit priest became inseparable from all three. This was a great strategic advantage for the evangelization of the indigenous people who understood the priest as representative of civil and military, as well as spiritual authority. The one major disadvantage for the priest in this miniature theocracy was that he became the object of all the discontent of the disenfranchised former indigenous chief, judge, shamans, and warriors who formerly gained their prestige in battle. The failure to use the indigenous leadership, the undermining and destroying of their positions and functions within the community, was both the primary objective, and the primary weakness of the Jesuit application of the Peace-by-Purchase system.

In the area of *apostolic practice*, once the actual Christian evangelism practices were separated from the social development and political reorganization, very little was changed from the previous epochs. The people were being taught the forms, symbols and respect for the priest as a political/spiritual leader, which really did not fit the pattern Christ himself taught as the servant-leader model, but it was all appropriate for the Tridentine Roman Catholic hierarchal model. After the adjustments made by Franciscans for apostolic practice in the second epoch, little additional advancement was made in this area of missiology through this fifth epoch.

In evaluating the *apostolic practice* of the sixth epoch of conquest into New Mexico, the stuttering start of the Spanish penetration seems to be symbolic of the same stuttering evangelistic effort by the Franciscans. Two factors greatly influenced the imposition of Christianity in practice: maintaining intact the Puebloan priesthood and allowing indigenous priests to maintain their houses of worship within the town complexes of the Pueblo. With the Pueblos, it was the Roman Catholic Church that was outside the gate, a foreign religion.

This was the first time in New Spain that the Roman Catholic priests had to minister and coexist with direct competition; they had to face-off, head to head on level ground with another highly traditional religion. Converts had to be persuaded and convinced of the new religion to be baptized, and after baptism the new religion had to keep proving itself better than the former religion to keep its membership. But the healthy continuing worship patterns of the Kachina cults indicate that the friars were not succeeding in this direct competition with a functioning indigenous worship system.

For the seventh Epoch, in the area of *Apostolic Practice* there was a marked advance in methodology that would continue to be a key to successful missionary work for ages to come: the specialized training of missionary candidates. For the friars going to minister on frontier mission fields, there began to be a focus on their spiritual character, their preparations in cross-cultural communications, and the need to develop the whole being of the indigenous people to whom they were being sent. The area of *apostolic practice* and mission theory took a giant step forward as Antonio Linaza de Jesús María established his first apostolic training center in Queretaro. Two concepts, pre-field training and post-field debriefing and renewal, have become kingpins in the management of cross-cultural Christian missions and the administration of orders and mission agencies. Another missiological issue that Linaz dealt with was the problem of inter-missionary relationships by requiring a two-year, pre-field period of spiritual formation as a ministry team—in other words, learning how to get along with each other. These were the first major developmental strides the Franciscans had made in *apostolic practice* and missiology since their initial entrance into the New Spain mainland in the second epoch.

In the last of these eight epochs of conquest, New Spain becomes divided between the United States of Mexico and the United States of America. Circumstances dictated that *apostolic practice* of missiology drop several notches in any evaluation of the California missionary effort. The church was being used for secular purposes and the primary objective of the California missions was to divorce the indigenous people from their land and their own culture, and make them culturally Spanish. In geopolitical terms, the Upper California missions were a successful frontier institution for geographical expansion with minimal exertion and expense. Serra was compromised with worldly pursuits from the beginning of the project. The attractions to the mission were numerous and many natives responded voluntarily, but not to learn a new belief system. As seen before, there were church buildings and many thousands of indigenous people were baptized into the new Spanish colonial culture, but few theologians could say that actual *conversion* to Christianity was taking place.

Therefore, in the evolution of Tridentine Roman Catholic missiology as touching upon *apostolic practices* of the friars in the context of North American conquests, there is a halting but clear developmental trend toward more effective missionary practice. This developmental process started with conquer, kill or enslave, and baptize when and if possible in the first epoch, and culminated in the seventh epoch with a clearly defined strategy implemented by well trained, highly motivated clergy who accomplished their objectives in the most efficient manner to date, and as painlessly as possible for the indigenous people. Yet the friars still labored severely handicapped by an incomplete and warped tridentine gospel message, and a great deal of symbolism that took on indigenous meanings creating yet another local, composite religion for the indigenous people, but still received within the Roman Catholic Church.

Church and Mission Structure

The second area of missiology is that of the relationship between the secular or hierarchal church structure and those of the apostolic or missionary orders. The question asked is: How did the constraints of Tridentine theology affect the development of *church and mission structure* during the invasion and conquest of New Spain? As noted at the beginning of this study, the mendicant orders came into existence as revitalization movements that believed one had to be taken out of the secular world with its secular church in order to achieve true spirituality. They built convents to isolate themselves and ventured out of their place of discipline and solitude only when necessary. These orders were undergoing revitalization themselves at the time of the Reformation movements in Europe and the discovery of the New World. Because of this, Cortéz pleaded for mendicants to come and evangelize the peoples of New Spain instead of the secular church. In Europe, as long as the mendicants were cloistered and did not interfere with the outsiders or secular church, there was no institutional conflict. They were all Roman Catholic Christians and the friars were usually the best model of a real Christian.

However, in order to do their ministries without interference from the secular church or to function as the church where there was no other church, the mendicant orders all sought and received Papal authority to function directly under the authority of the Pope on the new mission fields, practicing all the rights and privileges of ordained priests with their organizations functioning on the same level as a bishoprics of the secular church. It was always understood that the fruit of their ministries would eventually be passed on to local, secular church jurisdiction. The friction came as to when that transfer of jurisdiction should occur in the development of any specific local church.

The pattern that was emerging was that the orders were *apostolic;* they were *sent,* or *sent ones.* When the root Greek verb is translated into Latin it is *missionary.* They were sent to where the secular church was weak or did not exist to rise up Roman Catholic local churches. Until the new ministries were turned over to the secular church, they were under the authority and jurisdiction of the friars who were empowered to *act* as priests. This theory of missions understood that once the new

Missionary Practices and Spanish Steel

works were turned over to the secular church, the mendicants were free to go start new ministries where there still was no church. Therefore this section is dealing with the evolution of relationships between different ecclesiastical delegated authorities, the structure of the secular church and the structure of mission orders, and the encounter of the secular church with other non-Roman Catholic Church structures. What comes to mind, in the European context at the time of discovery, was that the missiological doctrines were already very well established in regards to non-Roman Catholic churches. That is, there was no other Christian Church but Roman Catholicism; all others were infidels, pagans, and heretics. There was no other authority for the church but Papal authority whose seat was in Rome.

Since initially in the New Spain conquest no religion, Christian or otherwise, other than Roman Catholicism could be allowed to exist, and no other Christian expression could be permitted to enter the region, tridentine doctrine severely handicapped, in fact prohibited this area of missiological development. Only in the area of relationships between the Roman Catholic Secular Church and the Roman Catholic Orders can be traced a development of missiology for *church and mission structure.*

The epoch one church structure followed exactly the European patterns, was directly under the authority of European church structure, and drew all its leadership from the European church institutions. The same relationship existed between the two types of institutions as in Europe, co-existing but separated in line of authority. Both structures were doing the same work with New Spain Europeans for the most part.

In the second epoch of the Central Valleys, after a number of bishoprics had been organized in New Spain, Zumárraga, a Franciscan missionary, was appointed the first archbishop and for the first time, New Spain had a directly delegated authority of the Roman Church structure. The New Spain secular church was still culturally a European church and ministered mostly to the Europeans and their descendants, called *Criollos.* The structure of the secular church continued to establish itself and was slowly growing throughout this period. It was growing in the number of churches, in the number of priests serving, and establishing its ministries in the cities and towns of New Spain. The indigenous people, who were the vast majority of the people, were still basically the responsibility of the mendicant orders and under their line of authority. Strong resentments were beginning to develop between the two expressions over the economic base of their ministries and the separate lines of authority.

The fourth epoch brought to a head the divisions that were started in the second epoch between secular and apostolic structures. Through the defensive settlements and silver barons, the secular church became both much stronger and more evangelistic, while the orders fell into a more lax and less fruitful period of maintenance and pastoral ministry. Therefore this fourth epoch represents a changing of the guard for the Roman Catholic Church in New Spain. From this time foreword the secular church would become stronger and dominate the leadership of the Roman Catholic Church.

While the secular church exerted its dominance, the Society of Jesus came on the scene with a good working relationship with the secular church, and disdain for the other orders. Implementing the Peace-With-Purchase program in new unsettled regions, they set the example of an apostolic order penetrating, pacifying, and evangelizing; things the previous orders had become less energetic in accomplishing. The other orders diminished in leadership as rivals of the secular church but continued to spearhead new evangelistic efforts along the frontiers. In these new areas the orders continued to operate under direct authority of the Pope on a par with the secular church bishops. But time limits were being placed upon the orders to turn the fruit of their labors over to the jurisdiction of the secular church. In doing so principles were established that the fruit of the orders, the new churches, would become secular church members as soon as convenient; the priests within the orders were temporary pastors who soon would move on making room for secular church priests. The purpose of the orders in missions was to evangelize, disciple, and establish churches, not to maintain congregations or stay on as pastors.

In the fifth through eighth epochs of conquest that followed, this general pattern of church-mission relationships continued, with the expected local differences of opinion and working relationships being debated at several levels of authority. Later, by law, the new mission churches had to be turned over to the secular church within ten years of their founding. This latter stage of development approached the description of the convents in Europe before the discovery of New

Spain. Therefore in the area of *church and mission structure* a complete circle of relationships was accomplished in the New Spain conquest.

Through this whole New Spain conquest, one sees a process by which the symbiotic relationship between secular church and apostolic structure was being established and forged into a solid, workable missiology. However, tridentine doctrine severely limited the extent of possible growth of missiology in this area of *church and mission structure* to just *internal* relationships of Roman Catholicism.

The Gospel and Religions

In dealing with the Christian response to encounters with other religions that do not acknowledge the Lordship of Jesus Christ the question asked was: How did the constraints of tridentine theology affect the development of *the gospel and religions* during the invasion and conquest of New Spain? Based upon tridentine doctrine, no other religion was of God; indeed, they were all of the devil, including other Christian religious expressions other than Roman Catholic. This strongly held belief left no room for any other religious expressions. To the best of their ability, the friars destroyed all other religions in their paths.

This tridentine doctrine would not be changed throughout the conquest period. There was to be no relationship between the Roman Catholic Church and other religions. All had to submit to the authority of Rome; all had to be considered Roman Catholic to survive the encounter. This area of missiology, the *gospel and religions,* did not exist for Roman Catholics except to see other religious expressions as enemies to be eradicated or absorbed throughout the conquest period.

The one exception to this was the encounter with the Pueblo people and the implementation of the Peace-With-Purchase program. There the friars had to deal with another viable, highly traditional religion on the Pueblos own turf. Though the Franciscans had some initial success, the offensive methodology of the friars so incensed the Puebloan leaders that they revolted and destroyed everything Roman Catholic; including the lives of Puebloan converts to Christianity along with all the Spanish they could kill. This ended the initial period of evangelism. The Kachina worship patterns and the Puebloan culture are still viable today with traces of adapted Roman Catholic symbolism and practices.

Salvation and Non-Christians

How did the constraints of tridentine theology affect the development of *salvation and non-Christians* during the invasion and conquest of New Spain? Though the focus for this section is more theoretical and theological, the actual practice of the friars reveals something of the friars' theological position in this area. We know in depth what the tridentine theology was. Knowing that pagans who had never heard the gospel of Jesus Christ were forever lost was obviously the primary motivation for the friars to go and evangelize them. Since the efficaciousness of the redemptive work of Christ in tridentine doctrine was dependent upon baptism, pagans had to be baptized one way or another or they were lost for eternity. The ministries of the friars were predicated upon the basic understanding that it was God's will for the pagans to be saved from their pagan religions, lifestyles, and sinfulness. The pagans were already condemned and without excuse due to general revelation. Someone had to go tell them about the finished work of Christ and baptize them into the Roman Catholic Church so they could be saved and not perish in hell fires.

This was the basic theological position and primary motivation for apostolic ministry. Throughout the conquest period there was an intensity to evangelize that at times waned but was always there. It was a passion that compelled friars to go and to accomplish their high calling in Christ Jesus as his chosen ones to preach the gospel, to be apostles of the living God. The theology of salvation and the non-Christian was fully developed and unchanged throughout the various epochs of the conquest period. It was the bedrock of theology that kept the friars motivated to evangelize, and it was the foundation of their intolerance for other faiths.

Christianity and Culture

How did the constraints of Tridentine theology affect the development of the area of *Christianity and culture* during the invasion and conquest of New Spain? Each separate culture is a creation of God yet it is corrupted by the sinful nature of man. In practice this area deals with being respectful of diversity in cultural expressions within the native context that are not corrupted by sin and reflect the hand of their Maker, while still being faithful to the critical theological principles and values of Christianity.

Previous to their arrival in New Spain, the Spanish Roman Catholics, in most cases, were dealing with high cultural and moral religions such as the Jewish and Muslim cultures in their military domination and religious cleansing of the Iberian Peninsula. It is not difficult to imagine their shock when meeting the Native Americans. They saw absolutely no redeeming value to the native cultures or indigenous ways of life.

There was no apparent dialogue with the native shamans, only complete repudiation of their apparent demonic powers, false icons, a prohibition of their rituals, and utter destruction of anything physical that represented the native religions or was even thought to represent another religion. The strange images of gods were destroyed; the libraries and all historical, scientific, and intellectual writings were collected and burned. The temples that served as centers for learning were torn down; symbols were smashed, defaced, or covered with Christian symbols. The indigenous Aztec priests were homosexuals; they practiced human sacrifice for the nation, and cannibalism was commonly practiced among them. With reason these were immediately put to an end.

No attempt was made to understand culture as a means to communicate the redemptive power of Jesus Christ. It appears that the force of tridentine doctrine and a very anemic Franciscan evangelism caused a syncretic marriage of both Native American religious practices and Roman Catholicism which produced a new set of religious expressions that came to be known as *Folk Catholicism*, also classified as Christopaganism. This was using cultural diversity *without* being faithful to biblical principles and values. Folk Catholicism, or Christopaganism, is a result of the massive failure to use correctly the elements of the target culture to express Christian principles.

The indigenous cultural elements that the Chichimeca war did not destroy, the Peace-With-Purchase plan did. Peace with the Spanish meant acculturation to Spanish ways with the elimination of indigenous ways. The Reductions and Christian villages were death centers for indigenous cultures. Again, there was no attempt to understand native religious expressions, no attempt to use indigenous culture as a bridge to understanding, and no usage of acceptable native cultural expressions for Christian worship.

With the Franciscan and Puebloan encounter, the indigenous leadership was alienated forcing the Puebloan Kachina worship underground but still totally intact and functioning. The Pueblo leadership was promised that they would be allowed a free-will decision on accepting or rejecting of the new religion because of the Peace-With-Purchase philosophy. Most Roman Catholic Churches were constructed outside the Pueblo towns, while the Kiva meeting rooms were inside the towns. This maintained the appearance of the Kiva as Puebloan and the Roman Catholic Church as foreign, not a part of the Pueblo. The friars failed to use or understand the Puebloan culture. The friars could not control it militarily, and in the end, the Puebloan culture won out. Today it is the most intact Native American culture still surviving in North America.

The greatest tragedy may be the lack of understanding of the friars to the importance of communicating truth and knowledge in relevant ways that would allow indigenous people to understand Christian spiritual concepts. Throughout the whole conquest period, the friars understood their work was to convert the indigenous to Spanish culture as well as convert them to Christianity. Perhaps they were not able to find the strategic bridges of cultural relevance because they simply were not looking for them.

Concluding Statement

It has been my hypothesis for this book that the Council of Trent so constrained the development of missiology of the mendicant friars that they seldom if ever were able to preach the gospel of Jesus Christ to the North Americans as seen in the biblical command, "Go therefore and make disciples of all the nations, baptizing them . . . and teach them to observe all that I have commanded you . . ."[2] The research question that evolved from this hypothesis was: How did post-Tridentine Roman Catholicism affect the missiology of the mendicant friars laboring in the New Spain context of conquest and domination by Spain?

Using Glasser's five components of missiology as a framework for analysis I have shown that in the area of *Salvation and the Non-Christian* the Tridentine missiology was well developed with respect to the Lord's command to go and preach, resulting in both the Pope and the King energetically sending the friars who were well prepared by European cultural standards and who responded to God's call to go and preach to the lost. The Spanish did exactly as the Tarascan and Aztec did; they used war to spread their religion and force their opponents to submit to their gods. The only difference in all three conquering empires was the effective use of Spanish steel. However the tridentine gospel of salvation forced on the indigenous Americans lacked most of the biblical redemptive elements, being reduced to water baptism in most cases. It was a baptism into Spanish cultural expressions more than Christianity—to the Spanish of course they were the same thing.

In the area of *Apostolic Practice* the friars went progressively from almost no understanding of how to evangelize the Native Americans in the first epoch to a complete and effective manner of doing apostolic work successfully, within the constrictions of Tridentine dogma, in the seventh epoch of conquest 250 years later. The missiological methodologies of the friars were successful, but the doctrine they taught was so lacking in content it gave birth to a whole new religion. Much of the apostolic practice that evolved during this period is still fundamental to missions today and shapes both Roman Catholic and Protestant mission dogma.

In the area of *Church and Mission Structure*, tridentine theology and practice severely limited the possibility of interrelationships with other expressions of Christianity, but it did allow an interesting circular inter-play within the Roman Catholic fold. The other two areas of missiology, the *Gospel and Other Religions* and *Christianity and Culture*, were never really factors in Roman Catholic missiology during the conquest period. The tridentine doctrines and practices effectively disabled any possibility of an effective missiology developing or being practiced in these two areas.

Hence, Tridentine doctrine had a terribly crippling effect on the 300-year Spanish missionary movement in New Spain. Transcultrual ministry to the indigenous people was not effectively accomplished because of those doctrinal constrictions. The anemic gospel that was being preached to the Native Americans could not be construed as redemptive. This huge missionary movement was like a five cylinder engine running with only two pistons firing. Still, God is sovereign, and, "the Lord's hand is not so short that it cannot save."[3] The Word of God was brought to New Spain, and the Holy Spirit of the Living God was in New Spain because the friars were in New Spain. The sovereign Lord God could call individual Americans to Himself because the Roman Pontiff and the King of Spain in obedience to God's command in His Word had sent the mendicant friars to preach to the indigenous nations of North America.

CHAPTER XIII

THE MISSIONARY LEGACY: APPROACHING INDIGENOUS NORTH AMERICANS TODAY

This book would be no more than another academic exercise if it were not brought to bear on the actual situation of most surviving indigenous North Americans today. Where did that huge, 300 year missionary effort leave the original people of New Spain, which is now Central America, Mexico, most of the USA, and part of Canada; and what does it mean in terms of the biblical command to go into all the world and preach the gospel to all creation?

Though the Pueblo *Senior Pastor* leaders of the sixth epoch agreed to be instructed in all that was being proposed to them as necessary for this Roman Catholic salvation, they had wisely stated the conditions that if they liked what was being taught, they would gladly respond in a positive way. If they did not like what was being taught, it would not do well to force anyone to follow this new teaching that the Spanish proposed. Most of the Pueblo residents did not like it. Force was implemented by the friars to coerce the Pueblo people resulting in the utter destruction of the entire missionary exercise and great loss of life in the following rebellion. The Pueblo rebellion also resulted in the preservation to this day of the most complete Native American religion in North America. The huge adobe Catholic cathedral that dominates Acoma, New Mexico is empty of all but a few benches around the inside walls; it is reserved for the exercise of the mildly syncretic Kachina religious expressions. A small room in the old priest quarters is used for the handful of Acumens who see a value in meeting with a Catholic priest in his monthly visits.

Nearly all other indigenous groups still in existence today in North America have a much greater combination of syncretic practices and combinations of symbols with unique meanings totally distinct from their original Roman Catholic connotations. These are now established religious systems, syncretic but melded into one workable world view that satisfies explanations and religious beliefs of the indigenous people of today. Often still called Roman Catholic, these melded religious expressions have very little to do with biblical Christianity, or even the true meanings of Roman Catholic Tridentine expressions.

To further complicate the situation, on most reservations, there are now multiple attempts by many Protestant evangelical groups to establish churches or missions in an attempt to evangelize and disciple indigenous people. Most of these "missions" could not exist without continual subsidies and outside help. It is not the author's intention to criticize these ministries, but to point out that they are not reaching the indigenous people in numbers that would indicate a significantly altered world view of the target cultures. If the words of Jesus are true, "I am the way, the truth, and the life; no one comes to the Father, but through Me"[1] then the majority of indigenous people who maintain their traditional world views concerning God or the gods, are still without hope in the redemptive power of Christ.

The friars came to the Americas with ethnocentric and egotistical concepts that doomed their efforts to failure in the beginning. Over 250 years they evolved and perfected some methodologies that proved to be effective and up to the task of making indigenous Americans into New Spain citizens and baptized Catholics, accomplishing their two fold commission as missionaries. The effective methodologies of the friars did not necessarily make the Native Americans followers of Jesus Christ. The lack of discipleship, no indigenous leadership, all too often poor moral examples of godly character, and freedom to continue in pagan practices under the guise of Catholicism allowed the forging of syncretic but still pagan religions.

There are now several ministries led by members of indigenous groups that are biblically Christian in doctrine and practice, that are developing culturally indigenous expressions of their Christian principles particularly on the USA side of the border. It is my prayer that these expressions will address the lack of cultural relevance that is so common in the evangelical efforts. We need Christians from every tribe and linguistic group to be addressing these same issues. It must be remembered that the friars did effectively use cultural expressions in the second epoch with the Aztec, but still failed to communicate the Christian content. It is a very difficult thing to put new meanings and content into old expressions and traditional behaviors.

It is the theory of vaccinations that a small dose of weak, or dead disease germs injected into the body will allow the body to build up antibodies that will prevent the stronger living disease germs from becoming established in the body. This seems to describe the situation with indigenous people who were exposed to a doctrinally weak, anemic gospel which blended well with the body of beliefs currently held by the native people. The result is a resistance to the whole gospel of Jesus Christ which greatly hinders being able to communicate the salvation message that Christian missionaries are commanded to teach to every nation, tribe, and tongue.

It is necessary for those who would minister to the American Indigenous Nations still in existence today to understand this resistance and be prepared to teach the whole counsel of God with patience. We are commanded to make disciples of our Lord. Discipleship is a process of living, teaching, practicing, and being together. Discipleship takes time. Jesus needed three years to train his men. He did it within their culture using their way of life to illustrate his teachings. So often we insist on behaviors and traditional expressions from our cultures that alienate the individual indigenous believer from his own community. The new disciple must be salt and light in his community, not separated from it. Discipleship is finding God's way to be Christian within the community, to build integrity through character traits that define the new life in Christ while working and living in that context.

In ministries to the broken hearted, it is necessary for the minister to depend upon God for insight and perception of spiritual issues that allow the process to focus in on the root problems. Prayer must precede practice; words of wisdom and knowledge are spiritual gifts given by the Holy Spirit to shed light on the causes and nature of the problems. Every human being is distinct, his experience unique, and his response to events in his life depends upon a multitude of factors. This pattern for reaching out to others in need is of value in reaching out to a people who for 500 years have been abused, hurt, violated, and relegated to the bottom of society in their own land. Prayer and dependence upon the Spirit of the Living God to lead the cross-cultural missionary will allow God to do His redemptive work through the ministry to each individual He brings into relationship with the missionary. Expect the Holy Spirit's leading, His divine intervention and direction when as His ambassador one reaches out to those who have never understood the reality of life in Christ.

The biblical concept of discipleship has often been replaced in our time-conscious society with a basic bible study and a weekly time of fellowship, though often without the latter. Failure to disciple, or simply calling memorized catechisms discipleship, was a step above nothing for the friars, but still fell far short of what the Scriptures call discipleship. Syncretism and unchanged world views were the result of the friars' efforts. True, biblical discipleship must take place to bridge the syncretic expressions so ingrained into the minds and world view of Native American people today. The mentor must return to the basic concepts of biblical goals for character development, of planning and time-management for the necessary quality, productive interaction with the disciple, of finding and using inherent cultural values and expressions to enhance teaching while developing Christian cultural expression of faith that are a contribution to their understanding of the world they live in. Christian principles will always make indigenous world views better and cause an uplifting of their culture. God's principals are universal and must be allowed to fit into all cultures; our cultural norms and expressions are not universal and should never be forced into another cultural expression.

Another area in which the missionary to indigenous people must take upmost care is that of cultural arrogance, or the lack of respect for the target culture. The friars of New Spain were arrogant in the extreme thinking that their Spanish cultural norms were both the highest level of human culture and the highest expression of Christian culture. They only had to look in their Bible to understand how, rather than rich and not needing a thing, they were really wretched, pitiful, poor, blind, and naked in God's eyes. Yet from their exalted position in their own eyes the friars saw the indigenous people as wretched, pitiful, poor, naked savages with absolutely no redeeming value in their culture or way of life. Questioning their very humanity, and with the king's mandate to make New Spain citizens of the savages, the rebuilding began with no regards to the starting point. A building without a foundation will not stand for long. The missionary's cultural blindness can become his worst obstacle in accomplishing his mandate to make authentic disciples of Jesus Christ.

An opposite perception to arrogance is the missionary's own integrity. The popular adage, *your actions speak so loud I can't hear what you are saying*, contains an important warning for the cross-cultural missionary. Many missionaries never really gain a good command of the indigenous language. Without the language there is never a real understanding of the indigenous culture. In such instances, what comes across in the missionary's preaching is often utter nonsense or worse, a total misconception of what is being taught. In many cases the market language such as Spanish or English is the second or third language for indigenous people. Expressing spiritual concepts that are hard to grasp in one's own language become more difficult in second and third languages. Therefore what is really communicated is what is observed in the missionary's behavior.

Recall the description of the contemporaries to the Franciscan Friars and other clergy of Mexico in the fifth and sixth Epochs, with a notable exception of the Jesuits, they were described as, 'not only destitute of the virtues necessary to their station, but were in every respect profligate. Some of them, disregarding their vows of poverty, others, forgetting their oaths of chastity, indulged in the grossest licentiousness.' This was very close to the same description given to the indigenous people of that time by the Spaniards. Christian virtues were not being learned from the friar's behavior, and there was apparently no other teaching as long as infant baptism was being done and taxes or indentured service took place. Most learning accomplished from the missionaries' ministry takes place because of *who* they are and what they *do*, not what they think they are teaching. Although the Pueblos of the sixth epoch were only allowed to observe, but not experience for themselves the Spanish use of war horses, the use of fire arms, or the tactics of Spanish solders, they readily used all these skills against the Spanish during the rebellion that drove out or killed all of the Spanish soldiers, colonists, and Pueblo Roman Catholic believers—using skills they learned by watching.

The missionary must be careful to live what he is teaching before the people. He must respect the laws of his own country, the laws of the host country in as much as they do not negate scriptural mandate, and the cultural rules of the indigenous group. Showing respect for those in authority and cultural practices that do not violate scriptural mandates is showing respect and acceptance for the target culture and its people. A record of promises kept, of words spoken and fulfilled, and of projects completed speaks volumes while building trust. Integrity of character will speak the truths that the missionary has not yet mastered the vocabulary to express.

Trust: a word, a concept often expected, but seldom given without a period of testing. Trust will always include an element of hope. Hope that the trust is well placed and that the trust will not return void. Trust is a hard thing to earn and an easy thing to lose. For 500 years, the indigenous people of North America have had their trust violated and their hope crushed by the European conquerors. The very people that brought the knowledge and practice of Christianity are the people that taught by their actions cultural dominance, slavery and indentured service, the stealing of land, forced labor, violation of women, duel standards of living, prejudice and class divisions; the list could go on for several pages. And now the surviving indigenous people are being asked by the missionary to believe and to trust in what the invader has said all along is our foundational guide, our rules of conduct, and our faith in God. *The trust still remains to be earned.* The hope still has to be kindled and nurtured. Servants of integrity still have to be sent to cross the cultural barriers and be faithful, honest witnesses of the new life in Christ.

It is within the very nature of a society, of an integrated culture, to defend itself against all outside forces that would alter the balances that maintain the cultural integrity. The anemic gospel forced upon the indigenous Americans by the Spanish militias with their steel weapons and the friars with their crosses and paintings, as well as faithful Roman Catholic colonists, have resulted in a new syncretic religion that is now the normal standard of belief for many Native American societies. To attack their religion is to attack the society itself. Drunkenness, idol worship, illicit moral behavior such as incestuous relationships or homosexuality, and witchcraft are often accepted parts of indigenous societies. These elements have been there for 500 years under the Spanish, and they were there for centuries before that. It is said that morality cannot be legislated. The Spanish tried that but for all their laws they have changed very little; the laws simply forced the practices into the shadows while indigenous societies continued as before in their belief systems and world views.

It is not the changes in outward appearances and practices that the missionary seeks, but changes in the heart and spiritual realms that in turn change the outward behaviors. There are often opportunities to initiate change and see the beginnings of a new life in relationship with Christ as Lord. It is nonthreatening to bring a dentist or a doctor into the indigenous context to meet physical needs, particularly in emergency situations such as floods, drought, earthquakes, or hurricanes. Such acts of relief and kindness can result in decisions to follow Christ and open the door to implementing true discipleship. Far too often the relief effort ends, the doctors go home, and the new believer is left without the discipleship needed to continue in *the way* of Christ.

Other natural disasters such as crop failure, crop plagues, extreme weather, or communicable disease can provide the same type of opportunity for outsiders to enter into their world and culture legitimately. An undisturbed society presents a nearly impossible cross-cultural barrier to an outsider. This is especially true when local laws are designed to protect and maintain indigenous cultures. Forces that disrupt the natural order of their world open otherwise closed cultures for a brief window of opportunity to minister in the name of Jesus and have that ministry accepted for the benefit of the whole. These changes, being good for the culture, can often result in acceptance of the minister into their otherwise closed world. However, this must be seen as a beginning, not an end. Humanitarian outreach is good of itself, and many mission agencies are organized for these purposes. They are meeting the biblical commands to love others unselfishly in deeds. Christ did command to love in deeds *and in truth*. However, for Christian mission it is an opportunity wasted if a missionary is not part of the initial response; he must enter with plans to stay and disciple the fruit of the humanitarian effort. Meeting physical needs is a legitimate entrance cause. It also lends legitimacy to the continuing presence of the missionary which permits the mentoring of new disciples *as long as his continuing presence is legitimate indeed.*

There are other legitimate reasons for a missionary to be in an indigenous context. One is language learning. Most groups will even help an outsider who wants to learn their history, their language, their cultural expressions, and their hope for the future. It shows that the outsider values their way of life. The study must be legitimate of itself: learn the language; do a master's thesis; learn their style of weaving, pottery making, or herbal medicines. Become the outside expert in *their* skills. These will all build trust and open doors for true communications and permit the continuing discipleship of new believers.

An error continues to be made by Western Christianity, especially by churches that insist upon and provide for the building of a church in the indigenous area. There are very few things a missionary can do that will more quickly stop the growth of an infant church like building a church structure. Such a structure is a threat, an open challenge to the traditions and institutions of the functioning indigenous culture, a threat that calls for an organized defense of traditional ways of their society. Christ did not tell us to build a church: He said *He* would build His church. He did command us to make disciples. If the missionary will dedicate all his time and resources into making disciples for the time he has in the indigenous culture, he can leave a mature, educated, capable group of indigenous Christians who can stand on their own in the missionary's absence. They can continue to meet together for fellowship, worship, and teaching as before. They can build their church building, in their own way when they feel the need, and develop their own cultural expressions of biblical principles that stand a far better chance of being used by God to demonstrate a changed life in Christ to more men and women of their society.

Authority must be imparted to leaders of the new, indigenous expression of biblical truth, not the academic or religious institutional authority of the Western Church which only implies foreign control of the church, but spiritual authority released over the men and women of that culture and of the Spirit's choosing. Jesus gave the sacraments of Baptism and the Lord's Supper for the strengthening of the Body of Christ. Obeying the Lord in these commandments contains grace and edification for those participants. To deny authority is to deny the sacraments and force new believers into disobedience, or worse, dependence upon outsiders. This undermines and cripples the body of Christ before it ever gets organized in the new culture. One of the greatest challenges for the missionary is to release the new body of believers into their calling in Christ Jesus without jeopardizing the missionary's own credibility with his sending church whose rules he must surely break to accomplish his purposes as a cross-cultural missionary.

Some examples might illustrate this conflict and why a distinction must be made between what is biblical spiritual authority and what is academic or institutional authority. We debate the form of bread for communion: wafers, crackers, and loaves, leavened or unleavened bread—yet we smile at tortillas, the indigenous Mexican's daily bread, being used in the communion supper. We argue about a lot of water or a little water, and whether it is poured, dipped, sprinkled, or flicked to accomplish baptism; yet we are not bothered when nearly entire churches are not baptized at all because the missionary could give no one authority to baptize due to the high academic requirements of the sending church which are being forced on the new mission church's leadership. Our academic arguments become mute when we realize we have denied new believers the grace contained in the sacraments due to cultural rules that should never be carried into cross-cultural ministry. We look at Presbyterian, Anglican, Pentecostal or Baptist churches anywhere in the world, and they essentially look the same, like the culture they were birthed in. Why must a people adopt another culture's expressions of biblical principles to worship our Lord and the creator of all cultures?

Very few communities in North America are without electricity, either from public or private sources. Great teachings are available on CDs and DVDs in hundreds of languages. Christian Schools offer whole curriculums on the internet and special conferences are broadcast in their entirety. Local churches by the thousands offer their sermons and teachings by broadcasts, internet, and recordings. With a couple of hundred dollars whole Bible schools can be set up in local churches to teach the Word of God to new believers. But these marvelous resources are of little value if there are no disciples of Jesus Christ to use them for the building and strengthening of the new, local bodies of believers in the foreign context. This clearly is why Jesus commanded us to go and make disciples—and let them and the Holy Spirit do the rest. It is both ethnocentric and just a plain lack of faith in God's redemptive power to think that a discipled man of God, filled with the Holy Spirit, would not be able to *do church* in his culture at least as well as the missionary can, and probably a whole lot better.

The need for those who would follow the Lord's command has never been greater: "Go therefore and make disciples of all the nations . . ."[2] With new disciples, Christ will build his church. A culturally relevant church in the midst of a nation can change the kingdoms of this world into the Kingdom of our God. That is why Christ commanded us to pray: "Ask the Lord of the harvest therefore to send out workers into His harvest field."[3] The reason given is that Jesus saw the people who were harassed and helpless like sheep without a shepherd. That is the condition of most of the indigenous people today. A half truth is a lie. It is time the indigenous Americans be given the whole truth in a way they can understand, accept, and apply to their lives and their nations.

The great gathering referred to in Revelation, chapter seven, includes souls from all nations, tribes, peoples, and tongues standing before the throne and before the Lamb, clothed with white robes and crying out with a loud voice saying, "Salvation belongs to our God who sits on the throne, and to the Lamb."[4] The indigenous societies of North America will be represented before the throne of God. Our generation is not responsible for the works, or the sins, of the previous 500 years; though it is both necessary and wise to repent for both sins and broken covenants made by our forefathers. This generation is responsible for preaching and teaching the gospel of Jesus Christ to those who are alive and without the knowledge of our Lord today and in our time. Let us learn from history—both the mistakes and the great advances in missiology made by the friars and, walk worthy of the calling with which we are called. Our Lord sent us to do what He did: to preach the good news to the poor, to bind up the brokenhearted, to proclaim freedom for the captives and release from darkness for the prisoners, and to proclaim the Lord's favor.[5] Let us do so in a wisdom that transcends cultural boundaries.

ABOUT THE AUTHOR

Andrew Toth has been doing missionary work for 42 years. He and his wife grew up in Washington State; he graduated from LeTourneau University in Texas with a degree in Aeronautical Engineering and worked at McDonnell Douglas in North Long Beach, California, before responding to the call of missions.

As a missionary, he began his ministry running youth camps in Ecuador and then spent most of his life evangelizing and starting churches in Mexico, primarily with indigenous North Americans. He also founded the first legally organized missionary sending agency in Mexico. Under the Presbyterian Church, he founded numerous Bible schools and taught in both residential and extension seminaries in Mexico. His graduate degrees include a Master's of Arts in Missiology from Fuller Theological Seminary and a Doctorado en Teología from La Universidad de las Naciones in Mission, Texas. He is a Professor of Record for the *Perspectives on the World Christian Movement* course in central Texas.

His practical experience has been with the Quechua of Ecuador; the Aztec, Purépecha, Northern Pame, and Mayo of Mexico; and the Nez Pierce of Idaho. For the last four years he has been the Director of Candidate Training with World Indigenous Missions out of New Braunfels, Texas. He continues to teach special classes and seminars in Bible Schools and churches in Mexico. His vision is to see the Mexican Church equipped to reach all of Mexico with the whole gospel of Jesus Christ.

BIBLIOGRAPHY

Adams, Richard. *Ancient Civilizations of the New World.* Oxford: Westview Press, 1997.

Aguilar, Rocio, and Francisco Sanchez. *Notas Para la Historia del Colegio Apostolico de Propaganda Fide de Cholula.* historico, Puebla: niversidad de las Americas, 2006.

Allaire, Louis. *The Caribs of the Lesser Antilles.* Gainesville: University of Florida Press, 1997.

Arróniz, Othón. *Teatro de Evangelización en Nueva España.* Mexico, D.F.: Universidad Nacional Autónoma de México, 1979.

Bannon, John. *Indian Labor in the Spanish Indies, Was There Another Solution?* Boston: D.C. Heath & Co., 1966.

Barnhart, C. L., Ed. *The American College Dictionary.* New York: Random House, 1960.

Barquero, Magdiel Castillo. *Origen del Sincretismo en Mexico, 2000 Años de Herencia Cultural.* New York: The Edwin Mellen Press, 2003.

Beeching, Jack. *An Open Path, Christian Missionaries, 1515-1914.* Ross-Erikson Pub., 1979.

Berger, Thomas. *A Long and Terrible Shadow, White Values, Native Rights in the Americas, 1492-1992.* Seattle: University of Washington Press, 1992.

Bernal, Ignacio. *Bibliografía de Arqueología y Etnografía, Mesoamérica y Norte de México, 1514-1960*. Mexico, DF: Instituto Nacional de Antropología e Historia, 1960.

Blanton, Richard E. *Ancient Mesoamerica: A Comparison of Change in Three Regions*. Cambridge: Cambridge University Press, 1981.

Braden, Charles. *Religious Aspects of the Conquest of Mexico*. Durham: Duke University Press, 1930.

Brown, Jonathan. *Latin America, A Social History of the Colonial Period*. Austin: Thomson & Wadsworth, 2005.

Carmack, Robert. *Toltec Influence on the Post Classic Culture History of Highland Guatemala*. Tulane: University Press, 1968.

Chance, John K. "Taricuri's Legacy: The Prehistoric Tarascan State." *American Indian Quarterly*, 1994.

Clendinnen, Inga. *Ambivalent Conquests, Maya and Spaniard in Yucatan, 1517-1570*. New York: Cambridge University Press, 1987.

Coe, Michael. *The Maya*. New York: Thames & Hudson, 1999.

Cohn, Norman. *The Pursuit of the Millennium: Revolutionary Millenarians and Mystical Anarchists of the Middle Ages*. New York: Oxford University Press, 1990.

Columbus, Christopher. *The Journel of Christopher Columbus*. New York: Bramhall House, 1960.

Cook, Noble David. *Born to Die, Disease and New World Conquest, 1492-1650*. Cambridge: Cambridge University Press, 1998.

Cortes, Hernando. *Five Letters 1519-1526*. Translated by Morris Bayard. New York: W.W. Norton & Co., 1969.

Crosby, Harry. *Antigua California, Mission and Colony on the Peninsular Frontier, 1697-1768.* Albuquerque: University of New Mexico Press, 1994.

Deagan, Kathleen. *Spanish-Indian Interaction in Sixteenth-Century Florida and Hispaniola.* New York: Smithsonian Institution Press, 1988.

Deeds, Susan. *Indigenous Rebellions on the Northern Mexican Mission Frontier: From First-Generation to Later Colonial Responses.* Lincoln: University of Nebraska Press, 1998.

Diamond, Jared. *Collapse, How Societies Choose to Fail or Succeed.* New York: Penguin Books, 2005.

Diaz, Bernal. *The Conquest of New Spain.* New York: Penguin Books, 1963.

Dunne, Peter Masten. *Black Robes in Lower California.* Berkeley: University of California Press, 1968.

Dussel, Enrique. *The Church in Latin America: 1492-1992.* Maryknoll: Orbis Books, 1992.

Farnsworth, Paul, and Robert H. Jackson. *Cultural, Economic, and Demographic Change in the Missions of Alta California: The Case of Nuestra Señora de la Soledad.* Lincoln: University of Nebraska Press, 1995.

Fitzhugh, William. *Cultures in Contact, The Impact of European Contacts on Native American Cultural Institutions, A.D. 1000-1800.* Washington: Smithsonian Institution Press, 1985.

Floyd, Troy. *The Bourbon Reformers and Spanish Civilization, Builders or Destroyers?* Boston: D.C. Heath and Co., 1966.

Foundation, The Lockman. *New American Standard Bible.* Reference Edition. Chicago: Moody Press, 1974.

French, B. F. *Historical Collections of Louisiana and Florida.* Document, Ann Arbor: University of Michigan Library, 2005.

Gerhard, Peter. *The Northern Frontier of New Spain.* Princeton: Princeton University Press, 1982.

Gibson, Charles. *The Aztec Under Spanish Rule, A History of the Indians of the Valley of Mexico 1519-1810.* Stanford: Stanford University Press, 1964.

Gradie, Charlotte May. "Jesuit Missions in Spanish North America, 1566-1623." University of Connecticut, 1997. 23.

Guerra, Francisco. "The Earliest American Epicemic: The Influenza of 1493." *Social science History,* 1988: 305-325.

Gutierrez and Orsi, eds. *Contested Eden, California Before the Gold Rush.* Berkeley: University of California Press, 1998.

Haas, Lisbeth. *Conquests and Historical Identities in California, 1769-1936.* Berkeley: University of California Press, 1995.

Hanke, Lewis. *All Mankind Is One, A Study of the disputation Between Bartolomé de Las Casas and Juan Ginés de Sepúlveda in 1550 on the Intellectual and Religious capacity of the American Indians,.* DeKalb: Northern Illinois University Press, 1974.

Haring, Clarence. *The Spanish Empire in America.* New York: Harcourt, Brace & World, Inc., 1947.

Haro, Maria Paz. "Religious Orders, The Indian, And the Conquest: Fifty Years of Dispute and Contradiction." *AT&T Online,* 2004: 2.

Hernandez, Pedro, and Manuel Serrano y Sanz. *Cabeza de Vaca, Relación de los naufragios y Comentarios de Alvar Núñez Cabeza de Vaca.* Madrid: Google Documents, 1906.

Hiebert, Paul. *Transforming Worldviews: An Anthropological Understanding of How People Change.* Baker Book House, 2008.

Horgan, Paul. *The Great River, The Rio Grande in North American History.* Hanover: Wesleyan University Press, 1984.

Howell, Martha, and Walter Prevenier. *From Reliable Sources, An Introduction to Historical Methods.* Ithaca: Cornell University Press, 2001.

Hurtado, Albert. *Indian Survival on the California Frontier.* Yale University Press, 1988.

John, Elizabeth. *Storms Brewed in Other Men's Worlds, The Confrontation of Indians, Spanish, and French in the Southwest, 1540-1795.* College Station: A&M University Press, 1975.

Johnson, Harry Prescott. "Diego Martinez de Hurdaide: Defender of the Northwestern Frontier of New Spain." *The Pacific Historical Review,* 1942: 169-185.

Kay, Thomas, and Jennifer Trafton. "Illuminating Europe." 2007: 26.

Kessell, John. *Kiva, Cross, and Crown, The Pecos Indians and New Mexico, 1540-1840.* Washington: National Park Service, US Department of the Interior, 1979.

Kieza, John. *Resilient Cultures, America's Native Peoples Confront European Colonization, 1500-1800.* Upper Saddle River: Prentice Hall, 2003.

Knight, Alan. *Mexico, The Colonial Era.* Cambridge: Cambridge University Press, 2002.

Langer, Erick, and Robert Jackson. *The New Latin American Mission History.* Lincoln: University of Nebraska Press, 1995.

León-Portilla, Miguel. *The Broken Spears: The Aztec Account of the Conquest of Mexico.* Beacon Press, 2007.

Lingenfelter, Sherwood. *Agents of Transformation, A Guide for Effective Cross-Cultural Ministry.* Grand Rapids: Baker Books, 1996.

Lockhart, James, and Enrique Otte. *Letters and People of the Spanish Indies, Sixteenth Century.* New York: Cambridge University Press, 1976.

Lopes Don, Patricia. "Franciscans, Indian Sorcerers, and the Inquisition in New Spain." *Journal of World History*, Mar 2006: 27-48.

MacCulloch, Diarmaid. *The Reformation.* New York: Penguin Books, 2003.

Megged, Amos. *Exporting the Catholic Reformation: Local Religion in Early-Colonial Mexico (Cultures, Beliefs, and Traditions-Medieval and Early Modern Peoples.* Brill Academic Publishers, 2005.

Mendieta, Gerónimo de. *Historia Eclesiástica Indiana, A Franciscan's View of the Spanish Conquest of Mexico.* New York: The Edwin Mellen Press, 1997.

Menzies, Gavin. *1421, The Year China Discovered America.* Perennial, Harper, Collins, Publishers, 2003.

Meyer, Michael, and William Sherman. *The Course of Mexican History.* New York, 1987.

Miranda, Francisco. *Uruapan, Monografía Municipal (1500-1970).* Call Number 900m 504, Uruapan: H. Ayuntamiento de Uruapan, Presidencia Municipal, 1979.

Neill, Stephen. *A History of Christian Missions.* New York: Penguin Books, 1964.

Nold, Patrick. "Praedicatores, inquisitores." *The Journal of Ecclesiastical History,* 2006: 57:1:133.

Olsen, Glenn. "Converting Europe." *Christian History & Biography,* 2007: 23.

Orr, William, and Robert Miller. *Daily Life in Colonial Mexico, The Journey of Friar Ilarione da Bergamo, 1761-1768.* Norman: University of Oklahoma Press, 2000.

Paredes, Américo. *With His Pistol in His Hand, A Border Ballad and its Hero.* Austin: University of Texas Press, 1958.

Phillippo, James. *Jamaica: Its Past and Present State.* Google Books, 1843.

Pool, Christopher. *Olmec Archaeology and Early Mesoamerica.* Cambridge: University Press, 2007.

Poole, Stafford. *Our Lady of Guadalupe, The Origins and Sources of a Mexican National Symbol, 1531-1797.* Tucson: The University of Arizona Press, 1996.

Powell, Philip. *Soldiers Indians and Silver, North America's First Frontier War.* Tempe: Center for Latin American Studies, 1975.

Prescott, William. *History of the Conquest of Mexico.* Philadelphia: J.B. Lippincott Co., 1843.

Reaman, Elmore. *The Trail of the Huguenots in Europe, the United States, South Africa and Canada.* Great Britain: Fredrick Muller Limited, 1964.

Reff, Daniel. *Depopulation and Culture Change in Northwestern New Spain, 1518-1764.* Salt Lake City: University of Utah Press, 1991.

Reyhner, Jon. *Teaching Indigenous Languages.* Flagstaff: Northern Arizona University, 1997.

Riding, Alan. *Distant Neighbors, A Portrait of the Mexicans.* New York: Random House, 1984.

Rivera, Luis. *A Violent Evangelism, The Political and Religious Conquest of the Americas.* Louisville: John Knox Press, 1990.

Roberts, David. *The Pueblo Revolt, The Secret Rebellion That Drove the Spaniards Out of the Southwest.* New York: Simon & Schuster, 2004.

Robertson, William, and John Frost. *The History of the Discovery and Settlement of America.* Grand Rapids: Harper & Brothers, 1843.

Robinson, W.W. *Land in California.* Berkeley: University of California Press, 1948.

Roth, Cecil. *The Spanish Inquisition.* New York: W.W. Norton & Co., 1964.

Sahagún, Bernardino de. *La Conversión de Los Indios de la Nueva España, Con el Texto de los Coloquios de los doce de Bernardino de Sahagún (1564).* Abya'Yala, 1990.

Sherman, William. *Forced Native Labor in Sixteenth-Century Central America.* Lincoln: University of Nebraska Press, 1979.

Shipek, Florence C. "Mission Indians and Indians of California Land Claims." *American Indian Quarterly,* 1989: 409-420.

Simpson, Lesley. *Studies in the Administration of the Indians in New Spain.* Berkeley: University of California Press, 1934.

Spicer, Edward. *Cycles of Conquest: The Impact of Spain, Mexico, and the United States on the Indians of the Southwest, 1533-1960.* Tucson: University of Arizona Press, 1997.

Tanner, Norman. *Decrees of the Ecumenical Councils, Vol 2.* Washington, 1990.

Thomson, A, and M. Ata'ur-Rahim. *Islam in Andalus*. London: Ta-Ha Publishers, 1996.

Tinker, George E., Deloria Vine, and Leslie Marmon Silko. *God is Red, A Native View of Religion*. Golden: Fulcrum Publishing, 1993.

Turner, Christy. *Man Corn, Cannibalism and Violence in the Pre-History American Southwest*. Salt Lake City: University of Utah, 1999.

Vaillant, George. *Aztecs of Mexico, Origin, Rise, and Fall of the Aztec Nation*. New York: Penguin Books, 1944.

Vecsey, Christopher. *On The Padres' Trail*. Notre Dame: University of Notre Dame Press, 1996.

Verástique, Bernardino. *Michoacán and Eden, Vasco de Quiroga and the Evangelization of Western Mexico*. Austin: University of Texas Press, 2000.

Vernon, Edward. *Las Misiones Antiguas, The Spanish Missions of Baja California, 1683-1855*. Santa Barbara: Viejo Press, 2002.

Von Hagen, Victor. *The Ancient Sun Kingdoms of the Americas*. Great Britain: Thames & Hudson, 1962.

Waters, Frank. *Mexico Mystique, The Coming Sixth World of Consciousness*. Chicago: The Swallow Press Inc., 1975.

Weber, David. *The Spanish Frontier in North America*. New Haven: Yale University Press, 1992.

Wigal, Donald. *Historic Maritime Maps, Used for Historic Exploration, 1290-1699*. New York: Parkstone Press, 2000.

Zampelli, Michael. "Trent Revisited: A Reappraisal of Early Modern Catholicism's Relationship with the Commedia Italiana." *The Journal of Religion and Theatre*, 2002: 120-130.

NOTES

Chapter I

[1]   The marriage procedure for the Northern Pame was that a young man and woman, usually between 12-14 years of age, would decide to marry. He would secretly then build a lean-to in the woods well away from the village; she would gather food stuffs to last them a good while. Then one day they would simply disappear. They would live together until the food ran out or some other pressing need would force them home. They would then live together as children of the home with the man's parents. When the new bride became pregnant, then the family would begin to set aside materials to build a new one room house. The house should be finished by the time the new borne appeared on the scene and the young family would then move into their new home within the father's family compound.

[2]   Juan Zumárraga was a Spanish friar (1468-1548). His accomplishments include the education of Indian youth establishing the Colegio de Santa Cruz de Tlatelolco in 1536 to train the sons of Indian aristocracy, producing a generation of Indian scholars who assisted Spanish friars in the writing of important works on history, religion, and customs of the preconquest era. He was appointed the first archbishop of Mexico in 1547. He served as Inquisitor in Mexico, and as such there is no doubt he is responsible for the destruction of the preconquest Aztec codices and other relics of the past. (In Spanish see: Greenleaf, Richard E. *Zumárraga and the Mexican Inquisition, 1536-1543*. 1962.)

[3]   Charles Samuel Braden, *Religious Aspects of the Conquest of Mexico* (Durham: Duke University Press, 1930), 76-81.

[4]   The *Black Legend* phrase was coined by Julian Juderías in his *La Leyenda Negra y la Verdad Histórica*. This legend holds that the Spanish murdered, maimed, tortured, and in general made life miserable for the Indians through cruelty, exploitation, religious intolerance, capture,

enslavement, and sexual abuse. The Black Legend can also be traced to published self-criticism from within Spain itself. As early as 1511, some Spaniards criticized the legitimacy of the Spanish colonization of the Americas. In 1552, the Dominican friar, Bartolomé de las Casas, published his famous *Brevísima relación de la destrucción de las Indias*, [A Brief Tale of the Destruction of the Indians] an account of the abuses that accompanied the colonization of New Spain. (Juderías, Julián, *La Leyenda Negra* (2003; first Edition of 1914) ISBN 84-9718-225-1; Keen, Benjamin. 1969. The Black Legend Revisited: Assumptions and realities. *The Hispanic American Historical Review*. Volume 49. No. 4. pp.703-719)

5   Hernando Cortes, *Five Letters 1519-1526*, Translated by Morris Bayard (New York: W.W. Norton & Co., 1969), 3-447. This translation contains the full text of all five known letters of Cortes from Mexico.

6   James Lockhart and Enrique Otte, *Letters and People of the Spanish Indies, Sixteenth Century* (New York: Cambridge University Press, 1976) This is an excellent collection of letters, with commentary, from officials, merchants, and ordinary settlers of various kinds.

7   Gavin Menzies presents a very convincing argument that the source of anomalies in European maps available to Spanish and Portuguese captains that indicated lands to the West, were derived from Chinese navigations of the Atlantic, Indian, and Pacific waters.

8   Lewis Hanke has presented an analysis and discussion of the debate between Las Casas and Sepúlveda over the nature and 'humanism' of the American indigenous people. Lewis Hanke, *All Mankind Is One, A Study of the disputation Between Bartolomé de Las Casas and Juan Ginés de Sepúlveda in 1550 on the Intellectual and Religious capacity of the American Indians* (DeKalb: Northern Illinois University Press, 1974).

9   Thomas Berger, *A Long and Terrible Shadow, White Values, Native Rights in the Americas, 1492-1992* (Seattle: University of Washington Press, 1992), xi.

10   Gavin Menzies, *1421, The Year China Discovered America* (New York: Perennial, Harper, Collins, Publishers, 2003), 267.

11   Eamon Duffy, *Saints & Sinners: A History of the Popes* (New Haven: Yale University Press, in association with S4C, 1997).

12   David Weber, *The Spanish Frontier in North America* (New Haven: Yale University Press, 1992), xiii.

[13] The lists of martyrs are quite long and seldom appreciated outside of the Roman Catholic Church. Fifteen clerics had lost their lives with the expeditions of Narvaez and De Soto; four Jesuits had drowned at sea returning to Cuba from Florida in addition to those lost at Chesapeake Bay; some starved to death on pioneer expeditions. Many others drowned or were killed going and returning from the Americas as storms and English pirates battered the Spanish fleets.

[14] Matthew 7.16, 20 NASB "By their fruits ye shall know them. Do *men* gather grapes of thorns, or figs of thistles? Therefore by their fruits ye shall know them."

[15] A survey using the names of the Roman Catholic Orders will give the reader a sketch of the history, as well as numerous links to a vast amount of information for each of the Orders' activities in the Americas.

[16] See: Erick Langer and Robert Jackson, *The New Latin American Mission History* (Lincoln: University of Nebraska Press, 1995), ix; John Kicza, *Resilient Cultures, America's Native Peoples Confront European Colonization, 1500-1800* (Upper Saddle River: Prentice Hall, 2003), 1; Charles Braden, *Religious Aspects of the Conquest of Mexico* (Druham: Duke University Press, 1930), ix; William Fitzhugh, Cultures in Contact, The Impact of European Contacts on Native American Cultural Institutions, A.D. 1000-1800 (Washington: Smithsonian Institution Press, 1985); Stafford Poole, Our Lady of Guadalupe, The Origins and Sources of a Mexican National Symbol, 1531-1797 (Tucson: The University of Arizona, 1996).

[17] Erick Langer and Robert Jackson, The New Latin American Mission History (Lincoln: University of Nebraska Press, 1995) ix-xii; For an example see: Gerónimo de Mendieta, *Historia Eclesiástica Indiana, A Franciscan's View of the Spanish Conquest of Mexico* (New York: The Edwin Mellen Press, 1997).

[18] Magdiel Castillo Barquero, *Origen del Sincretismo en Mexico, 2000 Años de Herencia Cultural* (New York: The Edwin Mellen Press, 2003), i-iii.

[19] David F. Salisbury, "Brief History of Cannibal Controversies" *Exploration* 15 August 2001.

[20] Thomas Berger, *A Long and Terrible Shadow, White Values, Native Rights in the Americas, 1492-1992* (Seattle: University of Washington Press, 1992), 49.

21   Martha Howell and Walter Prevenier, *From Reliable Sources, An Introduction to Historical Methods* (Ithaca: Cornell University Press, 2001), 19.

22   The Reduction was established by the Ordinances of Francisco de Alfaro, Judge of Charcas, in 1611. These Reduction laws gave great importance to the process of forming sedentary societies, not only as instruments of "humanization" and control of the indigenous Americans, but also as centers where they could be protected. It was said that for nomadic or seminomadic Indians not to be harmed would depend upon them being 'reduced' into settlements. Reductions kept in general terms to the rules laid down by Viceroy Toledo between 1570-1580, and the plans of 1573. All Reduction villages had the same basic elements such as church, school, priests' quarters, workshops, and dwellings. See: Enrique Dussel, *The Church in Latin America: 1492-1992* (Maryknoll: Orbis Books, 1992), 357-358.

23   Bernal in his monumental *Bibliografía de Arqueología y Etnografía* covers approximately the same geographic area as this study with an emphasis on the ethnology when making up his divisions. That resulted in 20 major divisions, but not taking into consideration the timeframe, the orders involved in the evangelism, the climatic considerations and their affect on culture, nor the political situations (Bernal 1960). Ignacio Bernal, *Bibliografía de Arqueología y Etnografía, Mesoamérica y Norte de México, 1514-1960* (Mexico, DF: Instituto Nacional de Antropología e Historia, 1960).

24   Matthew 28.19-20 NASB

Chapter II

1   It could be said that the renaissance led directly to the rebellion of evangelical Roman Catholics and the repeated attempts at reformation within the Latin Church. The Latin Church demanded blind faith in itself and pretended that the new perspectives were of no import. The Roman Catholic faith was corporate, not individual; therefore they were opposed to the concepts of the Enlightenment (Floyd 1966, iii). In New Spain this corporate, medieval concept of liberty would not be challenged until the New Spain northern frontiers were settled, where owner and peon fought side by side for their lives. This would bring about a more

individually based, egalitarian society and eventually lead to the war for Mexican independence from Spain.

2   Cecil Roth, *The Spanish Inquisition* (New York: W.W. Norton & Co., 1964), 20-24.

3   Paul Hiebert, *Transforming Worldviews: An Anthropological Understanding of How People Change* (Grand Rapids: Baker Book House, 2008), 307-333.

4   It should be noted that the Inquisition did not start in Spain. Pope Innocent III and Pope Gregory IX established the dreaded institution in the thirteenth century to combat heretical groups. The Inquisition was essentially a religious tribunal, bound fully as much by precedent and rule as any Court of Justice. The Dominican Order, founded in the thirteenth century as a teaching order with activities directed against heresy, was early associated with the Papal Inquisition, though it was only sporadically being implemented. When Spain successfully petitioned permission to appoint Inquisitors, the unique Spanish Inquisition came into being. The Inquisition was a spiritual body and did not carry out the convictions of the tribunal—that was the work of secular authorities. The public reading and execution of the sentences became a popular spectacle of the fifteenth and sixteenth centuries. Those who confessed were strangled before the fire was lit. Those who refused to admit wrongdoing, or those who defiantly clung to their "heresies" were burned alive. The Inquisition was exported to New Spain in 1569-70, under Philip II of Spain. The native population was in fact, exempt from the jurisdiction of the Inquisition, though that exemption was not always respected.

5   Max Leopold Margolis and Alexander Marx, *A History of the Jewish People* (New York: Scribner Pub., 1969).

6   A. Thomson and M. Ata'ur-Rahim. *Islam in Andalus* (London: Ta-Ha Publishers, 1996).

7   (Braden 1930, 7-14) Charles Samuel Braden, *Religious Aspects of the Conquest of Mexico* (Durham: Duke University Press, 1930), 7-14.

8   (Cohn 1990) Norman Cohn, *The Pursuit of the Millennium: Revolutionary Millenarians and Mystical Anarchists of the Middle Ages* (New York: Oxford University Press, 1990).

9   This directly affected Columbus, who had great difficulty finding ships to carry out his new plans to find India by sailing west from Europe. Frank Waters, Mexico *Mystique* (Chicago: The Swallow Press Inc., 1975), 24.

10 Donald Wigal, *Historic Maritime Maps, Used for Historic Exploration, 1290-1699* (New York: Parkstone Press, 2000), 115.

11 Diarmaid MacCulloch, *The Reformation* (New York: Penguin Books, 2003), 58.

12 It was inevitable, given the highly religious and nationalistic character of their long crusade against the Moors, that the Spaniards should seek to impose upon the New World the burning ideals of that crusade: one God, one king, one creed, one way of life—Spanish. John Bannon, *Indian Labor in the Spanish Indies, Was There Another Solution?* (Boston: D.C. Heath & Co., 1966), 11.

13 The term "regeneration" distinguishes baptism from every other sacrament, for although in theory penance revivifies men spiritually, this is resuscitation, a bringing back from the dead, rather than a rebirth. Penance does not make one Christian. On the contrary, it presupposes that one has already been born of water and the Holy Ghost to a life of grace, while baptism as taught by Roman Catholics was instituted to confer upon men the very beginnings of the spiritual life, to transfer them from the state of enemies of God to the state of adoption, as sons of God. *The Catholic Encyclopedia, 1914.* [The Catholic Encyclopedia Classic 1914 Edition—CD-ROM/DVD by Remy Lafort, S.T.D. and Arthur J. Scanlan, D.D.—Imprimatur: John Cardinal Farley and Patrick J. Hayes, Archbishops of N.Y. Nihil Obstat 19007-1914 (2003)], "Baptism" by Fanning, W.

14 It is interesting to note that first-level conversion of Jews and Moors was seen as insincere in Spain and an excuse for utter destruction and expulsion. After Trent, the fist-level conversion of native North Americans was seen as normal and sufficient for their eventual salvation. Perhaps the persecution of Jews and Moors in Spain was politically and economically motivated, rather than based upon their religious convictions.

15 Charles Samuel Braden, *Religious Aspects of the Conquest of Mexico* (Durham: Duke University Press, 1930), 12-14.

16 Prescott says: "We contemplate with indignation the cruelties inflicted by the early conquerors. But indignation is qualified with contempt when we see them thus ruthlessly trampling out the spark of knowledge, the common boon and property of all mankind. We may well doubt which has the stronger claim to civilization, the victor or the vanquished." William Prescott, *History of the Conquest of Mexico* (Philadelphia: J.B. Lippincott Co., 1843; reprint, Phoenix Press, 2002), 49.

[17] G. R. Evans, *John Wyclif: Myth & Reality* (Downers Grove: IVP Academic Pub., 2006).

[18] The Christian Library, *Foxe's Christian Martyrs of the World* (New Jersey: Barbour and Company, Inc., 1985), 264-270.

[19] Julius Kostlin and John G. Morris, *The Life Of Martin Luther* (Whitefish: Kessinger Publishing, LLC, 2007), 97-250.

[20] T.H.L. Parker, *John Calvin—A Biography* (Westminster: John Knox Press, 2007), 30-69.

[21] Ibid.

[22] Barbara B. Diefendorf, *The St. Bartholomew's Day Massacre: A Brief History with Documents* (Bedford Series in History & Culture. Bedford/ St. Martin's Pub., 2008).

[23] Elmore Reaman, *The Trail of the Huguenots in Europe, the United States, South Africa and Canada* (Great Britain: Fredrick Muller Limited, 1964), 9.

[24] It could be argued that France never did recover from the expulsion of the Huguenots for over a century, and simply ceased to be a power in Europe. Louis XIV soon realized it was a suicidal policy, for France lost most of her skilled artisans who also took the secrets of many French manufacturers to the Netherlands, England, and Germany. The expulsion was a death blow to several branches of French industry. Enormous amounts of wealth went out with the Huguenots and French commerce was stagnated. The French military alone lost 500 experienced officers, 12,000 soldiers, and 9,000 sailors. One hundred years later the French revolution finally lifted the country out of its self-imposed mediocrity, the Catholic monarchy was beheaded, and the stage was set for Napoleon and Republicanism (Reaman 1964, 61). Many of these Huguenots ended up in both French and English colonies of North America and would contribute to the strengthening of Protestant communities there, as well as foster a lingering hatred of the Spanish Catholics in New Spain.

[25] Merle D'Aubigné, *History of the Great Reformation of the Sixteenth Century in Germany* (Switzerland, &c.: Nabu Press, 2010).

[26] Jack Beeching, *An Open Path, Christian Missionaries, 1515-1914* (Ross-Erikson Pub., 1979), 14.

[27] Amy Turner Bushnell, *"Missions and Moral Judgment."* Organization of American Historians. Available from: http://www.oah.org/pubs/ magazine/Spanish frontier.html

²⁸   Erick Langer and Robert Jackson, *The New Latin American Mission History* (Lincoln: University of Nebraska Press, 1995), 31-32.

²⁹   The apocrypha was confirmed officially by Trent as canonical, but that inclusion did not alter the moral position of the Scriptures significantly. The apocrypha was accepted by the first millennium of Christianity only as 'highly useful' information. See: Merrill F. Unger, *Unger's Bible Dictionary* (Chicago: Moody Press, 1966), 70-71.

³⁰   Parker observed that the European Reformation enjoyed neither uniform success nor deep popular support in the sixteenth century, and ". . . the surviving evidence indicates a widespread inability on the part of the reformers . . . to create an acceptably pious laity within the first century of the Reformation. Amos Megged, *Exporting the Catholic Reformation: Local Religion in Early-Colonial Mexico (Cultures, Beliefs, and Traditions-Medieval and Early Modern Peoples* (Boston: Brill Academic Publishers, 2005), 18.

³¹   Erick Langer and Robert Jackson, *The New Latin American Mission History* (Lincoln: University of Nebraska Press, 1995), 42.

³²   Romans 10.9-10 NASB.

³³   Luis Rivera, *A Violent Evangelism, The Political and Religious Conquest of the Americas* (Louisville: John Knox Press, 1990), 231.

³⁴   Jack Beeching, An Open Path, Christian Missionaries, 1515-1914 (Ross-Erikson Pub., 1979), 18.

³⁵   "Tariácuri y El reino de Los Purépechas." *Pasajes de la Historia* (No. 8, enero 2003). [Translated by the author from the Spanish publication.]

³⁶   Las Casas received his call to ministry during the conquest of Cuba, joined the Dominicans, and fought for American indigenous rights for the rest of his life.

³⁷   Troy Floyd, *The Bourbon Reformers and Spanish Civilization, Builders or Destroyers?* (Boston: D.C. Heath and Co., 1966), xii.

³⁸   But one should also ask as to whether the new movements of evangelicalism and Protestantism do what Jesus did on earth? Did they follow his example, as Jesus commanded, that is, *be imitators* of the Son of God? Jesus did say, "By their fruits you will know them." In the *Great Commission* Jesus said, go and make disciples, baptizing them and teaching them. This is the heart of evangelism for any Christian expression; it is the root meaning of being evangelical. Yet we see that the evangelical movements of that time did little more than substitute another form of institutional church, retaining much of the older symbols and

forms by their own admission, but failed as the Roman Catholic Church failed, to make disciples and teach the indigenous Americans to walk as Jesus walked. Indeed, by their example, Europeans of both Roman Catholic and Evangelical persuasions, taught to invade, make war, hate, enslave, violate, and murder their neighbors. At least the Spanish, in general, attempted to justify their actions by baptizing the Americans in the process of destroying their cultures and societies. The English, in general, simply killed off the Americans and took the land for themselves. John Kieza, *Resilient Cultures, America's Native Peoples Confront European Colonization, 1500-1800* (Upper Saddle River: Prentice Hall, 2003), 125.

Chapter III

[1] Michael Zampelli, "Trent Revisited: A Reappraisal of Early Modern Catholicism's Relationship with the Commedia Italiana." *The Journal of Religion and Theatre*, 2002: 120-130.

[2] Christopher Vecsey, *On The Padres' Trail* (Notre Dame: University of Notre Dame Press, 1996), xi.

[3] Raymond F. Bulman, Frederick J. Parrella, and Jill Raitt, *From Trent to Vatican II: Historical and Theological Investigations* (Oxford University Press, USA, 2006), 19-39.

[4] Ibid.

[5] Ibid.

[6] Norman Tanner, *Decrees of the Ecumenical Councils*, Vol 2 (Washington, Herder & Herder, 1990), 657-799.

[7] Of course, any group of two or three Christians could use the same argument according to the statement of Jesus Christ in Mathew 18.20. Roman theologians said the explanation that Matthew 18:20 refers to an agreement and verification of inspired revelation more properly fits the context than the conclusion that Jesus was saying He would be present, in a special sense, even in the smallest assembly of the saints, when they gathered in His name.

[8] Jared Diamond, *Collapse, How Societies Choose to Fail or Succeed* (New York: Penguin Books, 2005), 431.

[9] Norman Tanner, *Decrees of the Ecumenical Councils*, Vol 2 (Washington, Herder & Herder, 1990), 657-799.

10   Purgatory was a relatively new concept for the Latin Church. By the 12th century, western Christians were taking this idea of intercession for the dead a bit further than just prayer during the Mass. The theologians developed a more sophisticated geography of the afterlife than was found in the biblical or early church documents. It was natural for creative Christian thinkers to speculate about some middle state in which those whom God loved would have a chance to perfect themselves and thus complete salvation. These concepts jelled into the definition of purgatory. This soul-prayer industry became a major source of income for the church, thus assuring its own "inspiration" at the Council of Trent based solely upon the traditions. Diarmaid MacCulloch, *The Reformation* (New York: Penguin Books, 2003), 11.

11   Norman Tanner, *Decrees of the Ecumenical Councils*, Vol 2 (Washington, Herder & Herder, 1990), 657-799.

12   These decrees were later supplemented by the Vatican Council of 1870. None of the continuing reforms after Trent would affect these basic Roman Catholic doctrines. There were elements of reform in structural reconfigurations, in religious Orders, and there were spiritual movements within the continuing Catholic responses to the ever growing Evangelical or Protestant movements.

13   The Sacred Congregation is a department of the pontifical administration. The system of government by Congregations, or administrative departments adopted during the counter-reformation period, took decades to implement the Tertian decrees and in doing so, established themselves as part of the bureaucracy of Rome.

14   Raymond F. Bulman, Frederick J. Parrella, and Jill Raitt, *From Trent to Vatican II: Historical and Theological Investigations* (Oxford University Press, USA, 2006), 19-39.

15   Michael Meyer and William Sherman, *The Course of Mexican History* (New York: Oxford University Press, 1987), 189-190.

16   Isaiah 6.8b NASB

Chapter IV

1   As touching this book, it may be noted that Columbus preceded the Council of Trent by half a century. It also should be noted that Spain

preceded Trent in nearly all aspects of doctrine and practice which Trent was to standardize in a rigid and unchangeable expression of Roman Catholicism. Spain's Crown had stood for the Dark-Age, imperial institutions of Roman Catholicism in their spiritual and physical battles against Jewish and Moorish institutions and their expressions of faith. They had kept evangelical reformers and their movements out of Spain. Spain was the model of Tridentine Roman Catholicism long before Trent froze Roman Catholicism in its Dark-Age expressions. It is correct to think of Spain at the time of conquest as Tridentine Roman Catholic.

2   Juan de Abreu Galindo, *The History of the Discovery and Conquest of the Canary Islands* [This Elibron Classics Replica Edition is an unabridged facsimile of the edition published in 1764.] (R. and J. Dodsley, T. Durham, London. Adamant Media Corporation, 2005), 11-18.

3   Ibid., 137-140.

4   Felipe Fernández-Armesto. *The Canary Islands after the Conquest: The Making of a Colonial Society in the Early Sixteenth Century* (Oxford: University Press, 1982).

5   Juan de Abreu Galindo, *The History of the Discovery and Conquest of the Canary Islands* [This Elibron Classics Replica Edition is an unabridged facsimile of the edition published in 1764.] (R. and J. Dodsley, T. Durham, London. Adamant Media Corporation, 2005), 146-165.

6   Diarmaid MacCulloch, *The Reformation* (New York: Penguin Books, 2003), 67.

7   Ibid.

8   Despite the large number of immigrants, the Guanches did not disappear, being assimilated rather than exterminated. Gaspar Fructuoso writing at the end of the 16th century described the population of La Palma [Canary Islands] as being evenly divided between Castilian, Portuguese and indigenous peoples. He reported these elements of the population as already being largely interbred, indistinguishable in faith and custom, and coexisting as equals. Gaspar Fructuoso, *Saudades da Terra* (Vol.1-6), [Originally published 1873.] (São Miguel: Instituto Cultural de Ponta Delgada, 1966), Book I.

9   Thomas Berger, *A Long and Terrible Shadow, White Values, Native Rights in the Americas, 1492-1992* (Seattle: University of Washington Press, 1992), xiii.

10 This was not a new concept for monks. Pope Gregory the Great (590-604) was the first to imagine evangelism beyond the Roman borders. He felt

that missionaries should adapt to existing societies as much as possible by establishing communities within those societies. Benedict wrote his Rule about half a century earlier; Boniface, apostle to the Germans, engaged in a type of theater to win converts and present the gospel in a comprehensible form; Anskar, apostle to the Scandinavians, was always trying to find common ground for understanding with those he was evangelizing; monasteries played a vital role in Charlemagne's vision of Christian civilization; so major elements of monastic missions were there even at that early stage.

[11] Romans 10.14 NASB

[12] Clarence Haring, *The Spanish Empire in America* (New York: Harcourt, Brace & World, Inc., 1947), 5.

[13] Ibid.

[14] Michael Craton, *Empire Enslavement and Freedom in the Caribbean* (Princeton: Markus Wiener Publishers, 1997), 1-32.

[15] Irving Rouse, *The Tainos: Rise and Decline of the People Who Greeted Columbus* (New Haven: Yale University Press, 1993), 105-133.

[16] Jerald T. Milanich, *Florida Indians and the Invasion from Europe* (Gainesville: University Press of Florida, 1998), 38-55.

[17] This was something that arrogance and pride prevented the Spanish from learning about construction from the Taino people. The first town of Santo Domingo was utterly destroyed by a hurricane.

[18] Michael Craton, *Empire Enslavement and Freedom in the Caribbean* (Markus Wiener Publishers, 1997), 1-32.

[19] Robert Henderson Fuson, *Juan Ponce de Leon: And the Spanish Discovery of Puerto Rico and Florida* (Blacksburg: McDonald and Woodward Publishing Company, 2000), 19-50.

[20] Ibid.

[21] Isaac Dookhan, *History of the Virgin Islands* (Puerto Rico: Canoe Pr, 2000), 1-30.

[22] Walter, Elis de, B. Leah, and Linda Criswell, eds. *Estudiemos las culturas indígenas de Colombia.* [Let's Study the Indigenous Cultures of Columbia] (Loma Linda: SIL, Editorial Townsend, 1984).

[23] Alan Riding, *Distant Neighbors, A Portrait of the Mexicans* (New York: Random House, 1984), 22.

[24] William Prescott, *History of the Conquest of Mexico* (Philadelphia: J.B. Lippincott Co., 1843; Reprint, Phoenix Press, 2002), 38.

[25] Bernal Diaz, *The Conquest of New Spain* (New York: Penguin Books, 1963), 104.

[26] Christy Turner, *Man Corn, Cannibalism and Violence in the Pre-History American Southwest* (Salt Lake City: University of Utah, 1999).

[27] Jack Beeching, *An Open Path, Christian Missionaries, 1515-1914* (Ross-Erikson Pub., 1979), 54.

[28] Noble David Cook, *Born to Die, Disease and New World Conquest, 1492-1650* (Cambridge: Cambridge University Press, 1998), 20.

[29] William Prescott, *History of the Conquest of Mexico* (Philadelphia: J.B. Lippincott Co., 1843; Reprint, Phoenix Press, 2002), 41.

[30] Kathleen Deagan, *Spanish-Indian Interaction in Sixteenth-Century Florida and Hispaniola* (New York: Smithsonian Institution Press, 1988), 283.

[31] Clifford L. Staten. *The History of Cuba* (Palgrave Essential Histories) (New York: Palgrave Macmillan, 2005), 1-30.

[32] Clarence Haring, *The Spanish Empire in America* (New York: Harcourt, Brace & World, Inc., 1947), 8.

[33] J. M. Cohen, ed. & trans. *The Four Voyages of Christopher Columbus* (New York: Penguin Books, 1969), 118.

[34] Kathleen Deagan, *Spanish-Indian Interaction in Sixteenth-Century Florida and Hispaniola* (New York: Smithsonian Institution Press, 1988), 282.

[35] Some sources say 1,200 men.

[36] Gavin Menzies, 1421, *The Year China Discovered America* (New York: Perennial, Harper, Collins, Pub. 2003), 267-270.

[37] The Caribs would capture boys, castrate them, and then use them for domestic and menial chores until they were old enough for consumption. Only boys born of Carib men were treated as sons, all others were eaten (J. M. Cohen, ed. & trans. *The Four Voyages of Christopher Columbus* (Penguin Books, 1969), 136-137.

[38] Ibid., 118.

[39] Noble David Cook. *Born to Die, Disease and New World Conquest, 1492-1650* (Cambridge: Cambridge University Press, 1998), 51.

[40] Ibid., 28.

[41] Cook's *Born to Die* is an excellent book for an analysis of the effects of epidemic disease on Amerindian peoples at the time of the conquest. Also see: Alfred Crosby, The Columbian Exchange: Biological and Cultural Consequences of 1492 (Westport: Greenwood Press, 1972), 42. Thomas Whitmore, *Disease and Death in Early Colonial Mexico: Simulating Amerindian Depopulation* (Boulder: Westview Press, 1992).

42 Francisco Guerra, "The Earliest American Epicemic: The Influenza of 1493." *Social Science History,* 1988: 305-325.

43 Noble David Cook. *Born to Die, Disease and New World Conquest, 1492-1650* (Cambridge: Cambridge University Press, 1998), 23, 30-33, 35, 38, 58.

44 Ibid., 39, 42-49.

45 All attempts at calculating demographic distributions at this point in time are superfluous. Even during the first ten year period the numbers vary widely. Educated guesses by demographers vary widely. This statement is based upon the authors own estimate considering the many different accounts of population and death rates of the indigenous people. See: Noble David Cook, *Born to Die, Disease and New World Conquest, 1492-1650* (Cambridge University Press, 1998, p 23) for a list of estimates from various sources.

46 "III-Until the Tridentine Reform (1492-1574)" *Order of the Blessed Virgin Mary of Mercy* (http://orderofmercy. org/?s=History) Accessed: Sept 21, 2007. Mercedarian Friars.

47 Enrique Dussel, *The Church in Latin America: 1492-1992* (Maryknoll: Orbis Books, 1992), 376.

48 *The Catholic Encyclopedia, 1914.* [The Catholic Encyclopedia Classic 1914 Edition—CD-ROM/DVD by Remy Lafort, S.T.D. and Arthur J. Scanlan, D.D.—Imprimatur: John Cardinal Farley and Patrick J. Hayes, Archbishops of N.Y. Nihil Obstat 19007-1914 (2003)] "Catholic Indian Missions of the United States."

49 Ibid.

50 Enrique Dussel, *The Church in Latin America: 1492-1992* (Maryknoll: Orbis Books, 1992), 375.

51 The other two 'religious' were an Order of Knights friar, and a Jeronymite lay brother.

52 Ibid.

53 Luis Rivera, *A Violent Evangelism, The Political and Religious Conquest of the Americas* (Louisville: John Knox Press, 1990), 219.

54 Enrique Dussel, *The Church in Latin America: 1492-1992* (Maryknoll: Orbis Books, 1992), 375.

55 Ibid. 376

56 (Fitzhugh 1985, 273) William Fitzhugh, *Cultures in Contact, The Impact of European Contacts on Native American Cultural Institutions, A.D. 1000-1800* (Washington: Smithsonian Institution Press, 1985), 273.

57 Maria Paz Haro, "Religious Orders, The Indian, And the Conquest: Fifty Years of Dispute and Contradiction." *AT&T Online*, 2004: 2.
58 Diarmaid MacCulloch, *The Reformation* (New York: Penguin Books, 2003), 68.
59 Much of the source data from these first ten years is questionable and at times contradictory. The majority of the surviving primary sources about Columbus were intended to be read by others for specific purposes. Foremost among these sources are the journals written by Columbus himself for his sovereigns, one for the first voyage now lost, though partly reconstructed; one for the second almost wholly gone; and one for the third which is accessible through reconstructions made by using later quotations. Each of the journals are supplemented by letters and reports to sovereigns and their trusted officials and friends, provisioning decrees from the sovereigns, and in the case of the second voyage, letters and reports of letters from fellow voyagers. There is no journal and only one letter from the fourth voyage, but a complete roster and payroll do survive from this alone of all the voyages. An eyewitness account survives that has been plausibly attributed to Columbus's younger son, Ferdinand who traveled with the admiral. (This is a condensation of an explanation of the problems in documentation that appears as a note to the Encyclopedia Britannica article on Christopher Columbus which highlights the difficulty of finding primary source data from this time period.) See: *Britannica Concise Encyclopedia, 2007* ed., s.v. "Christopher Columbus."
60 Kathleen Deagan, *Columbus's Outpost among the Taínos: Spain and America at La Isabela, 1493-1498* (New York: Yale University Press, 2002), 47-70. The source data is very weak; the conclusions are very probable.
61 Noble David Cook, *Born to Die, Disease and New World Conquest, 1492-1650* (Cambridge: Cambridge University Press, 1998), 61.
62 Troy Floyd, *The Bourbon Reformers and Spanish Civilization, Builders or Destroyers?* (Boston: D.C. Heath and Co., 1966), 24-27.
63 Ibid.
64 Noble David Cook, *Born to Die, Disease and New World Conquest, 1492-1650* (Cambridge: Cambridge University Press, 1998), 16.
65 Ibid.
66 Troy Floyd, *The Bourbon Reformers and Spanish Civilization, Builders or Destroyers?* (Boston: D.C. Heath and Co., 1966), 44-45.

67   (Neill 1964, 143-150)

68   Ibid.

69   This census figure was based upon the *encomienda* indigenous American people. It did not attempt to count all the Taino that still lived outside of slavery or in isolated parts of Hispaniola outside of Spanish supervision.

70   Noble David Cook, *Born to Die, Disease and New World Conquest, 1492-1650* (Cambridge: Cambridge University Press, 1998), 1.

71   Enrique Dussel, *The Church in Latin America: 1492-1992* (Maryknoll: Orbis Books, 1992), 5.

72   Las Casas is so well known I will just mention here that La Casas was ordained a deacon in Seville, studied for the priesthood, took a degree in Cannon Law at Salamanca, and then went to Hispaniola. He taught the catechisms to indigenous students, and was known as a gentlemen-cleric. He was an encomienda holder, but worked as a supply agent for the islands, until his conversion in Cuba and his radical defense of the indigenous people began.

73   Thomas Berger, *A Long and Terrible Shadow, White Values, Native Rights in the Americas, 1492-1992* (Seattle: University of Washington Press, 1992), 3.

74   Jack Beeching, *An Open Path, Christian Missionaries, 1515-1914* (Ross-Erikson Pub., 1979), 18.

75   Irving Rouse, *The Tainos: Rise and Decline of the People Who Greeted Columbus* (New Haven: Yale University Press, 1993), 150-161.

76   R. A. Van Middeldyk, *The History of Puerto Rico: From the Spanish Discovery to the American Occupation* (Seattle: CreateSpace Publishing, 2010), 8-22.

77   Ibid.

78   Ibid.

79   One source says 80,000 to 100,000 Tainos at the time of discovery. See: James Phillippo, *Jamaica: Its Past and Present State* (London [Google Books]: John Snow Patermoster Row, 1843), 1-14.

80   Clarence Haring, *The Spanish Empire in America* (New York: Harcourt, Brace & World, Inc., 1947), 18.

81   W. J. Gardner, *History of Jamaica* (Londen: Frank Cass & Co. Ltd., 1971), 2-16.

82   James Phillippo, *Jamaica: Its Past and Present State* (London: John Snow Patermoster Row [Google Books], 1843), 1-14.

83 *The Catholic Encyclopedia, 1914.* [The Catholic Encyclopedia Classic 1914 Edition—CD-ROM/DVD by Remy Lafort, S.T.D. and Arthur J. Scanlan, D.D.—Imprimatur: John Cardinal Farley and Patrick J. Hayes, Archbishops of N.Y. Nihil Obstat 19007-1914 (2003)] "Archdiocese of Santo Domingo."

84 Tinker has said [George E. Tinker, Deloria Vine, and Leslie Marmon Silko. God is Red, A Native View of Religion (Golden: Fulcrum Publishing, 1993), vii.] that the church has functioned to provide theological justification for acts of conquest, even when it protested to the contrary . . . at the surface level. The Dominicans in particular took the fight for indigenous rights all the way to the courts of the King, initiated and established fundamental laws for their protection, and then fought the colonists for their implementation at a grass roots level. This was somewhat more than *surface level.*

85 Simpson, Lesley Bird. The laws of Burgos of 1512-1513: Royal ordinances for the good government and treatment of the Indians. J. Howell Pub., 1960.

86 Christopher Vecsey, *On The Padres' Trail* (Notre Dame: University of Notre Dame Press, 1996), 6.

87 The cultural disintegration was manifested in group suicide, in hopelessness, in mothers who chose for their infants' death rather than a life of pain and anguish, in loss of procreation because males and females, suffering a profound "culture shock," had chosen not to procreate. Life without purpose was manifested in descriptions such as those found in Sepulveda's writings: They [the indigenous] are poor and detestable people, full of vicious and criminal customs, sodomy, cowardice, suicide . . . laziness, lack of gratitude, bestial understanding, incapable, natural slaves, immoral. See also: Lewis Hanke, *All Mankind Is One, A Study of the disputation Between Bartolomé de Las Casas* and Juan Ginés de Sepúlveda in 1550 on the *Intellectual and Religious capacity of the American Indians* (DeKalb: Northern Illinois University Press, 1974), 40-45.

88 Noble David Cook, *Born to Die, Disease and New World Conquest,* 1492-1650 (Cambridge: Cambridge University Press, 1998), 59-63.

89 Enrique Dussel, The Church in Latin America: 1492-1992 (Maryknoll: Orbis Books, 1992), 204.

90 Ibid.

91   Robert Henderson Fuson, *Juan Ponce de Leon: And the Spanish Discovery of Puerto Rico and Florida.* (Blacksburg: McDonald and Woodward Publishing Company, 2000), 83-90.

92   Inga Clendinnen, *Ambivalent Conquests, Maya and Spaniard in Yucatan, 1517-1570* (New York: Cambridge University Press, 1987), 16.

93   Bernal Diaz, *The Conquest of New Spain* (New York: Penguin Books, 1963), 102.

94   Ibid., 280-283.

95   For details of the effects of smallpox on the armies read: Bernal Diaz, *The Conquest of New Spain* (New York: Penguin Books, 1963), and Miguel León-Portilla, The Broken Spears: *The Aztec Account of the Conquest of Mexico* (Boston: Beacon Press, 2007).

96   University of North Texas, TSHA. "Álvarez de Pineda, Alonso." [Cited December 14, 2007] Available from: http://www.tshaonline.org/handbook/online/articles/fal72

97   Bernal Diaz, *The Conquest of New Spain* (New York: Penguin Books, 1963), 132-134.

98   Donald E. Chipman, *Nuno De Guzman and the Province of Panuco in New Spain, 1518-1533* (Glendale: Arthur H. Clark Co., 1967), 59-65, 141-154, 225.

99   The Catholic Encyclopedia, 1914. [The Catholic Encyclopedia Classic 1914 Edition—CD-ROM/DVD by Remy Lafort, S.T.D. and Arthur J. Scanlan, D.D.—Imprimatur: John Cardinal Farley and Patrick J. Hayes, Archbishops of N.Y. Nihil Obstat 19007-1914 (2003)] "Juan de Zumárraga."

100   Cabeza De Vaca, *Alvar Nunez. Chronicle of the Narvaez Expedition. Translated by Fanny Bandelier.* New York: Penguin Classics, 2002.

101   Paul Horgan, *The Great River, The Rio Grande in North American History* (Hanover: Wesleyan University Press, 1984), 95-108.

102   The Catholic Encyclopedia, 1914. [The Catholic Encyclopedia Classic 1914 Edition—CD-ROM/DVD by Remy Lafort, S.T.D. and Arthur J. Scanlan, D.D.—Imprimatur: John Cardinal Farley and Patrick J. Hayes, Archbishops of N.Y. Nihil Obstat 19007-1914 (2003)] "Catholic Indian Missions of the United States."

103   Elizabethen Era.Org, "Lucas Vázquez de Ayllon." [Cited December 20, 2007] Available from: http://www.elizabethan-era.org.uk/lucas-vasquez-de-ayllon.htm

104 S.C. Department of Archives & History. "The Spanish in South Carolina: Unsettled Frontier." 1989. Access: http://www.state.sc.us/webdev/acrobat/ pkt.pdf

105 Noble David Cook, *Born to Die, Disease and New World Conquest, 1492-1650* (Cambridge: Cambridge University Press, 1998), 47.

106 Jack Beeching, *An Open Path, Christian Missionaries, 1515-1914* (Ross-Erikson Pub., 1979), 39.

107 William Sherman, *Forced Native Labor in Sixteenth-Century Central America* (Lincoln: University of Nebraska Press, 1979), 39.

108 Clarence Haring, *The Spanish Empire in America* (New York: Harcourt, Brace & World, Inc., 1947), 12.

109 William Sherman, *Forced Native Labor in Sixteenth-Century Central America*(Lincoln: University of Nebraska Press, 1979), 77-78.

110 Jonathan Brown, *Latin America, A Social History of the Colonial Period* (Austin: Thomson & Wadsworth, 2005), 85.

111 Florida Center for Instructional Technology, College of Education, University of South Florida. "Exploring Florida; Tequesta of Biscayne Bay," 2002. Available from: http://fcit.usf.edu/florida/lessons/tequest/tequest1.htm.

112 Bob Leonard. *The Floridians, A Social History of Florida*, "Florida of the Conquistador" Tampa, Available at: http://floridanabob.hypermart.net/floridians.htm

113 Ibid.

114 A quote from Las Casas—"Nay, they have consistently afflicted and persecuted the monks, to prevent them from preaching, because it seemed to the Spaniards that this might be an impediment to their acquisition of gold and wealth . . ." John Bannon, Indian Labor in the Spanish Indies, Was There Another Solution? (Boston: D.C. Heath & Co., 1966), 39.

115 Jack Beeching, *An Open Path*; Noble David Cook, *Born to Die*; William Prescott, *History of the Conquest of Mexico*; John Bannon, *Indian Labor in the Spanish Indies*; Elizabeth John, *Storms Brewed in Other Men's Worlds*.

116 Caribindians.net. "Caribindians." Available from: http://www.caribindians.net/

117 Exploring Florida. "Florida Map: Florida Indian Reservations." Available from: http://fcit.usf.edu/Florida/maps/nat_am/nat_am01.htm

118 The Order of Blessed Virgin Mary of Mercy, "Mercedarian Historical Survey." [Cited December 30, 2009] Available from: http://orderofmercy.org/?s =History

[119] The introduction of the Carmelite order in New Spain was in 1585, after having overcome the initial reluctance of the Crown that controlled very carefully which Orders were allowed into New Spain.

[120] The History of Texas. "Missions and Missionaries." © 2003-2008 Son of the South [Cited December 31, 2009] Available from: http://www.sonofthesouth.net/texas/missions.htm

[121] The author has found no records to date to either verify or contradict this statement. The author feels it is a valid assumption.

[122] Nold, Patrick. "Praedicatores, inquisitores." *The Journal of Ecclesiastical History*, 2006:57:1:133.

[123] Arthur F. Glasser. "Missiology, What's It all About?" *Missiology Review* (Miss Rev 6:3-10).

[124] Mathew 28.18-20, NASB.

[125] Romans 1.18-2.11, NASB.

[126] Christopher Vecsey, *On The Padres' Trail* (Notre Dame: University of Notre Dame Press, 1996), 6.

[127] William Robertson and John Frost. *The History of the Discovery and Settlement of America* (Grand Rapids: Harper & Brothers, 1843), 365.

[128] The *Catholic Encyclopedia, 1914.* [The Catholic Encyclopedia Classic 1914 Edition—CD-ROM/DVD by Remy Lafort, S.T.D. and Arthur J. Scanlan, D.D.—Imprimatur: John Cardinal Farley and Patrick J. Hayes, Archbishops of N.Y. Nihil Obstat 19007-1914 (2003)] "Archdiocese of Santo Domingo."

[129] Paul Hiebert, *Transforming Worldviews: An Anthropological Understanding of How People Change* (Grand Rapids: Baker Book House, 2008), 42-48.

Chapter V

[1] La Malinche was one of twenty slave girls given to Cortéz by a Mayan Cacique in Tabasco. She was formerly an Aztec noblewoman but rejected by her mother in favor of a half-brother, sold into slavery, and sent off to the land of the Maya. See: Shep Lenchek, "La Malinche—harlot or heroine?" *El Ojo del Lago*. Dec (1997) Volume 14, Num 4.

[2] Ibid.

[3] Ibid.

4   Doing the math: 35 soldiers had been lost in Tabasco in skirmishes and sickness (Dias 1963:99). A number of men were left along the way to advise allies and to hold different strong points and Villa Rica on the coast. Some accounts would say only 450 Europeans actually went with Cortéz.

5   Bernardino Verástique, *Michoacán and Eden, Vasco de Quiroga and the Evangelization of Western Mexico* (Austin: University of Texas Press, 2000), 39.

6   (Adams 1997) Richard Adams, *Ancient Civilizations of the New World* (Oxford: Westview Press, 1997).

7   Robert Carmack, *Toltec Influence on the Post Classic Culture History of Highland Guatemala* (Tulane: University Press, 1968).

8   Richard E. Blanton, *Ancient Mesoamerica: A Comparison of Change in Three Regions* (Cambridge: Cambridge University Press, 1981).

9   Victor Von Hagen, *The Ancient Sun Kingdoms of the Americas* (Great Britain: Thames & Hudson, 1962).

10   Bernardino de Sahagún. *La Conversión de Los Indios de la Nueva España, Con el Texto de los Coloquios de los doce de Bernardino de Sahagún (1564)* (Quito: Abya'Yala, 1990).

11   Some sources would place the beginnings of the Tarascan Empire nearer to 1000 AD. See: Richard E.W. Adams, *Prehistoric Mesoamerica* (Norman: University of Oklahoma Press, 1991).

12   Michael D. Coe, *Mexico: From the Olmecs to the Aztecs (Ancient Peoples and Places)* (London: Thames & Hudson, 1994) 171.

13   Julie Adkins, "Mesoamerican anomaly? The Pre-Conquest Tarascan State" Department of Anthropology, SMU: Syllabus Anth 3311.

14   Ibid.

15   Ibid.

16   Ibid.

17   Ibid.

18   The Aztec had distorted the spiritual values of the early Toltec religion of Quetzalcoatl in which the mass of people still believed the fundamental precepts. See: "Toltec" in: Susan Toby Evans and David L. *Webster. Archaeology of Ancient Mexico and Central America: An Encyclopedia* (Special-Reference) (New York: Routledge, 2000).

19   Victor Von Hagen, *The Ancient Sun Kingdoms of the Americas* (Great Britain: Thames & Hudson, 1962), 100.

20 George Vaillant, *Aztecs of Mexico, Origin, Rise, and Fall of the Aztec Nation* (New York: Penguin Books, 1944), 180.

21 Ibid.

22 Sahagún, Bernardino de. *La Conversión de Los Indios de la Nueva España, Con el Texto de los Coloquios de los doce de Bernardino de Sahagún (1564).* Quito: Abya'Yala, 1990.

23 Bernal Diaz, *The Conquest of New Spain* (New York: Penguin Books, 1963), 107-108, 110, 236, 239.

24 Ibid (112, 120, 123-125)

25 The giving of young girls by officers to reward men for their loyalty seems to have been a common practice even though slavery was prohibited, except where indigenous people had taken up arms against the Crown; obviously young girls normally did not do that. There are no marriage ceremonies mentioned in most cases which causes one to wonder why fornication and/or adultery were such an acceptable, or at least a very common practice, in violation of the standards of their Holy Roman Catholic faith, and these were supposedly very devout men.

26 Bernal Diaz, *The Conquest of New Spain* (New York: Penguin Books, 1963), 135, 140-188.

27 These dates of plagues and epidemics are mostly taken from: Noble David Cook, *Born to Die, Disease and New World Conquest, 1492-1650* (Cambridge University Press, 1998).

28 This title, of course, ignores the whole Caribbean Epoch and the many friars and priests that served in the Caribbean.

29 Charles Samuel Braden. *Religious Aspects of the Conquest of Mexico* (Durham: Duke University Press, 1930), 131.

30 Lesley Bird Simpson. The laws of Burgos of 1512-1513: Royal ordinances for the good government and treatment of the Indians (J. Howell Pub., 1960), 35.

31 Christopher Vecsey. *On The Padres' Trail* (Notre Dame: University of Notre Dame Press, 1996), 16.

32 This title ignores the schools for the training of the priesthood in most of the great indigenous centers and the entire system of sciences and higher learning well established before the Spanish arrived.

33 Cortes and those with him knelt and kissed their hands [Franciscans] with the deepest respect, and then conducted them to the lodgings prepared for them. The Indians wondered much when they saw those whom some considered supernatural beings prostrate at the feet of these

humble and apparently despicable men. Cortes seized the opportunity to address a discourse to the *caciques* (chiefs) and lords who accompanied him recommending due veneration and respect, as he himself had shown, for those who had come to teach them the Christian religion. See: William Prescott, *History of the Conquest of Mexico* (Philadelphia: J.B. Lippincott Co., 1843; reprint, Phoenix Press, 2002).

34 *The Catholic Encyclopedia, 1914.* [The Catholic Encyclopedia Classic 1914 Edition CD-ROM/DVD by Remy Lafort, S.T.D. and Arthur J. Scanlan, D.D. Imprimatur: John Cardinal Farley and Patrick J. Hayes, Archbishops of N.Y. Nihil Obstat 19007-1914 (2003)] "Martin of Valencia, O.F.M."

35 Ibíd., "Toribio de Benavente Motolinía."

36 William Prescott, *History of the Conquest of Mexico* (Philadelphia: J.B. Lippincott Co., 1843; reprint, Phoenix Press, 2002), 276-277.

37 *The Catholic Encyclopedia, 1914.* [The Catholic Encyclopedia Classic 1914 Edition CD-ROM/DVD by Remy Lafort, S.T.D. and Arthur J. Scanlan, D.D.—Imprimatur: John Cardinal Farley and Patrick J. Hayes, Archbishops of N.Y. Nihil Obstat 19007-1914 (2003)] "Toribio de Benavente Motolinía."

38 Bernardino Verástique, *Michoacán and Eden, Vasco de Quiroga and the Evangelization of Western Mexico* (Austin: University of Texas Press, 2000), 97-99.

39 Adrian Blázquez, Guadalajara y el Nuevo Mundo: Nuño Beltrán de Guzmán, Semblanza de un Conquistador (Virrey Mendoza). [Guadalajara and the New World: Nuño Beltrán de Guzmán, the Image of a Conqueror] Guadalajara: Institución Provincial de Cultura "Marquesde Santillana," 1992.

40 As founder and officer-in-charge of the Nazi concentration camps and the infamous *Einsatzgruppen* death squads, Himmler held final command responsibility for annihilating "sub humans" who the Nazis deemed unworthy to live. Contact: Jim Tuck © 2008.

41 Adrian Blázquez, *Guadalajara y el Nuevo Mundo: Nuño Beltrán de Guzmán, Semblanza de un Conquistador (Virrey Mendoza).* [Guadalajara and the New World: Nuño Beltrán de Guzmán, the Image of a Conqueror] Guadalajara: Institución Provincial de Cultura "Marquesde Santillana," 1992.

42 Ibid.

43 Ibid.

44   This is from a document found in the official library of the municipal government of Uruapan, Michoacán. The document is full of flowery legal expressions, and I have taken considerable liberty in the translation of the portions cited for this research project (Miranda 1979).

45   Alan Knight, Mexico, *The Colonial Era* (New York: Cambridge University Press, 2002), 1-30.

46   Ortega Noriega Sergio, *Breve historia de Sinaloa (Vida y Pensamiento de Mexico), [A Short History of Sinaloa, Life and Thought in Mexico]* (Mexico City: Fondo de Cultura Económica: 2005).

47   Vicente Riva Palacio. *México a Través de los Siglos,* Vol. II [Mexico Across the Centuries] (Barcelona: Espasa, cited in Juan Dijes Antón, and Manuel Sagrado y Martín. Biografías de Hijos Ilustres de la Provincia de Guadalajara. [Biographies of Illustrious Sons of the Province of Guadalajara] (Guadalajara, Spain, 1889), 45.

48   John Bannon, *Indian Labor in the Spanish Indies, Was There Another Solution?* (Boston: D.C. Heath & Co., 1966), vii.

49   Bernardino de Sahagún, *La Conversión de Los Indios de la Nueva España, Con el Texto de los Coloquios de los doce de Bernardino de Sahagún (1564).* [The Conversion of the Indians of New Spain] (Quito: Abya'Yala, 1990).

50   There is also a contradictory note of testimony from the Tlamatinime—Aztec priests: "You said our gods are not true gods. Calm and amiable, consider, oh lords, whatever is best. We cannot be tranquil, and yet we certainly do not believe; we do not accept your teachings as truth, even though this may offend you." See: Bernardino Verástique, *Michoacán and Eden, Vasco de Quiroga and the Evangelization of Western Mexico* (Austin: University of Texas Press, 2000), v.

51   Bernardino de Sahagún, *La Conversión de Los Indios de la Nueva España, Con el Texto de los Coloquios de los doce de Bernardino de Sahagún (1564).* [The Conversion of the Indians of New Spain] (Quito: Abya'Yala, 1990), 8.

52   Vecsey, Christopher. *On The Padres' Trail.* Notre Dame: University of Notre Dame Press, 1996, 17.

53   Tinker presents an argument (Tinker 1993, 4) that Christian missionaries unwittingly (he also uses the phrases: 'thoroughly blinded by their own enculturation' 'unintended evil' 'confused gospel values') were guilty of complicity in the destruction of indigenous cultures and tribal social structures. The fact is the Roman Catholic missionaries had indigenous

enculturation to Spanish cultural mores as a major part of their reason for being sent to the indigenous people. Sodomy, cannibalism, inter-tribal warfare, bigamy, revenge killings, nudity, and human sacrifice were all cultural elements that the Spanish always put to a halt immediately. Tinker calls this cultural genocide and indicts the missionary as the cause for indigenous cultural cessation. Actually the failure, if it could be called that, of the Spanish was the failure to recognize the difference between destructive behavior and cultural behavior that was inherently good—just different. Nevertheless, whether good or destructive, the Spanish objective was still to convert all indigenous people to the Spanish culture. It was not unwitting complicity on the part of the friars, it was their job.

54 Bernardino de Sahagún, *La Conversión de Los Indios de la Nueva España, Con el Texto de los Coloquios de los doce de Bernardino de Sahagún (1564).* [The Conversion of the Indians of New Spain] (Quito: Abya'Yala, 1990), 8.

55 Christopher Vecsey, On The Padres' Trail (Notre Dame: University of Notre Dame Press, 1996), 17.

56 Both were formed and perfected in the Dark Ages; both represented a degradation of a higher religious expression: the Aztec religion was a traditional corruption of the Toltec religious philosophies; the Roman Catholic, a traditional corruption of New Testament Christianity. Both had a mundane, common expression that was a far cry from their philosophical or high form of religious belief.

57 The Spanish Inquisition was a public spectacle that served both judicial punishment and a public warning against violation of religious rules. See: Orr and Millar for a description of traditional religious Autos de Fe. William Orr and Robert Miller. Daily Life in Colonial Mexico, *The Journey of Friar Ilarione da Bergamo, 1761-1768* (Norman: University of Oklahoma Press, 2000), 151.

58 (Arróniz 1979, Introduction) Translation is by the author. Arróniz, Othón. Teatro de Evangelización en Nueva España. [The Evangelization Theater in New Spain] (Mexico, D.F.: Universidad Nacional Autónoma de México, 1979), Introduction.

59 John Bannon, *Indian Labor in the Spanish Indies, Was There Another Solution?* (Boston: D.C. Heath & Co., 1966), 1.

60 Christopher Vecsey. *On The Padres' Trail* (Notre Dame: University of Notre Dame Press, 1996), 18.

61   The *Leyes de Burgos*, the first law code of the Spanish in the New World, charged the encomenderos with the indoctrination of the Indians, and decreed that the Indians should live near Spanish settlements, so that the continuous conversion of those that would have it—through going to church on the feast days to hear mass, the divine rites, and seeing how the Spanish live—would be quickly accomplished.

62   John Bannon, *Indian Labor in the Spanish Indies, Was There Another Solution?* (Boston: D.C. Heath & Co., 1966), 2.

63   Even today it seems the majority of Mexican Soap Operas on TV are based upon the son or daughter of the *encomendero* (who is usually presented as a religious, just man) and the sibling's abuse of authority or their exploitation of the *peon*, the indigenous residents of the *encomienda*.

64   John Bannon, *Indian Labor in the Spanish Indies, Was There Another Solution?* (Boston: D.C. Heath & Co., 1966), 3-4.

65   The first attempts at formulating autonomous theories of international law occurred in Spain in the 16th century. Most prominent among the early thinkers were the theologians Francisco de Vitoria and Francisco Suárez. Suárez is especially notable in this regard in the rights of peoples which correspond to modern international law.

66   Lesley Simpson, *Studies in the Administration of the Indians in New Spain* (Berkeley: University of California Press, 1934), 31.

67   A civil war was provoked in Peru when the Viceroy there attempted to implement the New Laws with the elimination clause for *encomiendas*. See: William H. Prescott, *Conquest of Peru* (New York: The Book League of America, 1847), 290-302.

68   John Bannon, *Indian Labor in the Spanish Indies, Was There Another Solution?* (Boston: D.C. Heath & Co., 1966).

69   Having a mistress is still considered an acceptable practice among many Mexican males today causing one to wonder about the implementation of this ruling.

70   Philip Powell, *Soldiers Indians and Silver, North America's First Frontier War* (Tempe: Center for Latin American Studies, 1975), 5.

71   Miguel León-Portilla, *The Broken Spears: The Aztec Account of the Conquest of Mexico* (Boston: Beacon Press, 2007).

72   Bernardino Verástique, *Michoacán and Eden, Vasco de Quiroga and the Evangelization of Western Mexico* (Austin: University of Texas Press, 2000), v.

73   Ibid.

74 Ibid.

75 Ibid.

76 Juan Miguel Zarandona, "The Biography of Vasco de Quiroga (1470-1565), Bishop of Utopia, by Benjamín Jarnés (1888-1949)," Spaces of Utopia: An Electronic Journal, nr. 3, Autumn/Winter 2006, pp. 69-83.

77 Ibid.

78 Ibid.

79 Ibid.

80 John Bannon, *Indian Labor in the Spanish Indies, Was There Another Solution?* (Boston: D.C. Heath & Co., 1966), 57.

81 It is of interest that we see the foundations of the concept that children belonging to the State, or in this case to the Church, in the insistence of infant baptism by the State-Church—there being no difference in the two at this time. See: Christopher Vecsey. *On The Padres' Trail* (Notre Dame: University of Notre Dame Press, 1996), 17.

82 Bernardino de Sahagún, *La Conversión de Los Indios de la Nueva España, Con el Texto de los Coloquios de los doce de Bernardino de Sahagún (1564).* [The Conversion of the Indians of New Spain] (Quito: Abya'Yala, 1990), 8.

83 C. L. Barnhart, ed. *The American College Dictionary* (New York: Random House, 1960), 764.

84 The *untainted blood* was a Spanish citizen born in New Spain. This ever increasing percentage of the Spanish citizenry residing in Mexico and always considered second-class to the citizen born in Spain, would eventually become so powerful that they would lead the Mexican revolution to separate from Spain.

85 Bernardino de Sahagún, *La Conversión de Los Indios de la Nueva España, Con el Texto de los Coloquios de los doce de Bernardino de Sahagún (1564).* [The Conversion of the Indians of New Spain] (Quito: Abya'Yala, 1990), 8.

86 The manuscript was made to disappear by the agents of the Inquisition into the secret vaults of the Vatican until the twentieth century. One can understand why when one of the purposes of the book is to show the extent of corruption of the Roman Catholic religion by the indigenous populace of New Spain.

87 Hanke, Lewis. *All Mankind Is One, A Study of the disputation Between Bartolomé de Las Casas and Juan Ginés de Sepúlveda in 1550 on the*

Intellectual and Religious capacity of the American Indians (DeKalb: Northern Illinois University Press, 1974).

[88] Christopher Pool. *Olmec Archaeology and Early Mesoamerica* (Cambridge: University Press, 2007), 1.

[89] Ibid.

[90] Poole, Stafford. Our Lady of Guadalupe, The Origins and Sources of a Mexican National Symbol, 1531-1797 (Tucson: The University of Arizona Press, 1996).

[91] "The story of the apparition of the Virgin of Guadalupe to a poor indigenous man less than fifteen years after the Spanish conquest of Mexico did not come into prominence until the mid-seventeenth century. The first known telling of the tale appeared in a book published in Spanish in 1648 by the priest Miguel Sánchez. On the heels of the Sánchez version, the story was included in the book *Huei tlamahuiçoltica* published in 1649 by Luis Laso de la Vega, the vicar of the Guadalupe chapel and a friend of Sánchez. It had little impact initially, but by the twentieth century, with indigenism triumphant, it had become the best known version. "There have been a few translations of Laso de la Vega's apparition story into English but only on a popular or devotional level. The present edition offers a translation and transcription of the complete text of the 1649 edition, together with critical apparatus, including comparisons of the Sánchez and Laso de la Vega texts, and various linguistic, orthographic, and typographical matters that throw light on the date and manner of composition." From the inside flap of the text: Lisa Sousa, Stafford Poole C.M. and James Lockhart, *The Story of Guadalupe: Luis Laso de la Vega's Huei tlamahuiColtica of 1649 (UCLA Latin American Studies,* V. 84) (Stanford University Press, 1998).

[92] Bernal Diaz, *The Conquest of New Spain* (New York: Penguin Books, 1963), 366, 400-405.

[93] Charles Gibson, *The Aztec Under Spanish Rule, A History of the Indians of the Valley of Mexico 1519-1810* (Stanford: Stanford University Press, 1964), 99.

[94] Magdiel Castillo argues that, "The mission given to friars consisted of learning both the scientific and technological skills that the Indians had developed and used for several millennia . . . To further this mandate, churches and atrios were built over existing Pre-Columbian temples thereby creating a forum where the Spanish were able to obtain this knowledge under the auspices of religious training. [This interaction

called] syncretism was principally the result of an exchange of scientific and technological information" (Barquero 2003, iii). This author has completely ignored the very nature of the religious clerics, attributing to them the scientific mentality of the enlightenment which Spain missed for this epoch, still being in the dark ages and approaching everything from a correct religious standpoint—a Catholic Religious standpoint; nothing else mattered. The Spanish did learn from the Aztec their essentials of agronomy, but not through the scientific method of the enlightenment; the Spanish learned indigenous agronomy because they liked to eat.

95 Mathew 7.16-20 NASB

96 Mathew 28.18-20 NASB

97 Charles Gibson, *The Aztec Under Spanish Rule, A History of the Indians of the Valley of Mexico 1519-1810* (Stanford: Stanford University Press, 1964), 99.

98 Christopher Vecsey. *On The Padres' Trail* (Notre Dame: University of Notre Dame Press, 1996), 17.

99 Lopes Don, Patricia. "Franciscans, Indian Sorcerers, and the Inquisition in New Spain." *Journal of World History*, Mar 2006: 27-48.

100 Ibid.

101 William Orr and Robert Miller. *Daily Life in Colonial Mexico, The Journey of Friar Ilarione da Bergamo, 1761-1768* (Norman: University of Oklahoma Press, 2000), 151.

102 Bernardino de Sahagún, *La Conversión de Los Indios de la Nueva España, Con el Texto de los Coloquios de los doce de Bernardino de Sahagún (1564).* [The Conversion of the Indians of New Spain] (Quito: Abya'Yala, 1990), 8.

103 William Prescott, *History of the Conquest of Mexico* (Philadelphia: J.B. Lippincott Co., 1843; reprint, Phoenix Press, 2002), 49.

104 Charles Gibson, *The Aztec Under Spanish Rule, A History of the Indians of the Valley of Mexico 1519-1810* (Stanford: Stanford University Press, 1964), 100.

Chapter VI

[1] Inga Clendinnen, *Ambivalent Conquests, Maya and Spaniard in Yucatan, 1517-1570* (New York: Cambridge University Press, 1987), 3, 4-14, 17-18.

[2] This resulted in Sahagún's, *General History of the Things of New Spain*, one of the very few classic histories of this time period.

[3] Inga Clendinnen, *Ambivalent Conquests, Maya and Spaniard in Yucatan, 1517-1570* (New York: Cambridge University Press, 1987), 85.

[4] West Robert C. and J.P. Augelli. *Middle America: Its Land and People* (New Jersey: Prentice Hall, 1971).

[5] Michael Coe. *The Maya* (New York: Thames & Hudson, 1999), 191.

[6] Maya-Toltec Controversy in Chichen Itza: It has been a millennium since the fall of Chichen Itza. Information about Chichen Itza is mostly drawn through the analysis of its art and architecture. This, and the scarcity of texts prior to the Spanish conquest of Mesoamerica, has led to a dearth of information about Chichen Itza and spawned a great many theories. The gaps in information that exist in the history both of Chichen and of Tula are often filled with speculative migrations, invasions, and other events. It is in large part because of this that no consensus can be drawn as to the reason for this connection. There are enough gaps in information that many different theories can 'answer' why there is this connection. See: Lindsay Jones, "Conquests of the Imagination: Maya-Mexican Polarity and the Story of Chichén Itzá" *American Anthropologist, New Series*, Vol. 99, No. 2 (Jun., 1997), pp. 275-290

[7] See chapter 4 of this book.

[8] Inga Clendinnen, *Ambivalent Conquests, Maya and Spaniard in Yucatan, 1517-1570* (New York: Cambridge University Press, 1987), 19-26.

[9] Athena Review, "The Spanish Conquest of Yucatán (1526-46)" *Journal of Archaeology, History, and Exploration*, Athena Publications, Inc: Vol. 2, No. 1, 1999.

[10] Ibid.

[11] Ibid.

[12] Ibid.

[13] Ibid.

[14] *The Catholic Encyclopedia*, 1914. [The Catholic Encyclopedia Classic 1914 Edition—CD-ROM/DVD by Remy Lafort, S.T.D. and Arthur J. Scanlan, D.D.—Imprimatur: John Cardinal Farley and Patrick J.

Hayes, Archbishops of N.Y. Nihil Obstat 19007-1914 (2003)] "Mayan History."

[15] Ibid.

[16] Ibid. Several authors are in agreement on the number of Franciscans, but the dates vary considerably as to when they actually came. The original records are lost. Also see: Inga Clendinnen, *Ambivalent Conquests, Maya and Spaniard in Yucatan, 1517-1570* (New York: Cambridge University Press, 1987), 72.

[17] *The Catholic Encyclopedia, 1914.* [The Catholic Encyclopedia Classic 1914 Edition—CD-ROM/DVD by Remy Lafort, S.T.D. and Arthur J. Scanlan, D.D.—Imprimatur: John Cardinal Farley and Patrick J. Hayes, Archbishops of N.Y. Nihil Obstat 19007-1914 (2003)] "Mayan History."

[18] Ibid.

[19] Inga Clendinnen, *Ambivalent Conquests, Maya and Spaniard in Yucatan, 1517-1570* (New York: Cambridge University Press, 1987), 57, 58, 72, 74-77, 94.

[20] The Catholic Encyclopedia, 1914. [The Catholic Encyclopedia Classic 1914 Edition—CD-ROM/DVD by Remy Lafort, S.T.D. and Arthur J. Scanlan, D.D.—Imprimatur: John Cardinal Farley and Patrick J. Hayes, Archbishops of N.Y. Nihil Obstat 19007-1914 (2003)] "Mayan History."

[21] (Clendinnen 1987, 49, 98) Inga Clendinnen, *Ambivalent Conquests, Maya and Spaniard in Yucatan, 1517-1570* (New York: Cambridge University Press, 1987), 49, 98.

[22] In the twentieth century the Maya have been an exceedingly fertile ground for evangelism by the evangelical church like the Presbyterians and Pentecostals.

Chapter VII

[1] *Chichimeca* is nearly an exact equivalent of the American slang term S.O.B.

[2] Based on the authors observations and notes taken while inspecting the ruins and hearing the presentations at the La Quemada site.

3   Clean rats—these live in the maguey cactus plant and eat only cactus leaves; they are as nourishing as the guinea pig and can easily be captured and prepared.

4   Richard E. Adams and Murdo J. MacLeod, eds. *The Cambridge History of the Native Peoples of the Americas,* Vol. 2: Mesoamerica, Part 2. (Cambridge University Press, 2000), 12, 13, 112-114.

5   Philip Powell, *Soldiers Indians and Silver, North America's First Frontier War* (Tempe: Center for Latin American Studies, 1975), 7-9, 37, 236.

6   Ibid., 37)

7   P. J. Bakewell, *Silver Mining and Society in Colonial Mexico: Zacatecas, 1546-1700 (Cambridge Latin American Studies 15)* (Cambridge University Press, 1971), 4-25.

8   Ibid.

9   Ibid.

10   Ibid.

11   Philip Powell, *Soldiers Indians and Silver, North America's First Frontier War.* Tempe: Center for Latin American Studies, 1975, 181-183.

12   John Kessell, *Kiva, Cross, and Crown, The Pecos Indians and New Mexico, 1540-1840.* Washington: National Park Service, US Department of the Interior, 1979, 33.

13   Philip Powell, *Soldiers Indians and Silver, North America's First Frontier War* (Tempe: Center for Latin American Studies, 1975), 183-185.

14   P. J. Bakewell, *Silver Mining and Society in Colonial Mexico: Zacatecas, 1546-1700 (Cambridge Latin American Studies 15)* (Cambridge University Press, 1971), 4-25.

15   Philip Powell, *Soldiers Indians and Silver, North America's First Frontier War* (Tempe: Center for Latin American Studies, 1975), 185-188.

16   Ibid.

17   Ibid.

18   John Bannon, *Indian Labor in the Spanish Indies, Was There Another Solution?* (Boston: D.C. Heath & Co., 1966), 4-6.

19   Immediately the Moravian model of a Christian evangelistic community comes to mind, but that would not occur for another 170 years.

20   Alan Knight, *Mexico, The Colonial Era* (New York: Cambridge University Press, 2002), 71.

21   Philip Powell, *Soldiers Indians and Silver, North America's First Frontier War* (Tempe: Center for Latin American Studies, 1975), 141.

22   Ibid., 149.

23 Alan Knight, Mexico, *The Colonial Era* (New York: Cambridge University Press, 2002), 63.

24 In 1612 the Zacatecas cathedral was started on the site of a previous church, and then renovated again in the 1700s. The Santiago Cathedral of Queretaro was started in 1531, and modified several times as the convent was added and it evolved into a center for training missionaries. In the 1560s the Cathedral of Guadalajara was started; it took 50 years to complete it.

25 In the cathedral of San Luis Potosi, the first room to the left has an open coffin with the life-size figure of a dead, crucified son of Mary laid out, still with his crown of thorns on his bleeding head.

26 Saints and holy places still occupy much of the religion of the rural areas in the Gran Chichimeca today. In the front of the cathedrals and churches it is the symbols of Mariology, or even Saint Louis the 14th, but very seldom if ever the resurrected Christ. San Luis de la Paz, one of the first towns founded on the *Silver Highway* in San Luis Potosí, has stain glass windows, statuary, and carving of 'beautified' Louis the 14th in the cathedral, the churches and chapels. The "saint" has usurped the worship of all other expressions, including Roman Catholic and indigenous gods.

27 Ephesians 2.8-9 NASB

28 Charlotte M. Grady, *Latin American Studies Consortium of New England,* *"Jesuit Missionaries and Native Elites in Northern Mexico, 1572-1616.* Occasional Papers, University of Connecticut, 1997.

29 The Protestant church still has not been able to resolve this issue of ecclesiastic authority. They use the term *para-church* structure to distinguish the many mission and evangelistic associations from the *real* church structure, though what defines a real church is still quite ambiguous. The question is still the line of ecclesiastic authority. What has happened is that a church or mission is defined by their legal documents required by governmental authorities, thus by default the secular governments define the church or mission structure. Both church and mission expressions trace their beginnings from the book of Acts. In general, the protestant church ordains its leadership; the protestant mission structures have their leaders *commissioned* by the church and send them out to their mission function. When a missionary is ordained by the church and sent out by a mission they find themselves serving two masters in line authority. When a missionary is only commissioned,

they are usually forbidden to administer the sacraments of the church, resulting in the same type of limited Christian practices as the Roman Catholic priests that refused to give all the common teaching and sacraments to the indigenous people.

30 People have been taking bits of their old paths that matter to them and incorporating them into new ones for a very long time. From one perspective this is called syncretism or Cristo-paganism. Writers on the old Spanish Catholic colonies in particular have used the latter term. (See: Alan R. Tippett, "Cristo-paganism or Indigenous Christianity?" http://www.globalmissiology.org/english/indices/ by_section.htm

Chapter VIII

1 Susan Deeds, *Indigenous Rebellions on the Northern Mexican Mission Frontier: From First-Generation to Later Colonial Responses* (Lincoln: University of Nebraska Press, 1998), 1-29.

2 Cleve Hallenbeck, *The Journey of Fray Marcos De Niza* (Southern Methodist University Press, 1987).

3 Richard Flint, *No Settlement, No Conquest: A History of the Coronado Entrada* (University of New Mexico Press, 2008).

4 Arthur Scott Aiton, *Antonio De Mendoza First Viceroy of New Spain* (London: Russell and Russell, 1967).

5 Enrique Dussel, *The Church in Latin America: 1492-1992* (Maryknoll: Orbis Books, 1992), 358.

6 Adolph Francis Alphonse Bandelier. "Historical Documents Relating to New Mexico, Nueva Vizcaya, and Approaches Thereto, to 1773 (Volume 2)" (Washington: General Books LLC, 2010).

7 La Forja de la Sinaloa, Sergio Ortega Noriega. "Grupos Acaxee y Xixime." Available from: http://bibliotecadigital.ilce.edu.mx/sites/estados/libros/sinaloa/

8 Ibid.

9 Charlotte M. Gradie, *The Tepehuán Revolt of 1616: Militarism, Evangelism and Colonialism in Seventeenth-Century Nueva Vizcaya* (Chicago: University of Utah Press, 2000).

10 Ibid.

11 Charlotte M. Grady, *Latin American Studies Consortium of New England,* *"Jesuit Missionaries and Native Elites in Northern Mexico, 1572-1616.* Occasional Papers, University of Connecticut, 1997.

12 Jerald T. Milanich, *Florida Indians and the Invasion from Europe* University Press of Florida (1998).

13 Charlotte M. Grady, Latin American Studies Consortium of New England, "Jesuit Missionaries and Native Elites in Northern Mexico, 1572-1616." Occasional Papers, University of Connecticut, 1997.

14 Ibid.

15 Ibid.

16 Ibid.

17 Roberto Mario Salmon, *Indian Revolts in Northern New Spain (1680-1786)* (Lanham: University Press of America, Inc., 1991), 19-20.

18 Susan Deeds, *Indigenous Rebellions on the Northern Mexican Mission Frontier: From First-Generation to Later Colonial Responses* (Lincoln: University of Nebraska Press, 1998).

19 Charlotte M. Grady, *Latin American Studies Consortium of New England,* *"Jesuit Missionaries and Native Elites in Northern Mexico, 1572-1616.* Occasional Papers, University of Connecticut, 1997.

20 Translation: When Andrés Pérez de Ribas, in 1605 founded the Jesuit mission, the Indian catechist Luisa always accompanied him in his ministry; it was her job to gather the indigenous people, primarily the women and children to indoctrinate them, and in it's time to baptize them; the participation [in the work] of the Indian Luisa is described by Pérez de Ribas in the following manner: ". . . always the Indian Luisa went before me, chosen by God as an instrument for the healing of this nation." Roberto Acosta, *Apuntes históricos sonorenses La Conquista Temporal y Espiritual del Yaqui y del Mayo* (Hermosillo: Gobierno del Estado de Sonora, 1983).

21 Peter Gerhard discusses at least twenty five expeditions of foreigners, considered pirates by the Spanish, who reached the Pacific in the time frame of 1575-1742. See: Peter Gerhard, *Pirates of the Pacific, 1575-1742* (Lincoln: University of Nebraska Press, 1990). At a time when pirates are glorified in movies and even cartoons for children, it must be remembered that in the absence of declared war, it was necessary that there be no surviving witnesses to their gruesome deeds and all the victims of a captured ship's company were normally murdered or sold into slavery.

22 Peter Masten Dunne, *Black Robes in Lower California* (Berkeley: University of California Press, 1968(1, 2, 6, 9, 10, 12, 26, 27).

23 David Weber, *The Spanish Frontier in North America* (New Haven: Yale University Press, 1992), 241.

24 Edward Vernon, *Las Misiones Antiguas, The Spanish Missions of Baja California, 1683-1855* (Santa Barbara: Viejo Press, 2002), xii, xiii, xv, xvi.

25 Ibid.

26 José de Acosta, S.J. *Historia natural y moral de Indias* (Sevilla: Casa de Iuan de Leon, 1590).

27 Ordine Dei Carmelitani Scalzi. S.C. O'Mahony, trans. "Reinforcements: Domingo Ruzola and Thomas of Jesus" http://www.ocd.pcn.net/histo_16.htm

28 Most of this list are taken from: David Cook, *Born to Die, Disease and New World Conquest, 1492-1650* (Cambridge University Press, 1998), also from: John Schmal. "The History of Indigenous Durago" History of Mexico (Houston Institute: for Culture, http://www.houstonculture.org/mexico/durango.html)

29 "Horrorizaba especialmente a los españoles la antropofagia que acostumbraban los Xiximes, pues a decir del cronista, no era un rito para celebrar las victorias, como entre los acaxees y los Cahitas, sino una forma ordinaria de alimentación, y buscaban a hombres, mujeres y niños como presas de cacería." [Trans: Especially horrible to the Spanish was the anthropological custom of the Xiximes, as the historian writes, it was not a special rite to celebrate victories, as was among the Acaxees and the Cahitas, but it was an ordinary manner of eating; they looked for men, women, and children as prizes in hunting.] *Breve Historia de Sinaloa*, Sergio Ortega Noriega: "Grupos Acaxee y Xixime" [Accessed: Jan 8, 2008] http://bibliotecadigital.ilce.edu.mx/

30 Charlotte M. Gradie, *The Tepehuán Revolt of 1616: Militarism, Evangelism and Colonialism in Seventeenth-Century Nueva Vizcaya* (Chicago: University of Utah Press, 2000).

31 Charlotte M. Grady, Latin American Studies Consortium of New England, "Jesuit Missionaries and Native Elites in Northern Mexico, 1572-1616." Occasional Papers, University of Connecticut, 1997.

32 *History of Mexico.* "History of Indigenous Durango" [Cited January 10, 2008] Available from: http://www.houstonculture.org/mexico/durango.html

33 Charlotte M. Grady, Latin American Studies Consortium of New England, "Jesuit Missionaries and Native Elites in Northern Mexico, 1572-1616." Occasional Papers, University of Connecticut, 1997.

34 Harry Prescott Johnson, "Diego Martinez de Hurdaide: Defender of the Northwestern Frontier of New Spain." *The Pacific Historical Review,* 1942: 169-185.

35 N. Ross Crumrine, *The Mayo Indians of Sonora: A People Who Refuse to Die* (Phoenix: University of Arizona Press, 1977). And: *The Catholic Encyclopedia, 1914.* [The Catholic Encyclopedia Classic 1914 Edition—CD-ROM/DVD by Remy Lafort, S.T.D. and Arthur J. Scanlan, D.D.—Imprimatur: John Cardinal Farley and Patrick J. Hayes, Archbishops of N.Y. Nihil Obstat 19007-1914 (2003)] "Mayo Indians."

36 *History of Mexico*, "The History of Indigenous Sinaloa" [Cited January 10, 2008] Available from: http://www.houstonculture.org/mexico/sinaloa.html

37 Ted Glines, "The Great Yaqui Nation" Manataka, American Indian Council, See: http://www.manataka.org /page129.html

38 Ibid.

39 Ibid.

40 Sherwood Lingenfelter, Agents of Transformation, A Guide for Effective Cross-Cultural Ministry (Grand Rapids: Baker Books, 1996), 9-10.

41 John Kessell, Kiva, Cross, and Crown, *The Pecos Indians and New Mexico, 1540-1840* (Washington: National Park Service, US Department of the Interior, 1979), 68-69.

Chapter IX

1 John Kessell, Kiva, Cross, and Crown, *The Pecos Indians and New Mexico, 1540-1840* (Washington: National Park Service, US Department of the Interior, 1979), 68-69.

2 Paul Horgan, *The Great River, The Rio Grande in North American History* (Hanover: Wesleyan University Press, 1984), 16-68, 160-165.

3 David Roberts, *The Pueblo Revolt, The Secret Rebellion That Drove the Spaniards Out of the Southwest* (New York: Simon & Schuster, 2004), 36-40.

Andrew L. Toth

4   See: Elizabeth John, *Storms Brewed in Other Men's Worlds, The Confrontation of Indians, Spanish, and French in the Southwest, 1540-1795* (College Station: A&M University Press, 1975), 24-26. And, David Roberts, *The Pueblo Revolt, The Secret Rebellion That Drove the Spaniards Out of the Southwest* (New York: Simon & Schuster, 2004), 50.

5   Jeffrey D. Carlisle, "Apache Indians," *Handbook of Texas Online* (http://www.tshaonline.org/handbook/ online/articles/bma33), Accessed Nov 01, 2011. Published by the Texas State Historical Association.

6   Ibid.

7   Ibid.

8   Elizabeth John, *Storms Brewed in Other Men's Worlds, The Confrontation of Indians, Spanish, and French in the Southwest, 1540-1795* (College Station: A&M University Press, 1975), 22-24, 28-37, 47-49.

9   Another report says a total of one thousand died David Weber, *The Spanish Frontier in North America* (New Haven: Yale University Press, 1992), 86. And: Paul Horgan, Great River, *The Rio Grande in North American History* (Hanover: Wesleyan University Press, 1984), 208.

10 Christopher Vecsey, *On The Padres' Trail* (Notre Dame: University of Notre Dame Press, 1996), 125-127.

11 John Kessell, Kiva, Cross, and Crown, *The Pecos Indians and New Mexico, 1540-1840* (Washington: National Park Service, US Department of the Interior, 1979), 68-69.

12 David Roberts, *The Pueblo Revolt, The Secret Rebellion That Drove the Spaniards Out of the Southwest* (New York: Simon & Schuster, 2004), 127-168.

13 Ibid., 96-97.

14 David Weber, *The Spanish Frontier in North America* (New Haven: Yale University Press, 1992), 94-95.

15 (Horgan 1984, 159, 197, 198, 221) *Paul Horgan, The Great River, The Rio Grande in North American History* (Hanover: Wesleyan University Press, 1984), 159, 197, 198, 221.

16 John Kessell, *Kiva, Cross, and Crown, The Pecos Indians and New Mexico, 1540-1840* (Washington: National Park Service, US Department of the Interior, 1979), 75.

17 Christopher Vecsey, On The Padres' Trail (Notre Dame: University of Notre Dame Press, 1996), 130.

18 Ibid., 18.

[19]   John Kessell, *Kiva, Cross, and Crown, The Pecos Indians and New Mexico, 1540-1840* (Washington: National Park Service, US Department of the Interior, 1979), 106.

[20]   David Roberts, *The Pueblo Revolt, The Secret Rebellion That Drove the Spaniards Out of the Southwest* (New York: Simon & Schuster, 2004), 124.

[21]   Ibid.

[22]   Ibid., 126.

[23]   John Kessell, *Kiva, Cross, and Crown, The Pecos Indians and New Mexico, 1540-1840* (Washington: National Park Service, US Department of the Interior, 1979), 98-99.

[24]   Christopher Vecsey, *On The Padres' Trail* (Notre Dame: University of Notre Dame Press, 1996), 137.

[25]   This was in the Pecos cathedral once in operation.

Chapter X

[1]   Some sources say 117 men were actually abandoned. Some were wounded and died, some blended into society, most were captured and imprisoned.

[2]   Robert S. Weddle, "Carvajal y de la Cueva, Luis," *Handbook of Texas Online* (http://www.tshaonline.org/ handbook/online/articles/fcadn), accessed November 01, 2011. Published by the Texas State Historical Association.

[3]   Ibid.

[4]   William Foster and Johanna S. Warren (Translators). *The La Salle Expedition on the Mississippi River: A Lost Manuscript of Nicolas de La Salle* (Austin: Texas State Historical Association, 2003).

[5]   (French 2005)

[6]   *The History of Texas*. "Early History of Texas" (http://www.sonofthesouth. net/texas/history-texas.htm) Accessed: October 3, 2007. Published by Son of the South.

[7]   Ibid.

[8]   *The History of Texas*. "The French and Spanish War" (http://www. sonofthesouth.net/texas/history-texas.htm) Accessed: October 11, 2007] Published by Son of the South.

[9]   Cane River National Heritage Area Historic Sites. "Los Adaes State Historical   Site"   (http://www.caneriverheritage.org/main_file.php/

losadaes.php/) Accessed: October 11, 2007] Published by Cane River Heritage.Org.

10 *The History of Texas.* "The Spanish Settlement of Texas" (http://www. sonofthesouth.net/texas/history-texas.htm) Accessed: October 3, 2007. Published by Son of the South.

11 Ibid.

12 Indian Nations of Texas. "Indian Relations In Texas" *Texas State Library and Archives Commission* (http://www.tsl.state.tx.us/exhibits/indian/ intro/page2.html) Accessed: October 29, 2007.

13 "Tonkawa Indians," *Handbook of Texas Online* (http://www.tshaonline. org/ handbook/online/articles/bmt68), Accessed October 29, 2007. Published by the Texas State Historical Association.

14 Ibid.

15 Ibid.

16 Ibid.

17 Ibid.

18 "The Texas Coahuiltecan Indians" *Handbook of Texas Online* (http:// www.tsha.utexas.edu/handbook/online/articles/CC/bmcah.html), Accessed October 25, 2007. Published by the Texas State Historical Association.

18 Ibid.

19 R. E. Moore. "The Texas Coahuiltecan Indians" *Texas Indians* (http:// www.texasindians.com/coah.htm) Accessed: October 29, 2007. Texarch Associates.

20 "Tonkawa Indians" *Handbook of Texas Online* (http://www.tshaonline. org/handbook/online/articles/ KK/bmk5.html), Accessed September 7, 2007. Published by the Texas State Historical Association.

21 H. H. Lamb in H. Flohn (ed). *Climatic Fluctuations, World Survey of Climatology. Vol.2. General Climatology* (New York: Elsevier, 1969), 236.

22 "The Spanish Occupation of Texas 1519-1690" *Handbook of Texas Online* (http://www.tsha.utexas.edu/ handbook/online/articles/CC/ bmcah.html), Accessed November 20, 2007. Published by the Texas State Historical Association.

23 Herbert Eugene Bolton, ed. "Mendoza-Lopez Expedition of 1683-1684" (http://www.americanjourneys.org/aj-017/summary/index.asp) Accessed: November 20, 2007. American Journeys.

24 Herbert E. Bolton. "The Spanish Occupation of Texas 1519-1690" *The Handbook of Texas Online* (http://www.tshaonline.org/publications/

journals/shq/online/v016/n1/article_3.html) Accessed: November 20, 2007. Published by the Texas State Historical Association.

25   R. E. Moore. "The Texas Coahuiltecan Indians" *Texas Indians* (http:// www.texasindians.com/coah.htm) Accessed: October 29, 2007. Texarch Associates.

26   Clotilde P. García "José de Escandón" *The Handbook of Texas Online* (http://www.tshaonline.org/handbook/online/articles/EE/fes1.html) Accessed: December 3, 2007. Published by the Texas State Historical Association.

27   *Zorrilla, Juan Fidel and Carlos González Salas.* "José de Escandón y de la Helguera" *Diccionario Biográfico de Tamaulipas (Ciudad Victoria, 1984), 135-138.*

28   It would be clear into the twentieth century before an adequate road would be built to connect the Rio Grande valley area with the highlands of Central Mexico. Until then the safest transportation was to take a boat from Matamoros to Veracruz and then overland to Mexico City. The only less accessible area for Mexicans was California.

29   "Gestas: Escandón y la Colonización" *Tamaulipas Avanzamos.* (http:// www.tamaulipas.gob.mx/tamaulipas/historia/) Accessed: Dec 6, 2007. Publicado por: El Gobierno del Estado.

30   Raul N. Longoria "Nuevo Santander" (http://www.raullongoria. net/santander.htm) Accessed: Dec 10, 2007. Published by: The Longoria-Alcala family.

31   "Early Texas Missions and Missionaries" *The History of Texas* (http:// www.sonofthesouth.net/texas/ missions.htm) Accessed: Nov 10, 2007. Published by Son of the South.

32   Héctor Samperio Gutiérrez. "El Colegio Apostólico de San Francisco de Pachuca y sus Misiones del Noreste de México" *Consejo Estatal para la Cultura y las Artes de Hidalgo* (http://www.ofmmichoacan.org/) Accessed: Dec 10, 2007. Gobierno del Estado.

33   Ibid.

34   Ibid.

35   "The History of Texas—Missions and Missionaries" *Early Texas Missions and Missionaries* (http://www.sonofthesouth.net/texas/missions.htm) Accessed: Nov 10, 2007. Sons of the South.

36   The Catholic Encyclopedia, 1914. [The Catholic Encyclopedia Classic 1914 Edition—CD-ROM/DVD by Remy Lafort, S.T.D. and Arthur J. Scanlan, D.D.—Imprimatur: John Cardinal Farley and Patrick J. Hayes,

Archbishops of N.Y. Nihil Obstat 19007-1914 (2003)] "Reductions of Paraguay."

37 "The History of Texas—Missions and Missionaries" *Early Texas Missions and Missionaries* (http://www.sonofthesouth.net/texas/missions.htm) Accessed: Nov 10, 2007. Sons of the South.

38 Ibid.

39 Randel Tarin. "The Mission San Antonio de Valero" *Alamo de Parras* (http://www.tamu.edu/faculty/ccbn/dewitt/adp/history/mission_period/valero/) Accessed: Jan 10, 2008.

Chapter XI

1 Gutierrez and Orsi, eds. *Contested Eden, California Before the Gold Rush* (Berkeley: University of California Press, 1998) 82-90.

2 David Weber. The Spanish Frontier in North America (New Haven: Yale University Press, 1992) 237-243.

3 Junípero Serra in a letter several days after arrival states: "Here are also the two vessels, but the *San Carlos* without sailors, all having died of the scurvy, except two. The *San Antonio*, although she sailed a month and a half later, arrived twenty days before the *San Carlos*, losing on the voyage eight sailors." See: Genet, Donna. Father Junipero Serra: Founder of California Missions (Enslow Publishers, 1996).

4 David Weber. *The Spanish Frontier in North America* (New Haven: Yale University Press, 1992) 244-245.

5 Alberto Hurtado, *Indian Survival on the California Frontier* (New Haven: Yale University Press, 1988), 54.

6 Gutierrez and Orsi, eds. *Contested Eden, California Before the Gold Rush* (Berkeley: University of California Press, 1998) 48.

7 W. W. Robinson, *Land in California* (Berkeley: University of California Press, 1948), 5.

8 *The Catholic Encyclopedia, 1914.* [The Catholic Encyclopedia Classic 1914 Edition—CD-ROM/DVD by Remy Lafort, S.T.D. and Arthur J. Scanlan, D.D.—Imprimatur: John Cardinal Farley and Patrick J. Hayes, Archbishops of N.Y. Nihil Obstat 19007-1914 (2003)] "Mission Indians of California."

9 Ibid.

10 Ibid.

11   Gutierrez and Orsi, eds. *Contested Eden, California Before the Gold Rush* (Berkeley: University of California Press, 1998), 52, 55-63, 71.

12   Some Roman Catholic references say Otomí language. See: "Blessed Junípero Serra 1713-1784" Serra Club of Bethlehem (http://www. catholic-church.org/serra-beth/serra-4.htm).

13   Melba Levick, Stanley Young, and Sally B. Woodbridge. *The Missions of California* (San Francisco: Chronicle Books, 2004).

14   Shipek, Florence C. "Mission Indians and Indians of California Land Claims." *American Indian Quarterly*, 1989: 409-420.

15   These names being used are from the California Indian Library Collection (Ethnic Studies Library, Native American Studies Collection, 30 Stephens Hall, U.C. Berkeley, 94720. They are able to answer questions regarding the collection or concerning California Indians.) The Kumeyaay are also called Diegueño, obviously from the Spanish; around San Juan Capistrano they were called Acágchemem.

16   *The Catholic Encyclopedia, 1914.* [The Catholic Encyclopedia Classic 1914 Edition—CD-ROM/DVD by Remy Lafort, S.T.D. and Arthur J. Scanlan, D.D.—Imprimatur: John Cardinal Farley and Patrick J. Hayes, Archbishops of N.Y. Nihil Obstat 19007-1914 (2003)] "Mission Indians of California."

17   Ibid.

18   Lisbeth Haas, *Conquests and Historical Identities in California, 1769-1936* (Berkeley: University of California Press, 1995), 14.

19   Ibid 26.

20   Langer, Erick and Robert Jackson. *The New Latin American Mission History.* Lincoln: University of Nebraska Press, 1995), 4.

21   Ibid 32.

22   Lisbeth Haas, *Conquests and Historical Identities in California, 1769-1936* (Berkeley: University of California Press, 1995), 2-19.

23   Robet G. Schafer. "Critiquins the Critics: Assessing California's Native Peoples" (http://www.ca-missions.org/oldsite/schafer.html) Accessed: Jan 15, 2008 California Mission Studies Ass.

24   W. W. Robinson, *Land in California* (Berkeley: University of California Press, 1948), 97.

25   Rocio Aguilar and Francisco Sanchez. Notas Para la Historia del Colegio Apostolico de Propaganda Fide de Cholula. Puebla: Universidad de las Americas, 2006), 80.

26 Walter Feller. "Mojave Desert" *Desert Gazette* [January 10, 2008] Accessed: http://mojavedesert.net/california-indian-history/03.html

27 Amy Turner Bushnell. "Missions and Moral Judgment" *Organization of American Historians* (http://www.oah.org/pubs/magazine/spanishfrontier/bushnell.html) Accessed: Jan 20, 2008.

28 Paul Farnsworth and Robert H. Jackson. *Cultural, Economic, and Demographic Change in the Missions of Alta California: The Case of Nuestra Señora de la Soledad* (Lincoln: University of Nebraska Press, 1995), 126.

29 Noble David Cook. *Born to Die, Disease and New World Conquest, 1492-1650* (Cambridge: University Press, 1998), 11.

30 Amy Turner Bushnell. "Missions and Moral Judgment" *Organization of American Historians* (http://www.oah.org/pubs/magazine/spanishfrontier/bushnell.html) Accessed: Jan 20, 2008.

31 Ibid.

Chapter XII

1 It is ironic that Protestantism, which was so hated by the Roman Church, shares far more in essential doctrine with the Roman church than Christopaganism, which is still embraced and owned by the Roman Church. Seldom can this be seen more clearly than in the recent canonization of Juan Diego, a man who never existed according to history, whose life is most likely based upon a fictitious drama, and an image of the Virgin Mary borrowed from the plains of old Spain and brought to Mexico by Cortéz. The Virgin of Guadalupe is an ideal representation of the Mexican Christopaganism that came out of this Epoch.

This enigma of Christopagan acceptance can be explained, with the risk of oversimplification, by using the concept of spiritual authority. Rome had set itself up as the only valid operation of Christ's delegated authority on earth. This is the reason Roman Christian armies could sack Christian Constantinople opening the doors to conquest by the Arab armies and the spread of Islam into Europe. It is why the Thomas Christian Church of India was forced into Roman Catholicism thus destroying a native Asian Christian expression. Rome was defending the concept of exclusive representation of Christ's authority.

The Protestant Reformation based upon the Scriptures as a higher authority challenged the Roman Church's right to uphold Southern European Christianity as the only legitimate expression and to act as the sole authority in Christ's stead. For Rome, that Protestant challenge to their authority could not be tolerated. The Christopagan Church of Mexico submitted to the Roman Catholic Church's authority which was established on the Southern European traditions, not the Scriptures. For the New Spain Christopagan Church to retain its own pagan traditions and incorporate them into the fold of European traditions *did not violate the Roman Catholic Church's claim to sole authority* on earth. Christopaganism was not biblical, it was not Christian, but it was not a threat to the Roman Catholic Church's perceived line of spiritual authority. When the Council of Trent opened the door to *traditional authority* as superseding Scriptural authority in order to justify their European hierarchal power base in the face of Scriptural violations, they unknowingly opened the same door to all human traditions of any religious expression as long as the indigenous cultures could be said to be in submission to Rome.

It can be seen then why the Scriptures had to be withheld from all but the properly indoctrinated leaders of the New Spain cultures to protect the Roman Catholic line of authority and avoid another "Reformation" among the indigenous Americans. This logic led directly to closing the priesthood to all native leaders, which in turn led to the strengthening of indigenous traditions as their accepted leaders continued in their old ways under the Roman Catholic rites and symbols. As such, the indigenous Christopagan religion was never rejected from the Roman Catholic fold.

2   Matthew 28.18-19 NASB
3   Isaiah 59.1 NASB

Chapter XIII

1   John 14.6 NASB
2   Matthew 28.19 NASB
3   Matthew 9.38 NIV
4   Revelation 7.10 NIV
5   Isaiah 61.1-2 NIV